GRAPHICAL METHODS
FOR
DATA ANALYSIS

The Wadsworth Statistics/Probability Series

Series Editors

Peter J. Bickel, University of California
William S. Cleveland, Bell Laboratories
Richard M. Dudley, Massachusetts Institute of Technology

Bickel, P.; Doksum, K.; and Hodges, J.L., Jr.
Festschrift for Erich L. Lehmann.

Chambers, J.; Cleveland, W.; Kleiner, B.; and Tukey, P.
Graphical Methods for Data Analysis.

Graybill, F.
Matrices with Applications in Statistics, Second Edition.

GRAPHICAL METHODS
FOR
DATA ANALYSIS

John M. Chambers
William S. Cleveland
Beat Kleiner
Paul A. Tukey

Bell Laboratories

WADSWORTH INTERNATIONAL GROUP
Belmont, California

DUXBURY PRESS
Boston

This book is a co-publishing project of Wadsworth International Group and Duxbury Press, divisions of Wadsworth, Inc.

Library of Congress Cataloging in Publication Data

Main entry under title:

Graphical methods for data analysis.

(The Wadsworth statistics/probability series)
Bibliography: p.
Includes index.
1. Statistics—Graphic methods—Congresses.
2. Computer graphics—Congresses. I. Chambers, John M.
II. Series.
QA276.3.G73   1983   001.4'22   83–3660
ISBN 0–534–98052–X

Printed in the United States of America

87 86 85 84 83 — 1 2 3 4 5 6 7 8 9

ISBN 0-87150-413-8

ISBN 0-534-98052-X INTERNATIONAL

The text for the book was processed at Bell Laboratories on a VAX 11/780 computer running the UNIX* operating system and troff/mm software driving an APS-5 phototypesetter. The font is Palatino. Covers and text printing and binding by The Maple-Vail Book Manufacturing Group.

*UNIX is a trademark of Bell Laboratories, Inc.

To our parents

Preface

This book presents graphical methods for analyzing data. Some methods are new and some are old, some methods require a computer and others only paper and pencil; but they are all powerful data analysis tools. In many situations a set of data — even a large set — can be adequately analyzed through graphical methods alone. In most other situations, a few well-chosen graphical displays can significantly enhance numerical statistical analyses.

There are several possible objectives for a graphical display. The purpose may be to record and store data compactly, it may be to communicate information to other people, or it may be to analyze a set of data to learn more about its structure. The methodology in this book is oriented toward the last of these objectives. Thus there is little discussion of communication graphics, such as pie charts and pictograms, which are seen frequently in the mass media, government publications, and business reports. However, it is often true that a graph designed for the analysis of data will also be useful to communicate the results of the analysis, at least to a technical audience.

The viewpoints in the book have been shaped by our own experiences in data analysis, and we have chosen methods that have proven useful in our work. These methods have been arranged according to data analysis tasks into six groups, and are presented in Chapters 2 to 7. More detail about the six groups is given in Chapter 1 which is an introduction. Chapter 8, the final one, discusses general principles and techniques that apply to all of the six groups. To see if the book is for you, finish reading the preface, table of contents, and Chapter 1, and glance at some of the plots in the rest of the book.

FOR WHOM IS THIS BOOK WRITTEN?

This book is written for anyone who either analyzes data or expects to do so in the future, including students, statisticians, scientists, engineers, managers, doctors, and teachers. We have attempted not to slant the techniques, writing, and examples to any one subject matter area. Thus the material is relevant for applications in physics, chemistry, business, economics, psychology, sociology, medicine, biology, quality control, engineering, education, or virtually any field where there are data to be analyzed. As with most of statistics, the methods have wide applicability largely because certain basic forms of data turn up in many different fields.

The book will accommodate the person who wants to study seriously the field of graphical data analysis and is willing to read from beginning to end; the book is wide in scope and will provide a good introduction to the field. It also can be used by the person who wants to learn about graphical methods for some specific task such as regression or comparing the distributions of two sets of data. Except for Chapters 2 and 3, which are closely related, and Chapter 8, which has many references to earlier material, the chapters can be read fairly independently of each other.

The book can be used in the classroom either as a supplement to a course in applied statistics, or as the text for a course devoted solely to graphical data analysis. Exercises are provided for classroom use. An elementary course can omit Chapters 7 and 8, starred sections in other chapters, and starred exercises; a more advanced course can include all of the material. Starred sections contain material that is either more difficult or more specialized than other sections, and starred exercises tend to be more difficult than others.

WHAT IS THE PREREQUISITE KNOWLEDGE NEEDED TO UNDERSTAND THE MATERIAL IN THIS BOOK?

Chapters 1 to 5, except for some of the exercises, assume a knowledge of elementary statistics, although no probability is needed. The material can be understood by almost anyone who wants to learn it and who has some experience with quantitative thinking. Chapter 6 is about probability plots (or quantile-quantile plots) and requires some knowledge of probability distributions; an elementary course in statistics should suffice. Chapter 7 requires more statistical background. It deals with graphical methods for regression and assumes that the reader is already familiar with the basics of regression methodology. Chapter 8 requires an understanding of some or most of the previous chapters.

ACKNOWLEDGMENTS

Our colleagues at Bell Labs contributed greatly to the book, both directly through patient reading and helpful comments, and indirectly through their contributions to many of the methods discussed here. In particular, we are grateful to those who encouraged us in early stages and who read all or major portions of draft versions. We also benefited from the supportive and challenging environment at Bell Labs during all phases of writing the book and during the research that underlies it. Special thanks go to Ram Gnanadesikan for his advice, encouragement and appropriate mixture of patience and impatience, throughout the planning and execution of the project.

Many thanks go to the automated text processing staff at Bell Labs — especially to Liz Quinzel — for accepting revision after revision without complaint and meeting all specifications, demands and deadlines, however outrageous, patiently learning along with us how to produce the book.

Marylyn McGill's contributions in the final stage of the project by way of organizing, preparing figures and text, compiling data sets, acquiring permissions, proofreading, verifying references, planning page lay-outs, and coordinating production activities at Bell Labs and at Wadsworth/Duxbury Press made it possible to bring all the pieces together and get the book out. The patience and cooperation of the staff at Wadsworth/Duxbury Press are also gratefully acknowledged.

Thanks to our families and friends for putting up with our periodic, seemingly antisocial behavior at critical points when we had to dig in to get things done.

A preliminary version of material in the book was presented at Stanford University. We benefited from interactions with students and faculty there.

Without the influence of John Tukey on statistics, this book would probably never have been written. His many contributions to graphical methods, his insights into the role good plots can play in statistics and his general philosophy of data analysis have shaped much of the approach presented here. Directly and indirectly, he is responsible for much of the richness of graphical methods available today.

John M. Chambers

William S. Cleveland

Beat Kleiner

Paul A. Tukey

Contents

1 Introduction 1

    1.1   Why Graphics? 1
    1.2   What is a Graphical Method for Analyzing Data? . . . 3
    1.3   A Summary of the Contents 4
    1.4   The Selection and Presentation of Materials 7
    1.5   Data Sets 7
    1.6   Quality of Graphical Displays 8
    1.7   How Should This Book Be Used? 8

2 Portraying the Distribution of a Set of Data . . . 9

    2.1   Introduction 9
    2.2   Quantile Plots 11
    2.3   Symmetry 16
    2.4   One-Dimensional Scatter Plots 19
    2.5   Box Plots 21
    2.6   Histograms 24
    2.7   Stem-and-Leaf Diagrams 26
    2.8   Symmetry Plots and Transformations 29
  *2.9   Density Traces 32
   2.10 Summary and Discussion 37
   2.11 Further Reading 41
         Exercises 42

3   Comparing Data Distributions 47

3.1   Introduction 47
3.2   Empirical Quantile-Quantile Plots 48
3.3   Collections of Single-Data-Set Displays 57
*3.4   Notched Box Plots 60
*3.5   Multiple Density Traces 63
*3.6   Plotting Ratios and Differences 64
3.7   Summary and Discussion 67
3.8   Further Reading 69
      Exercises 69

4   Studying Two-Dimensional Data 75

4.1   Introduction 75
4.2   Numerical Summaries are not Enough 76
4.3   Examples 77
4.4   Looking at the Scatter Plots 82
4.5   Studying the Dependence of y on x
      by Summaries in Vertical Strips 87
4.6   Studying the Dependence of y on x
      by Smoothing 91
4.7   Studying the Dependence of the Spread of y on x
      by Smoothing Absolute Values of Residuals 105
4.8   Fighting Repeated Values with Jitter and
      Sunflowers 106
4.9   Showing Counts with Cellulation and Sunflowers . . 107
*4.10 Two-Dimensional Local Densities and Sharpening . . 110
*4.11 Mathematical Details of Lowess 121
4.12 Summary and Discussion 123
4.13 Further Reading 124
      Exercises 125

5   Plotting Multivariate Data 129

5.1   Introduction 129
5.2   One-Dimensional and Two-Dimensional Views . . . 131
5.3   Plotting Three Dimensions at Once 135
5.4   Plotting Four and More Dimensions 145
5.5   Combinations of Basic Methods 171
5.6   First Aid and Transformation 175
*5.7   Coding Schemes for Plotting Symbols 178

5.8   Summary and Discussion 181
5.9   Further Reading 183
      Exercises 187

6   Assessing Distributional Assumptions About Data 191

6.1   Introduction 191
6.2   Theoretical Quantile-Quantile Plots 193
6.3   More on Empirical Quantiles and Theoretical Quantiles 194
6.4   Properties of the Theoretical Quantile-Quantile Plot 197
6.5   Deviations from Straight-Line Patterns 203
6.6   Two Cautions for Interpreting Theoretical Quantile-Quantile Plots 210
6.7   Distributions with Unknown Shape Parameters . . 212
6.8   Constructing Quantile-Quantile Plots 222
*6.9   Adding Variability Information to a Quantile-Quantile Plot 227
*6.10   Censored and Grouped Data 233
6.11   Summary and Discussion 237
6.12   Further Reading 237
      Exercises 238

7   Developing and Assessing Regression Models . . 243

7.1   Introduction 243
7.2   The Linear Model 245
7.3   Simple Regression 247
7.4   Preliminary Plots 255
7.5   Plots During Regression Fitting 264
7.6   Plots After the Model is Fitted 278
7.7   A Case Study 290
*7.8   Some Special Regression Situations 296
7.9   Summary and Discussion 305
7.10   Further Reading 306
      Exercises 307

8   **General Principles and Techniques** 315

    8.1   Introduction 315
    8.2   Overall Strategy and Thought 316
    8.3   Visual Perception 320
    8.4   General Techniques of Plot Construction 326
    8.5   Scales 328

References 333

Appendix: Tables of Data Sets 345

Index 387

1

Introduction

1.1 WHY GRAPHICS?

There is no single statistical tool that is as powerful as a well-chosen graph. Our eye-brain system is the most sophisticated information processor ever developed, and through graphical displays we can put this system to good use to obtain deep insight into the structure of data. An enormous amount of quantitative information can be conveyed by graphs; our eye-brain system can summarize vast information quickly and extract salient features, but it is also capable of focusing on detail. Even for small sets of data, there are many patterns and relationships that are considerably easier to discern in graphical displays than by any other data analytic method. For example, the curvature in the pattern formed by the set of points in Figure 1.1 is readily appreciated in the plot, as are the two unusual points, but it is not nearly as easy to make such a judgment from an equivalent table of the data. (This figure is more fully discussed in Chapter 5.)

The graphical methods in this book enable the data analyst to explore data thoroughly, to look for patterns and relationships, to confirm or disprove the expected, and to discover new phenomena. The methods also can be used to enhance classical numerical statistical analyses. Most classical procedures are based, either implicitly or explicitly, on assumptions about the data, and the validity of the analyses depends upon the validity of the assumptions. Graphical methods provide powerful diagnostic tools for confirming assumptions, or, when the assumptions are not met, for suggesting corrective actions.

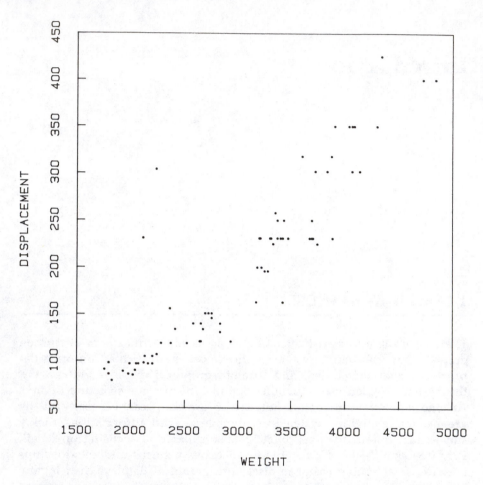

Figure 1.1 Scatter plot of displacement (in cubic inches) versus weight (in pounds) of 74 automobile models.

Without such tools, confirmation of assumptions can be replaced only by hope.

Until the mid-1970's, routine large-scale use of plots in data analysis was not feasible, since the hardware and software for computer graphics were not readily available to many people and making large numbers of plots by hand took too much time. We no longer have such an excuse. The field of computer graphics has matured. The recent rapid proliferation of graphics hardware — terminals, scopes, pen plotters, microfilm, color copiers, personal computers — has been accompanied by a steady development of software for graphical data analysis. Computer graphics facilities are now widely available at a reasonable cost, and this book has a relevance today that it would not have had prior to, say, 1970.

1.2 WHAT IS A GRAPHICAL METHOD FOR ANALYZING DATA?

The graphical displays in this book are visual portrayals of quantitative information. Most fall into one of two categories, displaying either the data themselves or quantities derived from the data. Usually, the first type of display is used when we are exploring the data and are not fitting models, and the second is used to enhance numerical statistical analyses that are based on assumptions about relationships in the data. For example, suppose the data are the heights x_i and weights y_i of a group of people. If we knew nothing about height and weight, we could still explore the association between them by plotting y_i against x_i; but if we have assumed the relationship to be linear and have fitted a linear function to the data using classical least squares, we will want to make a number of plots of derived quantities such as residuals from the fit to check the validity of the assumptions, including the assumptions implied by least squares.

If you have not already done so, you might want to stop reading for a moment, leaf through the book, and look at some of the figures. Many of them should look very familiar since they are standard Cartesian plots of points or curves. Figures 1.2 and 1.3, which reappear later in Chapters 3 and 7, are good examples. In these cases the main focus is not on the details of the vehicle, the Cartesian plot, but on what we choose to plot; although Figures 1.2 and 1.3 are superficially similar to each other, each being a simple plot of several dozen discrete points, they have very different meanings as data displays. While these displays are visually familiar, there are other displays that will probably seem unfamiliar. For example, Figure 1.4, which comes from Chapter 5, looks like a forest of misshapen trees. For such displays we discuss not only what to plot, but some of the steps involved in constructing the plot.

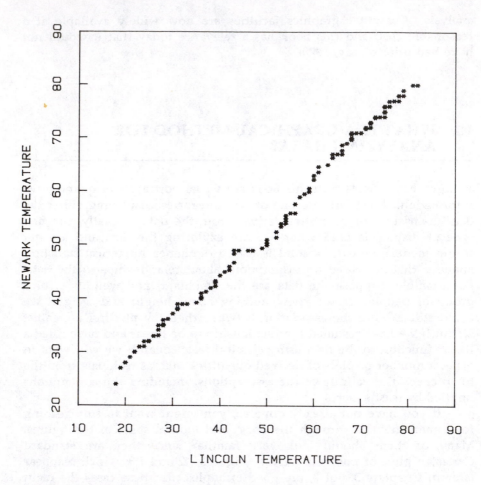

Figure 1.2 Empirical quantile-quantile plot of Newark and Lincoln monthly temperatures.

1.3 A SUMMARY OF THE CONTENTS

The book is organized according to the type of data to be analyzed and the complexity of the data analysis task. We progress from simple to complex situations. Chapters 2 to 5 contain mostly exploratory methods in which the raw data themselves are displayed. Chapter 2 describes methods for portraying the distribution of a single set of observations, for showing how the data spread out along the observation scale. Methods for comparing the distributions of several data sets are covered in Chapter 3. Chapter 4 deals with paired measurements, or two-

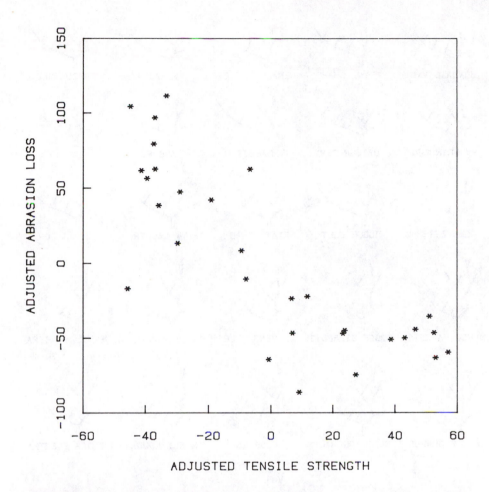

Figure 1.3 Adjusted variable plot of abrasion loss versus tensile strength, both variables adjusted for hardness.

dimensional data; the graphical methods there help us probe the relationship and association between the two variables. Chapter 5 does the same for measurements of more than two variables; an example of such multidimensional data is the heights, weights, blood pressures, pulse rates, and blood types of a group of people.

Chapters 6 and 7 present methods for studying data in the context of statistical models and for plotting quantities derived from the data. Here the displays are used to enhance standard numerical statistical analyses frequently carried out on data. The plots allow the investigator to probe the results of analyses and judge whether the data support the

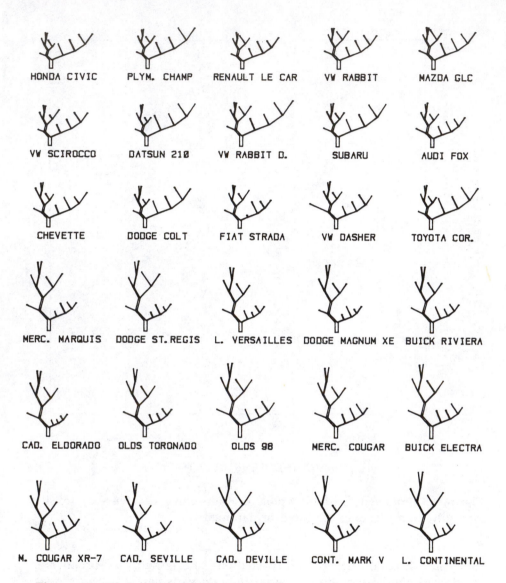

Figure 1.4 Kleiner-Hartigan trees.

underlying assumptions. Chapter 6 is about probability plots, which are designed for assessing formal distributional assumptions for the data. Chapter 7 covers graphical methods for regression, including methods for understanding the fit of the regression equation and methods for assessing the appropriateness of the regression model.

Chapter 8 is a general discussion of graphics including a number of principles that help us judge the strengths and weaknesses of graphical displays, and guide us in designing new ones.

The Appendix contains most of the data sets used in the examples of the book and other data sets referred to just in the exercises.

1.4   THE SELECTION AND PRESENTATION OF MATERIALS

We have selected a group of graphical methods to treat in detail. Our plan has been first to give all the information needed to construct a plot, then to illustrate the display by applying it to at least one set of data, and finally to describe the usefulness of the method and the role it plays in data analysis.

The process for selecting methods to feature was a parochial one: we chose methods that we use in our own work and that have proved successful. Such a selection process is necessary, for we cannot write intelligently about methods that we have not used. We have had to exclude many promising ones with which we are just beginning to have some experience and others that we are simply unfamiliar with. Some of these are briefly described and referenced in "Further Reading" sections at the ends of chapters.

1.5   DATA SETS

Almost all of the data sets used in this book to illustrate the methods are in the Appendix together with other data sets that are treated in the exercises. There are two reasons for this. One is to provide data for the reader to experiment with the graphical methods we describe. The second is to allow the reader to challenge more readily our methodology and devise still better graphical methods for data analysis. Naturally, we encourage readers to collect other data sets of suitable nature to experiment further.

1.6   QUALITY OF GRAPHICAL DISPLAYS

The plots shown in this book are generally in the form we would produce in the course of analyzing data. Most of them represent what you could expect to produce, routinely, from a good graphics package and a reasonably inexpensive graphics device, such as a pen plotter. A few plots have been done by hand. None were produced on special, expensive graphics devices. The point is that the value of graphs in data analysis comes when they show important patterns in the data, and plain, legible, well-designed plots can do this without the expense and delay involved with special presentation-quality graphics devices.

Naturally, when the plots are to be used for presentation or publication rather than for analysis, making the graphics elegant and aesthetically pleasing would be important. We have deliberately not made such changes here. These are working plots, part of the everyday business of data analysis.

1.7   HOW SHOULD THIS BOOK BE USED?

Readers who experiment with the graphical methods in this book by trying them in the exercises, on the data in the Appendix, and on their own data will learn far more from this book than passive readers.

It is usually easy to understand the details of making a particular plot. What is more difficult is to acquire the judgment necessary for successful application of the method: When should the method be used? For what types of data? For what types of problems? What patterns should be looked for? Which patterns are significant and which are spurious? What has been learned about the data in its application context by looking at the plots? The book can go just so far in dealing with these matters of judgment. Readers will need to take themselves the rest of the way.

2

Portraying the Distribution of a Set of Data

2.1 INTRODUCTION

A simple but common need arises in data analysis when we have a single set of numbers that are measurements, observations, or values of some variable, and we want to understand their basic characteristics as a collection. For example, if we consider the gross national product of all countries in the United Nations in 1980, we might ask: What is a "typical" or "average" or "central" value for the whole set? How spread out are the data around the center? How far are the most extreme values (both high and low) from the typical value? What fraction of the numbers are less than the value for one particular country (our own, say)?

In short, we need to understand the distribution of the set of data values: where they lie along the measurement axis, and what kind of pattern they form. This often means asking additional questions. What are the quartiles of the distribution (the 25 percent and 75 percent points along the observation scale)? Are any of the observations outliers, that is, values that seem to lie too far from the majority? Are there repeated values? What is the density or relative concentration of observations in various intervals along the measurement scale? Do the data accumulate at the middle of their range, or at one end, or at several places? Are the data symmetrically distributed?

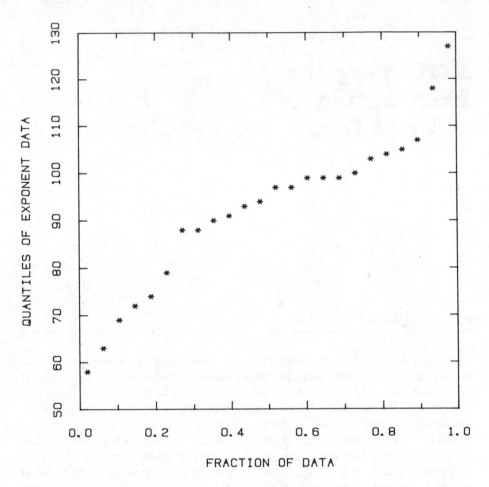

Figure 2.1 Quantile plot of the exponent data. The y coordinates of the plotted points are the ordered observations.

One way to present the distribution of a set of data is to present the data in a table. Many questions can be answered by carefully studying a table, especially if the data have first been ordered from smallest to largest (or the reverse). In a sense, a table contains all the answers, because apart from possible rounding, it presents all of the data.

However, many distributional questions are difficult to answer just from peering at a table. Plots of the data can be far more revealing, even though it may be harder to read exact data values from a plot. This chapter discusses a variety of plots designed for studying the distribution of a set of data.

Two sets of data will be used to illustrate the methodology. One is the daily maximum ozone concentrations at ground level recorded between May 1, 1974 and September 30, 1974 at a site in Stamford, Connecticut. (There are 17 missing days of data due to equipment malfunction.) The current federal standard for ozone states that the concentration should not exceed 120 parts per billion (ppb) more than one day per year at any particular location. A day with ozone concentration above 200 ppb is regarded as heavily polluted. The data are given in the Appendix.

The second set of data is from an experiment in perceptual psychology. A person asked to judge the relative areas of circles of varying sizes typically judges the areas on a perceptual scale that can be approximated by

$$\text{judged area} = \alpha(\text{true area})^{\beta}.$$

For most people the exponent β is between .6 and 1. Apart from random error, a person with an exponent of .7 who sees two circles, one twice the area of the other, would judge the larger one to be only $2^{.7} = 1.6$ times as large. Our second set of data is the set of measured exponents (multiplied by 100) for 24 people from one particular experiment (Cleveland, Harris, and McGill, 1982).

In this chapter we are concerned only with data values themselves, not with any particular ordering of them. (The ozone data have an ordering in time, for instance, and the exponent data could be ordered, say, by the ages of the people in the experiment.) We will usually refer to raw (unordered) data by "y_i for $i = 1$ to n", and to ordered data by "$y_{(i)}$ for $i = 1$ to n." The parentheses in the subscript simply mean that $y_{(1)}$ is the smallest value, $y_{(2)}$ is the second smallest, and so on.

2.2 QUANTILE PLOTS

A good preliminary look at a set of data is provided by the quantile plot which is shown for the exponent data in Figure 2.1. Before describing it, we must define "quantile".

The concept of quantile is closely connected with the familiar concept of percentile. When we say that a student's college board exam score is at the 85th percentile, we mean that 85 percent of all college board scores fall below that student's score, and that 15 percent of them fall above. Similarly, we will define the .85 quantile of a set of data to be a number on the scale of the data that divides the data into two groups, so that a fraction .85 of the observations fall below and a fraction .15 fall above. We will call this value $Q(.85)$. The only difference between percentile and quantile is that percentile refers to a percent of the set of data and quantile refers to a fraction of the set of data. Figure 2.2 depicts $Q(.85)$ for the ozone data plotted along a number line.

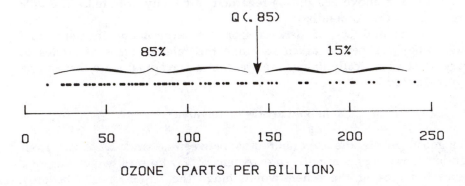

Figure 2.2 The Stamford ozone data, showing the .85 quantile.

Unfortunately, this definition runs into complications when we actually try to compute quantiles from a set of data. For instance, if we want to compute the .27 quantile from 10 data values, we find that each observation is 10 percent of the whole set, so we can split off a fraction of .2 or .3 of the data, but there is no value that will split off a fraction of exactly .27. Also, if we were to put the split point exactly at an observation, we would not know whether to count that observation in the lower or upper part.

To overcome these difficulties, we construct a convenient operational definition of quantile. Starting with a set of raw data y_i, for $i = 1$ to n, we order the data from smallest to largest, obtaining the sorted data $y_{(i)}$, for $i = 1$ to n. Letting p represent any fraction between 0 and 1, we begin by defining the quantile $Q(p)$ corresponding to the fraction p as follows: Take $Q(p)$ to be $y_{(i)}$ whenever p is one of the fractions $p_i = (i-.5)/n$, for $i = 1$ to n.

Thus, the quantiles $Q(p_i)$ of the data are just the ordered data values themselves, $y_{(i)}$. The quantile plot in Figure 2.1 is a plot of $Q(p_i)$ against p_i for the exponent data. The horizontal scale shows the fractions p_i and goes from 0 to 1. The vertical scale is the scale of the original data. Except for the way the horizontal axis is labeled, this plot would look identical to a plot of $y_{(i)}$ against i.

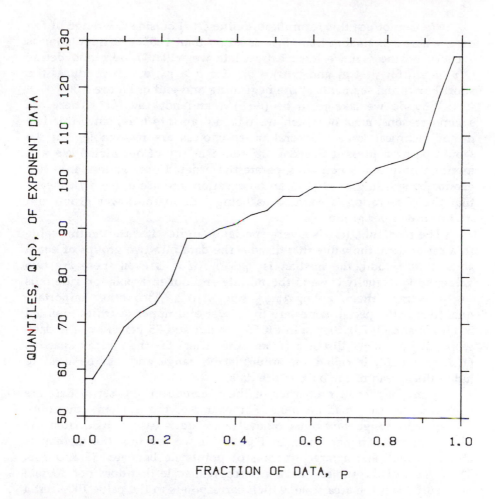

Figure 2.3 Interpolated quantiles for the exponent data.

So far, we have only defined the quantile function $Q(p)$ for certain discrete values of p, namely p_i. Often this is all we need; in other cases, we extend the definition of $Q(p)$ within the range of the data by simple interpolation. In Figure 2.1 this means connecting consecutive points with straight line segments, leading to Figure 2.3. In symbols, if p is a fraction f of the way from p_i to p_{i+1}, then $Q(p)$ is defined to be

$$Q(p) = (1-f)Q(p_i) + fQ(p_{i+1}).$$

We cannot use this formula to define $Q(p)$ outside the range of the data, where p is smaller than $.5/n$ or larger than $1-.5/n$. Extrapolation is a tricky business; if we must extrapolate we will play safe and define $Q(p) = y_{(1)}$ for $p < p_1$ and $Q(p) = y_{(n)}$ for $p > p_n$, which produces the short horizontal segments at the beginning and end of Figure 2.3.

Why do we take p_i to be $(i-.5)/n$ and not, say i/n? There are several reasons, most of which we will not go into here, since this is a minor technical issue. (Several other choices are reasonable, but we would be hard pressed to see a difference in any of our plots.) We will mention only that when we separate the ordered observations into two groups by splitting exactly on an observation, the use of $(i-.5)/n$ means that the observation is counted as being half in the lower group and half in the upper group.

The median, $Q(.5)$, is a very special quantile. It is the central value in a set of data, the value that divides the data into two groups of equal size. If n is odd, the median is $y_{((n+1)/2)}$; if n is even there are two values of $y_{(i)}$ equally close to the middle and our interpolation rule tells us to average them, giving $(y_{(n/2)} + y_{(n/2+1)})/2$. Two other important quantiles with special names are the lower and upper quartiles, defined as $Q(.25)$ and $Q(.75)$; they split off 25 percent and 75 percent of the data, respectively. The distance from the first to the third quartile, $Q(.75) - Q(.25)$, is called the interquartile range and can be used to judge the spread of the bulk of the data.

Many important properties of the distribution of a set of data are conveyed by the quantile plot. For example, the medians, quartiles, interquartile range, and other quantiles are quite easy to read from the plot. For the exponent data in Figure 2.1 we see that the median is about 95 and that a large fraction of points lie between 85 and 105. Thus, most of the subjects have a perceptual scale that does not deviate markedly from the area scale, which corresponds to the value 100. But a few subjects do have values quite different from 100. In fact, the total range (maximum minus minimum) is seen to be about 70. The subject with the smallest exponent, 58, comes close to judging some linear aspect of circles, such as diameter, rather than area. (A value of 50 corresponds to judging linear aspects exactly.)

Figure 2.4 is a quantile plot of the ozone data. It shows that the median ozone is about 80 ppb. The value 120 ppb is roughly the .75 quantile; thus the federal standard in Stamford was exceeded about 25% of the time. The highest concentration is somewhat less than 250 ppb and only 8 values are above 200 ppb (corresponding to days heavily polluted with ozone). The two smallest values of 14 ppb seem somewhat out of line with the pattern of points at the low end.

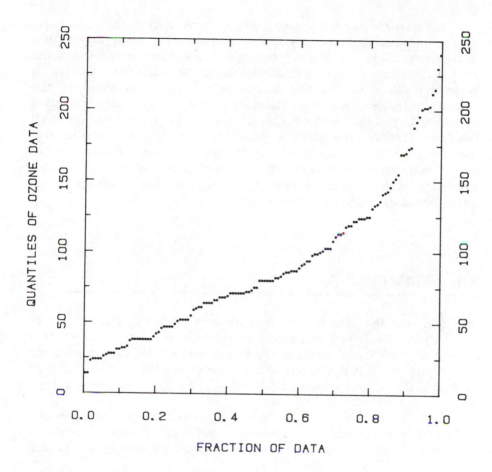

Figure 2.4 Quantile plot of the Stamford ozone data.

The local density or concentration of the data is conveyed by the local slope of the quantile plot; the flatter the slope, the greater the density of points. The rough overall density impression for the ozone data conveyed by Figure 2.4 is one in which the density decreases with larger ozone values. The highest local density of points occurs when there are many measurements with exactly the same value. This is revealed on the quantile plot by a string of horizontal points. For example, in Figure 2.4 there are two such strings of length 6 between 50 ppb and 100 ppb, and another of length 8 at about 35 ppb. A more detailed description of the ozone density will be given in Section 2.8 where a display specifically designed to convey density will be described.

The quantile plot is a good general purpose display since it is fairly easy to construct and does a good job of portraying many aspects of a distribution. Three convenient features of the plot are the following: First, in constructing it, we do not make any arbitrary choices of parameter values or cell boundaries (as we must for several of the displays to be described shortly), and no models for the data are fitted or assumed. Second, like a table, it is not a summary but a display of all the data. Third, on the quantile plot every point is plotted at a distinct location, even if there are exact duplicates in the data. The number of points that can be portrayed without overlap is limited only by the resolution of the plotting device. For a high resolution device several hundred points are easily distinguished.

2.3   SYMMETRY

We often use the idea of symmetry in data analysis. The essence of symmetry is that if you look at the reflection of a symmetric object in a mirror, its appearance remains the same. Since a mirror reverses left and right, this means that an object is symmetric if every detail that occurs on the left also occurs on the right, and at the same distance from an imaginary line down the center.

The distribution of a set of data is symmetric if a plot of the points along a simple number line is symmetric in the usual sense. The sketch in Figure 2.5 shows such a plot of six fictitious symmetric data values,

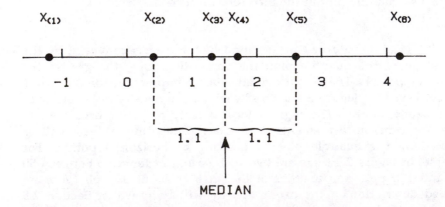

Figure 2.5 Six fictitious symmetric data values.

−1.2, 0.4, 1.3, 1.7, 2.6, and 4.2. The center of symmetry must be the median, and the sketch shows that $y_{(2)}$ and $y_{(5)}$ are equidistant from the center, that is,

$$\text{median} - y_{(2)} = y_{(5)} - \text{median} = 1.1.$$

The general requirement for symmetry is

$$\text{median} - y_{(i)} = y_{(n+1-i)} - \text{median}, \quad \text{for } i = 1 \text{ to } n/2.$$

(If n is odd we can use $(n+1)/2$ instead of $n/2$.) Of course, just as faces and others things that we regard as symmetric in real life are not exactly symmetric, so data will not be exactly symmetric. We will look for approximate symmetry.

We can also characterize symmetry in terms of the quantile function. Since the median is $Q(.5)$, we say that the data are symmetrically distributed if

$$Q(.5) - Q(p) = Q(1-p) - Q(.5) \quad \text{for all } p, \quad 0 < p < .5.$$

When data are asymmetric in a way that makes the quantiles on the right progressively further from the median than the corresponding quantiles on the left, then we say that the data are skewed to the right, or toward large values.

The quantile plot can be used to examine data for symmetry. If the data are symmetric the plot itself will not be symmetric in the usual sense; rather, the points in the top half of the plot will stretch out toward the upper right in the same way that the points in the bottom half stretch out toward the lower left. This is shown for our artificial data in Figure 2.6. When the data are skewed toward large values, then the top of the quantile plot extends upward more sharply. Figure 2.4 shows that the ozone data are skewed, but in Figure 2.1 the exponent data appear to be nearly symmetric. Section 2.8 discusses a plot specifically designed for investigating symmetry in data.

There are several reasons why symmetry is an important concept in data analysis. First, the most important single summary of a set of data is the location of the center, and when data are symmetric the meaning of "center" is unambiguous. We can take center to mean any of the following three things, since they all coincide exactly for symmetric data, and they are close together for nearly symmetric data: (1) the center of symmetry, (2) the arithmetic average or center of gravity, (3) the median or 50% point. Furthermore, if the data have a single point of highest concentration instead of several (that is, they are unimodal), then we can add to the list (4) the point of highest concentration. When data are far from symmetric, we may have trouble

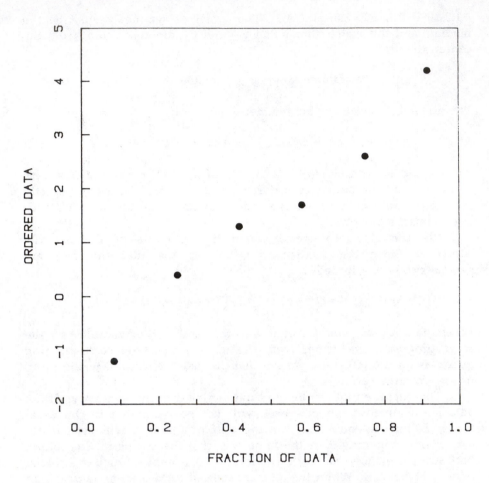

Figure 2.6 Quantile plot of the six fictitious symmetric data values of Figure 2.5.

even agreeing on what we mean by center; in fact, the center may become an inappropriate summary for the data.

Symmetry is also important because it can simplify our thinking about the distribution of a set of data. If we can establish that the data are (approximately) symmetric, then we no longer need to describe the shapes of both the right and left halves. (We might even combine the information from the two sides and have effectively twice as much data for viewing the distributional shape.)

Finally, symmetry is important because many statistical procedures are designed for, and work best on, symmetric data. For example, the simple and common practice of summarizing the spread of a set of data by quoting a single number such as the standard deviation or the interquartile range is only valid, in a sense, for symmetric data. For readers familiar with the normal or Gaussian distribution (which we do not discuss until Chapter 6), we mention that whereas the normal distribution is the foundation for many classical statistical procedures, symmetry alone underlies many modern robust statistical methods. The modern procedures have wider applicability because normality is often an unrealistic requirement for data, but approximate symmetry is often attainable. Interestingly, symmetry is a basic property of the normal distribution!

2.4 ONE-DIMENSIONAL SCATTER PLOTS

A simple way to portray the distribution of the data is to plot the data y_i along a number line or axis labeled according to the measurement scale. The resulting one-dimensional scatter diagram or scatter plot is shown in Figure 2.7 for the ozone data. Note that if we horizontally project the points on a quantile plot onto the vertical axis, the result is a vertical one-dimensional scatter plot. In this sense the quantile plot can be thought of as an expansion into two dimensions of the one-dimensional scatter plot.

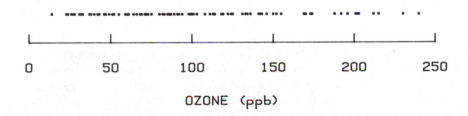

Figure 2.7 One-dimensional scatter plot of the ozone data.

The main virtue of the one-dimensional scatter plot is its compactness. This allows it to be used in the margins of other displays to add information. (An example will be shown later in the chapter.) In a one-dimensional scatter plot we can clearly see the maximum and minimum values of the data. Provided there is not too much overlap we can also get very rough impressions of the center of the data, the spread, local density, symmetry, and outliers. Furthermore the plot is easy to construct and to explain to others.

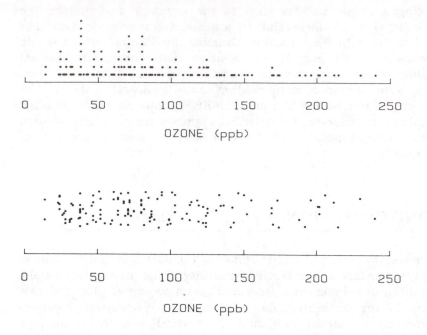

Figure 2.8 A one-dimensional scatter plot of the ozone data with stacking (top panel) and a jittered one-dimensional scatter plot (bottom panel).

However, a price is paid for collapsing the two-dimensional quantile plot to the one-dimensional scatter plot. Individual quantiles can no longer be found easily, and visual resolution of the points is more likely to be a problem even for moderately many points. We obtain maximum resolution by using a plotting character that is narrow such as a dot or a short vertical line instead of, say, an asterisk or an ×. But this does not solve the problem of exact duplicates. If $y_{(i)} = y_{(i+1)}$, then the plotting locations for $y_{(i)}$ and $y_{(i+1)}$ on the one-dimensional scatter plot are the same. (Note that this did not happen on the quantile plot.) For example, there are several repeated values in the ozone data which are not resolved in Figure 2.7. One way to alleviate this problem is to stack points, that is, to displace them vertically when they coincide with others. A one-dimensional scatter plot of the ozone data with stacking is shown in the top panel of Figure 2.8. This, however, is only a solution to the problem of exact overlap and does not help us when there are a lot of points that crowd one another. Another method that helps to alleviate both exact overlap and crowding is vertical jitter, which is illustrated in the bottom panel of Figure 2.8. Let u_i, $i = 1$ to n, be the integers 1 to n in random order. The vertical jitter is achieved by plotting u_i against y_i with u_i on the vertical axis and y_i on the horizontal axis. To keep the display nearly one-dimensional the range of the vertical axis — that is, the actual physical distance — is kept small compared to the range of the horizontal axis, and, of course, we do not need to indicate the vertical scale on the plot. The vertical jitter in Figure 2.8 appears to have done a good job of reducing the overlap in Figure 2.7.

2.5 BOX PLOTS

It is usually important to take an initial look at all of the data, perhaps with a quantile plot, to make sure that no unusual behavior goes undetected. But there are also situations and stages of analysis where it is useful to have summary displays of the distribution. One simple method of summarization, called a box plot (Tukey, 1977), is illustrated in Figure 2.9 for the ozone data and in Figure 2.10 for the exponent data.

In the box plot the upper and lower quartiles of the data are portrayed by the top and bottom of a rectangle, and the median is portrayed by a horizontal line segment within the rectangle. Dashed lines extend from the ends of the box to the *adjacent values* which are defined as follows. We first compute the interquartile range, $IQR = Q(.75) - Q(.25)$. In the case of the exponent data the quartiles are 83.5 and 101.5 so that $IQR = 18$. The upper adjacent value is defined to be the largest observation that is less than or equal to the upper quartile plus $1.5 \times IQR$. Since this latter value is 128.5 for the exponent data, the upper adjacent value is simply the largest observation, 127. The lower adjacent value is defined to be the smallest observation that is greater than or equal to the lower quartile minus $1.5 \times IQR$. For the exponent data, it is the smallest observation, 58. Thus for the exponent data, the adjacent values are the extreme values. If any y_i falls outside the range of the two adjacent values, it is called an *outside value* and is plotted as an individual point; for the exponent data there are no outside values and for the ozone data there are two.

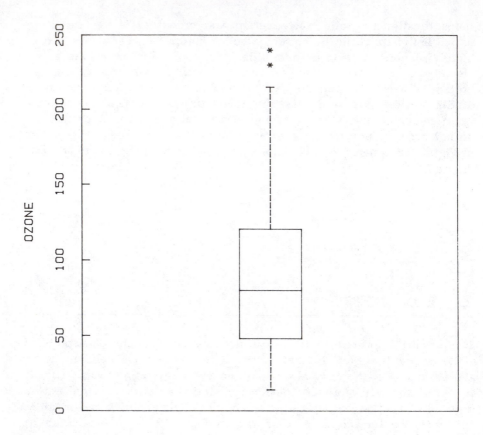

Figure 2.9 A box plot of the ozone data.

The box plot gives a quick impression of certain prominent features of the distribution. The median shows the center, or location, of the distribution. The spread of the bulk of the data (the central 50%) is seen as the length of the box. The lengths of the dashed lines relative to the box show how stretched the tails of the distribution are. The individual outside values give the viewer an opportunity to consider the question of outliers, that is, observations that seem unusually, or even implausibly, large or small. Outside values are not necessarily outliers (indeed, the ozone quantile plot suggests that the two ozone outside values are not), but any outliers will almost certainly appear as outside values.

The box plot allows a partial assessment of symmetry. If the distribution is symmetric then the box plot is symmetric about the median: the median cuts the box in half, the upper and lower dashed

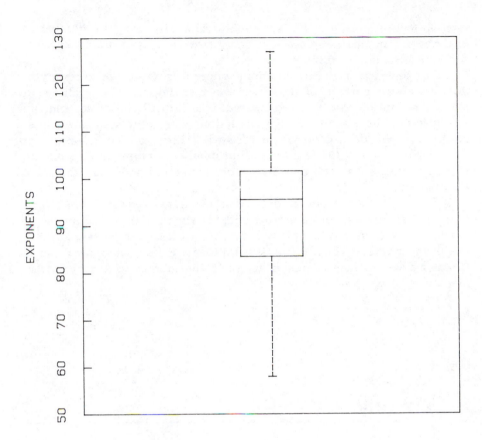

Figure 2.10 A box plot of the exponent data.

lines are about the same length, and the outside values at top and bottom, if any, are about equal in number and symmetrically placed. There can be asymmetry in the data not revealed by the box plot, but the plot usually gives a good rough indication. The box plot in Figure 2.9 shows that the ozone data are not symmetric. The upper components are stretched relative to their counterparts below the median, revealing that the distribution is skewed to the right. For the exponent data the box plot in Figure 2.10 suggests that the tails are symmetric, but that the median is high relative to the quartiles. Recall from Section 2.3 that the quantile plot of these data in Figure 2.1 suggests the data are approximately symmetric. To resolve this apparent contradiction, we can look more closely at Figure 2.1. Ignoring the two largest and two smallest values, the rest of the data appear slightly skewed toward small values, which explains the position of the median relative to the quartiles. But we should remember that the number of observations in this sample is small and that we would quite likely see different behavior in another sample.

Box plots are useful in situations where it is either not necessary or not feasible to portray all details of the distribution. For example, if many distributions are to be compared, it is difficult to try to compare all aspects of the distributions. In situations where the summary values of the box plot do a good job of conveying the prominent features of the distribution and the less prominent detailed features do not matter, it makes sense to use the box plot and eliminate the unneeded information.

The width of the box, as defined so far, has no particular meaning. The plot can be made quite narrow without affecting its visual impact so that it can be used in situations where compactness is important. This is useful in Chapter 3 when many distributions are being compared and in Chapter 4 when the box plot is added to the margin of another visual display.

2.6   HISTOGRAMS

Another way to summarize a data distribution, one that has a long history in statistics, is to partition the range of the data into several intervals of equal length, count the number of points in each interval, and plot the counts as bar lengths in a histogram. This has been done in Figure 2.11 for the ozone data. The relative heights of the bars represent the relative density of observations in the intervals.

The histogram is widely used and thus is familiar even to most nontechnical people and without extensive explanation. This makes it a convenient way to communicate distributional information to general audiences.

However, as a data analysis device it has some drawbacks. Figure 2.12 is a second histogram of the same ozone data. Below each histogram is a jittered one-dimensional scatter plot to show the relationship of the histogram to the original data. The two histograms give rather different visual impressions, and the differences depend on the fairly arbitrary choice of the number and placement of intervals. This choice determines whether we show more detail, as in Figure 2.12, or retain a smoothness or simplicity, as in Figure 2.11. But even Figure 2.11 is not genuinely smooth, because the bars have sharp corners. The

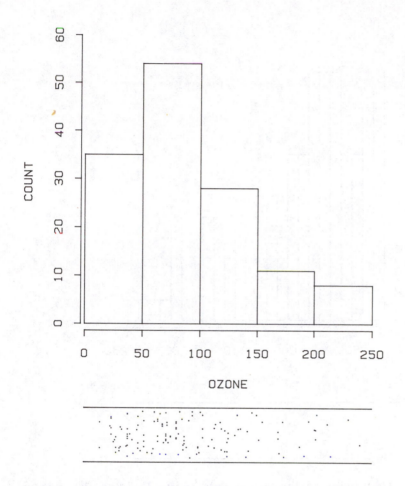

Figure 2.11 Histogram of the ozone data, with a jittered one-dimensional scatter plot.

positions of the corners have little to do with the data; they are an artifact of the histogram construction. (Smoother approaches are discussed in Section 2.9.) Figure 2.11 reveals an additional problem: following common practice, we put the ends of the intervals at convenient numbers (multiples of 50 ppb) so they can be easily read from the plot, but in doing so we have covered up the important nonzero lower bound for ozone and have created the erroneous impression that the density of the data points just below 50 ppb is much less than the density just above 50 ppb.

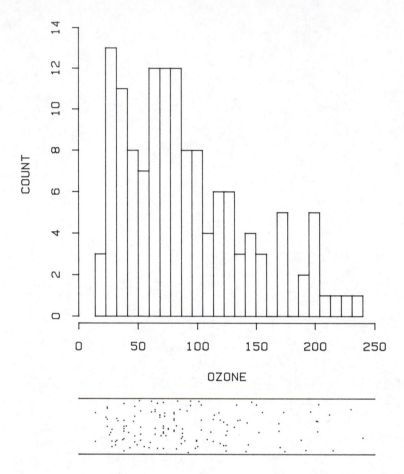

Figure 2.12 Histogram of the ozone data (with 25 intervals), with a jittered one-dimensional scatter plot.

2.7 STEM-AND-LEAF DIAGRAMS

Figure 2.13 shows a stem-and-leaf diagram of the ozone data (Tukey, 1977). It is a hybrid between a table and a graph since it shows numerical values as numerals but its profile is very much like a histogram.

To construct a stem-and-leaf diagram we first write down, to the left of a vertical line, all possible leading digits in the range of the data. Then we represent each data value by writing its trailing digit in the appropriate row to the right of the line. Thus the fifteenth row of the

Figure 2.13 Stem-and-leaf diagram of the ozone data.

```
 1 | 44
 2 | 3444467888
 3 | 1122378888888 8
 4 | 023677779
 5 | 1222259
 6 | 0114444668889
 7 | 11111122355
 8 | 000000223566 7779
 9 | 1244899
10 | 013338
11 | 1334899
12 | 2244455
13 | 1346
14 | 1236
15 | 025
16 | 99
17 | 034
18 | 8
19 | 26
20 | 1226
21 | 25
22 |
23 | 0
24 | 0
```

display in Figure 2.13 represents the observations 150, 152, and 155. Each number to the left of the vertical line is called a stem and each digit to the right of the vertical line is called a leaf.

The stem-and-leaf diagram is a compact way to record the data. Instead of the 319 digits that an ordinary table would require, Figure 2.13 uses only 175 digits. At the same time, the diagram gives us visual information; the length of each row shows the number of values in each row, so the display is essentially a histogram lying on its side. Regarded as a histogram, Figure 2.13 has interval length 10 ppb.

In Figure 2.13 we clearly see the asymmetry of the ozone data: there is a fairly sharp cutoff of the data on the top at about 20 ppb, but the large values trail off. We see that most days at Stamford have maximum ozone concentrations between 30 and 90 ppb, but there is an interesting slight dip in this range at about 50 ppb that is hard to appreciate in the quantile plot of this data in Figure 2.4. It may have an explanation or may be an accident of this particular set of data. The two values of 14 ppb look less exceptional in the stem-and-leaf diagram than they did in the quantile plot.

```
6 | 0 1 1 4 4 4 4 6 6 8 8 8 9
7 | 1 1 1 1 1 1 2 2 3 5 5
8 | 0 0 0 0 0 0 2 2 3 5 6 6 7 7 7 9
```

a

```
6 | 0 1 1 4 4 4 4
  | 6 6 8 8 8 9
7 | 1 1 1 1 1 1 2 2 3
  | 5 5
8 | 0 0 0 0 0 0 2 2 3
  | 5 6 6 7 7 7 9
```

b

```
6 ( 0 1 ) | 0 1 1
  ( 2 3 ) |
  ( 4 5 ) | 4 4 4 4
  ( 6 7 ) | 6 6
  ( 8 9 ) | 8 8 8 9
7 ( 0 1 ) | 1 1 1 1 1 1
  ( 2 3 ) | 2 2 3
  ( 4 5 ) | 5 5
  ( 6 7 ) |
  ( 8 9 ) |
8 ( 0 1 ) | 0 0 0 0 0 0
  ( 2 3 ) | 2 2 3
  ( 4 5 ) | 5
  ( 6 7 ) | 6 6 7 7 7
  ( 8 9 ) | 9
```

c

Figure 2.14 Stem-and-leaf diagrams for ozone data between 60 and 89 ppb.

In some applications the data have such a narrow range that they all fall into two or three stems, and the stem-and-leaf display shows too little detail. When this happens, we can alter the effective interval length of the stem-and-leaf diagram. Consider just the ozone observations between 60 and 89, which are shown in three stem-and-leaf diagrams in Figure 2.14. In panel (a) a diagram as we have just described it is shown; there are too few rows for the display to be very informative. In panel (b) each stem has two rows: the first is for the leaves 0 to 4 and the second for the leaves 5 to 9. With this modification the interval length is 5. In panel (c) the interval length is

2; the digits in parentheses, which serve to remind which digits go in each row, are useful when the display is being constructed by hand but are not necessary for final presentation.

In applications it is often necessary to change measurement units by multiplying by some power of 10, and to truncate the data (that is, to ignore some digits on the right) to get values suitable for a stem-and-leaf display. It is also sometimes useful to transform the data, for example by taking logarithms, as we will discuss in the next section. Furthermore, the rules for making the diagram can be modified if one finds that some other variation does a better job for a particular data set. For example, each leaf can be two digits rather than one, with a comma separating the leaves on a single row. Thus a row $5|21,36,97$ would represent 521, 536, and 597.

The stem-and-leaf diagram is particularly useful when it is important to convey both the numerical values themselves and graphical information about the distribution, for example in reports and published papers in which data are presented and analyzed.

The stem-and-leaf display is easy to construct by hand. In the examples we have shown, the leaves on each stem are ordered by magnitude because the ozone data were ordered in advance. However, we can make a stem-and-leaf display from unordered data, as well. The leaves will not be ordered within stems, but we can easily copy the display putting them in order. When we are working with paper and pencil, the stem-and-leaf diagram is an excellent tool for sorting the data from smallest to largest so that quantiles of various orders can be calculated.

2.8 SYMMETRY PLOTS AND TRANSFORMATIONS

All of the graphical displays discussed so far allow at least a partial assessment of the symmetry of a set of data. We can, however, design a graphical display specifically for this purpose.

In Section 2.3 we established that the data are symmetric if

$$\text{median} - y_{(i)} = y_{(n+1-i)} - \text{median}.$$

Thus we can check for symmetry by plotting $u_i = (y_{(n+1-i)} - \text{median})$ against $v_i = (\text{median} - y_{(i)})$, for $i = 1$ to $n/2$. (If n is odd we will use

$(n+1)/2$ instead of $n/2$.) If the points lie close to the line $u = v$, the distribution is nearly symmetric. A symmetry plot for the ozone data is shown in Figure 2.15, with the line $u = v$ drawn in.

As i increases, neither v_i nor u_i decreases, since $y_{(i)}$ and $y_{(n+1-i)}$ both move further from the median. Thus, going from left to right, the ordinates of the points on the symmetry plot are nondecreasing. Furthermore, as we go from left to right the fractions for the quantiles used on the horizontal axis go from .5 to 0, while the fractions for the quantiles used on the vertical axis go from .5 to 1. Thus the points in the lower left corner of the plot correspond to quantiles close to the median and to observations at the center of the distribution. The points in the upper right corner correspond to quantiles far from the median and to observations in the tails of the distribution. One interesting feature of the ozone symmetry plot in Figure 2.15 is that the points are relatively close to the line for v_i going from 0 to 40 ppb but diverge rapidly above 40 ppb. Overall the ozone data are skewed toward large values, but the skewness is largely due to the tails, not the central part of the distribution. The nature of the skewness would be difficult to capture with just a few summary statistics from the distribution.

When data are either amounts or counts of something, as with the ozone data, the distribution is frequently skewed to the right. This often arises because there is a lower bound on the data (usually zero) but no upper bound, which allows the measurements to stretch out to the right.

Frequently, for positive data skewed to the right, the asymmetry steadily increases in going from the center to the tails, as with the ozone data. When this happens, it may be possible to remove the asymmetry by a simple transformation of the data. One group of simple transformations for positive data is the class of power transformations which have the form

$$
\begin{array}{ll}
y_i^\theta & \text{if } \theta > 0 \\
\log y_i & \text{if } \theta = 0 \\
-y_i^\theta & \text{if } \theta < 0.
\end{array}
$$

For example, if $\theta = .5$, the transformation is the square root, $\sqrt{y_i} = y_i^{.5}$, while if $\theta = -1$ the transformation is the negative of the reciprocal, $-y_i^{-1}$. The reason for changing the sign when θ is less than 0 is to insure that the transformed values have the same relative order as the original values.

If the data are skewed to the right, then we might find a power transformation with $\theta < 1$ that makes the data nearly symmetric. ($\theta > 1$ can work for data skewed to the left, but left skewness occurs much less frequently.) A symmetry plot for the cube roots ($\theta = 1/3$) of the ozone

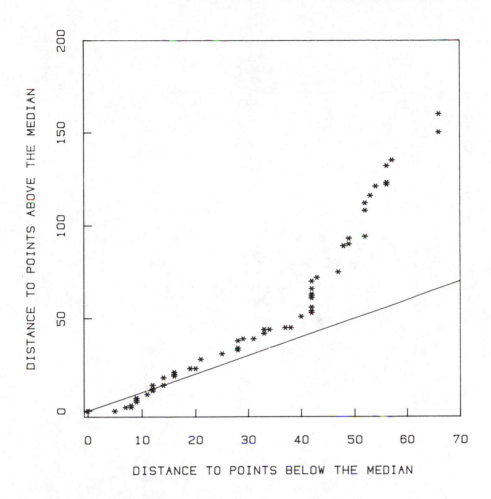

Figure 2.15 A symmetry plot of the ozone data.

data is shown in Figure 2.16. (Note that the original ppb scales for the
upper and lower halves of the data are shown along the right and top
edges of the plot to make it easier to match plotted points with original
data values.) Now the points lie reasonably close to the line $u = v$ so
that the data on the cube root ppb scale are nearly symmetric. To find
an adequate symmetrizing transformation we may have to try several
values of θ and make a symmetry plot for each.

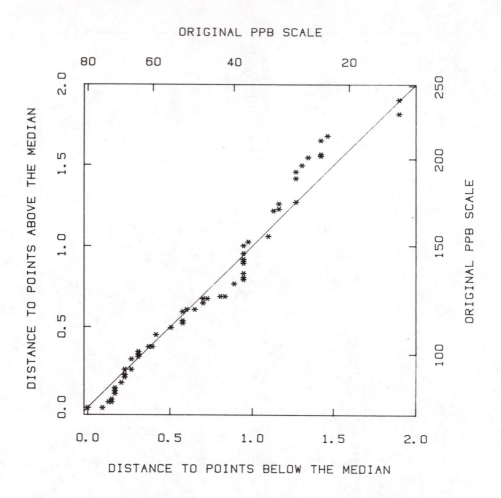

Figure 2.16 A symmetry plot of the cube roots of the ozone data.

*2.9 DENSITY TRACES

We have talked about density as meaning the relative concentration of data points along different sections of the measurement scale. To be more precise, we will say that the local density at any point y is the fraction of data values per unit of measurement that fall in some interval centered at y. Let us return to the histogram of the ozone data in Figure 2.11. In the interval 0-50 ppb there are 35 values; thus the density of the data in this interval is

$$\frac{35 \text{ observations}}{136 \text{ observations}} \Big/ 50 \text{ ppb} = 5.15 \times 10^{-3} \text{ ppb}^{-1}.$$

We will take this to be a measurement of the data density at the midpoint (25, in this case) of the interval.

The histogram does portray density, in a sense. The vertical scale is not the density scale as we have defined it, but if we divide the bar heights by the total number of observations and by the interval width (assumed to be equal for all bars) we would have the density scale. This does not change the relative bar heights, since all bars are divided by the same constant, and it can be accomplished simply by changing the labels on the vertical axis. Thus the appearance of the plot does not change. In fact, for data analysis purposes, the units on the vertical axis are of very little concern.

However, in either form, the histogram is typically not an adequate representation of local density because of the discontinuities in going from one interval to another. In most situations we would like something smoother than the "city skyline at dusk" look of the histogram. The problem is that for the histogram the local density is really only computed at the midpoint of each interval; then the bars are drawn as if the density were constant throughout each interval.

One remedy to this problem is to compute the local density at every value of y, and let the intervals in which we count observations overlap. We can fix some interval width, h, and define

$$\text{local density at } y = \frac{\text{number of observations in } [y-h/2, \, y+h/2]}{h \times \text{total number of observations}}.$$

In practice, we will compute the density at a number of equally spaced values of y and trace the data density over the range of the data by interpolating linearly between these values. A density trace has been computed in this way for the ozone data and displayed in Figure 2.17. The computation was carried out with $h = 75$ at fifty equally spaced values from the minimum measurement, $y_{(1)}$, to the maximum measurement, $y_{(136)}$. Each of these fifty density values is portrayed by an asterisk and successive points are joined by straight line segments.

It is helpful to think of this last *density trace* from a somewhat different perspective. Normally we think of each sample value y_i as a single isolated point. But instead let us think of "smearing" y_i over the interval from $y_i - .5h$ to $y_i + .5h$ according to a *weight function*. Let $W(u)$ be the "boxcar" weight function

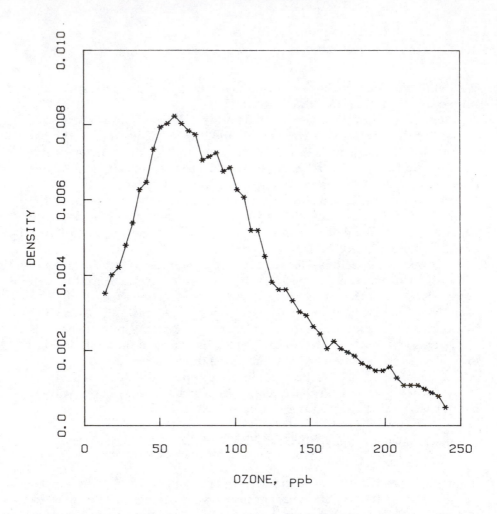

Figure 2.17 Density trace for the ozone data computed with the boxcar W function and $h = 75$.

$$W(u) = \begin{cases} 1 & \text{if } |u| \leqslant \tfrac{1}{2} \\ 0 & \text{otherwise.} \end{cases}$$

A picture of the boxcar function is shown in Figure 2.18. Smearing can be thought of as replacing y_i by a function of y, $W[(y-y_i)/h]/h$, which for each value of y is the smeared contribution of the observation y_i to the density at y. Instead of y_i contributing a count of 1 only at $y = y_i$ and 0 elsewhere, we now have $W[(y-y_i)/h]/h$ contributing a density of h^{-1} at all y in the interval $(y_i-.5h, y_i+.5h)$. The total area under the

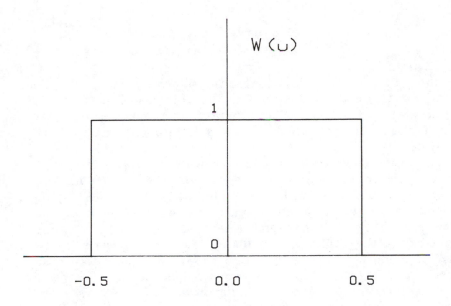

Figure 2.18 Boxcar W function for computing a density trace.

curve $W[(y-y_i)/h]/h$ is 1, which corresponds to the fact that each y_i formerly got a total count of 1. The density value at y, $f(y)$, can be thought of as the average of the smears of all y_i at y, given by the formula

$$f(y) = \frac{1}{hn} \sum_{i=1}^{n} W\left(\frac{y-y_i}{h}\right).$$

This formula is exactly equivalent to the rule given in the last paragraph for computing the density trace.

The density trace in Figure 2.17 is certainly an improvement over the histogram insofar as it eliminates the local discontinuity in going from one histogram interval to another. However, there is still some raggedness. The cause, it turns out, is the sharp cutoff of the boxcar function which goes abruptly from 0 to 1 at ±.5. To smooth things further we can replace the boxcar with a function which decreases gradually to 0 as u goes from 0 to .5 or −.5. One such function is based on the cosine and defined by

$$W(u) = \begin{cases} 1 + \cos 2\pi u & \text{if } |u| < \frac{1}{2} \\ 0 & \text{otherwise.} \end{cases}$$

A picture of the cosine weight function is shown in Figure 2.19. The formula for $f(y)$ is the same as before, but with the cosine version of $W(u)$ in place of the boxcar $W(u)$. The total area under the new $W(u)$ curve is also 1, so the smear for each point still contributes a total density of 1.

A density trace for the ozone data with the cosine function is shown in Figure 2.20. As in Figure 2.17, the computation has been carried out at 50 values with $h = 75$, but only the connecting line segments are drawn. Now the summary has a smoother appearance. Below the picture is a box plot which adds some exact quantile information to the display and facilitates comparison between the two graphical methods. The density trace shows that the peak density occurs around 70 ppb, a value somewhat less than the median. The fact that these data are skewed to the right means that the density trace stretches out further to the right than to the left. If the data were approximately symmetric then the density trace would be nearly symmetric.

The value of h determines how local and how smooth the density trace will be. There is a trade-off between smoothness and localness. As h decreases, $f(y)$ summarizes the density in smaller intervals centered at y, and $f(y)$ takes on a less smooth appearance as a function of y. For example, Figure 2.21 shows a density trace computed in the same manner as that in Figure 2.20 but with $h = 25$. It has a much rougher appearance due to the reduction in h. On the other hand, it reveals the drop in density near 50 that the smoother version cannot show.

The density traces in Figures 2.17, 2.20 and 2.21 all suffer from the same difficulty at the left hand edge of the data that was mentioned for the histogram. This kind of display cannot track the sudden drop of data density to zero and gives a misleading impression of the position of the lower boundary. Possible modifications to address this problem will not be pursued here. Figure 2.22 shows a density trace for the cube root of the ozone data that was depicted in a symmetry plot in Figure 2.16. The sharp cut off on the left does not occur on the cube root scale, and the plot works well at both ends.

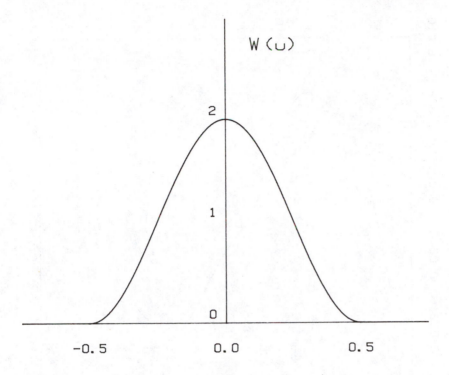

Figure 2.19 Cosine W function for computing a density trace.

2.10 SUMMARY AND DISCUSSION

We have presented a number of graphical methods for portraying the distribution of a simple set of observations. These techniques help us see many aspects of the distribution, including the extreme values, quantiles such as the median and quartiles, symmetry, changes in local density, repeated values, numbers of values in various intervals, and outliers.

The quantile plot is a good general-purpose plot. It is easy to construct and to explain, the plotted points do not coincide even if there are exact duplicates in the data. It is easy to read quantile information from the plot, and it can accommodate a large number of observations. The quantile plot gives rough information about the local density of the data and symmetry. In many instances it is a good way to study the data at the very start of the analysis. The quantile plot is not a summary but a display of all the data.

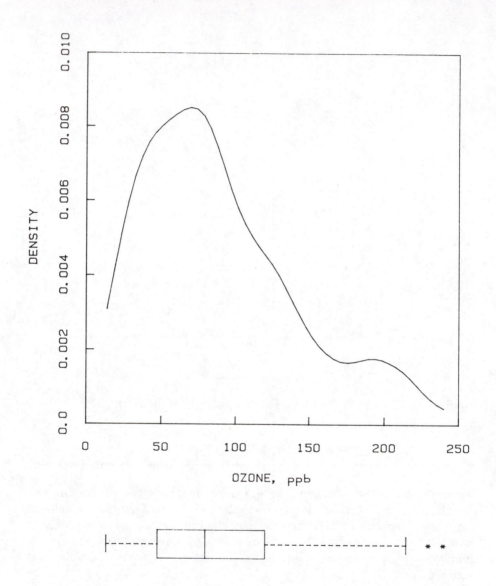

Figure 2.20 Density trace for the ozone data computed with the cosine *W* function and *h* = 75. A box plot of the data is added below the picture.

The one-dimensional scatter plot gives a quick, but sometimes misleading, view of the data. Overlap of plotted points is a serious potential problem. The overlap problem can be addressed by using a plotting character that is narrow or by using stacking or vertical jitter.

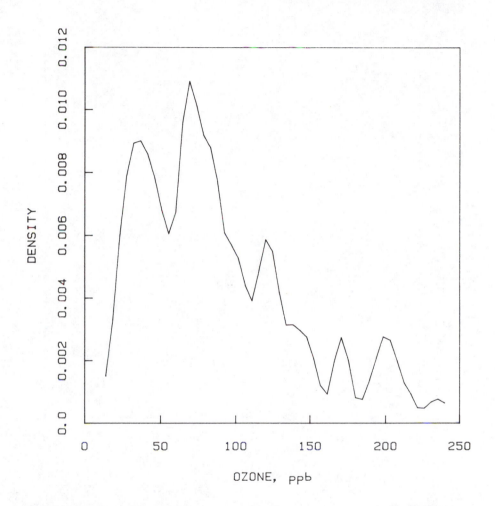

Figure 2.21 Density trace for the ozone data computed with the cosine W function and $h = 25$.

One useful property of the one-dimensional scatter plot is compactness. This means it can be added to the margins of other displays such as histograms.

Graphical summaries of data distributions are useful when it is either not feasible or not necessary to portray all the data. For example, in the next chapter we will encounter situations where a large number of distributions are to be compared so that a portrayal of all of the detail would result in an overwhelming amount of information. The box plot is a particularly effective summary which depicts extreme values and selected quantile information. Furthermore, because it is compact,.the

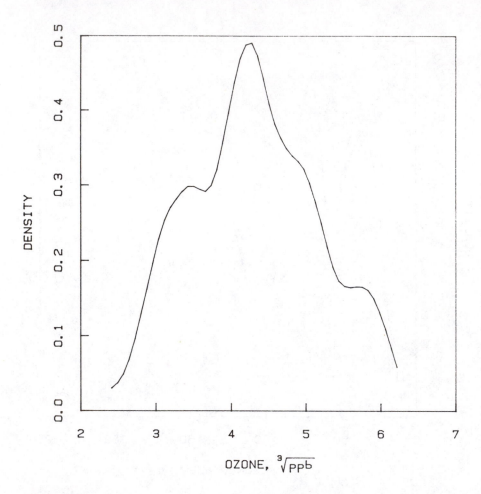

Figure 2.22 Density trace for the cube roots of the ozone data computed with the cosine W function and $h = 1$ (on the cube root ppb scale).

box plot can be used to supplement other displays.

Another type of summary, the histogram, requires minimal computation and is familiar to many people, so it is an attractive display when simplicity is important. This might occur, for example, in communicating with a nontechnical audience. But for data analysis purposes, it has some technical complications.

Stem-and-leaf diagrams combine the visual aspects of a histogram with the numerical information of a table. Typically they convey numerical values much more efficiently than a table (i.e., with fewer digits) and their graphical aspects allow a more effective understanding of the distribution than a table. Thus the stem-and-leaf diagram is an attractive alternative to a table when numerical values need either to be stored or to be communicated. The stem-and-leaf diagram is also a convenient graphical analysis tool, particularly when working by hand.

The symmetry plot helps us explore data for symmetry or deviations from symmetry. The plot can be useful for assisting the choice of a transformation to improve the symmetry of the data.

The density trace is designed for studying changes in local density over the range of the data. The user must choose a parameter value that prescribes how local the trace is and thus how smooth the appearance is.

2.11   FURTHER READING

Those interested in further reading on the graphical portrayal of distributions should proceed immediately to the excellent article by Wilk and Gnanadesikan (1968). It contains a discussion of the role of graphics in data analysis and further information about symmetry plots and plots related to the quantile plot. (What we call a quantile plot, they refer to as a plot of the empirical cumulative distribution function, or ecdf.) A similar treatment is given by Gnanadesikan (1977). Another good source for both philosophy and techniques is Tukey (1977), which is the basic reference for the box plots and stem-and-leaf diagrams. A lucid discussion of box plots and stem-and-leaf diagrams is given by Velleman and Hoaglin (1981), who also give computer programs for them.

Most accounts of density traces proceed from the assumption that the data are a sample from some random distribution, and that the purpose is to estimate the probability density of the underlying distribution. From a data analytic point of view this seems unnecessarily restrictive for a summary tool that can be used without imposing a probability mechanism on the data. But for balance the reader might want to peruse discussions of density estimation by Tarter and Kronmal (1976) and Wegman (1972).

The histogram is actually an eighteenth century data analytic tool (Playfair, 1786) which was invented as a data summary in the same spirit presented here. Thus for histograms we have returned to the original purpose. But for those who use histograms as probability density estimates both Diaconis and Freedman (1981) and Scott (1979) provide interesting reading on optimal procedures for choosing the interval width.

A simpler version of the box plot (see McGill, Tukey, and Larsen, 1978) has lines emanating from the rectangle to the extremes of the data so that neither adjacent values nor outside values can be perceived individually. The version we describe, which McGill, Tukey, and Larsen call a *schematic plot*, seems to be more versatile and informative. Of course, the two versions are identical when there are no outside values.

EXERCISES (Numbered data sets are in the Appendix. Starred exercises are more difficult.)

2.1. Given ten data points y_i, for $i = 1$ to 10, what are the fractions p_i for which $Q(p_i) = y_{(i)}$.

2.2. Given the ten data points $y = \{6, 3, 7, 2, 1, 10, 5, 4, 8, 9\}$, compute their median, quartiles, $Q(.1)$, $Q(.9)$, $Q(.01)$, $Q(.99)$, $Q(.0001)$, and $Q(.9999)$.

2.3. Compute the quantiles $Q(0.03)$, $Q(0.07)$, $Q(0.18)$, $Q(0.51)$, $Q(0.77)$, $Q(0.91)$ and $Q(0.98)$ of the ten data points in Exercise 2.2.

*2.4. Suppose that n is an integer and that 4 divides into $(n+2)$ k times with remainder r. Show that, using the linear interpolation rule for quantiles given in the text, the lower quartile or .25 quantile is

$$(1-\theta)y_{(k)} + \theta y_{(k+1)}$$

where $\theta = r/4$. What number should you use in place of $(n+2)$ above so that the same formula yields the upper quartile or .75 quantile?

2.5. Construct a quantile plot of the heights of all female singers in the New York Choral Society (Data Set 4). Discuss the properties of the distribution. What can you say about the data?

2.6. Make a quantile plot of the amounts of rainfall from the 26 seeded clouds in Data Set 5.

2.7. In certain experiments (like accelerated tests on how long light bulbs burn) only partial information about the data might be available. For instance, an experimenter's result sheet might list the days the tested bulbs lasted as follows: 1.01, 1.2, 1.4, 1.7, 2.2, 2.5, 3.1, 3.5, 4.4, 5.1, 6.1, 7.5, 8.9, 10.7, 12.6, 15.4, 18.3, 22.1, and 6 bulbs were still burning at the end of the 24-day test. How can the quantile plot be adapted to handle this kind of situation?

2.8. Make a one-dimensional scatter plot of the exponent data (Data Set 3).

2.9. Make a one-dimensional scatter plot of the female singer heights (Data Set 4).

2.10. Make a box plot of the female singer heights (Data Set 4).

2.11. Make a box plot of the amounts of rainfall from seeded clouds (Data Set 5). Why are there so many outside values?

2.12. How can you adjust box plots to show the data on light bulbs in Exercise 2.7?

*2.13. Suppose the data, $y_{(i)}$, for $i = 1$ to n, are exactly the quantiles for fractions $(i-.5)/n$ of the normal distribution, which means that if $\Phi(u)$ is the normal distribution function, then

$$\Phi(y_{(i)}) = \frac{i-.5}{n}.$$

For some fixed but large n, approximately what fraction of the observations would be beyond the adjacent values in a box plot? Do the same computation for the Cauchy distribution and for a t distribution with 4 degrees of freedom.

2.14. Make a histogram of the female singer heights (Data Set 4).

2.15. Make a histogram of the rain data (Data Set 5). Why is it so hard to pick good intervals for these data?

2.16. Make a stem-and-leaf diagram of the exponent data (Data Set 3).

2.17. Make a stem-and-leaf diagram of the prices of 74 automobile models for the year 1979 (Data Set 7).

2.18. Make a stem-and-leaf diagram of the batting averages of all players in the American League with 100 or more times at bat (Data Set 8).

2.19. Make stem-and-leaf diagrams with 10, 5 and 2 leaves per stem using the female singer heights (Data Set 4). Which of the three diagrams is most appropriate? Why?

2.20. The following data represent the percent of the clients of public defenders in 70 of the largest U.S. cities who were in jail prior to their trial (at the time of a recent study):

7, 10 (repeated 6 times), 12, 17, 20, 20, 20, 28, 25, 25, 22, 30, 35, 37, 30, 35, 33 (5 times), 40, 40, 45, 50 (7 times), 55 (4 times), 60 (5 times), 65, 67, 67, 70, 77, 75, 70, 75, 70, 75, 80 (5 times), 85 (4 times), 95 (4 times), 100, 100.

Make a stem-and-leaf diagram and a histogram. What characteristic of the data clearly shown in the stem-and-leaf diagram remains hidden in the histogram?

2.21. Make a stem-and-leaf diagram of the first 50 wind speed data values (Data Set 2). Are the leaves uniformly distributed within their respective stems? Do you think it likely that the original measurements were made in another unit such as knots (1 knot = 1.15 miles/hour) or km/hour (1 km = 1.604 miles)?

2.22. Stem-and-leaf diagrams are often used when one has to compute quantiles by hand. How would you proceed in doing this? Compute the octiles ($p = 0.125$, 0.25, 0.375, ..., 0.875) of the American League batting averages (Data Set 8).

2.23. Make a symmetry plot of the exponent data (Data Set 3). Comment on their symmetry.

2.24. Make a symmetry plot of the amounts of rainfall from seeded clouds (Data Set 5). What can you infer about the shape of the data distribution from the symmetry plot alone? Find a power transformation which makes the data approximately symmetric.

*2.25. Let m be the median of a distribution of positive measurements and let $Q(p)$ be the quantile function of the measurements. Show that if the logarithms of the measurements are symmetric, then, for $p < .5$,

$$[Q(1-p)-m] - [m-Q(p)]$$

decreases with increasing p. Which way are the data skewed?

*2.26. Compute and plot a density trace using the exponent data (Data Set 3).

*2.27. Compute and plot density traces of the female singer heights (Data Set 4) with $h = 5, 7$ and 9. Which h works best? Would $h = 6$ be a good choice?

*2.28. Make density traces of the wind speed data (Data Set 2) for several values of h. Which value of h is best? What does the plot show?

*2.29. Suppose the observations $y_{(1)}$ to $y_{(n)}$ are exactly symmetric about the median. Show that the density trace with the cosine function is symmetric in the sense that

$$f(median-u) = f(median+u).$$

*2.30. Let $y_{(i)}$ and $y_{(j)}$ be two values of a set of measurements with $y_{(j)} > y_{(i)}$. Show that the reciprocal of the slope of a line joining $y_{(i)}$ and $y_{(j)}$ on the quantile plot is nearly equal to the density trace at $y = (y_{(i)}+y_{(j)})/2$ with the boxcar function and with $h = (y_{(j)}-y_{(i)})/2$. Thus the reciprocal of the slope on the quantile plot portrays density.

2.31. Data Set 6 lists the birthdates of the signers of the Declaration of Independence. Modify the quantile plot in a way that displays the data including the uncertainty of the 8 inexact values. Make a histogram of the data. Do the ages that are not known exactly make any difference in the histogram? What did you do about people on the boundaries of the histogram cells?

2.32. Choose a data set from the Appendix and analyze it using the methods of this chapter.

3

Comparing
Data Distributions

3.1 INTRODUCTION

In many applications we have two or several groups of observations rather than a single set, and the goal of the analysis is to compare the distributions of the groups. For instance, we can again consider the gross national products of all countries in the United Nations in 1980, but separated into northern hemisphere and southern hemisphere countries. Probably the simplest comparison is to determine whether the "typical" value for one group is above or below the "typical" value for the other; however much more detailed comparisons are possible and often needed. Virtually any of the distributional questions posed for one group in Chapter 2 can be asked of two or more groups in comparison to each other.

Graphical methods can be used for making such distributional comparisons. We begin below by describing the empirical quantile-quantile plot. Then we discuss how the displays of Chapter 2 for each data set can be combined to allow effective visual comparisons. Finally, we show how certain kinds of derived plots based on differences and ratios can enhance our ability to perceive structure in the data.

One example that will be used to illustrate the methodology of this chapter is a set of data from a cloud-seeding experiment described by Simpson, Olsen, and Eden (1975). Rainfall was measured from 52 clouds, of which 26 were chosen randomly to be seeded with silver iodide. The data are the amounts of rainfall in acre-feet from the 52 clouds, and the objective is to describe the effect that seeding has on rainfall. The data for this and the two examples described below are given in the Appendix.

A second example is the average monthly temperatures in degrees Fahrenheit from January 1964 to December 1973 in Newark, New Jersey, and in Lincoln, Nebraska. Both the Newark and Lincoln data sets have 120 observations.

A third example is the maximum daily atmospheric ozone concentrations in Stamford, Connecticut, described in Chapter 2, together with a similar set of ozone measurements from Yonkers, New York, for the same time period. Although there are 136 Stamford values, the Yonkers data set has 148 observations, since Yonkers has fewer missing values.

3.2   EMPIRICAL QUANTILE-QUANTILE PLOTS

One very effective method for making detailed comparisons of the distributions of two data sets is the empirical quantile-quantile plot (Wilk and Gnanadesikan, 1968). It is constructed by plotting the quantiles of one empirical distribution against the corresponding quantiles of the other. If the two data sets are denoted by x_i, for $i = 1$ to n, and y_j, for $j = 1$ to m, then the empirical quantile-quantile plot is a plot of $Q_y(p)$ against $Q_x(p)$ for a range of p values. For example, the median is plotted against the median ($Q_y(.5)$ against $Q_x(.5)$), the upper quartile is plotted against the upper quartile, and so forth. If the two distributions were identical, all of the points would lie exactly on the line $y = x$; departures from this line give us detailed information about how the two distributions differ.

Figure 3.1 shows the empirical quantile-quantile plot for the cloud-seeding data with the line $y = x$ drawn in. We can denote the sorted data values for the seeded clouds as $y_{(1)}$ to $y_{(26)}$, and the sorted data values for the control clouds as $x_{(1)}$ to $x_{(26)}$. Then, since the number of observations is the same for the two sets, $x_{(1)}$ and $y_{(1)}$ are both the $(1-.5)/26$ quantiles for their respective sets. (Recall from Chapter 2 that $Q_x(p_i) = x_{(i)}$ and $Q_y(p_i) = y_{(i)}$ for $p_i = (i-.5)/26$ and $i = 1$ to 26.) Therefore, the point $(x_{(1)}, y_{(1)})$ appears in the empirical quantile-quantile plot. For similar reasons, the plot also contains the points $(x_{(2)}, y_{(2)})$, $(x_{(3)}, y_{(3)})$, and so on. In other words, as long as the two sets have the same number of observations, the empirical quantile-quantile plot is simply a plot of one sorted data set against the other. We will show below how to deal with unequal numbers of observations.

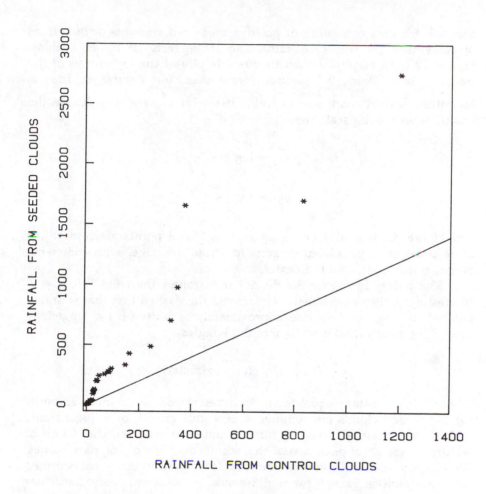

Figure 3.1 Empirical quantile-quantile plot of cloud seeding data, with the line $y = x$ drawn in. The points are the ordered rainfall values from the seeded clouds plotted against the ordered rainfall values from the unseeded clouds.

Figure 3.1 shows us several things about the rainfall data. Most striking is the fact that nearly all the points lie well above the $y = x$ line, and that the larger the values, the further the points are from the line. We clearly see that the seeded clouds produced more rain than the controls in this experiment.

Looking more closely, we notice that the points at the upper right are much more widely scattered than those at the lower left. In fact the lower left, which corresponds to low rainfall values, has quite a few points crowded together in a small space. This kind of configuration is common for data consisting of positive measured amounts or quantities of something (in this case, rain), and it suggests taking logarithms. Figure 3.2 is an empirical quantile-quantile plot of the logarithms of the two data sets. Base 10 logarithms were used, but natural, or base e, logarithms would work just as well. If we let $x_{(i)}^*$ and $y_{(i)}^*$ denote the quantiles on the log scale then

$$x_{(i)}^* = \log x_{(i)}$$

$$y_{(i)}^* = \log y_{(i)}$$

and Figure 3.2 is a plot of $y_{(i)}^*$ against $x_{(i)}^*$. The points are now much more uniformly spread out diagonally across the page, with somewhat denser concentration in the center.

The points in Figure 3.2 do not fall around the solid line $y = x$. Interestingly, they snake their way around the dashed line that is drawn parallel to $y = x$ and shifted approximately .4 units up (as judged by eye). This means that, if we ignore the wiggles,

$$y_{(i)}^* = x_{(i)}^* + c \quad \text{(approximately)},$$

where c is a constant equal to .4. In other words, the rainfall amounts for the seeded clouds are roughly .4 of a unit greater on a logarithmic scale than the rainfall amounts for the control clouds, and the .4 unit of additive increase applies across the whole distribution of data values. We can say that the two distributions (of logarithmically transformed data) are similar except for a difference in location. Any particular measure of location (e.g., the median or mean) for the $y_{(i)}^*$ would be equal to c plus the same measure of location for the x_i^*. A shift or change in the quantiles by an additive constant is one of the simplest ways that two distributions can differ.

But what does this mean in terms of the original data? Because the approximate relationship on the log scale is

$$\log y_{(i)} = \log x_{(i)} + c,$$

the approximate relationship on the original scale is

$$y_{(i)} = k \cdot x_{(i)},$$

where k is another constant equal to 10^c or about 2.5. Thus, the points in Figure 3.1 should fall near a straight line with slope k passing

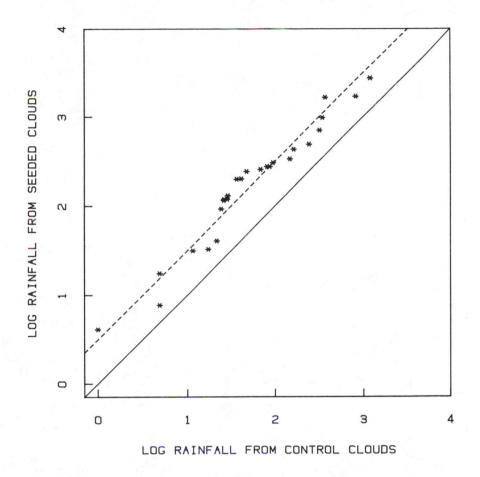

Figure 3.2 Empirical quantile-quantile plot of the logarithms of the cloud-seeding data. The solid line is $y = x$, and the dashed line is $y = x + 0.4$.

through the origin. Figure 3.3 reproduces Figure 3.1 but with the dashed line $y = kx$ added to the plot. We see that the dashed line is a reasonable approximation to the points and that the fit is worst at the upper right.

This plot has illustrated a second simple way that two data distributions can differ — by a positive multiplicative constant. Multiplying a set of data values by a positive k stretches them out or magnifies their pattern by a factor of k, but otherwise leaves the pattern or distributional shape unchanged. Any measure of location will be multiplied by k, and any measure of spread (e.g. standard deviation or

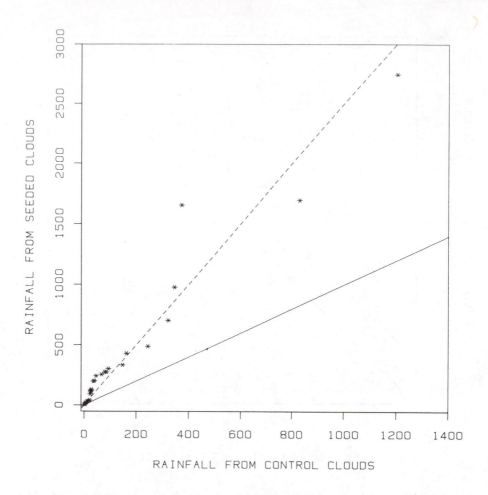

Figure 3.3 Like Figure 3.1, but with the dashed line $y = 2.5x$ drawn in.

interquartile range) also will be multiplied by k. For the rainfall data it seems that the effect of seeding clouds has been to increase their rain output in this experiment by a multiplicative factor of 2.5 rather than, say, by some additive amount. This could very well be an important fact about the intrinsic structure of these data and about the process of cloud seeding, and we have found it by looking at a few simple empirical quantile-quantile plots. It would have been difficult to discover this fact had we only computed simple numerical summaries such as means and standard deviations.

In some cases the points on an empirical quantile-quantile plot may lie near a straight line that neither passes through the origin nor has slope equal to 1. This combines the two ideas above, and would lead us to judge that the distributions were similar in "shape", but that the quantiles differed by both an additive constant and by a multiplicative constant. In symbols, this would mean that the two sets of sorted data values had the approximate relationship

$$y_{(i)} = k \cdot x_{(i)} + c,$$

or equivalently, in terms of quantiles,

$$Q_y(p_i) = k \cdot Q_x(p_i) + c.$$

The effect on location and spread would be, approximately,

$$\text{location}(y_1, \ldots, y_n) = k \cdot \text{location}(x_1, \ldots, x_m) + c$$

and

$$\text{spread}(y_1, \ldots, y_n) = k \cdot \text{spread}(x_1, \ldots, x_n).$$

Figure 3.4 is an empirical quantile-quantile plot for the temperature data described in Section 3.1, and it shows some rather interesting behavior. The temperature distributions for Newark and Lincoln are very similar for temperatures above 50 degrees, but below this value we see that the temperatures are higher in Newark since the points lie above the line $y = x$ in this region of the plot. Thus the hot weather in both places was about the same from 1964 to 1973, but the winter weather in Lincoln was generally colder than in Newark. In fact, by looking at the horizontal (or vertical) distance of the points from the line we can deduce that the coldest winter months are about 8° chillier in Lincoln than the coldest months in Newark.

In this example, since both data sets run over the same set of months, one might be tempted to plot a point for each month using the Lincoln and Newark temperatures as the x and y coordinates, instead of sorting each data set first before pairing them off. Such plots are called scatter plots and are the main subject of Chapter 4. (Note that there is no natural way to make a scatter plot of the cloud-seeding data, because there is no intrinsic pairing of the observations.) It is essential to understand the difference between a quantile-quantile plot and a scatter plot. Basically, a scatter plot is useful for studying such questions as "Is the monthly average temperature in Lincoln systematically related to the temperature in Newark?" or "If Newark has a hot month, is Lincoln likely to have hot weather in the same month?" On the other hand, the quantile-quantile plot is aimed at such questions as "Over a period of time, do the residents of Lincoln experience the same mixture of hot, mild, and cold weather as people living in Newark?" This question

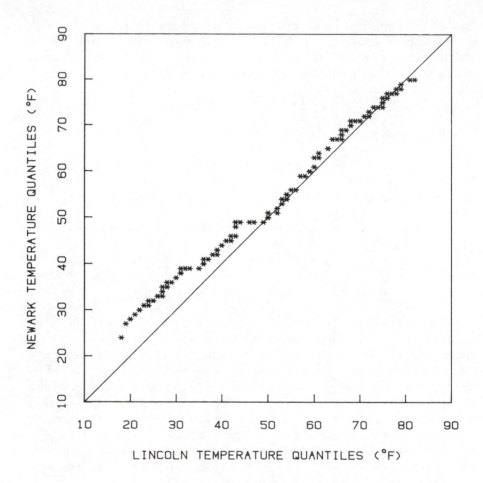

Figure 3.4 Empirical quantile-quantile plot for Newark and Lincoln temperatures.

would be meaningful even if the two data sets spanned different years, or if we were comparing autumn temperatures in Newark with spring temperatures in Lincoln, or if Newark were in another galaxy. It is the kind of question that a home owner in Lincoln and one in Newark might be interested in if they were concerned about the cost of heating in the winter and air conditioning in the summer at the two places but had no interest in whether they experienced hot and cold spells at exactly the same time.

Both data examples considered so far had equal numbers of observations in the two sets of measurements, so that finding pairs of matching quantiles was easy. Before making an empirical quantile-

quantile plot for the third example, the Yonkers and Stamford ozone data, we must decide what to do when the two data sets have unequal numbers of observations. The usual convention is to use the entire set of sorted values from the smaller data set and to interpolate a corresponding set of quantiles from the larger set. Suppose that $y_{(i)}$, for $i = 1$ to m, is the smaller set, and that $x_{(j)}$, for $j = 1$ to n, is the larger; that is, $n > m$. Then $y_{(i)}$, which is the $(i-.5)/m$ quantile of the y data, is plotted against the interpolated $(i-.5)/m$ quantile of the x data. We will use the quantile interpolation scheme mentioned in Section 2.2, which can be formulated in the following way. We need a value v such that

$$\frac{v-.5}{n} = \frac{i-.5}{m} ,$$

so we take

$$v = \frac{n}{m}(i-.5) + .5 .$$

If v turns out to be an integer, we simply plot $y_{(i)}$ against $x_{(v)}$. Otherwise, we let j be the integer part of v and let θ be the positive fractional part (that is, $v = j+\theta$, where j is an integer and θ is a number between 0 and 1). Then the interpolated quantile $Q_x((i-.5)/m)$ is calculated as

$$(1-\theta)x_{(j)} + \theta x_{(j+1)} .$$

In words, it is the number that falls a fraction θ of the way from $x_{(j)}$ to $x_{(j+1)}$. For example, suppose $m = 50$ and $n = 100$. Then

$$v = \frac{100}{50}(i-.5) + .5$$

$$= 2i - .5,$$

so that $j = 2i - 1$ and $\theta = .5$. This means that $y_{(1)}$ is plotted against $.5x_{(1)} + .5x_{(2)}$, that $y_{(2)}$ is plotted against $.5x_{(3)} + .5x_{(4)}$, and so forth.

For the ozone data, Stamford and Yonkers have 136 and 148 observations, respectively. Thus there are 136 points plotted on the empirical quantile-quantile plot, which is shown in Figure 3.5. The display demonstrates quite vividly that, overall, ozone concentrations are higher in Stamford than in Yonkers. Furthermore, as with the cloud-seeding data, the divergence from the line $y = x$ increases as the values increase. This means that large ozone concentration values differ more between the two sites than small values, ranging from 'nearly equal concentrations at the lower end, to a difference of about 100 ppb between Stamford and Yonkers at the high end.

A reasonable approximate description for the configuration in Figure 3.5 is a straight line with intercept 0 and slope 1.6. (A somewhat improved description is one straight line from 0 to the point where Stamford ozone is 100 ppb, and another straight line with a steeper slope from 100 ppb to 250 ppb.) The single straight line approximation with slope 1.6 means that, roughly, each Stamford quantile is about 60% larger than the corresponding Yonkers quantile. Thus, a reasonable summary conclusion from the plot is that the concentrations of ozone in Stamford are generally about 60% higher than in Yonkers.

As before, we must emphasize this does not mean that on any given day the ozone concentration is necessarily 60% greater in Stamford. (That is the sort of issue we will examine in Chapter 4.) Rather, over a period of time there is 60% more ozone experienced in Stamford, and the 60% increase is present across the whole range of observed ozone concentrations at the two sites.

If we were to summarize a given empirical quantile-quantile plot by saying that it closely follows a straight line, and if we were to report only the slope and intercept of the line but not show the plot or describe it further, this would be roughly equivalent to the standard practice of quoting the differences in means and standard deviations between the two sets of data, and doing nothing else. While a linear pattern might be the main message and serve as a good rough description for the relationship between two given sets of data, it rarely tells the whole story. The ozone empirical quantile-quantile plot allowed us to see at a glance that the ozone distribution in Stamford is roughly 1.6 times higher than in Yonkers, but it also allowed us to look harder and begin to see some of the more subtle differences between the two distributions. (They will be brought out even more sharply in Section 3.4.) Thus, the empirical quantile-quantile plot leads to a succinct summary comparison when it is appropriate, but also gives a detailed comparison when it is needed. For example, the more detailed comparison is needed for the Newark and Lincoln temperatures where the empirical quantile-quantile plot was not a simple straight line pattern.

So far in this section we have focused our attention on comparing only two data distributions. If we have r sets of data we can make the $r(r-1)/2$ empirical quantile-quantile plots for all pairs of distributions, provided this number is not too large. If there are many data sets, alternate methods are needed. Some will be described in the next section.

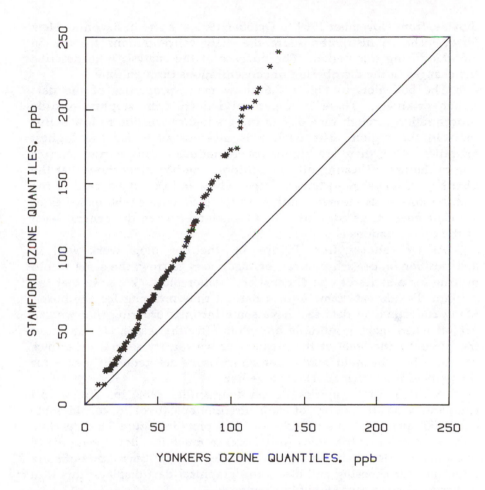

Figure 3.5 Empirical quantile-quantile plot for Yonkers and Stamford ozone concentrations.

3.3   COLLECTIONS OF SINGLE-DATA-SET DISPLAYS

Another approach to comparing distributions is to make any one of the displays in Chapter 2 for each distribution and place the plots in close proximity to enable a visual comparison. One possibility is to draw the plots alongside each other so that at least one scale axis is shared by all. An example is shown in Figure 3.6 where box plots are used to compare 36 distributions. The data in this case are daily maximum concentrations in parts per billion of another air pollutant, sulfur dioxide, from November 1969 to October 1972 at a site in Bayonne, New Jersey. The 36 distributions are the daily concentrations for the 36 months during this period. The purpose of the analysis is to describe the changes in the distribution of concentrations through time.

The box plots in Figure 3.6 show many properties of the data rather strikingly. There is a general reduction in sulphur dioxide concentration through time due to the gradual conversion to low sulfur fuels in the region. The decline is most dramatic for the highest quantiles. Also, there are higher concentrations during winter months due to the use of heating oil. In addition, the box plots show that the distributions are skewed toward large values and that the spread of the distributions — as measured either by the difference of the quartiles or the difference of the adjacent values — is larger when the general level of the concentrations is higher.

As we can see from Figure 3.6, the box plots work well in juxtaposition since each plot can be made very narrow; the same would be true for a series of one-dimensional scatter plots. We note that the sulphur dioxide data came with a natural time ordering for the boxes. Many collections of data sets have some intrinsic ordering that we can exploit when making multiple box plots. In other cases, we can order the boxes by the level of the median, or we can try several orderings. We must bear in mind that visual comparisons are generally easier for the pairs of boxes that are closer together.

Whereas the empirical quantile-quantile plot in Figure 3.4 compares a small number of data distributions (two) in considerable detail (all quantiles), the collection of box plots in Figure 3.6 displays a large number of distributions (thirty-six) in much less detail (essentially five quantiles for each, plus a few outside values). Such trade-offs are important for choosing and designing graphical data displays; this idea is discussed more thoroughly in Chapter 8.

Another way to compare two distributions is to make a stem-and-leaf diagram (or a histogram) for each, and to arrange them in a back-to-back fashion. This has been done in Figure 3.7 for stem-and-leaf diagrams of the Newark and Lincoln temperature data. The two diagrams share one set of stems, with the Newark leaves extending to the right and the Lincoln leaves to the left. The property that the low temperatures in Lincoln are lower than the low temperatures in Newark is apparent but is not as visually striking as in the empirical quantile-quantile plot. On the other hand, we can clearly see the bimodality of each data set, a property that we could not see in the empirical quantile-quantile plot, and we can see that the peaks at higher temperatures line up.

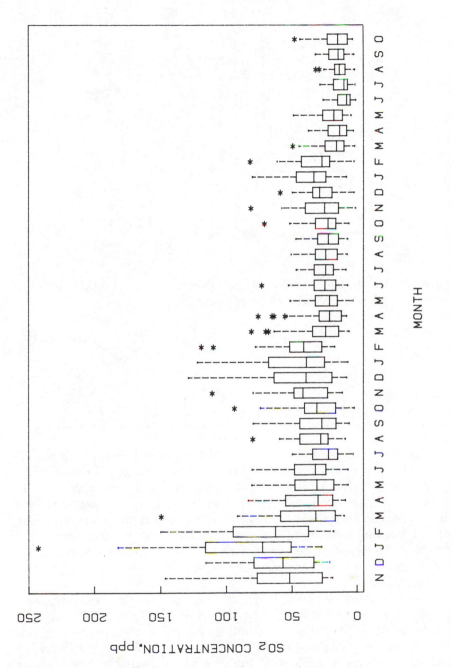

Figure 3.6 Box plots of daily maximum atmospheric SO$_2$ concentrations in Bayonne, New Jersey, for the months from November 1969 to October 1972.

```
              98 | 1 |
       443322100 | 2 | 4
  98888777766655 | 2 | 7889
         3221110 | 3 | 001112223334
       999876665 | 3 | 5555667889999999
       433332210 | 4 | 001122334
             976 | 4 | 556689999999
    444433322000 | 5 | 0011234444
       999987665 | 5 | 5566699
        44331100 | 6 | 00001334
     98888766665 | 6 | 557777899
    433322211100 | 7 | 001111122233 44444
99888776665555555 | 7 | 5566666777778889
              21 | 8 | 00
```

Figure 3.7 Back-to-back stem-and-leaf diagrams of monthly average temperatures for Lincoln (left) and Newark (right).

*3.4 NOTCHED BOX PLOTS

A pair of box plots for the logarithms of the rainfall data are shown in Figure 3.8. The two box plots depict the data from the control clouds and the seeded clouds, and an important question arises: should the difference in the locations of the distributions — as measured, for example, by the medians — be regarded as meaningful or simply as the result of random fluctuations that occur in data? Put another way, if we were to collect data from another similar set of seeded and control clouds, would we expect the medians to be as different as they were in this experiment?

The box plots as drawn in Figure 3.8 shed no light on this issue, since the answer depends critically on the number of observations that go into making each box, and the number of observations is not depicted. A box plot based on 10 observations would be rather variable from one experiment to another, but one based on 10,000 observations would probably be very stable.

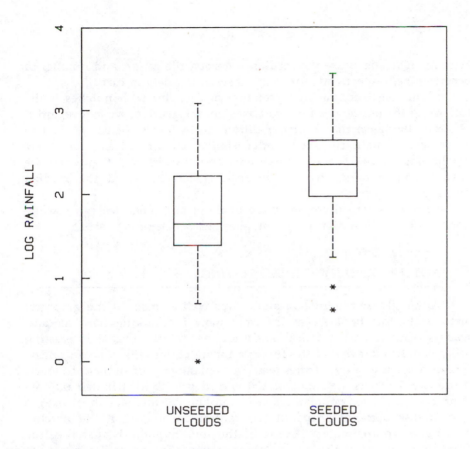

Figure 3.8 Box plots of the logarithms of the rainfall measurements from the unseeded and seeded clouds.

This was not a serious concern in Figure 3.6 because of the smooth time trend in those data. The vertical location of each box plot in Figure 3.6 is reinforced by the location of neighboring box plots and of box plots for the same month in other years; the smooth cyclical trend in that figure is unmistakable.

In applications where comparing locations is important, such as in the cloud-seeding experiment, box plots can be drawn with notches in their sides to help guide our assessment of relative locations. Figure 3.9 shows notched box plots (McGill, Tukey, and Larsen, 1978) for the log rainfall data, with the tops and bottoms of the notches computed from the formula:

$$M \pm 1.57 \times IQR/\sqrt{n}.$$

Here M, IQR and n are the median, interquartile range, and number of observations, respectively, for each subset of the data in turn.

A suitable informal interpretation of the plot with notches is the following: if the notches for two boxes do not overlap, we can regard it as strong evidence that a similar difference in levels would be seen in other sets of data collected under similar circumstances. Since the notches for the two sets of rainfall data do not overlap in Figure 3.9, we have strong evidence that cloud seeding has increased the median rainfall.

In cases where there are three or more box plots, we can use the notches to make a similar judgment about each pair of data sets.

NOTCHES AND HYPOTHESIS TESTING

Although we regard box plots — as well as most of the graphical methods in this book — as informal tools for looking hard at data, readers familiar with classical statistical theory may find it interesting background to know that the formula for notch lengths is based on the formal concept of a hypothesis test. In the language of statistical theory, if the two data sets are independent and identically distributed random samples from two populations with unknown medians but with a normal distributional shape in the central portion, then the notches provide an approximate 95% test of the null hypothesis that the true medians are equal: if the two notches overlap, then we fail to reject the null hypothesis with (approximate) 95% confidence. Alternatively, the difference between the medians could be described as "statistically significant at the .05 level."

We mention this not to encourage readers to regard notches on box plots as a way to make formal hypothesis tests, but to show that statistical theory can help in the design of informal tools for data analysis. The fact is that notches on box plots are useful guides for comparing median levels even when the requirements for the hypothesis test are not strictly met — which is very frequently the case!

When there are more than two sets of data each pair of notched box plots provides a test of significance for the difference of the medians of the two corresponding distributions. But the notches are not adjusted in any way to take into account that several hypothesis tests are being carried out simultaneously. (If there are p data sets then there are $p(p-1)/2$ pairs of medians being compared by notches.) It should be kept firmly in mind in interpreting the plot that even under the null hypothesis that all of the p medians are equal, the probability that at

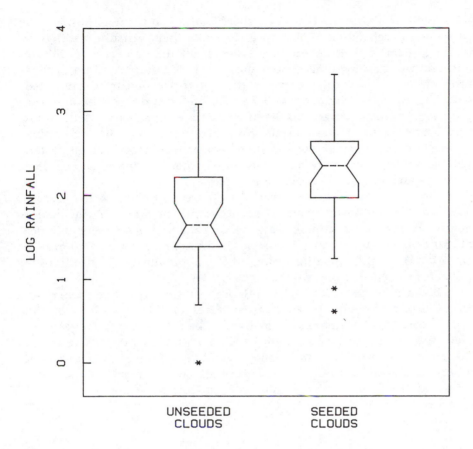

Figure 3.9 Notched box plots of the logarithms of the rainfall measurements from the unseeded and seeded clouds.

least one of the pairs of notches do not overlap will be greater than .05. This is the so-called "multiple comparisons" problem. Technical adjustments are possible, but generally unnecessary, as long as the notched box plots are used in the informal way discussed above.

*3.5 MULTIPLE DENSITY TRACES

If we choose to use density traces to depict data distributions, we can compare two or more data sets by plotting their density traces in the same plotting region so that they share both x and y axes. Since the traces cross each other, it is helpful to make them visually distinct by plotting them with different line types or in different colors. Figure 3.10 shows density traces for the Yonkers and Stamford ozone concentrations. The solid curve is the Yonkers ozone trace computed with the cosine W function and $h = 75$, and the dotted curve is the same kind of density trace for Stamford. In a comparison of densities it is important to use the same smoothing function W and the same value of the smoothing parameter h. Otherwise it would be difficult to tell whether differences in the curves resulted from differences in the data or in the method used to compute the traces.

The superposed density traces in Figure 3.10 show rather clearly that Yonkers has lower ozone concentrations. Stamford has a greater number of high concentration days while Yonkers has a greater number of low concentration days. However, we cannot see, as we could on the empirical quantile-quantile plot, the approximate multiplicative relationship between the two sets of quantiles.

Because of the multiplicative relationship that we found earlier, we might expect the superposed density traces of the logarithms of the ozone data to be more informative. The logarithm changes any multiplicative factor into an additive shift, so the two density traces of the log-transformed data may look more like shifted versions of each other. This is indeed the case in Figure 3.11 which depicts the density traces of the logs of the ozone data (calculated using a cosine W function with $h = .35$).

*3.6   PLOTTING RATIOS AND DIFFERENCES

One good plot frequently suggests another. Often when we see an interesting pattern in one plot, we will choose a second plot specifically to display the pattern in a better way. Consider the empirical quantile-quantile plot in Figure 3.4, which clearly shows the colder temperatures in Lincoln for the lower portion of the distributions. The plot not only provides this qualitative information but also allows an assessment of the magnitude of the temperature differential since the horizontal or vertical distances of the points from the line $y = x$ are the differences $y_{(i)} - x_{(i)}$. But we can get a better look at these differences by plotting $y_{(i)} - x_{(i)}$ against $x_{(i)}$. For the temperature data this has been done in Figure 3.12. (Notice the magnification of the vertical scale relative to Figure 3.4.) In addition, a smooth curve, whose computation will be discussed in the next chapter, has been superposed on the plot to

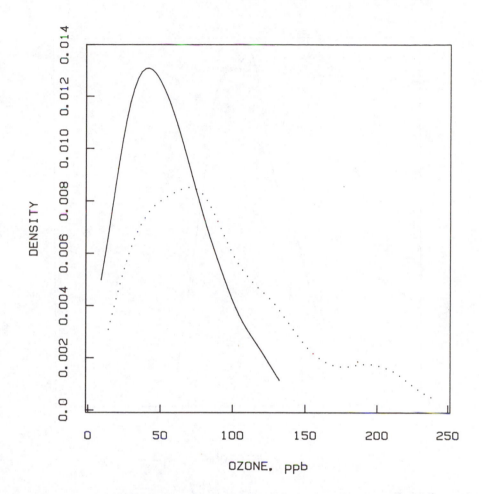

Figure 3.10 Density traces for Yonkers ozone concentration (solid) and Stamford ozone concentration (dotted).

summarize the behavior. We can now see more clearly that the magnitudes of these differences are as large as 8 degrees and that the differences tend to be smaller for higher temperatures.

For the empirical quantile-quantile plot of the ozone data in Figure 3.5 we concluded that, to a reasonable approximation, the two distributions appear to differ by a multiplicative constant. Thus if $y_{(i)}$, for $i = 1$ to 136, are the Stamford ozone quantiles and $x^*_{(i)}$, for $i = 1$ to 136, are the interpolated Yonkers quantiles, we have seen that $y_{(i)}$ is approximately $cx^*_{(i)}$. This implies that $y_{(i)}/x^*_{(i)}$ should be approximately

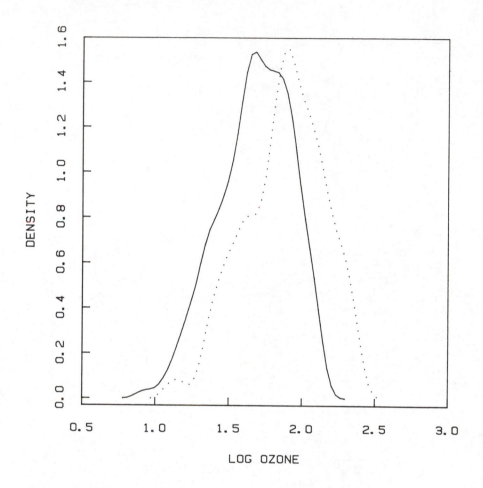

Figure 3.11 Density traces for log of Yonkers ozone concentration (solid) and log of Stamford ozone concentration (dotted).

the constant c. We get a more detailed look at the ratios and the adequacy of the approximation by plotting $y_{(i)}/x^*_{(i)}$ against $x^*_{(i)}$ as in Figure 3.13 and superposing a smooth curve. The display shows that the general level of the ratios is not actually constant; rather there is an increase from about 1.4 for low values of the distributions to about 1.8 for high values. Thus the percent increase in Stamford ozone concentrations over Yonkers concentrations gets larger as the concentrations get large. For low concentrations the increase is about 40% while for high concentrations it is about 80%. This gradual increase corresponds to the slight upward curvature in Figure 3.5.

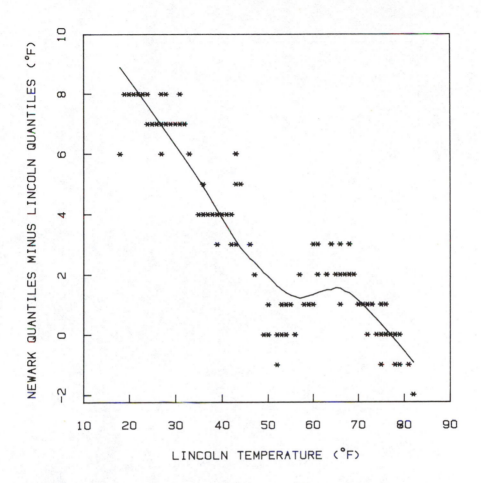

Figure 3.12 Newark temperature quantiles minus Lincoln quantiles plotted against the Lincoln quantiles.

3.7 SUMMARY AND DISCUSSION

In this chapter we have presented methods for comparing data distributions. The need for such comparison arises frequently in data analysis, and the number of distributions to be compared can range from two to very many.

A sensitive method for comparing two distributions is the empirical quantile-quantile plot, which allows a detailed comparison over the entire range of the distributions. This contrasts sharply with the common practice of comparing distributions by comparing only a

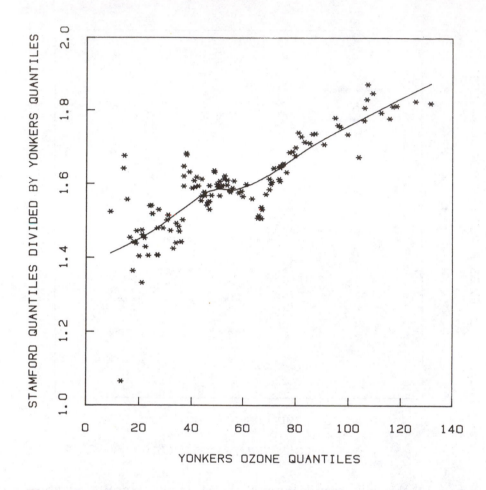

Figure 3.13 Ratios of Stamford ozone quantiles to Yonkers ozone quantiles plotted against the Yonkers quantiles.

small number of summary statistics such as means and standard deviations. Distributions can differ in such interesting and varied ways that one or two summary statistics are often simply inadequate. In fact, the empirical quantile-quantile plot allows us to decide whether a simple summarization of the relationship between the distributions is appropriate — whether, for instance the distributions really do differ only by additive or multiplicative constants. If the distributions differ in a more complex way, the empirical quantile-quantile plot, or one of the related ratio or difference displays, will usually help tell the story.

Several data distributions can be compared by making a collection of empirical quantile-quantile plots, one for each pair of data sets. If the number of distributions is large and making all pairs of empirical quantile-quantile plots is impractical, multiple box plots with a common vertical axis can be effective. Other displays, such as one-dimensional scatter plots, histograms, and stem-and-leaf diagrams can also be juxtaposed. Provided there are not too many distributions to be compared, several density traces can be superposed using different line types to help discriminate the curves.

3.8 FURTHER READING

Histograms, as we indicated earlier, are one of the oldest graphical data displays. With a history of nearly 200 years, quite a few variations have been suggested. A relatively recent paper by Dallal and Finseth (1977) presents four histograms by a combination of superposition and juxtaposition. Joiner (1975) shows that over a period of two centuries almost anything can happen. He uses pictures of students, standing in rows according to their heights, to form histograms of their heights. The purpose is to illustrate that "statistics is a 'live' subject."

Box plots and variations on them are described by Tukey (1977) who refers to them as box-and-whisker plots and schematic plots, and by McGill, Tukey, and Larsen (1978). One useful variant is to portray the sample sizes of the data sets by making the width of the box depend on the number of observations. Velleman and Hoaglin (1981) also give a clear account of box plots, and provide computer programs in Fortran and Basic.

Andrews, Snee and Sarner (1980) describe a display similar to multiple notched box plots, but designed for comparisons of means rather than medians.

EXERCISES

3.1. Make an empirical quantile-quantile plot of the salaries of chauffeurs and of mechanics in 44 cities around the world (Data Set 11). Comment on the result.

3.2. Who is better paid, teachers or cooks? Find out by making an empirical quantile-quantile plot of their salaries (Data Set 11). Comment. Could you have obtained the same information by simply computing means?

3.3. Make an empirical quantile-quantile plot of the first 60 average monthly temperatures in Eureka against the first 60 average monthly temperatures in Newark (Data Set 9). How different are the medians? The extremes? Can you easily describe the relationship between the two sets of quantiles?

3.4. Make an empirical quantile-quantile plot of the salaries of managers against the salaries of teachers (Data Set 11). Can you easily describe the relationship between the quantiles of the two professions? What if you leave the three topmost points out?

3.5. Given two data sets x_i, $i = 1$ to 10 and y_j, $j = 1$ to 20, which combination of ordered values of y_j would you plot against each ordered value, $x_{(i)}$, in an empirical quantile-quantile plot.

3.6. Given two data sets x_i, $i = 1$ to 13 and y_j, $j = 1$ to 20, which combination of ordered y-values would you plot against each ordered value, $x_{(i)}$?

3.7. Make an empirical quantile-quantile plot of the heights of Soprano 1 singers and the heights of Soprano 2 singers in the New York Choral Society (Data Set 4). If we connect successive points on the plot, the resulting curve has several horizontal and vertical pieces. Why?

3.8. Make an empirical quantile-quantile plot of the Tenor 1 heights and the Alto 2 heights (Data Set 4). Are the first tenors, who are men, taller than the second altos, who are women? By how much at the median, the quartiles, the extremes?

3.9. Make an empirical quantile-quantile plot of the daily maximum temperatures in New York City in June against those in July (Data Set 2).

3.10. Make an empirical quantile-quantile plot of the daily ozone measurements in New York City in May against those in June (Data Set 2).

3.11. Where did Sunday get its name from? Find out by making an empirical quantile-quantile plot of the daily amount of sunshine (solar radiation) in New York City (Data Set 2) on Sundays against workdays (Monday through Friday will be a good enough approximation).

3.12. Make an empirical quantile-quantile plot of the data portraying areas of graphs in one-column and multi-column journals (Data Set 10). Comment.

*3.13. If there are $n = 5$ values of x_i and $m = 25$ values of y_j, then the quantiles of $y_{(j)}$ that correspond to $x_{(1)}$, $x_{(2)}$, $x_{(3)}$, $x_{(4)}$, and $x_{(5)}$ on an empirical quantile-quantile plot are exactly $y_{(3)}$, $y_{(8)}$, $y_{(13)}$, $y_{(18)}$, and $y_{(23)}$ respectively. Thus no interpolation needs to be done. Find general conditions on n and m that insure no interpolation.

3.14. Compare salaries around the world (Data Set 11) of cashiers, teachers, cooks, electrical engineers, and managers by means of box plots.

3.15. Compare the four categories of heights of female singers in the New York Choral Society (Data Set 4) by means of box plots. Comment on the relationship between height and voice part.

3.16. Compare the four categories of heights of male singers in the New York Choral Society (Data Set 4) using box plots. Comment on the relationship between height and voice part.

3.17. Make box plots of logarithms of the amounts of rainfall from seeded and from unseeded (control) clouds (Data Set 5). Compare with Figure 3.2.

3.18. Make stem-and-leaf diagrams for the Yonkers and Stamford ozone data (Data Set 1), and contrast their effectiveness with Figure 3.5 as a device for comparing the two distributions.

3.19. Make stem-and-leaf diagrams for daily amounts of sunshine in New York City (Data Set 2) on Sundays and on workdays (use Monday through Friday as an approximation). Compare them and comment.

3.20. Compare salaries around the world (Data Set 11) of cashiers, teachers, cooks, electrical engineers, and managers by means of notched box plots. For which professions is there strong evidence that salaries are different?

3.21. Make notched box plots for the 8 categories of heights of singers (Data Set 4). Comment.

*3.22. List some conditions under which the notch of a notched box plot might reach outside the box.

*3.23. Why is the size of the notch of a notched box plot a function of $\sqrt{n}$, where n is the number of observations?

*3.24. Make superposed density traces for the Newark and Lincoln temperature data (Data Set 9), and try two or three values of the smoothing parameter h. Can you draw the same (or different) conclusions from these plots as we did from the empirical quantile-quantile plot in Figure 3.4.

*3.25. Superimpose density traces for the daily amounts of sunshine (Data Set 2) in New York City on Sundays and on workdays (Monday through Friday). Compare and comment.

*3.26. Plot the differences between *corresponding* quantiles of the heights of the Bass 1 singers and Soprano 1 singers in the New York Choral Society (Data Set 4) against the quantiles of the heights of the Soprano 1 singers. Comment on the result.

*3.27. Plot the ratios of the quantiles of the first 60 average temperatures in Eureka (Data Set 9) and the quantiles of the first 60 temperatures in Newark against the quantiles of the Eureka temperatures.

3.28. In the first paragraph of this chapter (or in any piece of text of comparable length), find and mark every occurrence of the letter r. Then count and record the number of letters that occur between every consecutive pair of r's (ignoring spaces between words), using a stem-and-leaf diagram to record the data. Next repeat the whole process for another letter, say d. What do you learn by comparing the two stem-and-leaf diagrams? Make an empirical quantile-quantile plot of the two sets of data, and see what further conclusions you can draw from it.

3.29. Compare the batting averages of baseball players in the American League and the National League (Data Set 8) using the graphical methods of this chapter. How are the distributions similar, how do they differ?

4

Studying
Two-Dimensional Data

4.1 INTRODUCTION

The scatter plot may well be the single most powerful statistical tool for analyzing the relationship between two variables, x and y. Suppose x_i and y_i for $i = 1$ to n are measurements or observations of x and y. Then a plot of y_i against x_i will be referred as a *scatter plot* of y_i against x_i. An example, with some familiar data that we have seen in Chapter 3, is shown in Figure 4.1. The variable y on the vertical axis is the concentration of ozone in Stamford, Connecticut, on the ith day, and the variable x on the horizontal axis is the concentration of ozone in Yonkers, New York, on the same day. Thus each point on the plot portrays the Stamford and Yonkers concentrations on one day.

A scatter plot can tell us much about the relationship between two variables, such as the ozone in Stamford and the ozone in Yonkers, particularly if we plan the plot carefully and use graphical enhancements to bring out features that would otherwise be hard to see. In this chapter we will discuss how to make scatter plots and how to add to them.

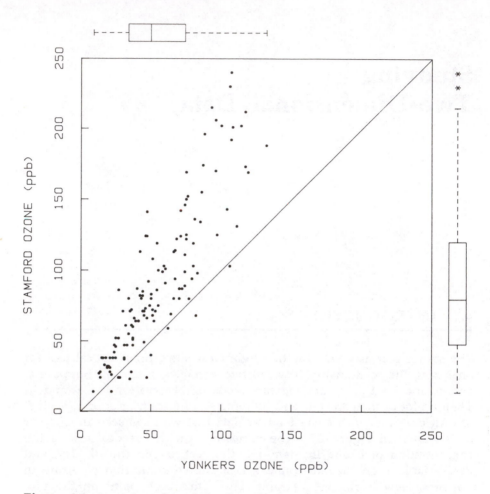

Figure 4.1 A scatter plot of the Stamford and Yonkers ozone data. Box plots are shown in the margins of the plot.

4.2 NUMERICAL SUMMARIES ARE NOT ENOUGH

One major feature of a scatter plot is that it shows all of the data. If we were to rely only on numerical summaries, we would have to take it on faith that the summaries capture the salient features of the relationship between the variables. Using one or a few numerical summaries to characterize the relationship between x and y runs the risk of missing important features, or worse, of being misled.

The Pearson product-moment correlation coefficient, r, is a popular numerical summary of the relationship between measured variables. The formula for r is

$$r = \frac{\sum\limits_{i=1}^{n} (x_i - \bar{x})(y_i - \bar{y})}{\left[\sum\limits_{i=1}^{n} (x_i - \bar{x})^2 \sum\limits_{i=1}^{n} (y_i - \bar{y})^2 \right]^{\frac{1}{2}}}$$

where $\bar{x}$ and $\bar{y}$ are the sample means of x_i and y_i. r measures the amount of *linear* association between x_i and y_i. If $r = 0$, there is no linear association; if $r = 1$, the maximum value, there is perfect positive linear association, that is, the points lie along a line with a positive slope; if $r = -1$, the minimum value, there is perfect negative linear association, that is, the points lie along a line with negative slope.

But r all by itself with no other information about the data tells us little about the relationship between y and x. This is demonstrated in Figures 4.2 and 4.3. The values of r for the eight scatter plots are all equal to the same value, 0.70, but the nature of the relationship between the two variables on the plots varies enormously. For example, in the upper right panel of Figure 4.2, the observations of the two variables are highly related to one another except for one unusual value. By contrast, in the upper left panel of Figure 4.2 the vast majority of the observations show no relationship, but the one dissenting point makes the correlation coefficient equal to 0.70. Even though the correlation is the same on all plots, the point configurations range from one indicating a very strong relationship between y and x to one indicating a very weak relationship between y and x. Clearly the scatter plots are vital for helping us to gain real insight into the nature of the data.

4.3 EXAMPLES

We will work with several data sets in exploring the ideas of this chapter. The examples fall into two categories: (1) those whose purpose is to explore the dependence of one variable, the response, on the other variable, the factor, and (2) those in which neither variable is a factor or response and the purpose is simply to explore the relationship between the variables.

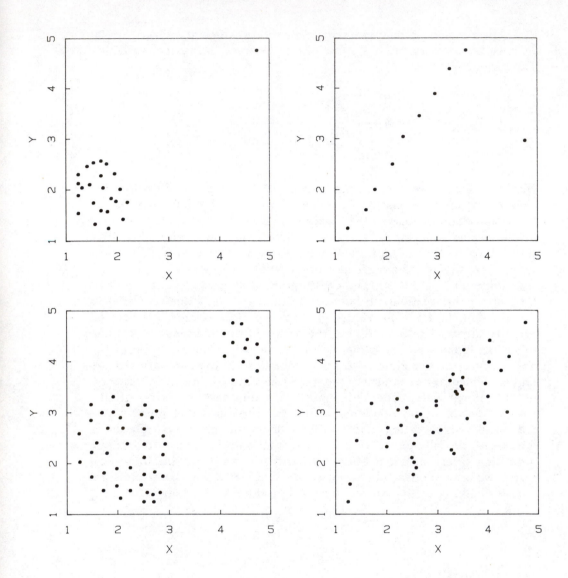

Figure 4.2 The four scatter plots all have correlation coefficient equal to 0.70.

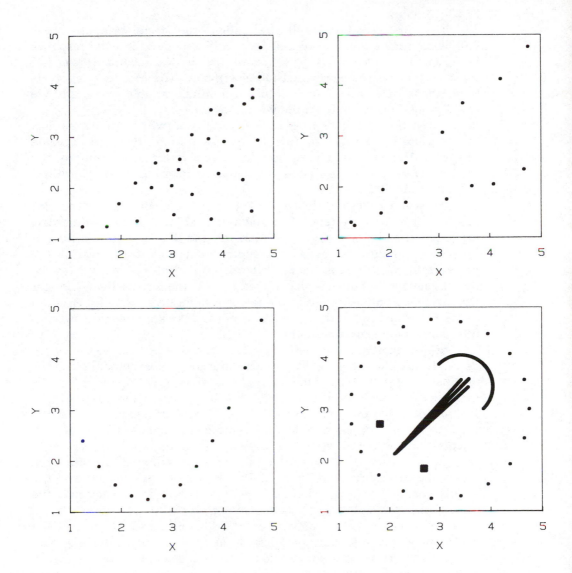

Figure 4.3 The four scatter plots all have correlation coefficient equal to 0.70.

The first category will be called the factor-response case. Following convention, we will denote the factor by x and the response by y, and we will plot the y_i values on the vertical (ordinate) axis and the x_i values on the horizontal (abscissa) axis. The second category is the exchangeable case since we could call either variable y or x and we could plot either variable on the vertical axis.

Given the basic objectives of the study from which the ozone data in Figure 4.1 were taken, this is an example of the exchangeable category. Neither variable is thought of as a factor or a response; the purpose is simply to see how closely related ozone is at two locations that are about 30 km apart.

A second example, shown in Figure 4.4, consists of data on 288 hamsters from an experiment by Lyman et al. (1981). The experimenters measured the life span of each hamster and the amount of time it hibernated. Figure 4.4 is a scatter plot of age at death against the percentage of lifetime spent hibernating. The purpose was to investigate the hypothesis that increased hibernation results in longer life. In this example we are in the factor-response case with hibernation as the factor and age at death as the response. We are investigating how life span depends on hibernation.

Scatter plots are often very useful when one or both variables are derived variables, that is, values resulting from computations on the original observed data. One example is shown in Figure 4.5. The variable portrayed on the horizontal axis is the square root of the fraction of space devoted to graphs for 57 scientific journals, and the variable on the vertical axis is an estimate of the standard error of each fraction. These data are from a survey (Cleveland, 1982) in which 50 articles from each of 57 scientific journals were sampled, and for each article measurements were made of the total area of the article and the area devoted to graphs. The fractional graph area for a journal is the sum of the 50 graph area measurements divided by the sum of the 50 total area measurements, and the estimate of the standard error of the fractional graph area is a complicated function of the graph area and total area measurements for that journal. This example is in the factor-response category since the purpose of the analysis is to discover (for statistical reasons that we do not need to go into here) whether and how the standard error depends on fractional graph area. In Chapter 7 we will encounter many scatter plots like Figure 4.5 in which variables derived from data are plotted.

One special case of the factor-response category is a time series: a sequence of y_i values measured at points in time, and the x_i are the consecutive observation times. The ozone data from Stamford are an example. Figure 4.6 is a plot of Stamford ozone against time, measured in days. For each day from May 1, 1973 to September 30, 1973 (except

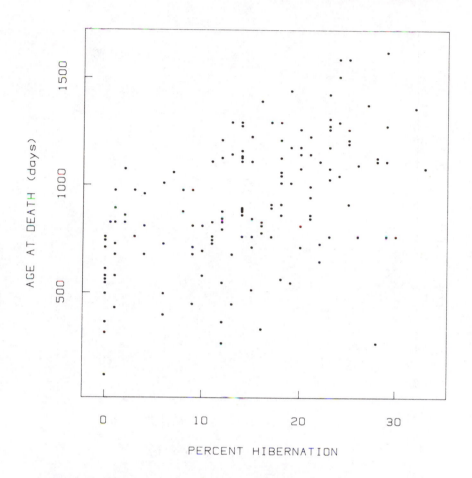

Figure 4.4 A scatter plot of age at death against percent of lifetime spent hibernating for 144 hamsters.

when the equipment was malfunctioning), the maximum ozone was recorded. The sequence of maximum ozone measurements through time is a time series. For most time series data encountered in practice, the x_i are equally spaced through time, but for the Stamford ozone data the equipment broke occasionally causing data values to be missed, so the x_i are not all equally spaced. For time series data, we are in the factor-response category, since the objective of the analysis is to see how the measured variable y_i changes with time.

Our final two examples bring us back to the exchangeable case. One consists of the prices and weights of 74 models of automobiles sold in the United States in 1979. A scatter plot of weight against price is

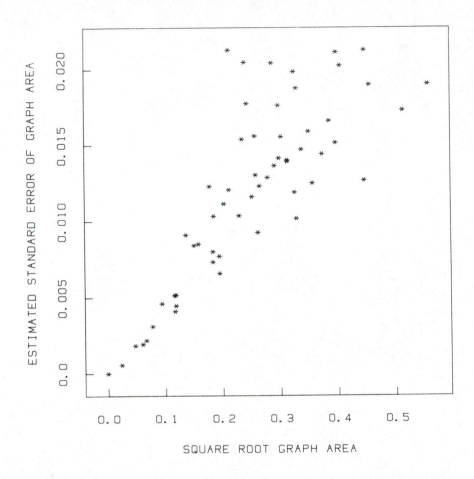

Figure 4.5 A scatter plot of the fraction of space devoted to graphs and an estimate of the standard error of the fraction for 57 scientific journals.

shown in Figure 4.7. The other consists of measurements of widths and lengths of petals from 150 iris flowers. The measurements are part of the Anderson (1935) iris data made famous by Fisher (1936). A scatter plot of width against length is shown in Figure 4.8.

4.4 LOOKING AT THE SCATTER PLOTS

Before we consider ways to enhance scatter plots, it is instructive for us to take a closer look at the simple scatter plots for our examples.

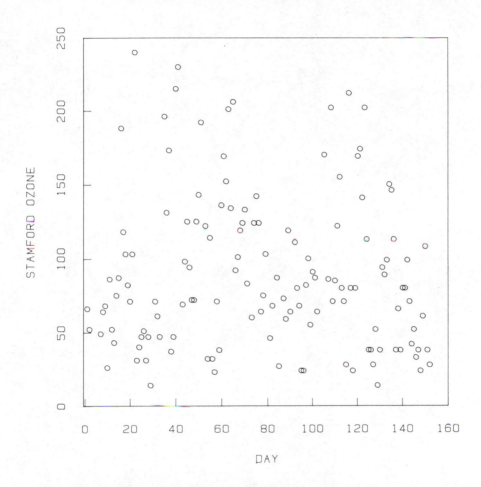

Figure 4.6 A scatter plot of Stamford ozone against time.

BIVARIATE OZONE DATA

In Chapter 3 we used an empirical quantile-quantile plot to compare the empirical distribution of the Yonkers data and the empirical distribution of the Stamford data. That analysis did not give us a look at the day-by-day relationship between ozone in Yonkers and ozone in Stamford.

The scatter plot in Figure 4.1 shows the ozone measurements' *empirical bivariate distribution*; it shows how the points (x_i, y_i) spread out in the plane. In Chapter 2 we had measurements of one variable and studied their empirical distribution along a line; here the measurements are pairs of numbers, so we depict them in a plane. (In the next chapter

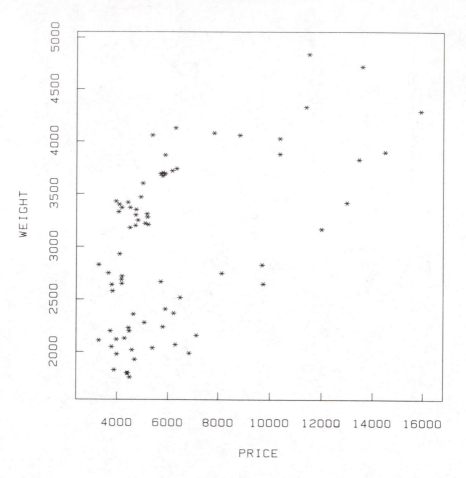

Figure 4.7 A scatter plot of weight and price for 74 automobile models.

our measurements will be 3 or more numbers requiring 3 and higher dimensional spaces.)

If we projected the points in Figure 4.1 onto the horizontal axis of the graph and plotted them along the axis, we would have a one-dimensional scatter plot of the Yonkers ozone data which would allow us to see the empirical distribution of Yonkers ozone by itself in the same plot. We have not actually done this in Figure 4.1, but instead have drawn a box plot of the Yonkers data positioned in the margin above the graph so that its scale is the same as the horizontal scale of the scatter plot. Similarly, the projection of the points onto the vertical axis would be the marginal empirical distribution of the Stamford data, which we have portrayed to the right of the scatter plot with a box plot.

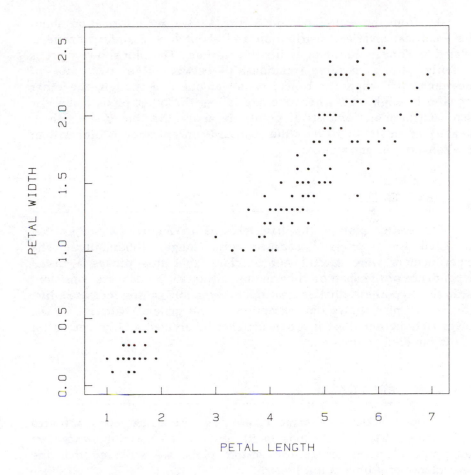

Figure 4.8 A scatter plot of width against length for 150 iris petals.

A scatter plot with box plots in the margins does, to a certain extent, facilitate a visual comparison of the two individual empirical distributions. In Figure 4.1 we have enhanced this comparison by making the scales on the vertical and horizontal axes the same. It is quite clear from the scatter plot that ozone concentrations in Stamford are higher than those in Yonkers, but we do not get as thorough a comparison of the two empirical distributions as the empirical quantile-quantile plot in Figure 3.5 provides. For example, we cannot see from the scatter plot that the Stamford quantiles are, roughly, 1.6 times the Yonkers quantiles.

But from the scatter plot in Figure 4.1 we get information about the empirical bivariate distribution and about how Stamford ozone is related to Yonkers ozone at each point in time. The plot shows there is a fairly strong positive relationship between the two sets of measurements; when the concentration at one site is high, the other tends to be high, and when one site is low the other tends to be low also. Furthermore, almost all points lie above the line $y = x$, which means that on almost all days the Stamford concentration is higher than the Yonkers concentration.

HAMSTER DATA

The scatter plot of the hamster data in Figure 4.4 shows that increased life span is associated with longer hibernation. The experimenters were careful not to claim that this proves a casual dependence of life span on hibernation, although the data are consistent with the hypothesis that increasing hibernation causes increased life. The scatter plot shows one exception to the general pattern. In the lower right corner there is a hamster that hibernated a large percent of its life but died young.

GRAPH AREA DATA

The plot of estimated standard error against square root graph area in Figure 4.5 has a linear look to it, but in a later section, where we superimpose smooth curves on scatter plots, we will see that the dependence of y on x is not linear.

STAMFORD OZONE TIME SERIES DATA

The time series plot in Figure 4.6 does not reveal any striking dependence of ozone on time. But in a later section we discuss ways of enhancing scatter plots that will reveal some patterns.

AUTOMOBILE WEIGHT-PRICE DATA

The scatter plot of the weight-price data in Figure 4.7 shows two branches of points, each going from the lower left to the upper right, separated by a wide gap. Seeing such a pattern, or any other kind of clustering of points, should immediately make us look for explanations or seek some other variables that may be associated with the grouping. For example, the sample of automobiles in Figure 4.7 contains both U.S. and foreign cars. Could it be that one branch is foreign and the other branch U.S.? We explore this possibility in Chapter 5, where we learn to look at three and more variables at once.

IRIS DATA

The flower measurements in Figure 4.8 also show two clusters of points. Here the reason is that there are three varieties of irises in the sample; one variety makes up the cluster in the lower left and the other two make up the cluster in the upper right.

But it turns out that Figure 4.8 is a poor scatter plot. In fact, in certain ways it is misleading. All of the length and width measurements have been rounded to the nearest .1 cm, which accounts for the lining up of the points in both the horizontal and vertical directions. The result of the rounding is that there is substantial overplotting, that is, many of the dots account for several data points. In fact, only 102 distinct dots appear on the scatter plot, although there are 150 data values in the sample. The plot is misleading, for it does not give a correct impression of how dense the points are in different regions of the scatter plot. In a later section we will discuss procedures for dealing with overlap.

4.5 STUDYING THE DEPENDENCE OF y ON x BY SUMMARIES IN VERTICAL STRIPS

In the factor-response situation it is conventional to denote the response by y_i and the factor by x_i, and to plot y_i on the vertical axis with x_i on the horizontal axis. Thus in Figures 4.4, 4.5, and 4.6 the responses (age at death, graph area standard error, and ozone) are plotted on the vertical axes, and the factors (percent hibernation, square root graph area, and time) are plotted on the horizontal axes.

Our goal in the factor-response case is to study *how the empirical local distribution of y changes as a function of x*. Suppose we consider the values of y_i for those points whose x_i values lie in some interval. To see what we mean, look at the top panel of Figure 4.9. The plotting region has been divided into 5 vertical strips in such a way that the numbers of points in the strips are as nearly equal as possible. Within each strip we can study the empirical distribution of the y_i values, and we can ask

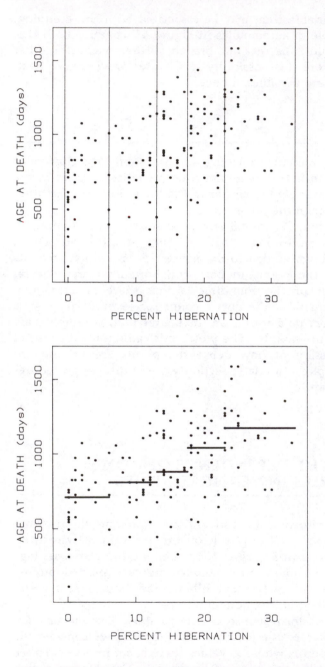

Figure 4.9 In the upper panel, the hamster scatter plot has been divided into strips with nearly equal numbers of points in the strips. In the lower panel, strip medians are shown by horizontal lines.

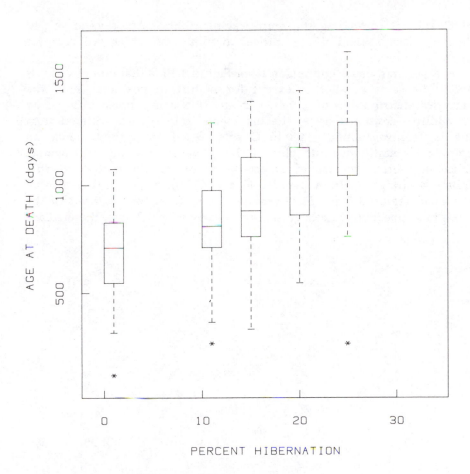

Figure 4.10 Strip box plots for the hamster data.

how the five empirical distributions differ, that is, how the empirical distribution of y changes as x changes. The bottom panel of Figure 4.9 depicts the median of the y_i values in each interval as a horizontal line segment, and shows that the median of y increases with x.

There is no reason why we should stop with the middles (medians) of the empirical distributions. In Figure 4.10, box plots portray medians together with other aspects of the local distributions. For each vertical strip a box plot is constructed from the y_i values in the strip, and the box plot is positioned horizontally at the median of the x_i values in the strip. These box plots show us how the median, quartiles, adjacent values, and values beyond the adjacent values of the y empirical distribution change as x increases. In effect, we are back in the situation of Chapter 3 comparing the empirical distributions of several sets of data; the strips yield five empirical distributions which we compare using box plots.

A general visual impression from Figure 4.10 is that one box plot is about the same as another except for a shift in position. Thus the empirical distributions of y_i values in any two strips appear to differ by an additive constant, just as the log seeded rainfall data differed from the log control rainfall data in Chapter 3. If we were to make an empirical quantile-quantile plot of the y_i values in one strip against those in another, we would expect the points on the plot to roughly follow a straight pattern parallel to the 45° line, just as the rainfall points in Figure 3.2 do. Furthermore, the shift in the positions of the box plots appears to be related nearly linearly to x. That is, the medians

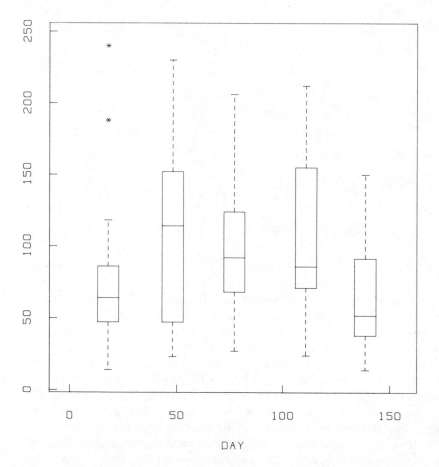

Figure 4.11 Strip box plots for the Stamford ozone time series.

increase linearly, the upper quartiles increase linearly, and so forth, all with the same slope. A mathematical description of how the median of y changes as x changes would be

$$\text{median}(y) \approx a + bx.$$

Any other quantile also changes in a linear way and with the same value of b.

Box plots for 5 vertical strips are shown for the Stamford ozone time series in Figure 4.11. Now we can see something that we could not see in the scatter plot of ozone against time in Figure 4.6; there is less ozone at the beginning and at the end of the time span. This is not surprising since the generation of ozone depends, in part, on solar radiation. At the beginning of the data in May, and at the end in September, there is less solar radiation than in between and therefore less ozone.

4.6 STUDYING THE DEPENDENCE OF y ON x BY SMOOTHING

One nice thing about the strip y medians in the bottom panel of Figure 4.9 is that they are easy to compute and to understand. But in a sense they are a crude summary, for they show us nothing about how the middle of the empirical distribution of y changes *within* a strip. A procedure called smoothing can be used to do this; smoothing is far more complicated than strip medians but shows us much more.

Before describing the details of a particular kind of smoothing, we will discuss the end product and say something about its purpose. The open circles in Figure 4.12 are the scatter plot of a set of made-up data. The solid dots on the plot portray another set of points called *smoothed values*. For each point (x_i, y_i) on the scatter plot there is a smoothed point, $(x_i, \hat{y}_i)$, whose abscissa, x_i, is the same as the abscissa of (x_i, y_i) and whose ordinate, $\hat{y}_i$, we will refer to as the *fitted value* or *smoothed value* at x_i.

The intent of the fitted value $\hat{y}_i$ is to portray the middle of the empirical distribution of y at $x = x_i$. Since we don't usually have enough repeated observations at $x = x_i$ to get a good estimate of the middle of this distribution, $\hat{y}_i$ is based on the y values of points whose x values are in a neighborhood, or interval, centered at x_i. The pattern formed by the smoothed points $(x_i, \hat{y}_i)$ is a smooth curve through the data; since the smooth curve describes how the middle of the local

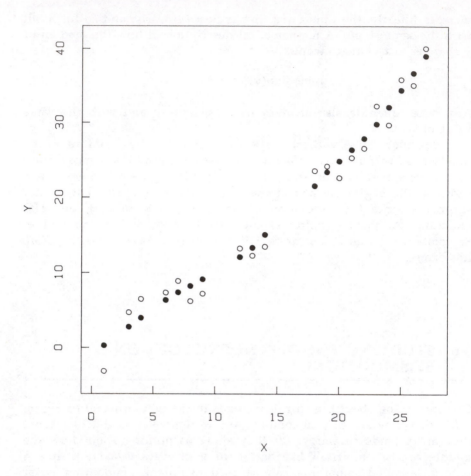

Figure 4.12 The open circles are a scatter plot of made-up data. The filled circles are smoothed values.

empirical distribution of y changes as x changes, it is what statisticians would call a *regression curve of y on x*.

The visual impression conveyed by the smoothed values in Figure 4.12 is two straight lines that come together somewhere between $x = 15$ and $x = 20$. This is clearly a much more refined description than we could have obtained from strip medians.

In Figure 4.13 smoothed values are portrayed for the hamster data. This time, line segments have been drawn connecting consecutive smoothed points (consecutive in the x direction), but the smoothed points themselves have not been plotted individually. The visual impression is a smooth curve, and in Figure 4.13 it is quite close to a

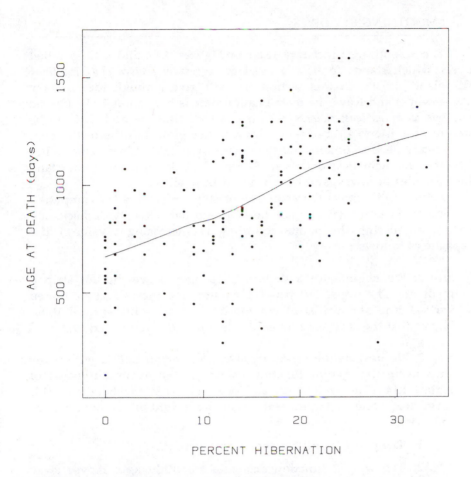

Figure 4.13 The curve portrays smoothed values for the hamster data.

line; this suggests that the middle of the empirical distribution of *y* as a function of *x* can be reasonably well described by a line. The line

$$y = 678 + 18.3x,$$

fit to the curve by eye, indicates that each additional percent of hibernation time corresponds, on average, to about 18 additional days of life.

SMOOTHING BY LOWESS

The smoothing procedure used in Figures 4.12 and 4.13 is called *lowess*, which stands for *locally weighted regression scatter plot smoothing* (Cleveland, 1979). In this section we will give a rough idea of how lowess works and leave the mathematical details to Section 4.11. Lowess employs *weighted least squares*, which is a statistical method that can be used to fit a line to a set of points on a scatter plot. But the reader does not actually need to understand the details of weighted least squares nor the other mathematical details in Section 4.11, in order to understand the basic idea of lowess and how to use it in practice.

Figure 4.14 depicts the sequence of steps in lowess for computing one smoothed point, $(x_6, \hat{y}_6)$, for the made-up data. (For this discussion we are numbering the points according to increasing x-values.) The steps are as follows:

Step 1: We begin with a vertical strip, just as we did for strip y medians. The upper left panel of Figure 4.14 shows x_6 by a dotted vertical line and the strip boundaries by two solid vertical lines. Notice that the strip is centered on the point of interest, (x_6, y_6).

Step 2: We next define *neighborhood weights* for all points within the strip using the weight function shown in the lower left panel of Figure 4.14. The weight for any point (x_i, y_i) is the height of this curve at x_i. The important features of the weight assignment are the following:

1. The point (x_6, y_6) has the largest weight.

2. The weight function decreases smoothly as x moves away from x_6.

3. The weight function is symmetrical about x_6.

4. The weight function hits zero just as x reaches the boundary of the strip.

The formula for the neighborhood weight function is given in Section 4.11.

Step 3: A line is fitted to the points of the scatter plot that lie within the strip, using weighted least squares. The fitted line describes in a linear way how y depends on x within the strip. The upper right panel of Figure 4.13 shows the points within the strip along with the fitted line. How much influence any one point has on the fitted line depends on the neighborhood weight associated with it; a point, such as (x_6, y_6), with large weight has a large influence and a

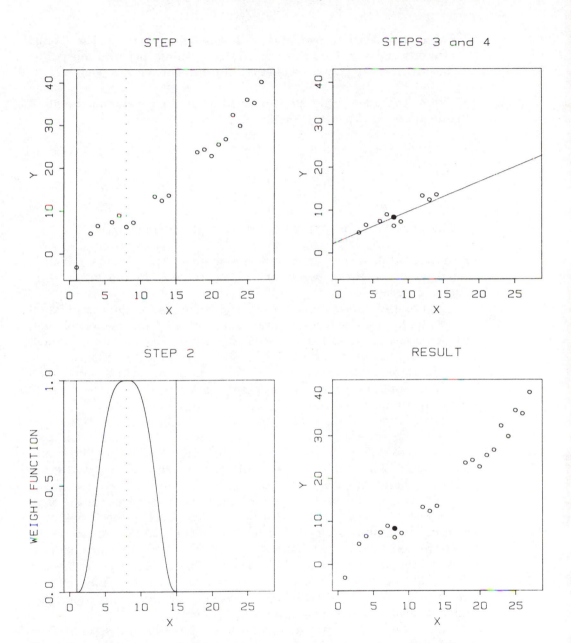

Figure 4.14 The four panels depict the computation of a smoothed value at x_6, using neighborhood weights.

point with smaller weight has a smaller influence. The points closest to x_6 play the major role in determining the line, and points outside the strip play no role at all, since they have zero weight.

Step 4: The fitted value, $\hat{y}_6$, is defined to be the y value of the fitted line at $x = x_6$. That is, if the fitted line is

$$y = \hat{a} + \hat{b}x,$$

then

$$\hat{y}_6 = \hat{a} + \hat{b}x_6.$$

The solid dot in the upper right panel is the point $(x_6, \hat{y}_6)$.

The result of all of this effort is one smoothed value $(x_6, \hat{y}_6)$, which is shown, along with the points of the scatter plot, in the lower right panel of Figure 4.14.

Figure 4.15 shows the same sequence of steps for the computation of the fitted value for (x_{20}, y_{20}), the rightmost point on the scatter plot. The details of the steps are similar, and the result is another smoothed value, $(x_{20}, \hat{y}_{20})$, shown by the solid dot in the lower right panel.

The steps above are carried out for each point on the scatter plot. The final result is the set of smoothed points $(x_i, \hat{y}_i)$, for $i = 1$ to 20, shown by the dots in Figure 4.12.

Notice that in Figures 4.14 and 4.15 the widths of the vertical strips for x_6 and x_{20} are not equal. The strip in Figure 4.15 is wider than that in Figure 4.14 (although part of it falls off-scale). This is due to the rule that is used to form the strips: the strip for x_i is centered at x_i and made just wide enough to cover 10 points.

For any point on the scatter plot, the distance to its strip boundaries is equal to the distance to its 10th nearest neighbor (counting the point as a neighbor of itself). For $x_{20} = 27$ we can see in the lower left panel of Figure 4.14 that the left boundary falls at $x_{11} = 18$, the 10th nearest neighbor of x_{20}. (The right bound is off-scale at $x = 36$.) In our example, since the distance to the 10th nearest neighbor varies for different x_i, the widths of the strips vary, and therefore the widths of the weight functions vary.

There is nothing sacred about 10 as the number, q, of nearest neighbors to use. We could have chosen q to be, say, 8 or 15; the choice will affect the appearance of the smoothed values in ways that we will discuss shortly. In practice we do not choose q directly. Instead, we choose a fixed fraction f between 0 and 1, and take q to be fn rounded to a whole number, where n is the total number of points. f is roughly the fraction of points that receive nonzero weight in the fitting of each line.

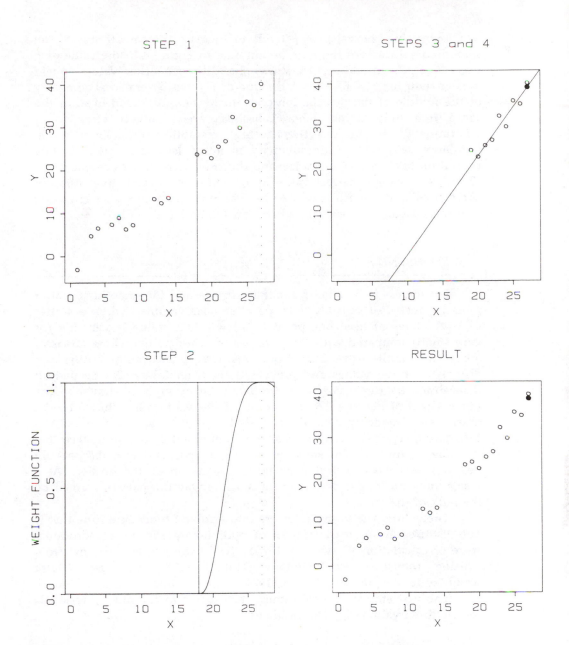

Figure 4.15 The four panels depict the computation of a smoothed value at x_{20}.

Increasing the value of f tends to increase the smoothness of the smoothed values. For the hibernation data in Figure 4.13 the value of f was set at .67. In Figure 4.16, f was .2 and the smoothed values appear noisier than for $f = .67$. A small value of f gives a very local summary of the middle of the distribution of y in the neighborhood of x, in the sense that only points whose abscissas are relatively close to x_i determine $\hat{y}_i$. In this case there is high resolution but a lot of noise. For large values of f the summary is much less local; there is low resolution but there is less noise, and the smoothed values are smoother. There is no single correct value of f. Different values give different summaries, and often it is wise to look at more than one. Current users of lowess usually choose values between 1/3 and 2/3.

ROBUSTNESS

For lowess to be a good general purpose tool for smoothing scatter plots it must deal sensibly with peculiar observations. Often a scatter plot will have at least one point (x_i, y_i) whose y value is very big (or very small) compared with the y values of other points whose abscissas are in the vicinity of x_i. Such a point, which we will call an outlier, can distort the fitted values and prevent them from following the pattern determined by the majority of the data. An example is shown in the upper panel of Figure 4.17. The points of the scatter plot, shown by the dots, are the made-up data of Figure 4.11, except that the y value of the 11th point, (x_{11}, y_{11}), has been changed from about 25 to about 40 so that it is now an outlier. The smoothed values for points whose abscissas are near x_{11} have been distorted by being pulled up by the outlier. As a result, they no longer describe in a sensible way the pattern formed by the bulk of the data.

The solution is to make lowess into a robust procedure (one that is not distorted by a small fraction of outliers) by adding an additional stage of calculation (Cleveland, 1979). To do this we will borrow from existing robustness methodology (Huber, 1973), and use *iterated* weighted least squares (Andrews, 1974).

The first step in the robustness iteration is to compute y residuals for the fitted values, $\hat{y}_i$. The residuals,

$$r_i = y_i - \hat{y}_i,$$

are the signed vertical distances from the smoothed points to the points on the scatter plot. The lower left panel of Figure 4.17 is a plot of these residuals against x_i for the made-up data. Notice that the place where the outlier occurred has a very large residual.

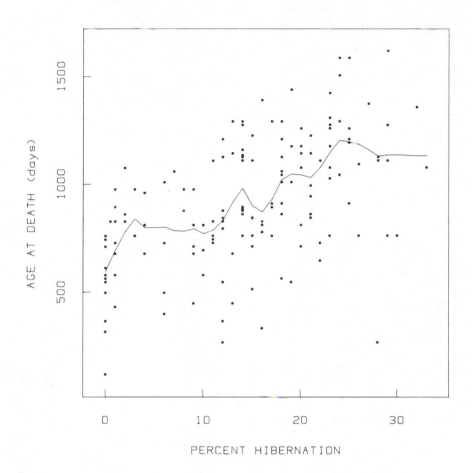

Figure 4.16 The curve portrays smoothed values for the hamster data with a smaller value of *f* than in Figure 4.13.

The next step in the robustness iteration is to define a set of *robustness weights* based on the sizes of the residuals. A weight function is portrayed in the lower right panel of Figure 4.17. Residuals close to zero receive large robustness weights, those far from zero receive small robustness weights.

Now we go back to the very beginning and refit a line in a vertical strip for each point of the scatter plot, this time using the robustness weights as well as the neighborhood weights. When fitting a line to get a smoothed value at x_{20}, say, the new weight for each point is the original neighborhood weight *multiplied by* the robustness weight for that point. Thus a point will have a small combined weight either if it

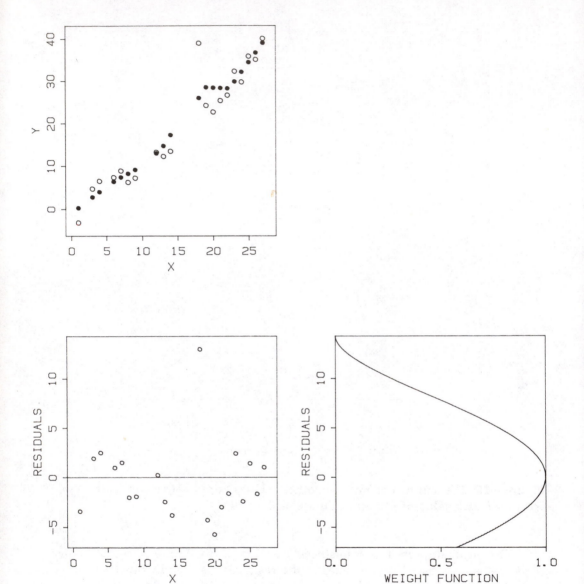

Figure 4.17 The three panels depict the computation of robustness weights for the made-up data with an outlier.

is far from x_{20} along the x axis or if it has a large residual in the initial stage. For example, the point (x_{11}, y_{11}) now gets no weight in the fitting of the line for any point, because it has a zero robustness weight.

For our made-up data with the outlier, the result of fitting the lines all over again using the robustness weights is shown in the top panel of Figure 4.18. The smoothed points have settled down, they are no longer distorted by the outlier, and they now do a good job of describing the pattern of the majority of the data.

In the bottom panel of Figure 4.18 the residuals for the new smoothed values are plotted against x_i. To get some added protection against outliers we can repeat the whole robustness step. We can define new robustness weights from the new residuals in the bottom panel of Figure 4.18 and then return again to the very beginning to compute smoothed values using the new robustness weights. The second robustness step is sensible to take routinely since in some cases the smoothed values do not rid themselves of the effects of outliers in one robustness step, although for our made-up data the second robustness step has little effect. In the remaining examples of this chapter, and in other chapters as well, we will use the robust version of lowess with two robustness steps.

WHY IS SMOOTHING SCATTER PLOTS IMPORTANT?

Superimposing smoothed values on scatter plots of factor-response data is important since in many cases it is difficult for our eye-brain system, as powerful as it is, to get an accurate impression of the pattern of dependence of y on x. The graph-area data in Figure 4.5 provide an example. Look at the graph and try to decide if the dependence of y on x is linear. There is a linear look to the point cloud but in fact the dependence is very nonlinear. We can see this clearly by splitting the scatter plot in two. In the top panel of Figure 4.19 y_i is plotted against x_i for $x_i < .2$ and in the bottom panel y_i is plotted against x_i for $x_i > .2$. Lines have been fitted to the two plots separately (using simple least squares regression) and their slopes and intercepts are very different. Thus the dependence of y on x over the entire range of the data is not a single linear function of x.

Figure 4.20 shows lowess smoothed values with $f = 1/2$. With the smoothed values superimposed we now see very clearly that there is a nonlinear dependence of y on x. Thus the smooth curve helps to keep us from making an erroneous judgement of linearity.

The classical procedure for smoothing scatter plots is to fit polynomials to the data, usually straight lines or quadratics. The problem with polynomials — even those with degrees higher than 2 —

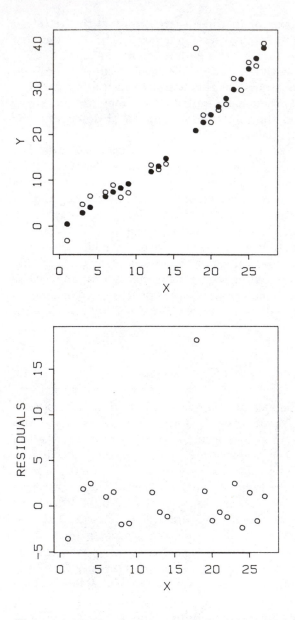

Figure 4.18 In the top panel the solid dots are smoothed values resulting from the first robustness step. The lower panel is a scatter plot of the residuals from the smoothed values against x.

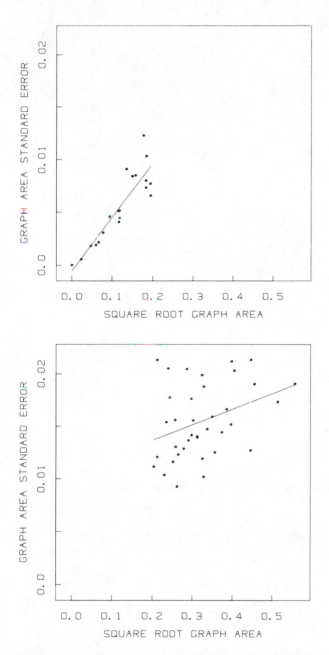

Figure 4.19 The top panel is a plot of the graph-area data for values of square root graph-area less than .2. In the lower panel the plot is for values of square root graph-area above .2. In both panels lines were fit by least squares.

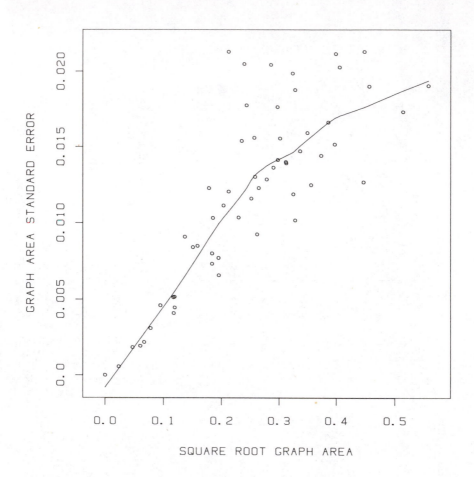

Figure 4.20 Graph-area data with lowess smoothed values.

is that they are neither flexible nor local. What happens on, say, the extreme right of the scatter plot can very much affect the fitted values at the extreme left. And polynomials have difficulty following patterns on scatter plots with abrupt changes in the curvature. For example, it would be difficult for a single polynomial to describe the broken-line pattern of the made-up data in Figure 4.12.

4.7 STUDYING THE DEPENDENCE OF THE SPREAD OF *y* ON *x* BY SMOOTHING ABSOLUTE VALUES OF RESIDUALS

We should remember that the smoothed values of the previous sections tell us only about the *middle* of the local distribution of y at x, but do not tell us anything else about other aspects of the distributions, such as spread and skewness.

In the strip box plots in Figures 4.10 and 4.11 we can perceive other aspects. For example, consider spread, as portrayed by the distance between the upper and lower quartiles. There is no clear, consistent change of the spread of y as x changes in Figure 4.10; that is, the spread appears to be nearly constant. However, with the strip box plots we do not get to see spread changes *within* a strip.

But it turns out that we can get a more detailed look at spread by applying smoothing in a particular way. Suppose $\hat{y}_i$ are the fitted values from a lowess smoothing. Let

$$r_i = y_i - \hat{y}_i$$

be the residuals. Now $|r_i|$, the absolute values of the residuals, tell us something about the spread of y. If the $|r_i|$ for x_i in some interval tend to be larger than the $|r_i|$ for x_i in some other interval, then the y_i are more spread out in the first interval than in the second. Thus, one way to study spread in detail is to plot $|r_i|$ against x_i and to plot a lowess smooth curve through the points $(x_i, |r_i|)$. This has been done in Figure 4.21. First, the $\hat{y}_i$ were computed with the robust lowess procedure with $f = 2/3$, then the r_i were computed from the $\hat{y}_i$, and then the robust lowess procedure with $f = 2/3$ was applied to $(x_i, |\hat{r}_i|)$ to get the smooth curve shown in the figure. In plotting this smooth curve we are using a graphical portrayal of the middle of the distribution of $|r_i|$ within neighborhoods to tell us about the changing spread of y_i.

The detailed look at spread in Figure 4.21 now shows us something we did not see in the strip box plots of Figure 4.10. There is a consistent but very mild increase in the spread of y as x increases. This should not surprise us. When the middle of the local distribution of y increases as x increases, it is common for the spread to increase as well; it is frequently nature's way to have the spread of measurements increase as their overall magnitude increases.

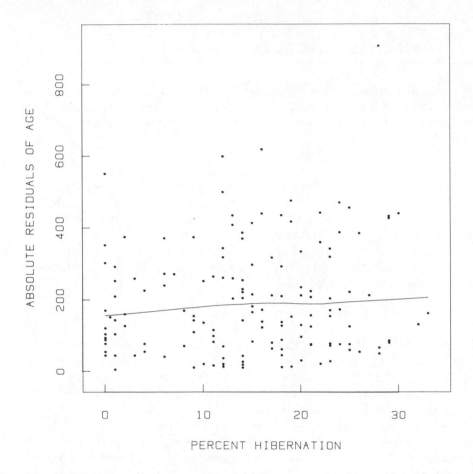

Figure 4.21 The smoothed absolute values of residuals show how the spread of y changes with x.

4.8   FIGHTING REPEATED VALUES WITH JITTERING AND SUNFLOWERS

In Section 4.2 we pointed out that the scatter plot of the iris data in Figure 4.8 was misleading because there was much overlap of plotted points; thus a single dot might mean one, two, or more points. Recall that in Chapter 2 we were faced with an overlap problem with one-dimensional scatter plots, and there the solution was to use vertical jitter or stacking to alleviate the problem. It turns out that we can use similar procedures on two-dimensional scatter plots.

We can jitter the points on a scatter plot by adding random noise to one or both of the variables. There are many ways to do this but here is one that is usually successful. Let u_i, for $i = 1$ to n, be n equally spaced values from -1 to 1 in random order. Let v_i, for $i = 1$ to n, be another random order of the equally spaced values. Then jittered values of the x_i and y_i are

$$x_i + \theta_x u_i$$

$$y_i + \theta_y v_i.$$

One way to choose θ_x is to make it some fraction, say .02 or .05, of the range of the x_i (i.e., the largest x_i minus the smallest) or for rounded data we could take θ_x to be 1/2 the rounding interval. θ_y can be chosen in a similar way. We want the fraction to be big enough to alleviate the overlap but not so big as to seriously corrupt the data.

The above jittering procedure has been used in Figure 4.22 with θ_x equal to .05 times the range of the x_i and θ_y equal to .05 times the range of the y_i. It is now clear that there are many more points in the lower left cluster than there appeared to be in Figure 4.8.

We cannot directly use the stacking procedure of Chapter 2 to alleviate overlap on scatter plots, but we can use a similar procedure, shown in Figure 4.23. The symbols, called sunflowers (Cleveland and McGill, 1982), show the number of observations that occur at the centers of the symbols. A dot means one observation, a dot with two lines means two observations, a dot with three line segments means three observations, and so forth. The sunflowers show, as did the jittered plot, that there is substantial overlap in the lower left cluster.

4.9   SHOWING COUNTS WITH CELLULATION AND SUNFLOWERS

With a single set of data we saw in Chapter 2 that the histogram could help us understand the one-dimensional, or univariate, distribution of the data by showing counts of points in intervals of equal length. Showing counts in squares of equal size can help us understand the bivariate distribution of x and y.

We can use the sunflower symbol of the previous section to show such counts. To describe the procedure we will use the ozone data of Figure 4.1. The making of the histogram begins with the frame around the scatter plot, which, as in Figure 4.1, we will suppose is square. Now

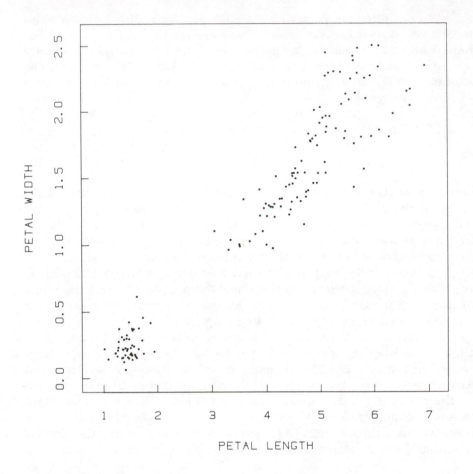

Figure 4.22 Petal width is plotted against petal length with jitter added.

take the region inside of the frame and divide it into square cells as shown in Figure 4.24. We will follow Tukey and Tukey (1981) and call this a *cellulation*. Now count the number of points in each cell and use a sunflower centered inside of each cell, as shown in Figure 4.25, to show the number of points.

Portraying counts in cells gives us information about the concentration of data points in different regions of the plot. For example, the sunflowers in Figure 4.25 show us that the counts are highest in the lower left portion of the point cloud and decrease as we move toward the upper right of the point cloud. That is, the density of the data is greatest in the lower left.

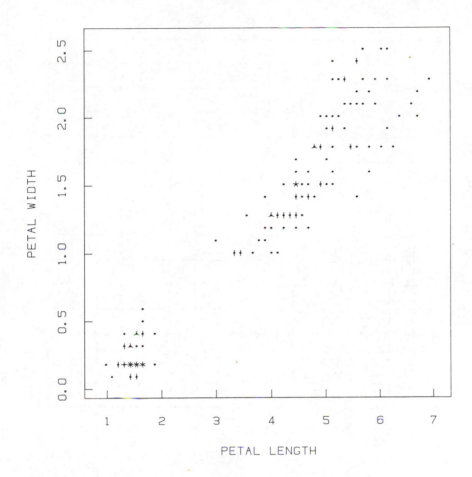

Figure 4.23 Sunflowers show the overlap in the iris data.

Figure 4.26 shows cellulation and sunflowers for the cube-root ozone data. Remember that in Chapter 2 we found that cube roots made the univariate empirical distribution of Stamford ozone nearly symmetric. In Figure 4.26 we see that for the bivariate distribution of Yonkers and Stamford ozone the cube root transformation moves the region of highest density to the central portion of the point cloud.

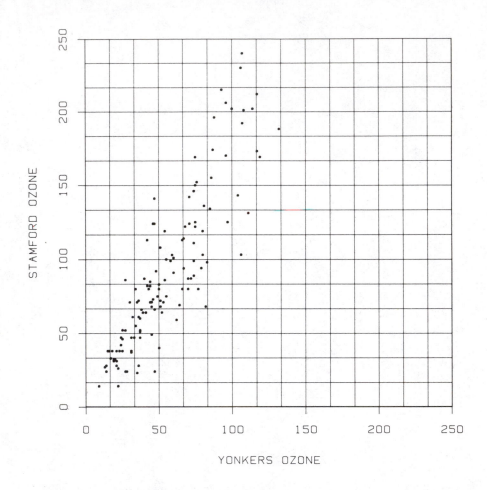

Figure 4.24 Cellulation of the ozone data.

*4.10   TWO-DIMENSIONAL LOCAL DENSITIES AND SHARPENING

When we study a scatter plot such as Figure 4.1 we get some appreciation of the relative *density* of the points in different regions of the plot. By "density" we mean simply the relative concentration of data points; for example, from Figure 4.25 we see that the density of the ozone data is higher in the lower left section of the point cloud than in the upper right.

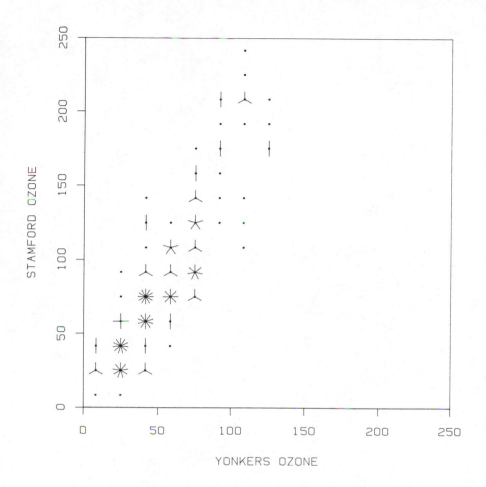

Figure 4.25 Sunflowers depict the number of data values in each cell.

This notion of the two-dimensional density of x and y is similar to the notion of the one-dimensional density of a single variable that was discussed in Section 2.9. There the local density at a point x was measured by

$$\frac{\text{fraction of data in an interval centered at } x}{\text{interval length}} .$$

For data in two dimensions we can measure density in a similar manner; the local density at (x,y) is

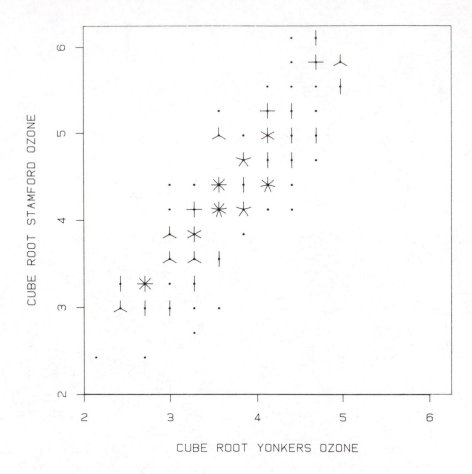

Figure 4.26 Sunflowers in cells for the cube root ozone data.

$$\frac{\text{fraction of data in a circle centered at } (x,y)}{\text{circle area}}.$$

For example, Figure 4.27 is the scatter plot of Figure 4.1 with two circles whose centers are shown by x's. The circle in the lower left, whose center is at $(27, 34)$, contains 37 data points and has an area of $1{,}963$ ppb^2. Since there are 136 points on the scatter plot, the local density at $(27, 34)$ is

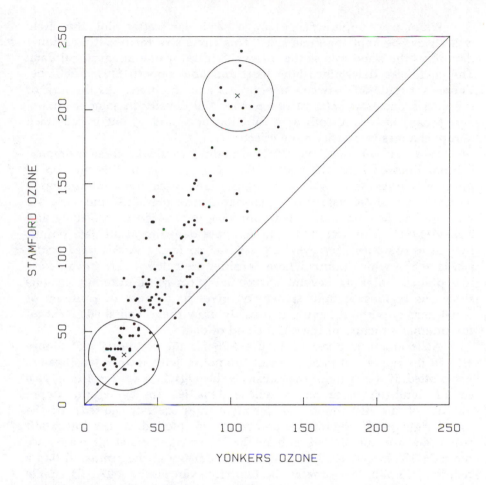

Figure 4.27 Stamford ozone data with two of the circles used to compute local densities.

$$f(27, 34) = \frac{37}{(136)(1963 \text{ ppb}^2)} = 13.86 \times 10^{-5} \text{ ppb}^{-2}.$$

The circle in the upper right, whose center is at (104, 209), has 9 points, so the local density at its center is

$$f(104, 209) = \frac{9}{(136)(1963 \text{ ppb}^2)} = 3.37 \times 10^{-5} \text{ ppb}^{-2}.$$

When we compute $f(x, y)$ for a particular scatter plot, the circle will always be kept the same size. This circle size for two-dimensional data plays the same role as the interval width for one-dimensional data. The circle size determines how local and how smooth $f(x, y)$ will be. There is a trade-off between smoothness and localness. As the size of the circles decreases, $f(x, y)$ summarizes the density in smaller circles, and $f(x, y)$ is less smooth as a function of x and y, but it can track abrupt changes in density more effectively.

How can we plot $f(x,y)$? One method would be to superimpose contour lines of f on the scatter plot of y_i and x_i. In this method of plotting, curves show values of equal density as the contours on a weather map show values of equal barometric pressure. But here we will use another method, called *sharpening*, which is due to Tukey and Tukey (1981). The first step is to compute densities at all data points, that is, to compute $f(x_1, y_1)$, $f(x_2, y_2)$, and so forth. A *sharpened scatter plot* is one in which points whose densities are below a certain value are not plotted. Making several sharpened plots with different cut-offs shows us regions of highest density, gives us a sense of contours of equal density without having to actually draw them, and sheds light on the internal structure of the point cloud of data.

An example is given in Figure 4.28 for the ozone data of Figure 4.1. In the upper left panel, 75% of the points with lowest densities are not plotted; if we think of the density values $f(x_i, y_i)$, for $i = 1$ to n, as a set of numbers, those points whose densities are below the upper quartile of the distribution of density values are not plotted. In the upper right panel 50% of the points are not plotted, in the lower left panel 25% are not plotted, and in the lower right panel all points are plotted. The circles used to compute the density at the points all had a radius of 25 ppb, the same as the two circles in Figure 4.27. To enable visual comparisons, it is essential to force all four of the plots in Figure 4.28 to have the same and x and y scales.

In the upper left panel of Figure 4.28 we see a tight cluster of points that indicates the region of highest density. As we move through the panels with the value of the density cut-off point decreasing we see the points spreading out from the lower left to the upper right; thus a rough overall impression is that the density values are highest in the lower left and decrease in going toward the upper right. Having a region of highest density at one end of a point cloud rather than in the middle is a kind of bivariate skewness that is analogous to the univariate skewness that we saw in Chapter 2 for the Stamford data by itself. Indeed, given the univariate skewness in each variable alone we would expect to see bivariate skewness in the point cloud.

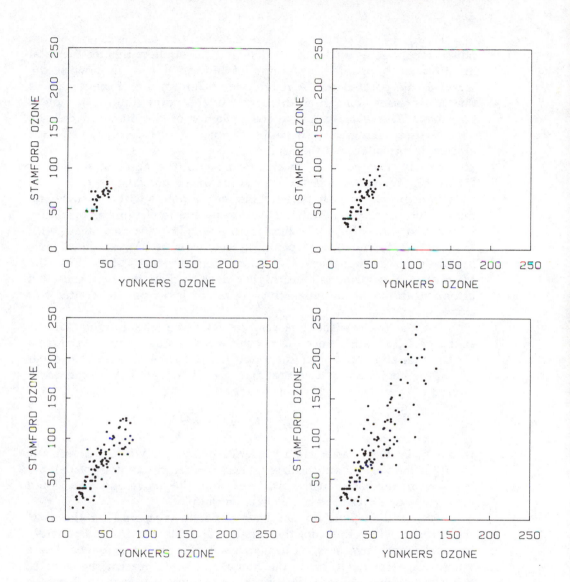

Figure 4.28 Four sharpened scatter plots of the ozone data.

Figure 4.29 is similar to Figure 4.28 except that the data used are now the cube roots of the ozone data and the circle radius for the local densities is .7 $ppb^{1/3}$. The region of highest density is now at the center of the point cloud. A rough overall impression of the density is that it decreases going from the center of the point cloud to the outer boundary. This corresponds to the behavior of the Stamford data by itself. After taking cube roots in Chapter 2, the local density was greatest in the middle of the data.

Let us now consider local densities for the automobile data in Figure 4.7. We will proceed as we did for the ozone data; for each point (x_i, y_i) on the plot we compute the number of points within a circle and divide this count by the circle area and by the total number of points. Figure 4.30 shows density values for the weight-price data, again with 75%, 50%, 25%, and 0% sharpening. Two areas of highest density are revealed by the upper panels. Also, the sharpened plots show the crescent in the lower left has higher density than the two arms that extend to the right, although this is evident just from the scatter plot alone.

For the ozone data it is easy to determine the formula for the circles on Figure 4.27; since the units of measurement, ppb, are the same for both variables, and since the graph has the same number of ppb per cm on the horizontal and vertical axes, a circle of radius h on the graph around the point (x_i, y_i) has the equation

$$(x - x_i)^2 + (y - y_i)^2 = h^2.$$

where x_i, y_i, x, y, and h are all in units of ppb. If we had chosen the scales on the vertical and horizontal axes so that the number of ppb per cm was not the same on the two axes, then the above equation would have given an ellipse and not a circle on the plot.

Most scatter plots do not have variables measured on the same scale. Even when they do, the number of units per cm is frequently unequal on the two axes, as in Figure 4.8. Figure 4.1 is a special case where we deliberately made the number of units per cm the same in order to enhance the comparison of the amount of ozone in Stamford with the amount in Yonkers. We are not comparing petal lengths with petal widths in Figure 4.8, so the number of units per cm is not forced to be equal on the two axes, but rather the scales are chosen so that the points fill up the plotting region vertically and horizontally.

To compute local density values we need to know the formula for a circle on the scatter plot. Our approach will be to compute standardized values of the data. Let x_{lo} and x_{hi} be the x values at the left and right edges of the plot (in the same units as the x_i), let r_x be the plotted range,

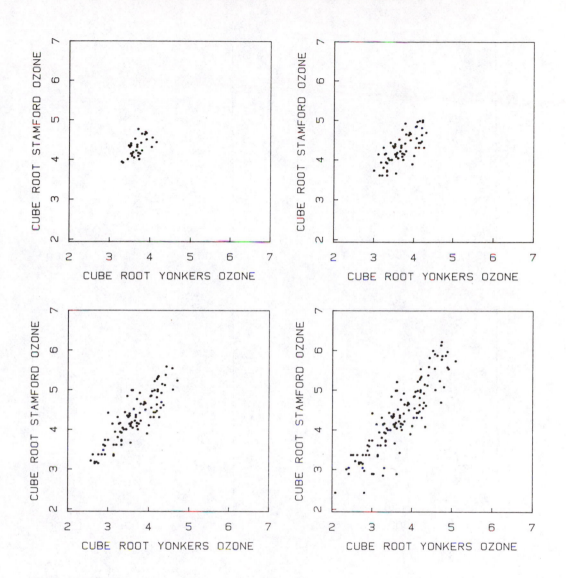

Figure 4.29 Four sharpened scatter plots of the cube root ozone data.

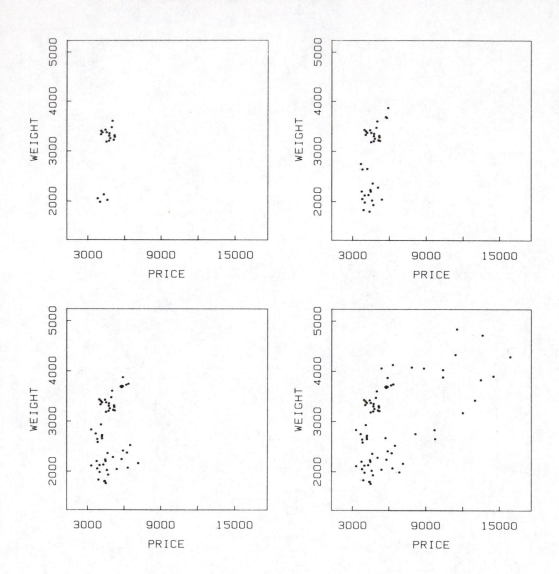

Figure 4.30 Four sharpened scatter plots of the automobile weight-price data.

$$r_x = x_{hi} - x_{lo},$$

and let w_x be the physical width of the plot in centimeters (or any other physical units). Also, let y_{lo}, y_{hi}, r_y and w_y be defined analogously for y, with w_y measured in the same units as w_x. Then the standardized values are

$$x_i^* = (x_i - x_{lo})/r_x$$

$$y_i^* = (y_i - y_{lo})(w_y/w_x)/r_y.$$

In these calculations, if the plot is square then the aspect ratio w_y/w_x is 1 and w_x and w_y can be ignored.

We will still make the scatter plot using the original x_i and y_i values, but we will scale the plot so that the values of x_i^* and y_i^* change by the same amount over one cm. This is illustrated in Figure 4.31 where both the x,y scales and the x^*,y^* scales are shown. Now when we compute a local density at (x_i, y_i) we work on the x^*,y^* scale. A circle of radius h around (x_i^*, y_i^*) is the set of points (x^*, y^*) with

$$(x^* - x_i^*)^2 + (y^* - y_i^*) = h^2.$$

When we computed densities for the weight-price data for Figure 4.30 we used standardized values and we took h to be .1. (h is, roughly, a fraction of the width of the plot.) Since the (x^*, y^*) scale is typically not needed to interpret the plot, it is not usually shown.

One might wonder why we have made such a fuss about circles and scales. The reason is this: we want our numerical computation of density to correspond to the visual information about density that we get from the scatter plot itself. Our eye-brain system gets this information from the amount of black that we see in different regions, and the extent to which points merge in our minds to form black or grey patches depends primarily on distance independently of direction. If we were to use highly elongated ellipses instead of circles to compute local densities we could get results that do not correspond to what our eyes see.

We can write a mathematical formula for the two-dimensional local density $f(x, y)$ similar to the one-dimensional density formula in Chapter 2. Let

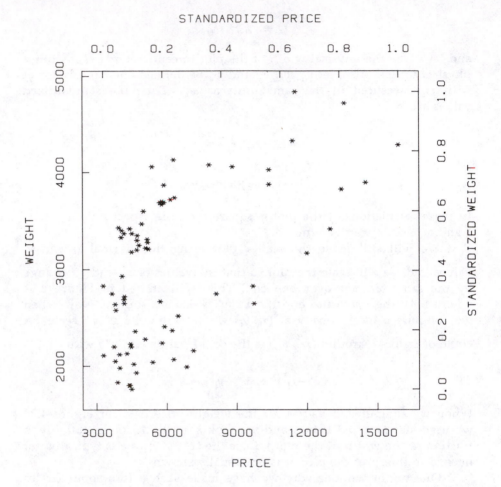

Figure 4.31 The weight-price data with original and standardized scales shown.

$$W(u, v) = \begin{cases} 1/\pi & \text{if } u^2 + v^2 \leqslant 1 \\ 0 & \text{otherwise} \end{cases}$$

This "cylinder" function, W, whose total integral is one, is analogous to the boxcar function that we defined in Section 2.9 and shown in Figure 2.18. Now we can express $f(x, y)$ by

$$f(x, y) = \frac{1}{h^2 n} \sum_{i=1}^{n} W\left(\frac{x-x_i}{h}, \frac{y-y_i}{h}\right)$$

(In practice, as mentioned above, we will usually be applying this formula to x^*, y^*, x_i^* and y_i^*, instead of x, y, x_i and y_i.)

As in the univariate case, we can think of $f(x, y)$ as the result of smearing the data points. Each (x_i, y_i) is replaced by a function of (x, y), namely $h^{-1}W\left(\frac{x-x_i}{h}, \frac{y-y_i}{h}\right)$, which is the smeared contribution of the observation (x_i, y_i) to the density at (x, y). Furthermore, since our cylinder smearing function has a discontinuity at all points on the unit circle $u^2 + v^2 = 1$, we might decide to replace the function with one that also has total integral one but decreases smoothly from a maximum at (0,0) to zero on the unit circle. This will remove the discontinuity. For example, we could use

$$W(u,v) = \begin{cases} \dfrac{1 + \cos \pi(\sqrt{u^2+v^2})}{\pi} & \text{if } u^2 + v^2 \leqslant 1 \\ 0 & \text{otherwise} \end{cases}$$

This function would give smoother two-dimensional local densities just as the cosine function in Section 2.9 gave smoother one-dimensional densities.

*4.11 MATHEMATICAL DETAILS OF LOWESS

In the lowess procedure the user chooses f, which is approximately the fraction of points to be used in the computation of each fitted value. Let q be fn rounded to the nearest integer. First, we will describe the computation of the neighborhood weight functions shown in the lower left panels of Figures 4.14 and 4.15. Let d_i be the distance from x_i to its qth nearest neighbor along the x axis. (x_i is counted as a neighbor of itself.) Let $T(u)$ be the *tricube weight function*:

$$T(u) = \begin{cases} (1 - |u|^3)^3 & \text{for } |u| < 1 \\ 0 & \text{otherwise} \end{cases}$$

Then the weight given to the point (x_k, y_k) when computing a smoothed value at x_i is defined to be

$$t_i(x_k) = T\left(\frac{x_i - x_k}{d_i}\right).$$

If d_i is 0, meaning that the q nearest neighbors of x_i all have abscissas equal to x_i, then points whose abscissas are equal to x_i are given weight 1 and all other points are given weight 0. In this case, since the slope of a fitted line cannot be estimated, a constant is fit instead of a line.

To compute a fitted value at x_i in the first stage of lowess, a line (or constant if $d_i = 0$) is fitted to the points of the scatter plot using weighted least squares with weight $t_i(x_k)$ at the point (x_k, y_k). That is, values of a and b are found which minimize

$$\sum_{k=1}^{n} t_i(x_k)(y_k - a - bx_k)^2.$$

If $\hat{a}$ and $\hat{b}$ are the values that achieve the minimum, then the initial fitted value at x_i is defined to be

$$\hat{y}_i = \hat{a} + \hat{b}x_i.$$

After the computation of initial fitted values for all x_i, residuals are computed,

$$r_i = y_i - \hat{y}_i,$$

and robustness weights are computed from them. Let $B(u)$ be the bisquare weight function:

$$B(u) = \begin{cases} (1-u^2)^2 & \text{for } |u| < 1 \\ 0 & \text{otherwise.} \end{cases}$$

Let m be the median of the absolute values of the residuals, that is,

$$m = \text{median}|r_k|.$$

The robustness weight for the point (x_k, y_k) is defined to be

$$w(x_k) = B\left(\frac{r_k}{6m}\right).$$

The median absolute residual, m, is a measure of how spread out the residuals are. If a residual is small compared with $6m$, the corresponding robustness weight will be close to 1; if a residual is greater than $6m$, the corresponding weight is 0. Suppose the r_i behave very much like a sample from a normal distribution. Then m nearly estimates $2\sigma/3$ where σ is the population standard deviation, and so $6m$ nearly estimates 4σ. Thus for well-behaved normal residuals we would very seldom have a weight as small as 0.

The next stage is to get updated fitted values, by fitting lines again, but this time incorporating the robustness weights. In the weighted linear regression for refitting $\hat{y}_i$, the point (x_k, y_k) is given weight $w(x_k)t_i(x_k)$. If (x_k, y_k) is a peculiar point with a large residual it will play a small role, or no role at all, in any of the fitted lines in this stage of the computation.

4.12 SUMMARY AND DISCUSSION

Scatter plots are a powerful tool for helping us to understand the relationship between two measured or observed variables, x and y. When x is a factor and y is a response, scatter plots can show us how the empirical distribution of y depends on x. In the exchangeable case, when neither x nor y is regarded as a factor or a response, scatter plots can tell us much about the bivariate empirical distribution of x and y.

Strip medians and strip box plots show how the empirical distribution of y in vertical strips varies from strip to strip on the scatter plot. They are an easy-to-make summary but the price paid is to display no information about the change in the distribution of y within strips.

Smoothing procedures require more computation but provide a more detailed look at how various aspects of the local distribution of y depend on x. Smoothed values from lowess show the middle of the distribution of y as it changes with x. If we compute residuals from these smoothed values, and plot the absolute values of the residuals against the x_i, along with smoothed absolute residuals, we can see how the spread of the distribution of y depends on x.

Repeated points on scatter plots are a problem that we cannot ignore. Both jittering and sunflowers can be used to address the problem. Sunflowers together with cellulation provide counts in square regions even when points do not exactly coincide.

Two-dimensional local densities can be computed in a manner analogous to one-dimensional local densities. Portraying the local density values using several sharpened scatter plots with different cutoff values shows regions of highest density, gives a sense of contours of equal density, and gives information about the internal shape of the point cloud.

4.13   FURTHER READING

Anscombe (1973) has an interesting discussion of scatter plots and demonstrates their value in regression analysis (which we will get to in Chapter 7). Figures 4.2 and 4.3 were inspired by scatter plots of Anscombe that have very different patterns but the same correlation and regression coefficients.

A number of procedures for smoothing scatter plots, frequently called nonparametric regression procedures, have been suggested. Tukey (1977), for example, combines moving medians and moving averages to smooth scatter plots, but the procedure does not take the x_i distances into account and proceeds as if the x_i were equally spaced. Stone (1977) has investigated the problem of a very wide class of smoothers and gives an extensive bibliography.

Friedman and Stuetzle (1982) have implemented a locally weighted regression procedure that runs fast enough to be used in projection pursuit regression (Friedman and Stuetzle, 1982). The speed-up necessitates ignoring the distances among the x_i. P. Tukey (1980) has suggested another speed-up for lowess which is simple and appears to work well. Lowess fitted values are computed at a subset of the points in such a way that a string of consecutive abscissas of points not in the subset are never more than a prespecified distance apart. Fitted values for points not in the subset are then computed using linear interpolation. In this way a limit is put on the total number of regressions for each iteration, independent of the number of points. This procedure has been implemented in a FORTRAN routine that computes lowess (Cleveland, 1981). This program also incorporates some special procedures to avoid numerical problems that can arise if the slope of a fitted line is poorly determined.

In Tukey and Tukey (1981) a number of issues about scatter plots, which they also call two-views, are discussed that are not included here. Among them are merging (making points blend to enhance overall impressions), separating (coding categories of points on a scatter plot), and alternating (superimposing contours on a scatter plot).

EXERCISES

4.1. Make a scatter plot of the first 60 average monthly temperatures in Eureka against the first 60 average monthly temperatures in Newark (Data Set 9).

4.2. Make a scatter plot of the salaries of chauffeurs against the salaries of teachers (Data Set 11). What can you say about the relationship between the salaries of these two professions?

4.3. Make a scatter plot of length against rear seat of the automobile data (Data Set 7).

4.4. Make a scatter plot of the salaries of electrical engineers against the salaries of teachers (Data Set 11). What do the outliers have in common?

4.5. Make a scatter plot of per capita disposable income against the percentage of the population below age 15 of 35 countries (Data Set 16). What do the countries with a large fraction of young people have in common?

4.6. Make a scatter plot of price against gear ratio of the automobile data (Data Set 7).

4.7. Make a scatter plot of murder-suicides against newspaper coverage (Data Set 17). Do the variables appear related?

4.8. Plot the number of telephones in the USA from 1900 to 1970 (Data Set 18) against time. Would smoothing these data help any? How can you check if the percentage growth in numbers of telephones over the last 20 years has been constant?

4.9. Make a scatter plot of fuel economy (mpg) against displacement for the automobile data (Data Set 7).

4.10. Make a scatter plot of brain weight against body weight of 62 mammals (Data Set 19). What problem arises? Take logarithms and make the plot again. Does this help? What rough numerical measure of intelligence does the plot suggest?

4.11. Let -20, -13, -10, -4, 2, 2, 3, 3, 5, 6, 6, 6, 7, 7, 7, 9, 9, 13, 13, 18, 30, 50, 100, 400 be 24 x values. Which x values would be involved in computing a lowess smoothed value at $x = -20$ if $f = 1/3$? Which values are involved when $x = 6$, when $x = 9$, and when $x = 13$?

*4.12. Why does the smoothing algorithm lowess compute a regression line through the nearest neighbors instead of simply taking their means? Construct a case where it makes a substantial difference.

4.13. What influences the weight of a particular point in the weighted regressions used in the smoothing algorithm lowess?

*4.14. Smooth the data on the scatter plot of displacement against trunk size (Data Set 7) by

1. Computing the medians in 5 vertical strips.

2. Fitting a regression line to the data in each of 5 vertical strips.

3. Computing the mean over the 10 nearest neighbors at each point.

4. Using the smoothing algorithm lowess.

Compare these smoothing methods with each other.

4.15. Make a scatter plot of the salaries of managers against the salaries of cooks (Data Set 11). Superimpose a smoothed curve if you have a way to compute it; if not use strip medians.

4.16. Make a scatter plot of displacement against turning diameter for the automobile data (Data Set 7) and superimpose a smoothed curve or strip medians.

4.17. Plot the temperature data in New York (Data Set 2) against time. Summarize the data by medians of vertical strips of width 2 weeks. Superimpose a smooth curve on the scatter plot. How does the smooth curve compare to the medians of the 2-week strips?

4.18. Make a scatter plot of the percent contribution to gross domestic product of agriculture against per capita disposable income (Data Set 16) and superimpose a smooth curve or strip medians.

4.19. Plot wind speed in New York City against time (Data Set 2) and superimpose a smooth curve or strip medians.

4.20. Jitter the points on a scatter plot of loaf volumes against protein content of 100 commercial Ohio wheats (Data Set 15). Replot the scatter diagram by using sunflowers. Compare the use of sunflowers with jittering.

4.21. Make a scatter plot of longitudinal girth against length of eggs of the common tern (Data Set 21). Jitter the points on the plot. Replot the scatter diagram by using sunflowers. How can the plot be modified to express the high number of data values at some of the points?

4.22. Make a scatter plot of years since highest degree against age of Bell Laboratories managers (Data Set 20).

    1. Make a sunflower plot of the data.

   *2. Make a sharpened scatter plot of the data. Which plot is more useful?

4.23.   1. Make a sunflower plot of % savings rate against per capita disposable income in 35 countries (Data Set 16).

   *2. Make a sharpened scatter plot. Compare the two plots.

5

Plotting
Multivariate Data

5.1 INTRODUCTION

Although scatter plots and related displays help us to study paired data values, many serious data analysis applications involve several or many variables, not just two. In Chapter 4 we studied a number of *bivariate* data sets, that is, paired measurements of two variables. One example is ozone measurements each day at Stamford, Connecticut and Yonkers, New York. But in reality this was just part of a much larger *multivariate* data set which included measurements of many variables. For example, along with Stamford and Yonkers there were daily measurements of ozone at Elizabeth, New Jersey, at Roosevelt Island, New York, at Springfield, Massachusetts, at Hartford, Connecticut and at 40 or so other sites. There were also meteorological measurements such as wind speed and direction, temperature, and precipitation. And ozone was not the only pollutant measured; there were nitric oxide, nitrogen dioxide, peroxyacetyl nitrate, formaldehyde, and many other unpleasant substances. Given the complexities of atmospheric chemistry and air mass movements, it was crucial in that study to consider more than two variables at a time.

Just as we can plot bivariate data in a two-dimensional coordinate system, we can imagine plotting three-variable or trivariate data in a three-dimensional coordinate system, and (stretching our imagination a bit) we can imagine plotting multivariate data in a multidimensional coordinate system. For this reason, we often refer to multivariate data as *multidimensional*, even though they are data generated by very real processes in our own three-dimensional world. They have not come from some abstract or imaginary space of four or more dimensions. Air pollution and weather are very real indeed.

We will illustrate the techniques of this chapter primarily with two data sets, both of which were partially examined in Chapter 4. The first is a set of four measurements on each of 150 iris flowers. The four measurements are sepal width, sepal length, petal width, and petal length for each flower; the sample contains 50 flowers from each of three varieties, *iris setosa*, *iris virginica*, and *iris versicolor*. (In an iris flower, the sepals look like three additional long and floppy petals.) We can regard these data as 150 four-dimensional observations, or points, in four-dimensional space. For some purposes we can think of iris variety as a fifth variable that is *qualitative* rather than *quantitative*, and use the (arbitrary) coding of 1, 2, and 3 to indicate the three iris varieties. This data set is moderately small, the variables are measured in the same units (centimeters) and span comparable ranges, there are no missing values, and, as we shall see, there are no wild or obviously erroneous values. In this sense, these data are well behaved.

The second data set consists of selected characteristics of 74 automobile models sold in the U.S. in 1979. The variables can be roughly categorized into three groups: performance, size, and price. The performance variables include fuel efficiency (mpg), turning diameter, gear ratio, and the repair records in the previous two years (1977 and 1978). The size variables are head room, spaciousness of the rear seat, size of the trunk, weight, length, and engine displacement. Purchase price is the single variable in the final category. The repair records are measured on a five-point scale ranging from "much worse than average" (coded as 1), to "much better than average" (coded as 5); three models first introduced in 1978 and five in 1979 have incomplete repair records.

In working with the automobile data, we encounter several of the complications that are common in practice. There are missing values, and there are different measurement scales (dollars, pounds, inches, etc.). Most of the variables are on essentially continuous scales, but two of them (the repair records) are on discrete scales. In addition, the model name can be regarded as a qualitative variable from which other coded qualitative variables can be constructed. For instance, we can easily create coded variables to indicate make (Lincoln, Mercury, Plymouth, etc.), manufacturer (General Motors, Ford, Volkswagen, etc.), country of manufacture, and so on.

The iris data set and the car data set each can be written down as an *n* by *p* matrix consisting of *n* observations on *p* variables. For example, the car data matrix is 74 × 12, each row is for a car model, and each column is one of the measured variables. We can think of the car data as being 74 points in a 12 dimensional space.

5.2 ONE-DIMENSIONAL AND TWO-DIMENSIONAL VIEWS

Although our ultimate interest in studying multivariate data usually centers on the relationships among the variables, it is often still worthwhile to study each variable by itself, paying attention to such things as ranges, skewness, outliers, repeated values, and discrete scales; sometimes this can help guide our choice and interpretation of subsequent multivariate displays. Thus, a sensible way to begin looking at a multivariate data set is to isolate individual variables and look at them one at a time, using the techniques of Chapter 2.

Figure 5.1 shows twelve stem-and-leaf displays for the twelve variables of the automobile data. We can quickly spot a number of features, such as: (i) The price distribution is highly skewed and the distribution of miles per gallon is slightly skewed, (ii) the repair records are discrete but fairly symmetrical and the 1978 repair record is, on the whole, somewhat better than 1977, (iii) there is one exceptionally low and one exceptionally high value among the rear-seat measurements, and both the head-room and and rear-seat measurements are rounded to the nearest 1/2 cubic foot, (iv) there is a curious gap at 19 in the trunk measurements, (v) the distributions of length and turning diameter are bimodal, and (vi) the gear ratio measurements bunch up at certain preferred values.

Having learned what we can from univariate displays of separate variables, we can select pairs of variables to examine with the scatter plotting techniques of Chapter 4. For instance, Figure 5.2 is a scatter plot of weight against length for the automobile data with a robust smooth curve superimposed. It reveals a gentle upward curvature at the lower left and two moderately unusual cars that are somewhat heavy for their length, the AMC Pacer and the Cadillac Seville. However, in general, weight seems to be roughly a linear function of length. We might reasonably have expected to see more curvature in this plot if we thought that width, height, and cross-section of frame members also increased with length, but the plot suggests that for this group of cars, heights, widths, and structure cross-sections do not increase, on average, with length. (We will show how to make some improvement to this plot in Section 5.6.)

Figure 5.3 shows the 1978 repair record plotted against price for the 69 automobile models for which 1978 repair records are available. It suffers from one of the problems discussed in Chapter 4: the discreteness of the repair record scale causes the points to line up essentially into five one-dimensional scatter plots with considerable overlap of the plotted symbols. To alleviate this, we can adopt one of the several strategies offered in Chapter 4. We could make a sunflower

Length
(10's of inches)

14 : 279
15 : 45567
16 : 133455589
17 : 00002234457999
18 : 02469
19 : 23356788889
20 : 0000111344667
21 : 2246788
22 : 00112
23 : 03

Gas Mileage
(miles per gallon)

12 : 00
13 :
14 : 000000
15 : 00
16 : 0000
17 : 0000
18 : 000000000
19 : 00000000
20 : 000
21 : 00000
22 : 00000
23 : 000
24 : 0000
25 : 00000
26 : 000
27 :
28 : 000
29 : 0
30 : 00
31 : 0
32 :
33 :
34 : 0
35 : 00
36 :
37 :
38 :
39 :
40 :
41 : 0

Weight (1000 lbs)

1 : 88889
2 : 000001111222223444
2 : 5666677777889
3 : 22222233333444444
3 : 567777778999
4 : 0111133
4 : 78

Turning Diameter
(feet)

32 : 0
33 : 00
34 : 000000
35 : 000000
36 : 000000000
37 : 0000
38 : 000
39 : 0
40 : 000000
41 : 00000
42 : 00000000
43 : 00000000000
44 : 000
45 : 000
46 : 00
47 :
48 : 000
49 :
50 :
51 : 0

Gear Ratio (times 10)

21 : 9
22 : 468
23 :
24 : 11137777
25 : 366
26 :
27 : 133333333355
28 : 7
29 : 33333333478
30 : 55568888888
31 : 5
32 : 013
33 : 077
34 :
35 : 444588
36 : 4
37 : 00234888
38 : 19

Headroom
(cubic feet)

1 : 5555
2 : 0000000000000
2 : 55555555555555
3 : 0000000000000
3 : 5555555555555555
4 : 000000000
4 : 5555
5 : 0

Rear Seat
(cubic feet)

18 : 5
19 :
20 :
21 : 05
22 : 000
23 : 00005555
24 : 005
25 : 000555555555
26 : 00005
27 : 000000005
28 : 0000055555
29 : 00000555
30 : 00005555
31 : 0555
32 :
33 :
34 :
35 :
36 :
37 : 5

Trunk (cubic feet)

5 : 0
6 : 0
7 : 000
8 : 00000
9 : 0000
10 : 00000
11 : 00000000
12 : 000
13 : 0000
14 : 0000
15 : 00000
16 : 0000000000000
17 : 0000000
18 : 0
19 :
20 : 000000
21 : 00
22 : 0
23 : 0

1977 Repair Record
(5 is best)

1 : 000
2 : 00000000000
3 : 000000000000000000000000000
4 : 00000000000000000000
5 : 00000

1978 Repair Record
(5 is best)

1 : 00
2 : 00000000
3 : 00000000000000000000000000000000000
4 : 000000000000000000
5 : 00000000000

Price ($1000)

3 : 33778889
4 : 0001112222344455555566777789
5 : 0112224477888999
6 : 2233358
7 : 18
8 : 18
9 : 77
10 : 44
11 : 45
12 : 0
13 : 056
14 : 5
15 : 9

Engine Displacement
(100's of cubic inches)

0 : 8899999
1 : 00000000001222222333444
1 : 5555666
2 : 0000223333333333333
2 : 5556
3 : 0000022
3 : 55555
4 : 002

Figure 5.1 Stem-and-leaf displays for all twelve variables of the automobile data. The decimal point is at the colon. There are 74 automobile models (observations); several repair records are missing.

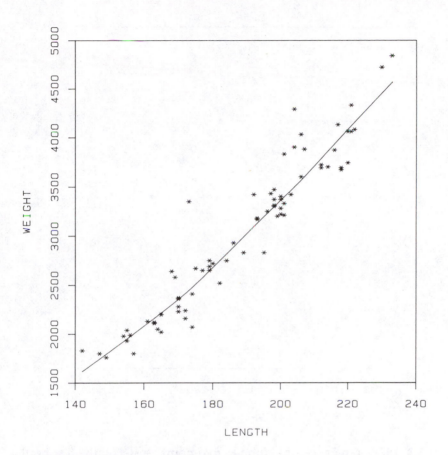

Figure 5.2 Scatter plot of automobile weight (in pounds) against automobile length (in inches) with a robust smooth curve.

plot or use five horizontal box plots, but for reasons of practical simplicity and flexibility that will become apparent later in this chapter, we will jitter both the 1977 and 1978 repair-record data values by adding random amounts in the range −.3 to +.3. This amount of jitter corrupts the data less than one might think, since the original data values can be easily recovered from the jittered values by rounding. The jittered values will be used for most of the plots involving repair records in this chapter. Figure 5.4 is the jittered version of Figure 5.3. The main visual message in this plot is the similarity of the 1978 repair records for models in different price ranges. Price alone does not determine mechanical reliability.

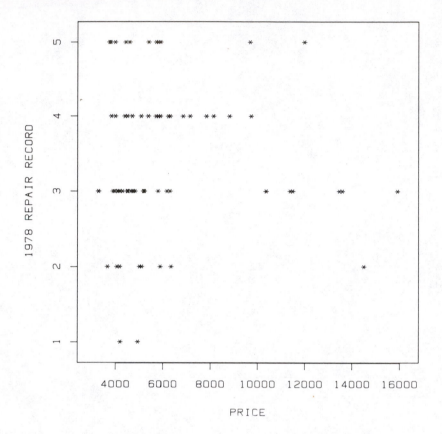

Figure 5.3 1978 repair record (on a five-point scale with 5 = best) plotted against price (in dollars) for all models that had a 1978 repair record.

We can proceed to plot and study other pairs of variables, but we must face the fact that with p variables there are $p(p-1)/2$ distinct pairs from which to choose. For example, the twelve automobile variables produce 66 pairs. A systematic approach becomes important, and in Section 5.4 we show a way to assemble all the scatter plots into a single composite display.

In fact, the scatter plot turns out to be the basic building block for most of the multivariate displays in this chapter.

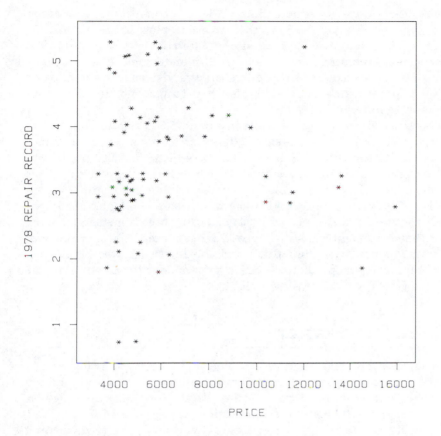

Figure 5.4 Jittered 1978 repair record plotted against price.

5.3   PLOTTING THREE DIMENSIONS AT ONCE

Before we tackle four and higher-dimensional data, it is important to have some techniques for looking at data in three dimensions. We will show three basic approaches, all of which involve two-dimensional scatter plots in special ways.

MULTIPLE VIEWS — DRAFTSMAN'S DISPLAY

Out of three variables (say, 1978 repair record, weight, and price of the 74 automobile models) there are three ways to choose two at a time, leading to three bivariate scatter plots. It is convenient to arrange them on the page as in Figure 5.5 so that adjacent plots share an axis in common. (Note that we have used the jittered version of the 1978 repair record.) This arrangement lets us eliminate some clutter by not showing two of the axis scales, and it enables a viewer to scan across or down the page matching up points that correspond to the same observation in different plots.

The array of *pairwise scatter plots* in Figure 5.5 is reminiscent of the drawings that a draftsman makes. If we imagine a physical three-dimensional "scatter plot" of these data in which the data points are tiny spheres suspended inside a cube, then the three component scatter plots of Figure 5.5 are the "front", "top" and "side" views of the data cube. For this reason, following Tukey and Tukey (1981 and 1983), we can call Figure 5.5 a *draftsman's display* of the three-dimensional data. Two of the component plots in Figure 5.5 have already been discussed. The top component was Figure 4.7, and the lower-left was Figure 5.4. In the third component plot we see a general decline in 1978 repair record associated with increasing weight.

SYMBOLIC SCATTER PLOTS

When the top component plot of Figure 5.5 occurred as Figure 4.7, we noted a curious separation of the points into two "branches", and we raised the question of whether the separation has any deeper significance. We will look into that question now.

In order to search for a meaningful way to characterize distinct clusters of points in a scatter plot, it can be helpful in some circumstances to replace the plotted points by descriptive labels (if available) and to examine the plot, bringing to bear any auxiliary information we may have regarding the points. Figure 5.6 shows the plot of Figure 5.5 with the first two characters of each model name as given in the table of the data in the Appendix.

Although Figure 5.6 has some shortcomings (for instance, there is overcrowding which makes it impossible to read some of the labels), the plot serves its purpose well, for a few moments of reflection reveals that many of the points in the lower branch are foreign car models, and many in the upper branch are manufactured in the U.S.

To explore this more carefully, we can construct a new variable that takes the value 0 for U.S. cars, and 1 for foreign cars (such a variable is often called an *indicator* or *dummy* variable), and replot weight against price using the symbols O and × for U.S. and foreign, respectively. The resulting Figure 5.7 confirms our suspicions. All of the points on the upper branch are U.S. cars, and most of the points on

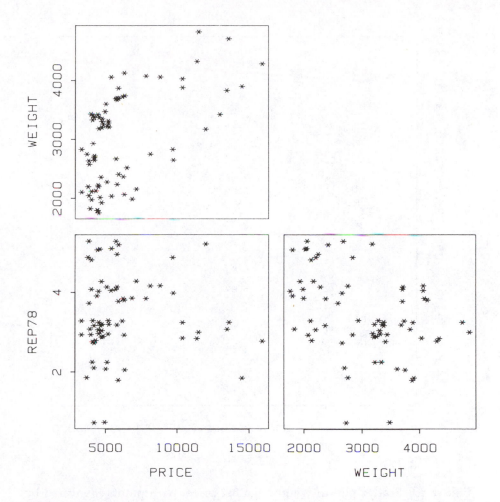

Figure 5.5 Draftsman's display of all three pairwise scatter plots involving price, weight and (jittered) 1978 repair record, for those cars that had a 1978 repair record.

the lower branch are foreign. An overall assessment is that for both U.S. and foreign car models (at least in this group of 74) weight generally increases with price, but that U.S. cars are generally heavier than foreign cars of comparable price. Equivalently, foreign cars are generally more expensive than U.S. cars of comparable weight.

If we focus on deviations from the general pattern we can observe that the increase of weight with price for U.S. cars levels off above $8,000. Beyond that point, price increases but weight only fluctuates. Interestingly, in terms of weight and price, three of the four most

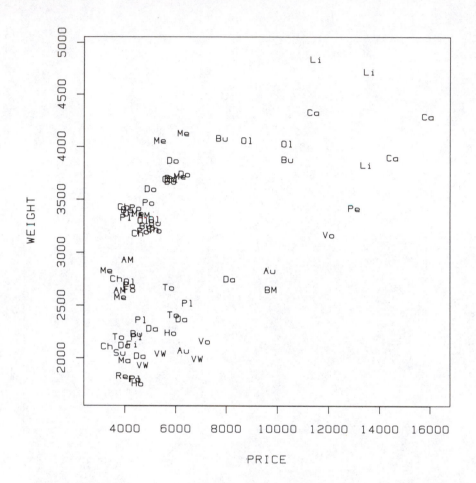

Figure 5.6 Scatter plot of weight against price, with points identified by the first two characters of the name of the make.

expensive U.S. cars (Cadillac Seville, Cadillac Eldorado, and Lincoln Versailles) fall in line with the foreign cars. At the low end of the scale, the eight U.S. cars seem to fit the pattern of the foreign cars. As it turns out, several of these cars are actually manufactured abroad on contract for U.S. automobile companies.

The two figures we have just seen are examples of a class of plots for three-dimensional data called *symbolic scatter plots*. Two variables are represented by the x- and y-coordinates of the plotted points, and a third variable is portrayed by the plotted symbol. In graphical terms, Figure 5.7 is more successful than Figure 5.6, because the categories in Figure 5.6 are too numerous and the symbols (the 2-character sequences)

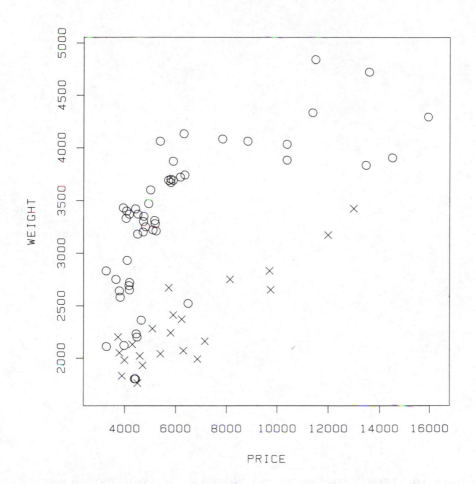

Figure 5.7 Symbolic scatter plot of weight against price, with U.S. cars coded as O and foreign cars as ×.

too complicated to allow meaningful visual patterns to emerge. Nevertheless, we might never have thought of making Figure 5.7 without having studied Figure 5.6 first.

The third variable depicted in Figure 5.7 takes on only discrete values, which makes it easy to assign symbols. One way to adapt the idea to variables measured on continuous scales is to code a third variable into the *size* of the plotted symbol (with some conveniently chosen largest and smallest size). Returning to the three variables, weight, price and 1978 repair record, we plot in Figure 5.8 the 1978 repair record against price, with weight coded by circle size. The *diameter* of the circle has been made proportional to weight. We see that

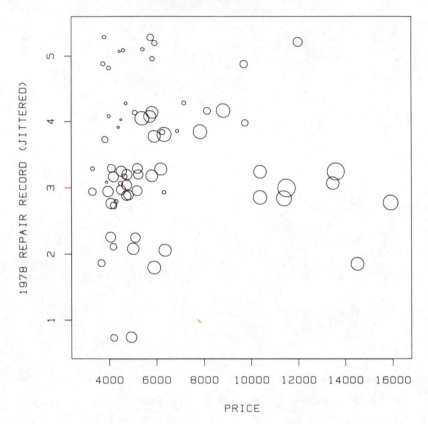

Figure 5.8 Symbolic scatter plot of jittered 1978 repair record against price, with automobile weight represented by the diameter of the circle.

the cars with the best repair records (fours and fives) tend to be light *and* inexpensive; only perhaps six of the smallest cars had repair records as low as 3. A few of the largest cars had "better than average" repair records, but none were "much better than average"; the two expensive cars with "much better than average" repair records are fairly light cars. Despite the general pattern, one of the two cars with dismal repair record is fairly light and inexpensive.

Various kinds of symbols can be used for representing data values. Other examples are shown below, and Section 5.7 discusses some considerations for choosing types of symbols that are appropriate for various kinds of applications.

We note that the sunflower plot in Chapter 4 is a kind of symbolic scatter plot, but the number of petals on a sunflower is used to portray the local density of points in the x-y plane, not a third variable.

PARTITIONING AND CASEMENT DISPLAYS

In symbolic scatter plots and draftsman's displays each component scatter plot shows the entire set of n observations. An alternative approach is to partition the n observations into subsets according to the values of one variable, and then for each subset to make a separate scatter plot of the other two variables. The plots can be arranged in a row (or in a column) according to increasing value of the partitioning variable.

Figure 5.9 again depicts weight against price for the car data, this time partitioned into five separate plots according to 1978 repair record. The increase of weight with price is evident in each repair-record category, and there is a striking appearance of distinct clusters of points. All of the cars that are both heavy and expensive form a cluster with repair record rated average (= 3) except for one that has slipped to a 2. There is a small cluster of heavy moderately priced cars with better than average repair record (= 4), and another cluster of light cars with better to much better than average repair records (= 5) and low to moderate prices. A large cluster of inexpensive cars have average repair records and low to medium weights, and all (but one) of the cars with worse or much worse than average repair records (4 or 5) form a cluster of inexpensive, medium-weight cars. The question of whether these clusters have any useful interpretations would have to be explored by studying the identities of the points in the various clusters.

If the partitioning variable is on a continuous scale, we can partition according to intervals, or bands, of values much as we do for histograms. Geometrically, this operation can be visualized, as suggested by Figure 5.10, by starting with a three-dimensional (x, y, z) scatter plot of the data inside a cube, and "slicing" the cubical region into several layers or strata with a series of planes parallel to the (x, y) coordinate plane but at different equally-spaced depths in z. Then the slices of the data space are flattened and placed side-by-side. This kind of plot has been called a *casement display* (Tukey and Tukey, 1983), since it is like cranking open a series of casement windows, drawing each data point to the nearest window, and then cranking them shut again.

Two technical issues should be mentioned. First, the number of partitions is often not critical. There may be a "natural" number, as there was for the 1978 five-point repair record scale. Otherwise, we can

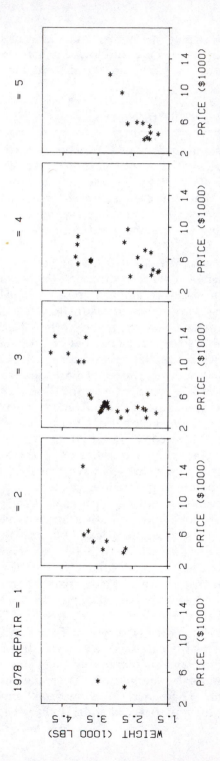

Figure 5.9 Casement display of automobile weight (in 1000's of lbs.) against price (in $1000's), partitioned by 1978 repair record.

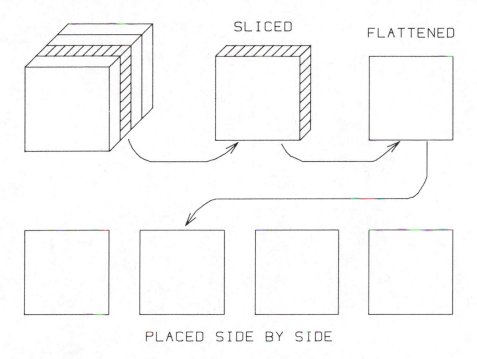

SLICED

FLATTENED

PLACED SIDE BY SIDE

Figure 5.10 Schematic view of the construction of a casement display showing a data space partitioned into slices, or strata.

usually choose a number between 2 and 8 that offers a reasonable trade-off, bearing in mind that with too few partitions we may lose much of the detailed structure as it relates to the sliced variable, but with too many partitions there may be too few points in each plot. Also, when there are many partitions the individual plots may have to be made small just to fit them on the page. To illustrate the trade-offs, in Figure 5.11 we have collapsed the outer pairs of categories of 1978 repair record into single categories, corresponding to "below-average", "average", and "above-average" repair records. All of the clusters described earlier are still apparent, but the viewer cannot appreciate, for instance, that the upper cluster in the right-hand plot consists entirely of 4's.

The second technical issue is that the plotted x and y axes must be identical on all the component scatter plots, even though some of the plots will typically not be filled up. The plotted range in each plot must be based on the entire data set.

There is a close connection between symbolic scatter plots and casement displays. If the component plots in a casement display are constructed with different plotting symbols, then the plots could be

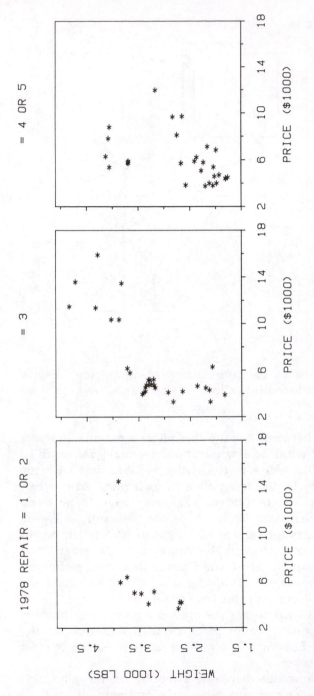

Figure 5.11 Casement display of automobile weight against price, partitioned by 1978 repair record, with below average repair records combined into a single category, and above average records into a single category.

superimposed to produce a symbolic scatter plot. Despite this close connection, in our experience both kinds of plots are useful, and each is capable of bringing out features in the data that the other does not. The casement display lets us see the shape of the point cloud in each partition more clearly, but the symbolic plot makes it easier to see the relationship between the clouds from one partition to the next.

5.4 PLOTTING FOUR AND MORE DIMENSIONS

The methods we have described for three-dimensional data underlie a variety of displays for data involving four and more variables. We will show how each basic approach for three dimensions (draftsman's display, symbolic scatter plot, and casement display) can be extended. Then in the subsequent section we will show how the approaches can be used in various combinations in a single display.

GENERALIZED DRAFTSMAN'S DISPLAY

The draftsman's display for three dimensions generalizes easily to applications involving multivariate data. We simply include one more row in the display for each additional variable. Figure 5.12 is a *generalized draftsman's display* of the four variables of the iris data.

As before, the essential property of this array of scatter plots is that any adjacent pair of plots have an axis in common. In Figure 5.12 this means that by scanning across the last row we see petal width plotted against each of the other variables in turn, and we can track an interesting point or group of points, such as the small cluster at the bottom, from plot to plot. Similarly, the first column shows each variable plotted against sepal length.

It is not as easy to scan the plots in Figure 5.12 involving sepal width (or petal length), since they do not line up; but we can do this in the full array of scatter plots shown in Figure 5.13. In return for this convenience, we pay the price of increasing the overall visual complexity of the display without adding any additional information, since the plots in the upper triangle are the same as those in the lower triangle except that the axes are reversed. We also require an extra row and column, which forces each component plot to be somewhat smaller so they all fit on a page. (If plotting time is a consideration, we should also realize that the full array takes twice as long to plot.)

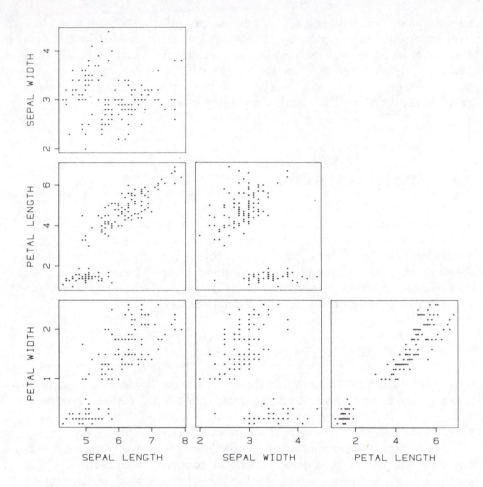

Figure 5.12 Generalized draftsman's display of the six pairwise scatter plots formed from the four variables of the iris data. Units are centimeters.

The most striking feature of the generalized draftsman's view of the iris data in Figure 5.13 is the separation of points into clusters. Knowing that the data sample includes three iris varieties, we should immediately suspect that the clusters are associated with variety. (Our suspicions will be confirmed by another plot below.) Two clusters occur in every plot, although in some they are more pronounced, and by scanning across rows and down columns of the display we can easily see that the clusters in the various plots correspond to the same subset of points. The last two rows of the display show that each petal measurement by itself separates the clusters. By contrast, the first two

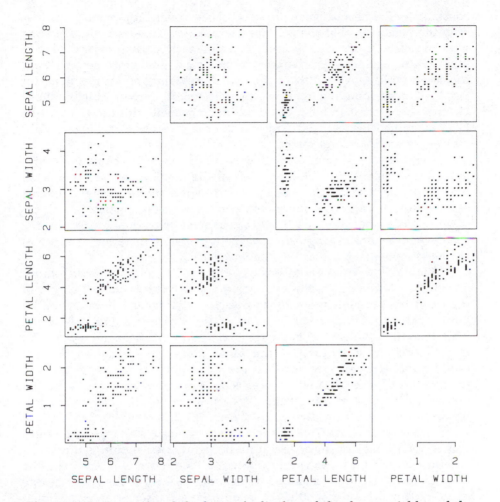

Figure 5.13 Generalized draftsman's display of the four variables of the iris data, extended to the full array.

rows show that neither sepal measurement alone separates them. Nevertheless, in terms of the two sepal measurements together (seen in the first plot in the second row), the clusters are separated by a space that stretches diagonally across the plot.

By thinking about what these variables mean, we can learn something about the shapes of petals and sepals in this collection of 150 iris flowers. In the plot of petal width against petal length (fourth row, third plot), the points stay fairly close to a line through the origin (width = constant × length). This means that the overall shape of petals, as described by their aspect ratio (length/width), remains fairly constant for large and small flowers. To a rough approximation, it is only the petal *sizes* that change, not their *shapes*. However, the situation with sepals is more complicated. Within each cluster in the plot of sepal width against sepal length (second row, first plot), sepal length increases with sepal width (although there is more scatter than for petals — corresponding to a greater variety of shapes). But between clusters there is a *decrease* of sepal width associated with the cluster that has generally *longer* sepals. This means the cluster in the lower right has longer and narrower sepals.

Looking at the four plots that compare sepal measurements with petal measurements (in the lower left of the display), we see that sepal length increases with petal size both within and across clusters, but that sepal width *decreases* with increasing petal size across clusters.

Roughly speaking, we have established that the flowers in the smaller cluster are distinguished by being smaller in terms of three of the measurements, but that they have *wider* sepals.

Some of the component plots in Figure 5.13 show isolated points, or outliers. For instance, there is such a point in the lower left corner of the third row, second plot. In no case in this example does an outlier have a value that is unusual in terms of any single variable; it is in the joint behavior of pairs of variables that the points seem unusual. We might consider whether it is the same flower that accounts for the outliers appearing in several plots, and how many variables are actually involved. In Figure 5.14 we have selected the flower associated with the outlier on the plot of petal width against sepal width, and plotted this flower as an asterisk on each panel. We now clearly see that this single iris flower stands apart from the rest in every plot involving sepal width and is accounting for all of the outliers; its unusual nature is due to its exceptionally small sepal width relative to its other measurements. The table from which these measurements come (Fisher, 1936) gives a value of 2.3 cm for the sepal width. This could be a transcription error, for if we reverse the digits, the value 3.2 cm would no longer be an outlier.

In principle, a generalized draftsman's display can be made for any number of variables, but when we have a large number of variables (more than, say, 7 to 10) the technique runs into some practical difficulties. If the component plots are made small enough so that the whole array fits onto a sheet of ordinary size paper, then they may be too small to be useful. (One solution is to generate the plot in sections on separate sheets that can be pasted together and hung on the wall.) When we see interesting patterns in individual component plots of the generalized draftsman's display, we can enlarge them for closer examination.

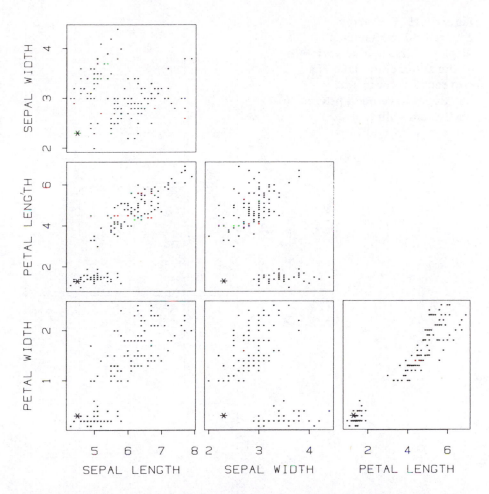

Figure 5.14 Generalized draftsman's display of the four-dimensional iris data (like Figure 5.11), with one flower plotted as an asterisk.

Figure 5.15 is a generalized draftsman's display of all twelve variables of the automobile data. Note that we have again used the jittered version of the 1977 and 1978 repair records. Headroom is jittered, as well; had we not used jitter, the overlap of plotted points at this small scale would have been severe. To fit Figure 5.15 into this book, we had to make the plots smaller than we would have liked.

Despite the small size of the plots in Figure 5.15 we can see a wealth of information (more, in fact, than we have space to comment on here). The (8,9) plot (eighth row down, ninth plot from the left), which we already saw in Figure 5.2, shows a fairly tight linear relationship

Figure 5.15 Full-array generalized draftsman's display of the twelve variables of the automobile data. The two repair records and headroom have been jittered to resolve crowding.

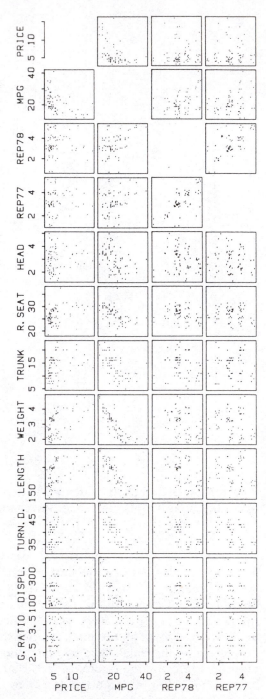

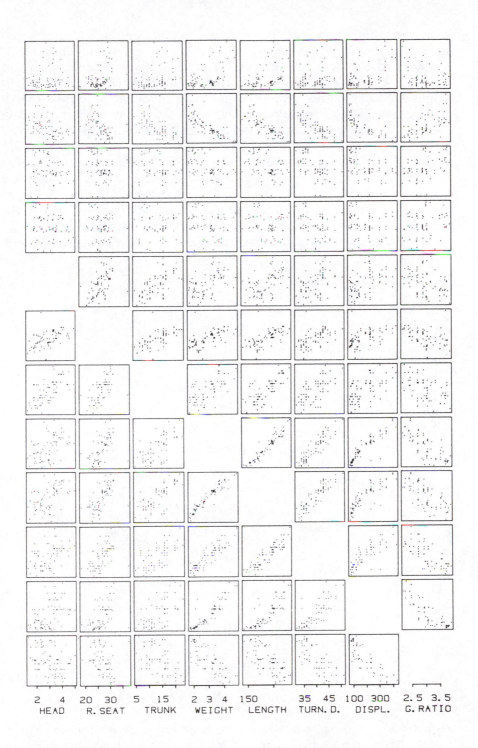

2   4   20   30   5   15   2   3   4   150   35   45 100 300   2.5 3.5
HEAD   R. SEAT   TRUNK   WEIGHT   LENGTH   TURN. D.   DISPL.   G. RATIO

between length and weight. We can regard length and weight as measuring nearly the same attribute for these cars, essentially size. If we need to condense our data set by leaving out a variable, we could probably drop one of these two without losing much information. (It might be even better to drop both and use a combination of the two as a size variable.) As a precaution, we can scan across the 8th and 9th rows to see whether weight and length have similar relationships to the other variables. In fact, they do, except that weight has a somewhat tighter relationship with mpg and with displacement than length does. For this reason, it might be better to retain weight as a size variable and eliminate length. We note, incidentally, that there are three bivariate outliers in the plot of displacement against length, but only two in the plot of displacement against weight. Of the three cars that are short for their displacement, two of them are also light for their displacement, but one of them is not.

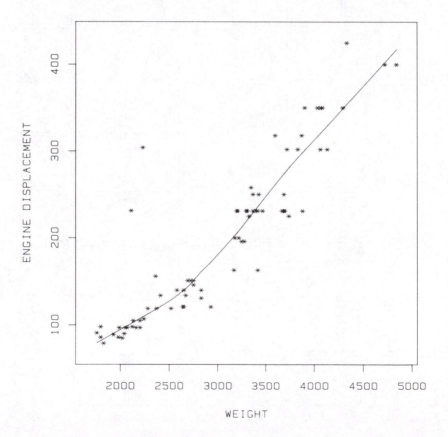

Figure 5.16 Scatter plot of engine displacement (in cubic inches) against weight (in pounds) for the automobile data, with a robust smooth curve.

There are definite curved relationships to be seen in several of these plots, especially those involving displacement. The curvature in some of the displacement plots looks like it could be roughly of the form $y \approx a(x-c)^3$. This suggests that (displacement)$^{1/3}$ might be a better variable to work with than displacement itself, for it might be more linearly related to the others. To test this assertion, Figure 5.16 is a blow-up of the (11,8) plot of displacement against weight, with a robust smooth curve, and Figure 5.17 is a similar plot of (displacement)$^{1/3}$ against weight. The latter is straighter, although the improvement is not dramatic.

The division of points into two branches, or arms, in the (1,8) plot (which was seen enlarged earlier in Figures 4.7 and 5.5) is still apparent, even at this scale. Moreover, there is a suggestion of two branches in several other plots involving price. Whether or not the branching is consistently related to country of manufacture could be explored by

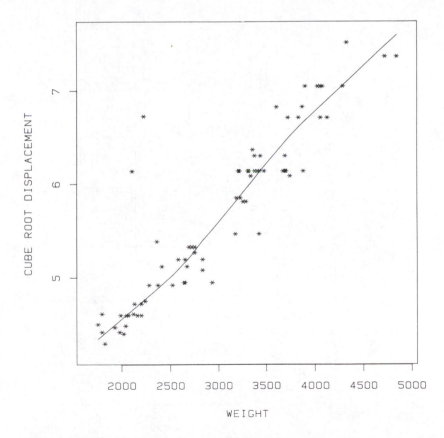

Figure 5.17 Cube root of engine displacement plotted against weight, with a robust smooth curve.

Figure 5.18 Generalized draftsman's display of the modified automobile data. Repair records, gear ratio and mpg have been negated, displacement is on a cube root scale, and the variables have been reordered.

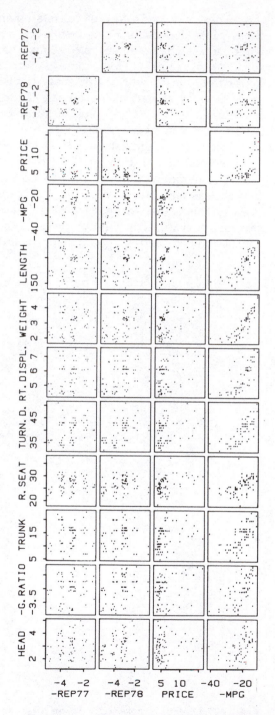

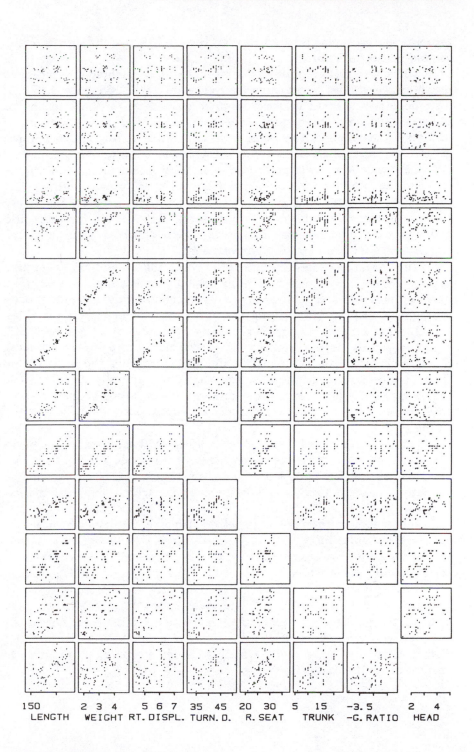

150   2 3 4   5 6 7   35   45   20   30   5   15   −3.5   2   4
LENGTH   WEIGHT RT. DISPL. TURN. D.   R. SEAT   TRUNK   −G. RATIO   HEAD

reproducing each plot in the top row, coding U.S. and foreign into the plotted points, as before.

Miles per gallon (mpg) is a variable of considerable interest to motorists. It should be no surprise to see in row 2 of Figure 5.15 that mpg decreases with an increase in price or with an increase in any of the size variables. The nature of the decrease, as well as the identity of outliers in these plots (cars with unusually high or low fuel economy, given their other characteristics) is of interest to the economy minded.

Gear ratio is a less familiar variable. Most motorists may not know, for instance, whether low mpg cars have high or low gear ratios. The (2,12) plot of Figure 5.15 shows that gear ratio and mpg are positively related, as gear ratio increases, so does mpg. By studying the gear ratio and mpg columns we see that these two variables have negative relationships with almost all other variables.

The variety of upward and downward trends and of linear and curved patterns in Figure 5.15 might seem bewildering. A simplified view of these data can be obtained by reconstructing the generalized draftsman's display after making the following changes to the variables: (1) replacing mpg by −mpg, (2) replacing gear ratio by −(gear ratio), (3) replacing both repair records by −(repair record), (4) replacing displacement by (displacement)$^{1/3}$, and (5) reordering the variables so that the ones involved in tighter patterns occur generally together. The result is Figure 5.18. A clearer picture of the whole situation now emerges, and we can more easily focus on subtler aspects of the patterns in these plots.

An important next step in the analysis of these data might be to "remove" the clear linear pattern in many of the plots, which is due to a dominant size effect. This could be done with the regression techniques of Chapter 7. Another is to take logarithms, which we shall discuss later in this chapter.

When looking at a generalized draftsman's display, which shows only two variables in each component plot, one should not draw strong conclusions about relationships that involve three or more variables or about causal relationships. For instance, the (5,7) plot in Figure 5.18 shows that greater length is associated with greater displacement, but it is probably not length *per se* that determines engine size in cars. Instead, longer cars are generally heavier, and it is the increase in weight that requires bigger engines. This general issue is explored more extensively in Chapter 7 which discusses a type of plot that takes account of multivariate effects.

MULTIPLE-CODE SYMBOLS ON SCATTER PLOTS

We have shown two examples of a third variable coded into the plotting symbol in a scatter plot in Figures 5.6 to 5.8. By using more complicated plotting symbols, we can code two or even several additional variables into each plotting symbol on a scatter plot in order to portray four-dimensional and higher-dimensional data.

This idea is not new. It is used routinely, for instance, by meteorologists whose weather map symbols, such as the one in Figure 5.19 simultaneously show cloud cover (by the fraction of shading), wind direction (by the direction of the flag) and wind speed (by the number of bars) at each of many monitoring stations.

Figure 5.20 is a scatter plot with two variables coded into the plotting symbols. As in Figure 5.8, weight is represented by the size of the symbols, but now foreign cars are represented as × and U.S. cars as O. As before, the x and y-coordinates portray price and (jittered) 1978 repair record. In this single plot we can see not only that smaller cars had generally better repair records (as we saw in Figure 5.8), but also that the foreign cars tended to be both (i) the smaller ones, and (ii) the ones with generally better repair records in all price ranges.

Many coding schemes can be devised for portraying two or more variables simultaneously in the plotting symbols. Figures 5.22 and 5.24 are examples of schemes for dealing with fairly large numbers of variables. Each symbol in these figures portrays all twelve automobile variables, as shown by the corresponding keys in Figures 5.21 and 5.23. We have chosen to display only the symbols for the 15 lightest and 15 heaviest cars. Also, instead of using two of the variables as x and y-coordinates we have coded *all* the variables into the symbols, and laid out the symbols in an array, ordered across rows by automobile weight. This insures that the symbols do not overlap, and treats all the variables in a symmetrical fashion. Figure 5.22 is a *symbolic star plot* in which the values of the variables are coded into the lengths of twelve rays, and Figure 5.24 is a *symbolic profile plot* in which the values of the variables are used to control the heights of the ends of the connected line segments.

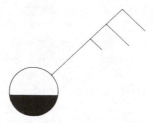

Figure 5.19 A typical weather map symbol. Wind direction and speed are shown by the direction of the flag and the number of bars; cloud cover is shown by shading.

The construction of star symbols in Figure 5.22 may require a few words of explanation. A convenient approach is the following:

1. Since the data values are used as lengths of rays, they should be all nonnegative and of rather similar sizes, so we first rescale each variable to range from c to 1, where c is the desired length of the smallest ray relative to the largest. (c may be zero.) If x_{ij} is the jth measurement of the ith variable then the scaled variable is

$$x_{ij}^* = (1-c)(x_{ij} - \min_i x_{ij})/(\max_i x_{ij} - \min_i x_{ij}) + c.$$

2. To portray p variables, we choose p rays whose directions are equally spaced around the circle, so that the jth ray is at an angle $\theta_j = 2\pi(j-1)/p$ from the horizontal, for $j = 1$ to p.

3. For the ith (rescaled) observation, consisting of the p-tuple $(x_{i1}^*, x_{i2}^*, \ldots, x_{ip}^*)$, we need a star whose jth ray is proportional to x_{ij}^*. If we set the plotting origin at the center of the star and want the maximum radius to be R, then the required star is obtained by computing and connecting the $p + 1$ points,

$$P_{ij} = (x_{ij}^* R \cos \theta_j, \, x_{ij}^* R \sin \theta_j),$$

for j ranging from 1 to p, then back to 1 again. (Repeating $j = 1$ at the end is necessary to "close" the star.)

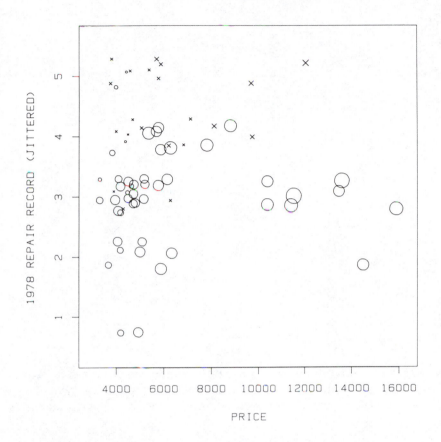

Figure 5.20 Symbolic scatter plot of 1978 repair record against price with two variables encoded into the symbols: diameter of the symbol shows automobile weight, and type of symbol shows nationality, O for U.S., × for foreign.

The construction of the profile symbols is similar but more straightforward. (Star symbols can in fact be regarded as profiles in polar coordinates.) To construct profiles, note that with all-positive data it is convenient to use the same kind of initial scaling and work with the same x_{ij}^{*} values. However, when the data can assume negative values, profiles have one advantage over stars in that the base line of the profile can be made to represent zero and the profile allowed to dip

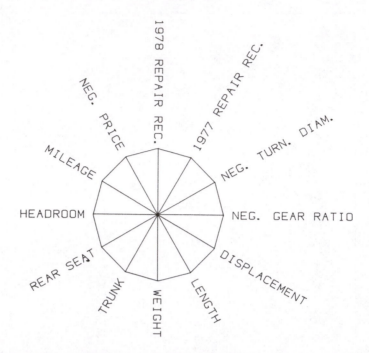

Figure 5.21 Key showing the assignment of automobile variables to rays of a star. Roughly, the horizontal and downward-pointing rays are size-linked variables, and the others are price and performance variables.

below the base line. A suitable scaling for the jth variable of signed data might be

$$x_{ij}^* = x_{ij}/\max_i |x_{ij}|$$

Figure 5.21 is a diagram showing the assignment of the twelve automobile variables to the rays of the star. It has been arranged, where possible, for large rays to represent "favorable" characteristics, which was achieved by changing the sign of the variables price, turning diameter, and gear ratio by multiplying them by -1. The order of assigning variables to rays has been chosen so that upward pointing rays are cost and performance variables, and horizontal rays (left and right) and downward rays are variables closely linked with size.

In Figure 5.22 we see that the star symbols for the lightest 15 cars (the top three rows) generally have large top halves (good price and performance) and small bottom halves (small sizes), but that the reverse

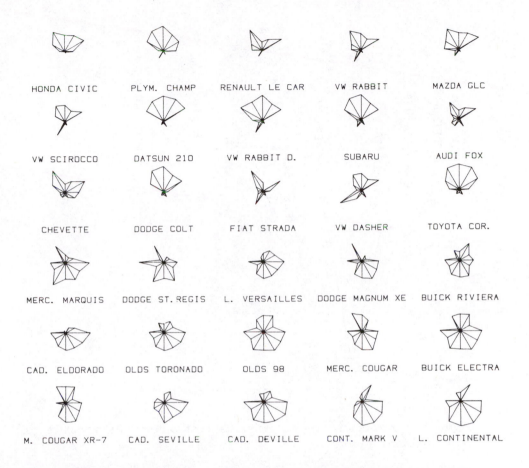

Figure 5.22 Star symbol plot of all twelve variables of the automobile data. Each star represents a car model, each ray a variable. Only the 15 lightest car models (top three rows) and 15 heaviest models (bottom three rows) are shown.

is true for the heaviest 15 cars. Among the top 15 symbols, five of them (the Plymouth Champ, Datsun 210, VW Rabbit Diesel, Subaru, and Toyota Corolla) fan out quite uniformly (favorably) on the upward-pointing price and performance variables, and two others (Mazda GLC and Dodge Colt) are not far behind. Among small cars, the VW Scirocco has an unusually large trunk, and the VW Dasher an unusually spacious rear seat.

Among the heavier cars (the bottom three rows) we can observe that the stars for the Oldsmobile 98 and Buick Electra are remarkably similar to each other (although the Oldsmobile 98 gets better mileage).

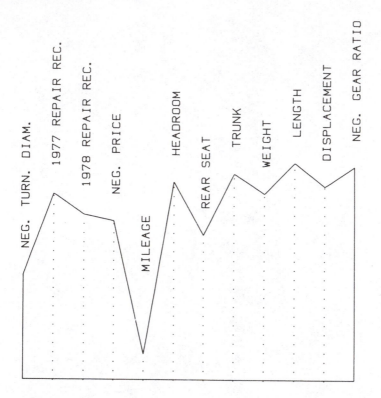

Figure 5.23 Key showing the assignment of automobile variables to positions along a profile.

In terms of the size variables alone, these two cars are also very similar to the Cadillac Deville and Lincoln Continental. Looking for unusual values, we might notice that the two Dodge models and three Mercury models have low prices for cars in this weight category, and that the two Dodge models share the dubious distinction of having both a low price and a poor 1978 repair record.

All of the features that we have pointed out in Figure 5.22 can also be seen in Figure 5.24. It could be argued that the stars form a more dramatic and memorable set of shapes. In particular, it is easier to decide at a glance whether a "spike" appearing in each of two stars corresponds to the same variable. With the profiles, the viewer might need to line up two symbols to find the answer.

When there are many variables involved in a symbol plot there is a serious question as to whether a viewer can get a visual impression of the behavior of a particular variable, or of the joint behavior of two

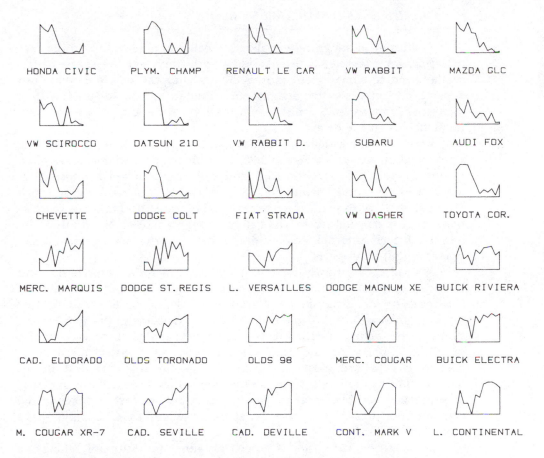

Figure 5.24 Profile symbol plot of all twelve variables of the automobile data. Each profile depicts a car model; positions along a profile correspond to variables. Only the 15 lightest models (top three rows) and 15 heaviest models (bottom three rows) are shown.

variables. (For instance, is it possible to see in Figures 4.22 and 4.24 that length and weight increase and decrease together, and that their relationship is nearly linear?) One of the main purposes of such multi-code schemes is to obtain a symbol with a distinctive shape for each observation (each automobile, in this case), so that a viewer can look for pairs or groups of symbols with similar shapes, or individual observations that are very different from the rest. It can be helpful to cut the symbols apart (along with their labels) onto separate slips of paper, and to slide them around on the table grouping them in interesting ways.

*KLEINER-HARTIGAN TREE SYMBOLS

The order of assigning variables to features in a symbol (to the rays in a star, for example) is usually rather arbitrary, yet the shape of the symbol, and to some extent the effectiveness of the whole display, can depend critically on the assignment. Replotting the display with a different assignment might emphasize different features and relationships in the data.

Kleiner and Hartigan (1981) have addressed this issue by designing a *tree* symbol, shown in Figure 5.25, in which each variable is assigned to one branch of a stylized tree, and the branches are connected, in turn, to limbs and eventually to the trunk. As with stars, each observation is portrayed by one tree symbol, and the branches of trees have lengths determined by the values of the variables. In addition, the length of each internal limb is determined by the average of all the branches that it supports.

Instead of arbitrarily assigning variables to branches, Kleiner and Hartigan perform an initial *hierarchical clustering* of the variables, and use the resulting dendrogram (or cluster tree) as the basis for their tree symbol. We will not explain hierarchical clustering in detail here, because the actual details of the clustering are not crucial to the graphical aspects of the tree symbol plots. In short, hierarchical clustering is a statistical procedure for repeatedly grouping things together (always two at a time), so that the things (variables in our case, or subsets of variables) that are most alike appear closest together in the tree. For our present purposes, variables are judged as alike if they have a high correlation.

In Figure 5.25 the Kleiner-Hartigan tree symbol shows a hierarchical clustering of 10 automobile variables (excluding turning diameter and gear ratio) for the 30 car models used in Figures 5.22 and 5.24. Not surprisingly, weight and length are very much alike and are close to all other variables which are positively correlated with size. Overall, this tree symbol shows two major groupings: size related variables on the left and economy related variables (negative price, repair records and mileage) on the right.

Figure 5.26 shows a Kleiner-Hartigan tree symbol plot for the 30 car models shown in Figures 5.22 and 5.24. One benefit of the tree symbol is that groups of variables that are similar to each other can act together in concert, reinforcing each other's influence on the lengths of shared internal limbs. This makes the tree symbol more sensitive to certain kinds of joint behavior among the variables; the large right-hand parts of the trees for the Datsun 210, the VW Rabbit Diesel and the Subaru, for instance, show that these three models are very economical cars (at least as measured by these variables), while the Cadillac

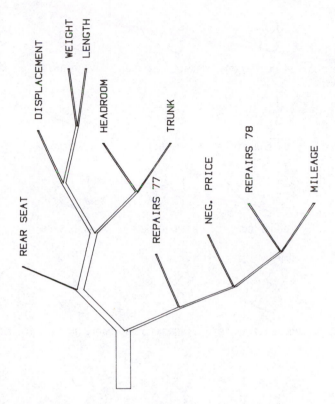

Figure 5.25 Key showing the assignment of ten automobile variables to branches of a tree symbol, determined by hierarchical clustering of the variables.

Eldorado is definitely not an economical car. Tree symbols are also sensitive to deviations from the joint behavior of closely related variables; for instance, in terms of most size variables VWs are small cars, but the VW Rabbits clearly have large trunks and headroom, and the VW Dasher has an extremely spacious rear seat. Also, the Fiat Strada has an unusually dismal 1977 repair record, given its other price/performance variables, and the price of the Cadillac Seville is seen to be disproportionately high.

PARTITIONING AND MULTIWINDOW DISPLAYS

The idea of partitioning a data set to create a casement display can be adapted to four-dimensional data. Earlier we showed a series of plots

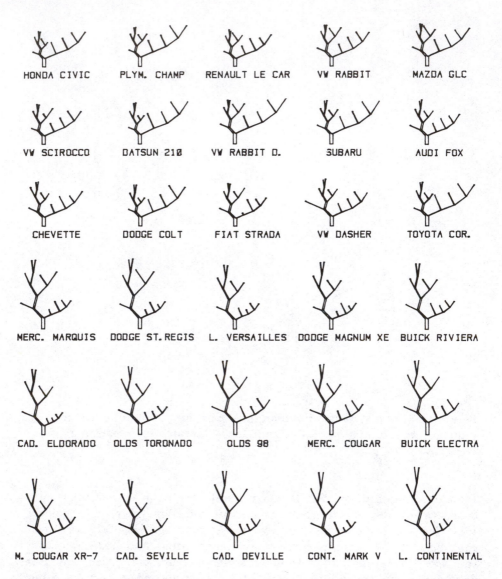

Figure 5.26 Tree symbol plot of ten automobile variables. Each tree represents a car model; terminal branches represent variables. Only the 15 lightest models (top three rows) and 15 heaviest models (bottom three rows) are shown.

of weight against price, one for each level of the 1978 repair record. Now we will partition the 74 data points according to both the 1978 *and* 1977 repair records simultaneously. Since there are five levels for each repair record, there are twenty-five pairs of levels altogether, leading to twenty-five scatter plots of weight against price, which can be conveniently arranged in a five by five array as shown in Figure 5.27. (Models with either repair record missing have been omitted.) Of course, some of the component scatter plots are empty, since there were, for instance, no models with repair record rated 1 in 1977 and 5 in 1978.

In the top margin of Figure 5.27 there is an additional row of scatter plots of weight against price. Each of these is the aggregate or superposition of all the plots below it in the display. As a result, the first five plots in the top row are exactly the casement display (shown earlier) of weight against price, partitioned by 1978 repair record. Similarly, the additional column of plots in the margin on the right are the aggregate plots for the rows of the array. They form a casement display of weight against price partitioned by 1977 repair record. Finally, there is a plot in the upper-right corner that is the superposition of all the other plots in the display. It is the complete scatter plot of weight against price for all car models (except those that had missing values for either repair record).

We call Figure 5.27 a *multiwindow display* because it can be thought of as looking into the "space" of two of the variables (the two repair records, in this case), carving out an array of cells or windows, and looking through each window at two other variables (weight and price, in our case). Such displays are likely to be particularly helpful for somewhat larger data sets.

As with casement displays, a multiwindow display can be constructed even if the partitioning variables are measured on continuous scales. For example, we can construct a multiwindow display of the iris data, using sepal length and sepal width as the two partitioning variables. Figure 5.28 shows the scatter plot of sepal length against sepal width for all 150 data points, partitioned with dashed lines into a six by six pattern of cells. Conceptually, at least, the multiwindow plot in Figure 5.29 is constructed from Figure 5.28 by taking each square cell and replacing it with a small scatter plot of petal length against petal width for just those points that fall into the cell.

In terms of the automobile data, the kind of question that can be addressed with a multiwindow display is, "Does the relationship of price to weight change from one joint (1977-8) repair-record category to another, and do such changes depend in any systematic way on the repair-record category?" In Figure 5.27 we can look for a positive relationship between weight and price within each repair-record category. The only two subplots that show such a pattern are the (3,3)

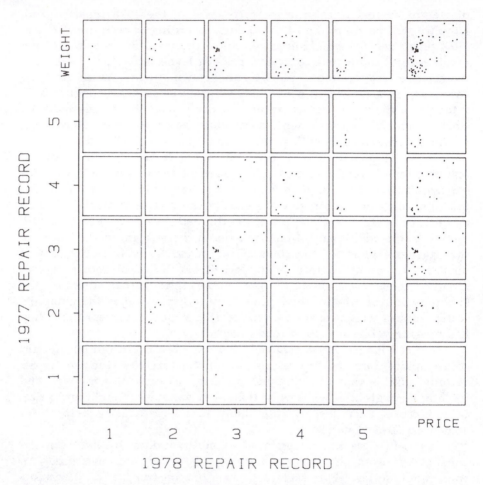

Figure 5.27 Multiwindow display of automobile price against weight (in each of the small squares), partitioned by 1977 repair record and 1978 repair record. The plots in the right and top margins are the superpositions of the plots in the corresponding rows and columns.

and (4,3) plots, and possibly the (2,2) plot. There are too few points in many of the squares to make such a judgment, however it is noteworthy that the (3,4), (4,4), (4,5) and (5,5) squares show no increasing relationship. This suggests that, outside the "average" repair record category (3,3) price and weight are linked closely enough to repair records so that there is little systematic pattern left between price and weight once a repair record category is isolated. We note that the points in the (4,3) plot form a linear price/weight pattern parallel to, but above

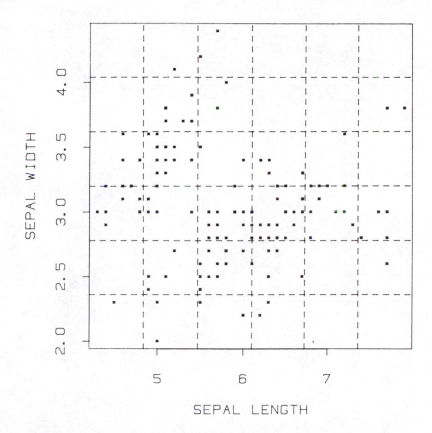

Figure 5.28 Scatter plot of sepal width against sepal length, partitioned into a 6 by 6 array of cells, as the first step in constructing a multiwindow plot.

(or to the left of), the pattern in the (3,3) plot. This means that the models that went from "above average" repair record in 1977 to "average" in 1978 are generally heavier and/or less expensive than the models that stayed in the "average" category both years, but that price increases at the same rate for both groups. We also see that the two models that made spectacular improvement from 1977 to 1978, going from "average" or "below average" repair record to "much better than average" (see the (2,5) and (3,5) plots), are both medium weight, expensive cars. The two branches that we know are linked to nationality are not seen clearly in any window except the (4,4), although they begin to emerge in the marginal windows, especially the (2,*), (4,*) and (*,4) plots. Certain other marginal plots seem to belong almost entirely to one branch or the other.

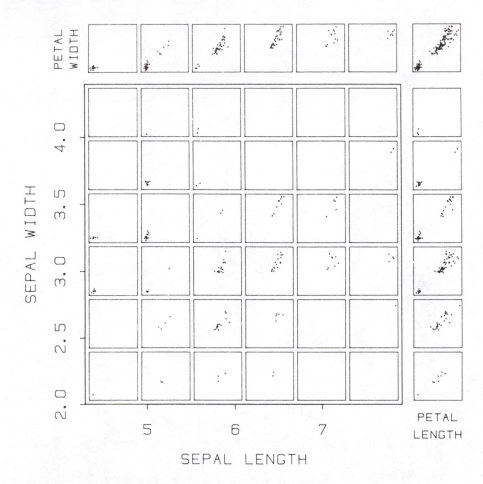

Figure 5.29 Multiwindow plot of the four-dimensional iris data. (jittered) petal width is plotted against (jittered) petal length, partitioned by sepal width and sepal length.

In the multiwindow display of the iris data in Figure 5.29, we see that virtually none of the cells in the main part of the display contain points from both clusters. This means that knowing sepal length and sepal width (that is, knowing which cell a point is in) clearly establishes which cluster it is in. This is not true for either set of marginal plots (those partitioned on a single sepal measurement), since several of the marginal plots straddle the two clusters. The increase of petal width with petal length within the large cluster is apparent in each window that contains enough points to establish a pattern. This is true in the margins, as well, except perhaps for the largest two categories of sepal width or sepal length. We also note that whereas the smaller cluster seemed to have little linear structure in the full plot of petal length against petal width (the upper-right plot in Figure 5.29, or the lower-right plot in Figure 5.12), there does now seem to be some structure in several of the sepal length/sepal width categories, especially the (3,1) and (3,2) windows and the (*,2) and (3,*) marginal windows. We could isolate and enlarge these plots for further study.

We mention two practical considerations for multiwindow plots. First, since the partitioning is done with respect to two variables, the number of partitions is fairly large, and if the number of data points is small or moderate, there may be very few data points in each window. This may make the display fairly uninformative. The technique works best when the data points are fairly numerous. The second practical point is that even when there are only four variables altogether (as with the iris data), there are still twelve distinct ways of making the multiwindow plot, depending on which two variables are used for partitioning and how the other two variables are assigned to the x and y-axes. It may be worthwhile to look at several or all of them.

5.5 COMBINATIONS OF BASIC METHODS

The three approaches that we have been describing for display of three- and higher-dimensional data — partitioning, symbols, and draftsman's displays — can be combined to produce various kinds of hybrid displays.

Perhaps the simplest way to combine these ideas is to take any of the multiple-scatter-plot displays (the draftsman's display, casement display, or multiwindow display) and to portray one or several additional variables by coding them into the plotted symbols. A good example is provided by the iris data. Regarding iris variety as a qualitative fifth variable, we can choose three distinct plotting symbols for the three varieties and convert the generalized draftsman's display of Figure 5.12 into the *symbolic generalized draftsman's display* in Figure 5.30. This plot clearly shows that one of the iris varieties accounts for the smaller cluster in every component plot. But it also shows that although the other two varieties are not well-separated by white space in any of the pairwise scatter plots, they nevertheless do not overlap by very much except in the sepal width against sepal length plot.

Other good examples can be constructed from the automobile data, coding U.S. and foreign into the plotting symbols on generalized draftsman's views of subsets of the variables. Figure 5.31 shows such a

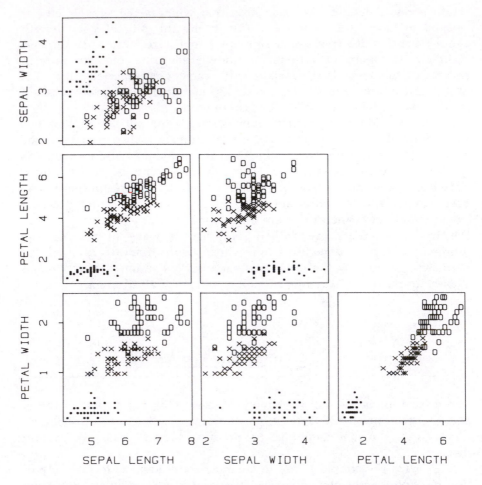

Figure 5.30 Symbolic draftsman's display of the four-dimensional iris data, with a fifth variable, iris variety, coded into the symbols.

plot for the variables weight, price, mpg and 1978 repair record. Besides the clear structure in the top plot that we have already described, we observe that 1978 repair record and weight together (in the center plot) separate most of the U.S. cars into a cluster with average to low repair records and medium to heavy weight, as compared to the cluster of foreign cars. There is a similar partitioning but less of a clear separation in terms of mpg and 1978 repair record taken together (in the right-hand plot). The plot of mpg against weight is perhaps the most surprising; although it is true (as expected) that mpg decreases with increasing weight and that the U.S. cars account for more of the heavier

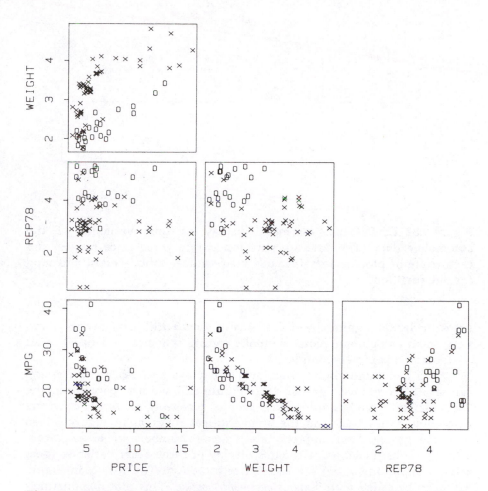

Figure 5.31 Symbolic draftsman's view of four variables of the automobile data (price, weight, 1978 repair record, and fuel economy), with a fifth variable, nationality, coded into the symbols. × represents U.S. cars and O represents foreign.

and less fuel-efficient models, the pattern of foreign cars seems to slide *under* the pattern of U.S. cars. This means that, apart from the few most efficient cars (which are foreign), foreign cars are generally *less* efficient than their U.S. counterparts of comparable weight!

In principle, symbols of any complexity could be used on any of the multiple-view displays, but there is an obvious practical limitation. If the points are at all crowded so that the symbols overlap, then the variable(s) coded into the symbols will not be perceived by the viewer.

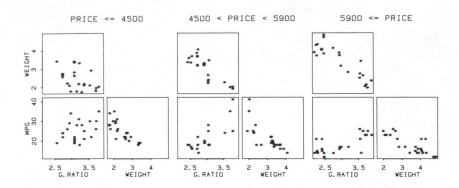

Figure 5.32 Draftsman's casement display of four variables of the automobile data. The data are partitioned into three price ranges, and each triple of plots is a draftsman's view of gear ratio, weight and mpg for one partition.

In particular, in a generalized draftsman's view with many variables and very small component plots, symbolic coding schemes — if used at all — should be kept very simple.

The ideas underlying draftsman's displays and casement displays can also be combined. To construct Figure 5.32 we first partitioned the 74 automobile models into three groups according to price, choosing price boundaries based on the stem-and-leaf diagram in Figure 5.1 so that the groups have approximately equal numbers of observations. Then we constructed a draftsman's display of three other variables (gear ratio, weight, and mpg) for each price category. The result, in Figure 5.32, can be called a *draftsman's casement display*. This plot demonstrates that the strength of the linear relationships among these three variables changes for different price ranges, both in terms of slope and the amount of scatter. In the middle price range, all pairs of the three variables show close connections, but in the low price range the relationship of gear ratio to the other two is more diffuse, and in the high price range the linear relationship between fuel economy and each of the other two has more moderate slope.

We can obviously go one step further and enhance Figure 5.32 by coding an additional variable, say U.S. versus foreign, into the plotting symbols. The resulting plot, shown in Figure 5.33, combines all three basic approaches into a single display.

At this point we should offer a word of caution. The variety of displays introduced in this chapter may well seem complicated and confusing. Indeed, it is easy to get carried away designing new kinds of

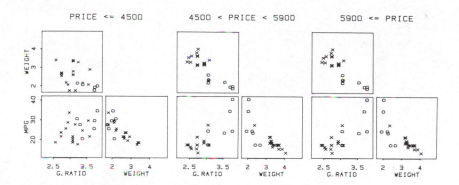

Figure 5.33 Symbolic draftsman's casement display. The plot is the same as Figure 5.32 except that now U.S. cars are coded by × and foreign cars by O.

displays for multivariate data, and to feel that the more information that is crammed into a display — the more data points, the more variables, and the more cleverly it is done — the better the display is. But we must remember that the objective is always to gain insight into the data. The truth is that one display is better than another *if it leads to more understanding*. Often a simpler display, one that tries to accomplish less at one time, succeeds in conveying more insight. In order to understand complicated or subtle structure in the data we should be prepared to look at complicated displays when necessary, but to see any particular type of structure we should use the simplest display that shows it.

5.6   FIRST AID AND TRANSFORMATION

It will often be true that our plots will be simpler and more understandable if the variables are transformed suitably. This can be done initially according to a set of general rules or by special procedures suggested by the data.

We already applied some of this "first aid", as Mosteller and Tukey (1977) call it, in going from the first draftsman's display in Figure 5.15 to the second in Figure 5.18. To make all relationships increasing ones we changed the signs of some variables; to enhance our understanding of the relationships we reordered the variables; and to remove some

Figure 5.34 Draftsman's display of automobile data after logs have been taken.

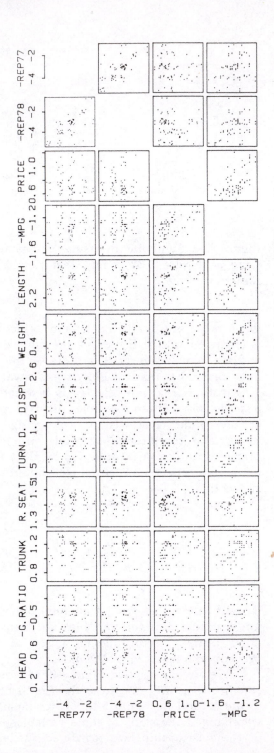

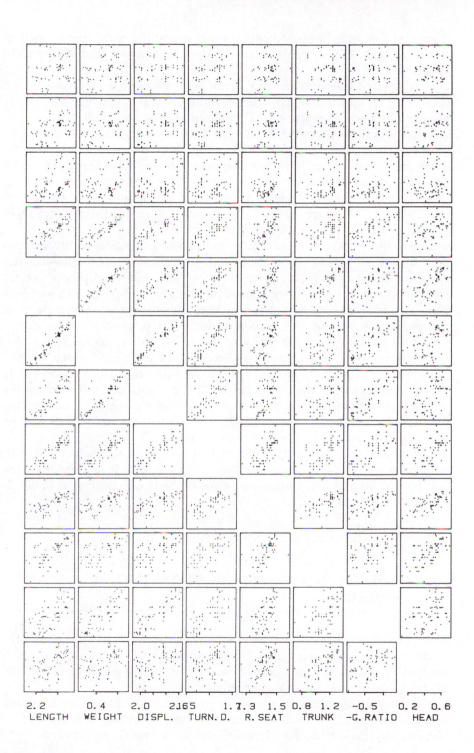

2.2   0.4   2.0   2.165   1.7.3   1.5 0.8 1.2   -0.5   0.2   0.6
LENGTH   WEIGHT   DISPL.   TURN. D.   R. SEAT   TRUNK   -G. RATIO   HEAD

curvature we transformed displacement by taking cube roots. All of these changes were suggested by the data themselves and the specific application.

A general rule of first aid given by Mosteller and Tukey is the following: reexpress (i.e., transform) variables that can never be zero or negative by taking logarithms. (We should apply any such general rule prudently and be prepared to alter it in ways suggested by the data.) This rule is applied in Figure 5.34, another draftsman's display of the automobile data. Logs have been taken of all variables except the 1977 and 1978 repair records, which, while positive, do not deserve logging since they are actually categorical variables given numerical values for convenience. In Figure 5.34 $-\log(y)$ is used for all variables y that were plotted as $-y$ in Figure 5.18.

A number of very nice things happen to the automobile variables as a result of taking logs. Some of the relationships between the variables now appear straighter than before. For example, a careful comparison of the plot of weight against length in Figures 5.18 and 5.34 (the (6,5) plot in both cases) shows that logs straighten the pattern of the points. A second even more vivid result is the reduction in the crowding of the points for many of the plots. For example, if we scan the plots in the third columns of Figures 5.18 and 5.34, which are the plots of all variables against price, we see that logs reduce the substantial crowding that occurred on the left side of each plot on the original scale. One reason for the reduction in crowding is that the log transformation removes most, if not all, of the substantial skewness in the empirical distribution of the price variable.

If we now compare Figure 5.15, the very first draftsman's display of the car data, and the new version in Figure 5.34, it is clear that first aid has lightened somewhat the difficult task of peering into a 12-dimensional space.

*5.7   CODING SCHEMES FOR PLOTTING SYMBOLS

The preceding sections have shown only a small selection of all the possibilities for plotting symbols. When choosing or designing a set of symbols for a particular application, one should keep several general points in mind, and avoid certain pitfalls.

In a general sense, there are only a limited number of graphical aspects that can be usefully controlled in a plotting symbol. These include size (of circles, for instance), shape (× and O, for instance), and orientation (direction of a flag in a weather vane symbol, for instance). Other possibilities include color (hue, saturation, or intensity), texture (such as solid, dotted and dashed lines), and heaviness of line.

If a single qualitative variable is to be represented by symbols, the different levels of the variable should be portrayed by symbols that are graphically distinct. For instance, the symbols a, b, c, d and e are not nearly as distinguishable as, say, the symbols O, ×, Δ, □ and *. Moreover, even a basically good set of symbols will become indistinct if either (i) they are plotted too small, (ii) the points are too numerous or overlap excessively, or (iii) too many categories are represented.

When a quantitative variable is portrayed, one should use a coding scheme that conveys magnitudes graphically. In particular, the numbers 1, 2, 3, 4, etc., do not have graded visual impact and are poor for this purpose.

When the data to be coded into the symbols can be either positive or negative, it is often important to allow positive and negative values of equal magnitude (absolute value) to have similar visual impact. Each of the data sets used in this chapter consisted of all positive measurements, so this was not a major concern, but it would be important if the variable were, say, gains and losses on the stock market, or residuals from a fitted model. In such cases it is poor practice to scale the minimum observation into the smallest symbol and the maximum into the largest, as we did for automobile weights. Instead, one can let the smallest symbol (a dot, say) represent zero, and use an expanding sequence of symbols of one type (+'s, say) to represent positive values, and an expanding sequence of symbols of a different type (O's, say) to represent negative values.

Another way to represent signed data is to use solid circles for positive values and dashed circles for negative values, with size determined by absolute value. To illustrate this, we will construct from the automobile data a new variable that takes positive and negative values. Recall that in the (3,2) plot of Figure 5.31 we noticed that the foreign cars seemed to be less fuel efficient than U.S. cars of comparable weight. To study this phenomenon more carefully, we can fit a line to the plot (using robust linear regression, the details of which are unimportant here since an eyeball fit or a robust smooth curve would suffice) and take the (signed) vertical distance to the line (that is, the residual) as a variable to be called "excess mpg." It is the increase or decrease in mpg that a car exhibits relative to cars of comparable weight, and in Chapter 7 it would be called "mpg adjusted for weight." A negative value represents relatively poor mpg.

Figure 5.35 is the familiar plot of weight against price, this time with excess mpg coded into the area of the plotted circles and negative values shown as dashed circles. Although there are several negative

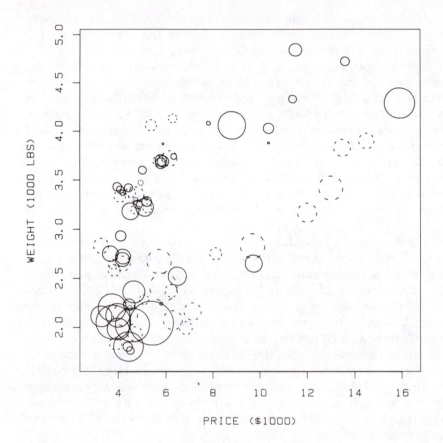

Figure 5.35 Symbolic scatter plot of automobile weight against price, with the variable "excess mpg" coded into the symbol. Area of a circle represents magnitude, and dashed circles mean negative values.

values of excess mpg (dashed circles) on the upper branch and two or three positive values on the lower branch, the preponderance of points on the upper branch (which we know to be U.S. cars) have positive excess mpg, and most of the points on the lower branch have negative excess mpg (and they are mostly foreign).

When two or more variables are to be represented in a single symbol, it is helpful to code them into different graphical aspects (size, shape, texture, etc.). In Figure 5.20 we used shape (× and O) and size to construct a double-code symbol. The star symbols work fairly well in graphical terms despite the many variables involved, because the variables are coded into rays with distinct orientations, which makes them visually distinguishable.

Unintentional graphical interactions can reduce the effectiveness of multiple-code symbols. For instance, when we use size together with coding by × and O, a very small size can make it impossible to distinguish × from O. For this reason, it is best to make the minimum size somewhat larger than a point.

The order of assigning variables to aspects of a symbol can have a major effect on the appearance of the collection of symbols and on the relationships in the data that the plot brings out. Removing some of the arbitrariness can help; for example, in the star symbols for the automobile data in Figure 5.22 we put the size-linked variables together in one group and the price and performance variables together in another. Also, it is often helpful to try several different assignments.

Missing data values pose a particularly sticky problem for symbols. For instance, if the ray corresponding to a missing value is simply left off of a star symbol, the result will be almost indistinguishable from a minimum (i.e., an extreme) value. It may be better either (i) to impute a value, perhaps a median for that variable, or a fitted value from some regression on other variables, (ii) to indicate that the value is missing, possibly with a dashed line, or (iii) not to draw the symbol for a particular observation if *any* value is missing.

We should not rely on symbols to convey detailed quantitative information. For instance, despite some recent experiments (Cleveland, Harris, and McGill, 1982), it is still uncertain whether it is more appropriate to code a variable by making it proportional to the diameter or the area of a circle, or some other measure of size. And even if we knew the answer, we could not rely on accurate judgments consistent through time and from one viewer to another.

On the whole, it is difficult visually to assess a whole plot filled with multiple-code symbols, so a good general rule is: keep it simple.

5.8 SUMMARY AND DISCUSSION

Three approaches have been presented — the full collection of pairwise scatter plots arranged in a draftsman's display, symbolic coding schemes, and data partitioning for casement and multiwindow displays. They form a basic set of graphical tools for looking in fairly direct ways at data in higher dimensions; they can be combined in several ways and applied either to raw data or to data that are derived as output from various stages of statistical analysis. None of these graphical techniques depends on any particular method of multivariate statistical analysis, although they all can help guide the choice of suitable models and analysis strategies.

There are many other multivariate graphical displays that are either designed for data with specific kinds of structure, specialized for certain kinds of applications, or closely linked to particular multivariate analysis methods. A small sampling is given in the next section.

Compared to plots of two-dimensional data, plots of three-(and higher)-dimensional data are more difficult to look at and to understand. This is true not necessarily because the plotting techniques are poorer, but because the problem is inherently more challenging; the viewer is asked to construct a three-(or higher)-dimensional mental image of a configuration of points from looking at two-dimensional plots. Moreover, the variety of patterns and relationships that can exist in higher dimensions is potentially richer.

When designing plots for three-dimensional data one always faces the problem that plotting devices can only draw two-dimensional pictures. Moreover, our eyes essentially see only two dimensions. It is true that the slight differences between the right-eye image and left-eye image convey some depth information to the brain, but human depth perception is much weaker and less reliable than the perception of up-down and right-left. Most of our knowledge about the three-dimensional nature of the things we see around us comes from viewing them from different angles.

Work with dynamic computer-driven displays has shown that simulating the rotation of an object or a cloud of points about an axis that is perpendicular to the line of vision is an effective way to convey the three-dimensional shape of the object or point cloud. But dynamic displays require fairly sophisticated computer hardware and software, and cannot be easily reproduced for publication. For these reasons, we have restricted ourselves to static displays. Thus, we have shown only two-dimensional pictures of data, from which the viewer must construct a mental image or model of the data configuration in three dimensions.

When plotting four-dimensional or higher-dimensional data, we face the same problem, and another more fundamental one, as well. Since we live in a three-dimensional world, we are likely to have little intuition about geometric shapes and spatial relationships in four and more dimensions. For instance, we have no difficulty imagining a three-dimensional scatter plot showing points suspended inside a cubical region (although it might be tricky to build one). However, we cannot even visualize a physical realization of a four-dimensional scatter plot.

Despite the perceptual difficulties, from a mathematical and computational viewpoint it is easy to deal with four or more dimensions. Points in four-dimensional space are represented by ordered quadruples of numbers, just as points in three and two dimensions are represented by ordered triples and ordered pairs of numbers. The formula for the Euclidean distance between two points (x_1, y_1, z_1, w_1) and (x_2, y_2, z_2, w_2) in four dimensions is

$$\text{distance} = \sqrt{(x_1-x_2)^2+(y_1-y_2)^2+(z_1-z_2)^2+(w_1-w_2)^2}$$

which is a straightforward generalization of the familiar distance formula for two dimensions, based on the Pythagorean Theorem. Similarly, the formula for the angle between two rays has an easy extension to higher dimensions. Most familiar geometrical shapes and relationships have analogues in four (and higher) dimensions, since most of them can be defined in terms of distances and angles. For instance, a four-dimensional sphere (often called a hypersphere) is the locus of points in four dimensions that are some fixed distance away from a given point. Similarly, we can talk about clusters of neighboring points in four dimensions, the diameters and orientations of the clusters, and the distances among them. Imagining four and more dimensions is possible, even if we cannot see them physically.

5.9 FURTHER READING

General references on graphical displays for multivariate data include the books by Gnanadesikan (1977), Everitt (1978), and Bertin (1980, and, in French, 1973 and 1977), as well as several chapters in books edited by Wang (1978) and by Barnett (1981). Gnanadesikan's book addresses multivariate data analysis in general but uses graphical methods heavily. Much of Bertin's work is related to cartography and to data that has a geographic component. In the book edited by Wang, see especially the chapters by Newton and by Chernoff. Three chapters by Tukey and Tukey in the Barnett volume constitute both a review article with a bibliography and a source of a number of new ideas. They are a basic reference for the three main approaches presented in this chapter.

Several review articles on graphical displays for multivariate data have appeared in journals. One is by Chambers and Kleiner (1982) who present many techniques not discussed in this chapter and another is by Gabriel (1983). Fienberg (1979) and Wainer and Thissen (1981) have written review articles on graphical data analysis in general but with considerable emphasis on multivariate graphics. All of these papers offer extensive bibliographies.

Many ideas have been proposed for coding data values into symbols on scatter plots in addition to those shown in this chapter. An early careful discussion of the idea was given by Anderson (1957, reprinted in 1960) whose symbols consist of a circle with whiskers of variable length at the top; they are called *glyphs* or, when used on scatter plots, *metroglyphs*. Stars were described by Friedman, Farrell, Goldwyn, Miller and Siegel (1972). Hartigan (1975a) proposed 3-dimensional *boxes* in perspective view as symbols. Bachi (1968) described a more complex set of symbols called *graphical rational patterns*. Chernoff (1973) devised the clever idea of using cartoon *faces* as symbols with data values coded into the facial features (curvature of smile, angle of eyebrow, etc.). The purpose, he argues, is to allow viewers to draw on their vast experience of interpreting facial expressions at a glance. Further suggestions and examples of symbolic plots are given in Bertin (1973), Everitt (1978), and Tukey and Tukey (1981).

An original idea related to symbols was suggested by Andrews (1972). Each multivariate data observation is mapped into a function by using the p coordinates of the observation as coefficients in a Fourier series. The n curves are then superimposed on a single plot for visual comparison.

Another idea related to symbols is the *symbolic matrix* (Bertin, 1973; Chambers and Kleiner, 1983). In effect, each numerical entry in the n by p data matrix is replaced by a single-character symbol whose darkness represents the magnitude of the data value relative to other data values in the column. Patterns of light and dark in the symbolic matrix show groups of high and low values. The patterns can be enhanced by permuting the rows (observations) and columns (variables). In this scheme, each row of the symbolic matrix can be regarded as a symbol representing a multivariate data observation.

Many classical methods of multivariate statistical analysis result in sets of linear combinations of the p variables. Suppose the n measurements of the ith variable are x_{ij} for $i = 1$ to n. A linear combination

$$u_i = \sum_{j=1}^{p} \alpha_j x_{ij}$$

can be interpreted as a new variable derived from the others, with properties that depend on the objectives of the method. For instance, *principal components* finds linear combinations that maximize the spread of the data values, subject to certain normalizing constraints, and in *discriminant analysis* the centroids of designated groups of observations (such as the three iris varieties) are maximally spread out. *Canonical correlation analysis* and *factor analysis* have similar interpretations. Also, any variable which consists of the residuals from a linear regression, such as the excess-mpg variable discussed in Section 5.7, is of this form. With any one of these techniques, a pair of linear combinations can be used as *x* and *y* coordinates for a scatter plot (Friedman and Tukey, 1974; Tukey and Tukey, 1981). Often these scatter plots of derived variables can be regarded as views of the multivariate point cloud from angles that are oblique to the original coordinate axes. Kruskal (1969) observed that this approach can be generalized by defining any "index of interest" as a function of the *n* values of the linear combination, then finding the linear combination that maximizes the index, using general computer software for numerical optimization. Kruskal defined an *index of condensation* to be used in this way. Friedman and Tukey (1974) named the general approach *projection pursuit* and offered a different index that tries to maximize "clottedness" or clustering in the view. The approach has recently been further extended and a modified form studied by Friedman and Stuetzle (1982).

The *biplot* devised by Gabriel (1971) is closely related to the scatter plot of the first two principal components, but in addition to *n* points plotted for the *n* observations, it shows *p* points for the *p* variables. The interplay between these two sets of points in the plot sheds light on the relationship between observations and variables in the data. (See also Gabriel, 1981, and Bradu and Gabriel, 1978). Some of the techniques of *correspondence analysis* produce similar kinds of plots (Benzecri, 1973; Greenacre, 1981).

The methods for selecting views of the data cloud mentioned in the previous two paragraphs are both (i) *linear*, since the plotted coordinates are linear functions of the variables, and (ii) *data-dependent*, since, unlike in the draftsman's display, the choice of view is determined as a function of the data. Tukey and Tukey (1981) suggest augmenting the draftsman's display with sets of data-independent views formed by projecting the data points onto the faces of a regular polytope, for instance a pentagonal dodecahedron. Such views are oblique to the original coordinate axes, and are, in a certain sense, maximally separated around the data cloud.

Several *nonlinear* methods exist for producing two-dimensional pictures of multidimensional data clouds. Wakimoto and Taguri's (1978) *constellation plot* shows centroids of points transformed by polar coordinates. Friedman and Rafsky's (1981) *multivariate planing* procedure derives from the minimal spanning tree of the data cloud a two-dimensional picture that tries to preserve the local structure of the configuration. See Everitt (1978) for other uses of the minimal spanning tree.

The collection of methods referred to as *multidimensional scaling* (see, for instance, Carroll and Kruskal, 1978, Kruskal and Wish, 1978, or Carroll and Arabie, 1980) can also be regarded as nonlinear graphical techniques. These methods were originally designed to deal with data collected directly in the form of inter-point distances (or distance-like quantities) between pairs of objects. For example, the data might be judgements made by experimental subjects of the dissimilarities between pairs of stimuli. Multidimensional scaling produces low-dimensional coordinate representations for the objects, and the output of the analysis is most commonly a scatter plot or a series of scatter plots.

A number of graphical displays have been devised for use in connection with cluster analysis. The *dendrogram* or *cluster tree* displays the result of a hierarchical clustering (see, for instance, Hartigan, 1975b, Chambers and Kleiner, 1983, or Knuth, 1969). Various specialized plots for studying collections of distances between cluster centroids and between objects and cluster centroids have been described by Carmichael and Sneath (1969), Dunn and Landwehr (1980), Fowlkes, Gabbe, and McRae (1976), and Gnanadesikan, Kettenring, and Landwehr (1977).

Gnanadesikan (1977, Chapter 5) discusses ways of using probability plotting techniques (which are presented in the next chapter) for studying distributional properties of multivariate point clouds, and gives a number of references. Wachter (1975) has developed a form of probability plotting as an adjunct to principal component analysis.

When a set of three-dimensional data points (x_i, y_i, z_i), for $i = 1$ to n, trace a fairly smooth surface $z = f(x,y)$ over the x-y plane, the surface can be depicted either by drawing a contour plot of the surface, or by showing a perspective view of a square grid projected from the x-y plane onto the surface. Chambers (1977) describes computer algorithms for making these plots.

Finally, we pointed earlier to the emerging opportunities for dynamic display of multivariate data. A prototype system of this sort, PRIM-9, was developed by Tukey, Friedman and Fisherkeller (1976; also Fisherkeller, Friedman, and Tukey, 1974). More recent descendents of PRIM-9 are PRIMH (Donoho, Huber, Ramos, and Thoma, 1982) and the Orion I system (Friedman, McDonald, and Stuetzle, 1982). In addition, Andrews (1982) has developed a program that can simulate the rotation of a cloud of points of moderate size on the screen of an Apple II home computer.

EXERCISES

5.1. Study the three-dimensional data on Bell Laboratories Managers (Data Set 20) by

1. Plotting age against years since highest degree and coding degree level by different symbols or colors.

2. Making a draftman's display.

Which of the two methods do you prefer in this case?

5.2. Display the variables per capita disposable income, % population under 15, and % population >75 in 35 countries (Data Set 16) by

1. Plotting income against % population under 15 and coding % population above 75 by the size of the plotting symbol.

2. Making a draftman's display.

5.3. Investigate the three variables tar content, temperature, and rotor speed for the tar content data (Data Set 23) by

1. Making a draftman's display.

2. Plotting tar content against rotor speed and coding temperature.

3. Constructing a casement display with two partitions formed by temperature.

5.4. Look at the daily readings for ozone, solar radiation, and temperature in the New York metropolitan area (Data Set 2) by

1. Making a draftsman's display.

2. Plotting ozone against solar radiation and coding temperature.

3. Making casement displays with 3 and 5 partitions formed by temperature.

5.5. Study the interactions between place of manufacture, price, and each of the other variables of the automobile data (Data Set 7) by plotting price against each variable and coding place of manufacture (foreign — U.S.). The cars made in the U.S. are AMCs, Buicks (except the Opel), Cadillacs, Chevrolets, Dodges (except the Colt), Ford Mustang, Lincolns, Mercuries, Oldsmobiles, Plymouths (except the Arrow, the Champ and the Sapporo) and Pontiacs. (The assignment used in the text is based on the nationality of the parent company rather than the actual country of manufacture.)

5.6. Investigate the rubber specimen data (Data Set 25) by

1. Plotting abrasion loss against tensile strength and coding hardness.

2. Making a casement display with two partitions formed by hardness.

5.7. Investigate the relationships among the three variables, air flow, water temperature, and acid concentration of the stack loss data (Data Set 22) by using the techniques described in this chapter.

5.8. Make a generalized draftsman's display of the four variables of the stack loss data (Data Set 22).

5.9. Pick out the outliers on each scatter plot of the generalized draftsman's display of the automobile data (Data Set 7) in Figure 5.18 and identify them on all other scatter plots. Which cars are outliers on more than one scatter plot? What does this mean?

5.10. Make a generalized draftsman's display of per capita disposable income, % savings rate, and the % contribution to gross domestic product of agriculture, manufacturing and service in 35 countries (Data Set 16). Mark the data points for India, Japan, Libya, Luxembourg, West Germany, USA and Zambia on each scatter plot. How does each of these countries differ from the bulk of the data?

5.11. Make a generalized draftsman's display of the four variables of the air quality data for the New York City metropolitan area (Data Set 2). How do you handle days with missing observations?

5.12. Compare the salaries in Amsterdam, Bahrain, Bogota, Buenos Aires, Geneva, Istanbul, Jakarta, Manila, New York, Rio de Janeiro, San Francisco, and Tokyo (Data Set 11) by means of

  1. Symbolic profile plots.

  2. Symbolic star plots.

  *3. Trees.

5.13. Divide the tooth measurements of humans, apes, and fossils (Data Set 24) into four groups by any two of the following methods:

  1. Symbolic profile plots.

  2. Symbolic star plots.

  *3. Trees.

Which technique do you prefer for these data?

5.14. Using the socioeconomic data (Data Set 16) represent the countries Australia, Canada, Denmark, West Germany, Honduras, Libya, Malaysia, Nicaragua, Panama, Tunisia, United States and Zambia by any one of the following methods:

  1. Symbolic profile plots.

  2. Symbolic star plots.

  *3. Trees.

Classify these countries into a few major groups.

5.15. Make a generalized draftsman's display of the 3 variables % population below 15, % contribution of agriculture and % contribution of service to gross domestic product for 35 countries (Data Set 16). Code % population above 75 by the size of the symbols on the scatter plots. What relationships are apparent in the plot?

5.16. Investigate the improvement in the automobile data (Data Set 7) when logarithms are taken as in Figure 5.34 by making 3 full-size scatter plots: log weight against log price, log displacement against log weight, and log weight against log length. Comment on the improvement in crowding and whether relationships appear to have improved by comparing with Figures 5.2, 5.7, and 5.16.

*5.17. Using the automobile data (Data Set 7) make a symbolic draftsman's casement display like Figure 5.33 but with 1978 repair record (compressed to three categories as in Figure 5.11) coded into the symbols. Interpret the plot. (For a list of cars manufactured in the U.S. see Exercise 5.5.)

6

Assessing Distributional Assumptions About Data

6.1 INTRODUCTION

At the heart of probabilistic statistical analysis is the assumption that a set of data arises as a sample from a distribution in some class of probability distributions. The reasons for making distributional assumptions about data are several. First, if we can describe a set of data as a sample from a certain theoretical distribution, say a normal distribution (also called a Gaussian distribution), then we can achieve a valuable compactness of description for the data. For example, in the normal case, the data can be succinctly described by giving the mean and standard deviation and stating that the empirical (sample) distribution of the data is well approximated by the normal distribution.

A second reason for distributional assumptions is that they can lead to useful statistical procedures. For example, the assumption that data are generated by normal probability distributions leads to the analysis of variance and least squares. Similarly, much of the theory and technology of reliability assumes samples from the exponential, Weibull, or gamma distribution.

A third reason is that the assumptions allow us to characterize the sampling distribution of statistics computed during the analysis and thereby make inferences and probabilistic statements about unknown aspects of the underlying distribution. For example, assuming the data are a sample from a normal distribution allows us to use the t-distribution to form confidence intervals for the mean of the theoretical distribution.

A fourth reason for distributional assumptions is that understanding the distribution of a set of data can sometimes shed light on the physical mechanisms involved in generating the data.

Analyses based on specific distributional assumptions about data are not valid if the assumptions are not met to a reasonable degree. "Garbage in, garbage out," as the quip goes. This chapter presents graphical displays for checking distributional assumptions about data.

When we use a phrase like "data generated from a normal distribution" it is important to keep firmly in mind that we do not mean it in a precise sense. Real data can never come from a genuine normal distribution, for that would require data with infinite precision and with the possibility of including arbitrarily large and small values. In practical terms, all data are discrete, since they have limited accuracy, and they are bounded above and below. When we ask, "Are the data normally distributed?" we are really asking "Is the empirical distribution of the data sufficiently well-approximated by a normal distribution for the purposes we have in mind?"

Recognizing that the second question is the relevant one leads us to pursue certain courses of action and discourages us from taking others. It discourages us from testing specific null hypotheses about distributions using formal significance tests, since we know in advance that a hypothesis such as normality cannot be precisely true. It encourages us to look in detail at *how* the empirical distribution of a set of data differs from the theoretical distribution. In some cases we might judge the departures of the data from the theoretical distribution to be unimportant; in other cases we might judge them to be a serious impediment. Our decision will be based on the nature of the departures and the use we plan to make of the result. For example, if we are checking the normality of a set of data for the purpose of justifying the use of least squares, we are not likely to be concerned if we find that the data are discrete due to rounding to two significant digits; but we are likely to abandon normality (and least squares) if we find that the empirical distribution has somewhat heavier tails than the normal, for we know that even mildly heavier-than-normal tails can seriously degrade least squares results (see Mosteller and Tukey, 1977, for more details).

In some cases the checking of distributional assumptions must alternate with other analysis steps. For instance, in the usual normal-theory regression, it is the error term that is assumed to have a normal distribution. One must first calculate a regression and get a set of residuals, which estimate the true errors, then check the normality of the residuals. Thus, in this chapter, the "data" to which we refer are not always raw data; frequently they are quantities that result from transforming and combining raw observations in various ways, or quantities that are the output from previous steps of analysis.

One data set for use in examples will be the results from a cloud-seeding experiment described by Simpson, Olsen, and Eden (1975). Rainfall was measured from 52 clouds, of which 26 were randomly chosen to be seeded with silver iodide. The data were presented in Chapter 3 where the focus was on a comparison of seeded and control (unseeded) clouds. In this chapter we will look at several probability distributions for the data.

A second set of data comes from an experiment with a special kind of stereogram, called a random dot stereogram, studied extensively by Julesz (1965 and 1971). A viewer sees a three-dimensional object that is formed by a left and a right image, each of which by itself has the appearance of densely packed random dots. A viewer typically does not immediately perceive the object in such a stereogram, but after several seconds the left and right images fuse in the brain and the object suddenly comes into view. The data are the lengths of time it took subjects in the experiment to see the three-dimensional object in a particular random dot stereogram (Frisby and Clatworthy, 1975). In the Frisby-Clatworthy experiment the object was a spiral ramp coming out of the page and different subjects were given varying kinds of prior information about it. We shall divide the subjects into two groups: those who were given a combination of visual and verbal prior information (35 subjects) and those who were given either no information at all or just verbal information (42 subjects).

6.2 THEORETICAL QUANTILE-QUANTILE PLOTS

In Chapter 3, we compared two empirical distributions using an empirical quantile-quantile plot. A *theoretical quantile-quantile plot* is obtained by replacing one of the empirical distributions by a theoretical distribution, thus plotting the quantiles of the data against the corresponding quantiles of the theoretical distribution. Theoretical quantile-quantile plots are also often called *theoretical Q-Q plots* or *probability plots*.

To describe this construction in more detail, let us suppose, as we did in Chapter 3, that y_1 to y_n are the raw data and that $y_{(1)}$ to $y_{(n)}$ are the values of the data sorted from smallest to largest, so that y_i is the p_i empirical quantile for $p_i = (i - .5)/n$. (The $y_{(i)}$ are sometimes called the *order statistics*.) Also, suppose $F(y)$ is the cumulative distribution function of the theoretical distribution in question. Now the p quantile of F, where $0 < p < 1$, is a number that we will call $Q_t(p)$ which satisfies

$$F(Q_t(p)) = p \qquad (6.1)$$

or

$$Q_t(p) = F^{-1}(p) . \qquad (6.2)$$

In words, this means that a fraction p of the probability of the distribution occurs for values of y less than or equal to $Q_t(p)$, just as a fraction p (approximately) of the data are less than or equal to $Q_e(p)$, the empirical p quantile of the data. (We are adding subscripts "t" and "e" to the quantile notation of Chapter 3 in order to distinguish the theoretical and empirical versions.)

In the theoretical quantile-quantile plot, $Q_e(p_i)$ is plotted against $Q_t(p_i)$, for $i = 1$ to n, where $p_i = (i - .5)/n$. For example, Figure 6.1 is a theoretical quantile-quantile plot for the logarithms of the seeded rainfall data; the empirical quantiles of the data are plotted against corresponding quantiles of a normal distribution. When the normal distribution is used, the result is also commonly called a *normal probability plot*. What to look for in probability plots and how to interpret them will be the topic of Section 6.4.

6.3   MORE ON EMPIRICAL QUANTILES AND THEORETICAL QUANTILES

In the quantile plot of a set of data (Chapter 2) the empirical quantiles, $Q_e(p_i)$ or $y_{(i)}$, were plotted against p_i as a way of studying the distribution of the data. Such an empirical quantile plot is shown in the top panel of Figure 6.2 for the log seeded-cloud rainfall data. (For the moment ignore the vertical and horizontal lines in the plotting region). We can also plot $Q_t(p)$ against p for any theoretical distribution and call the result a *theoretical* quantile plot, since it portrays a theoretical distribution rather than data. A quantile plot for the standard normal distribution with mean 0 and variance 1 is shown in the bottom panel of Figure 6.2.

It is not uncommon to see plots like those in Figure 6.2 with the axes reversed — that is, plots of p against $Q_t(p)$ and of p_i against $Q_e(p_i)$. In the theoretical version, a plot of p against $Q_t(p)$ is the same thing as a plot of $F(y)$ against y, so it is called a *cumulative distribution function plot*. For the data version, the empirical cumulative distribution function $\hat{F}(y)$

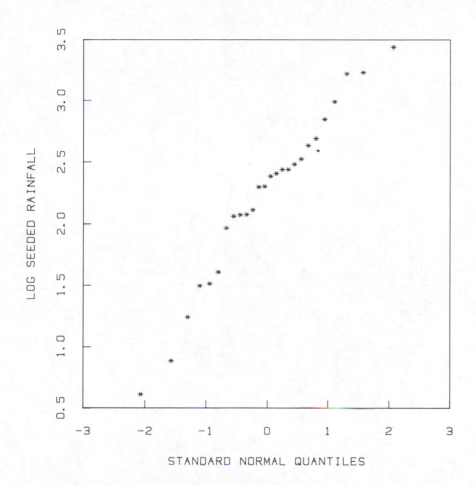

Figure 6.1 Theoretical quantile-quantile plot of the logarithm (base 10) of the seeded rainfall data against the quantiles of a normal distribution with mean 0 and variance 1.

is defined to be equal to p_i when $y = y_{(i)}$, so plotting p_i against $Q_e(p_i)$ is the same as plotting $\hat{F}(y_{(i)})$ against $y_{(i)}$ and is called an *empirical cumulative distribution function* plot.

Our stated goal was to compare the empirical and theoretical distributions. This could be done simply by staring at Figure 6.2 and considering "How similar in shape are the string of points and the curve?" Superimposing the plots might help some, but in general it is difficult to make an effective visual comparison of two curved patterns. A probability plot is an alternative that allows a much more effective comparison of the points with the curve.

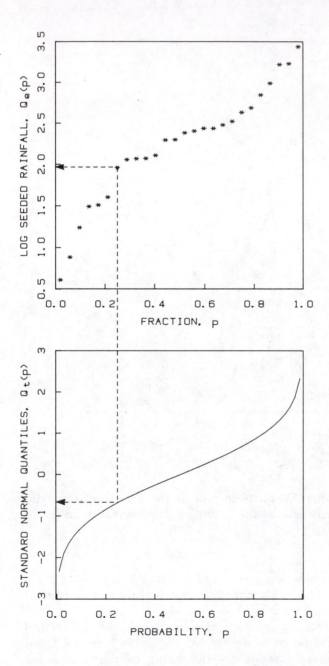

Figure 6.2 Constructing the theoretical quantile-quantile plot from the empirical quantiles (top) and the theoretical quantiles (bottom).

In a certain sense, in making the normal probability plot in Figure 6.1, we are plotting the points in the upper panel of Figure 6.2 against the curve in the lower panel. Let us see what we mean by this. The point $(p_7, y_{(7)})$ in the upper panel, which is shown by the dashed lines, has abscissa $p_7 = (7-.5)/26 = .25$ and ordinate $y_{(7)} = 1.97$, the seventh order statistic. As the vertical dashed line shows, we go down to the lower panel and find the ordinate of the curve at p_7. The number, $-.67$, is the point for which the normal cumulative distribution function takes on the value .25. We then use these two values, $-.67$ and 1.97, as coordinates for a point, $(-.67, 1.97)$, on the theoretical quantile-quantile plot. Each point in the upper panel of Figure 6.2 generates a point on Figure 6.1. We can now make our comparison of the two distributions (the empirical and the theoretical) by studying the single plot in Figure 6.1, instead of the two in Figure 6.2.

6.4   PROPERTIES OF THE THEORETICAL QUANTILE-QUANTILE PLOT

In many respects, the interpretation of a theoretical quantile-quantile plot, or probability plot, is similar to the interpretation of an empirical quantile-quantile plot, which was discussed in Section 3.2.

Consider a situation in which the theoretical distribution is a close approximation to the empirical distribution. Then the quantiles of the data will closely match the theoretical quantiles, and the points on the plot will fall near the line $y = x$, so the line $y = x$ is the null, or reference, configuration for the plot. Of course, the random fluctuations in any particular data set will cause the points to drift away from the line, but if the theoretical distribution is "correct", the points will remain reasonably close to the line. If any large or systematic departures from the line occur, they should be judged as indicating lack of fit of the distribution to the data.

Figure 6.3 shows four normal probability plots of data generated by a computer using a standard normal pseudo-random number generator. The sample sizes in the figure are $n = 20$, 50, 100, and 200. As the plots suggest, there is greater variability in the tails than in the center; this happens for any distribution whose density decreases gradually to zero in the tails.

What kinds of large or systematic departures from the line $y = x$ might one expect to see? As with empirical quantile-quantile plots, the points may fall near some line other than $y = x$. If the observed configuration follows a line that is parallel to the line $y = x$, then an

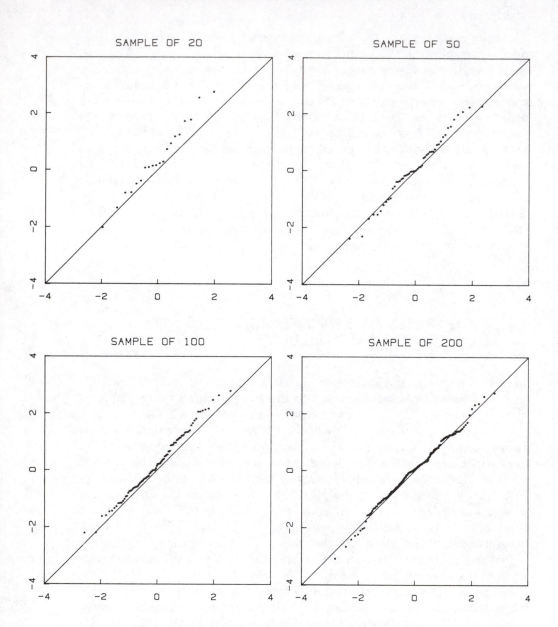

Figure 6.3 Normal quantile-quantile plots of four samples with sizes 20, 50, 100, and 200 from a normal pseudo-random generator.

appropriate constant (positive or negative) could be added to all data points to shift the configuration onto the line $y = x$. This is suggested by the top panel of Figure 6.4. We would conclude that the empirical distribution is compatible with the theoretical distribution, but that they have different locations (as measured by means or medians) or, equivalently, that they are centered at different values.

Another possibility is that the points may have a nearly straight configuration that passes through the origin but is not parallel to the line $y = x$. If so, then it is always possible to find a single positive constant by which to multiply all observations to, in effect, expand or compress the configuration vertically and make it follow the line $y = x$, as suggested by the bottom panel of Figure 6.4. In this case, we would conclude that the data and the theoretical distribution match, except for a difference in spread (as measured, for example, by the standard deviation or by the interquartile range). If adding a constant is also required to map the configuration onto the line $y = x$, then we would judge that the sample and the reference distribution differ both in location and spread. (The word "scale" is sometimes used in place of "spread" but we try to avoid its use here to avoid confusion with a scale on a graph.)

In either case, vertical shifts and changes in slope do not affect the straightness of the configuration. Thus, it is the straightness of the theoretical quantile-quantile plot that is used to judge whether the data and reference distribution have the same distributional shape, while shifts and tilts away from the line $y = x$ indicate differences in location and spread, respectively.

What we have established, really, is that a single theoretical quantile-quantile plot compares a set of data not just to one theoretical distribution, but simultaneously to a whole family of distributions with different locations and spreads. For instance, a single normal probability plot constructed using quantiles from the normal distribution with mean zero and variance one is sufficient to test the data against all normal distributions. This invariance to location and spread is a crucial property of the plot and one that makes it a particularly useful tool. In fact, the idea can be used in reverse to obtain informal estimates of location and spread of the data from the plot, say by drawing a line by eye and measuring its intercept and slope.

We can demonstrate several of the points above using the exponential distribution with unknown spread and location parameters applied to the random-dot stereogram data. The cumulative distribution function for the two-parameter exponential distribution is

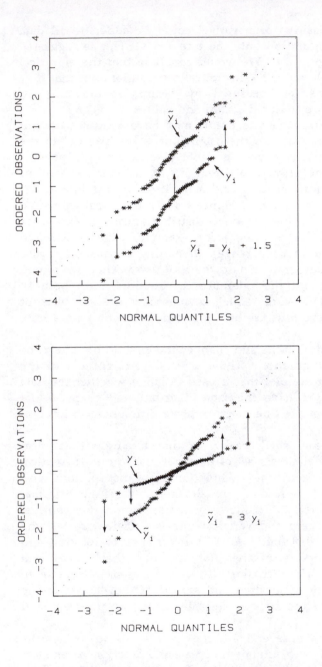

Figure 6.4 Effect of the addition of a constant (top panel) and of the multiplication by a constant (bottom panel) on a quantile-quantile plot.

$$F(y) = \begin{cases} 1 - \exp[-(y-\mu)/\lambda] & \text{for } y \geq \mu \\ 0 & \text{for } y \leq \mu \end{cases}.$$

If we let $Q_t(p_i;\mu,\lambda)$ represent the quantile for $p_i = (i-.5)/n$ from this distribution then

$$p_i = 1 - \exp\left[-\frac{Q_t(p_i;\mu,\lambda)-\mu}{\lambda}\right]$$

and solving for Q_t gives

$$Q_t(p_i;\mu,\lambda) = -\lambda \log_e(1-p_i) + \mu.$$

If our set of data did come from an exponential distribution with parameters λ and μ, then in a plot of $y_{(i)}$ against $Q_t(p_i;\mu,\lambda)$ the points would tend to follow the line $y = x$. Alternatively, in a plot of $y_{(i)}$ against $Q_t(p_i;0,1) = -\log_e(1-p_i)$, which are the theoretical exponential quantiles for parameter values $\mu = 0$ and $\lambda = 1$, the points would tend to follow the line $y = \lambda x + \mu$.

Figure 6.5 shows exponential probability plots of the stereogram fusion times for the two groups of subjects, those who received verbal and visual prior information, and those who received only verbal information or no information. In each case the ordered data are plotted against $Q_t(p_i;0,1)$ and the line drawn on the plot has intercept equal to one and slope equal to $\hat{\lambda}$, an estimate of λ. The choice of $\mu = 1$ arose from considerations external to the experimental data shown on the plots. The estimate of λ in each case is the maximum likelihood estimate from the experimental data (given $\mu = 1$), which is $\hat{\lambda} = \bar{y} - 1$ where $\bar{y}$ is the mean of the y_i. For the subjects with visual prior information, $\bar{y}$ is 5.6 seconds, and for the subjects with only verbal information or no information, $\bar{y}$ is 7.6 seconds. The plots appear to support two conclusions: one is that the data do have exponential distributions, since the points have reasonably linear patterns, and the second is that the maximum likelihood estimates of the parameters λ and μ appear acceptable, since the lines (based on those estimates) are reasonable approximations to the patterns of the points on the plots.

The satisfactory match of the exponential distribution to the stereogram data is interesting in its own right for it relates to theories about the visual and mental processes of image fusion. For instance, an exponential distribution would be consistent with a theory that says the probability of the images fusing in any given millisecond is constant and does not depend on how long the viewer has already stared at the stereogram. But the satisfactory match also allowed Cleveland and

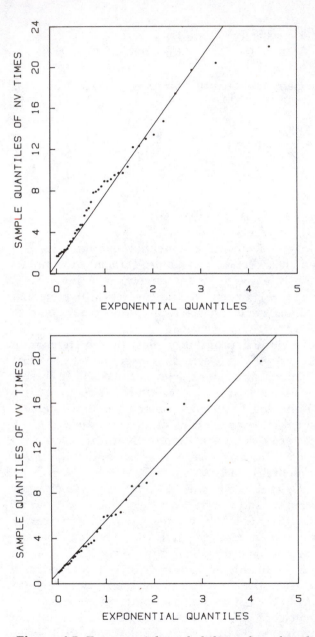

Figure 6.5 Exponential probability plots for the stereogram data. The top panel is the plot for the group of subjects that received only verbal information or no information (NV). The bottom panel is the plot for the group of subjects that received verbal and visual (VV) prior information.

Guarino (1978), in a reanalysis of the data, to compute confidence intervals for the mean fusion times under the two experimental conditions, and to reverse the original conclusion of Frisby and Clatworthy by showing that there *is* a statistically detectable reduction in fusion times when prior visual information is given to subjects.

6.5 DEVIATIONS FROM STRAIGHT-LINE PATTERNS

If large or systematic departures from straightness are observed in the theoretical quantile-quantile plot, they will indicate that, apart from location and spread, the shapes of the data distribution and theoretical distribution do not match. At this point a second crucial property of the plot comes into play. Not only does the plot provide a warning that the match is poor, but it may suggest the nature of the mismatch. For example, we can ask: What is the shape of the pattern of points in Figure 6.1? Is it straight? If not, how does it deviate from straightness?

To judge straightness it is helpful to fit a line, either by numerical estimation as we did for Figure 6.5, or by visual means. If we do it visually, we can fit the line either to the whole set of data or to a portion of the points that seems reasonably straight. For example, Figure 6.6 reproduces Figure 6.1, but with a line fitted visually to the points lying to the right of $y_{(6)}$. We can see fairly quickly that the pattern of data points curves down at the left, since the straight line lies well above the first 6 points.

When there are departures from linearity in a theoretical quantile-quantile plot, they frequently match one of the following descriptions:

- Stragglers (outliers) at either end

- Curvature at both ends, indicating long or short tails

- Convex or concave curvature, related to asymmetry

- Horizontal segments, plateaus, or gaps.

We will discuss each of these in turn.

OUTLIERS

It is an unfortunate fact of statistical life that samples of real data are often contaminated by a small fraction of aberrant observations.

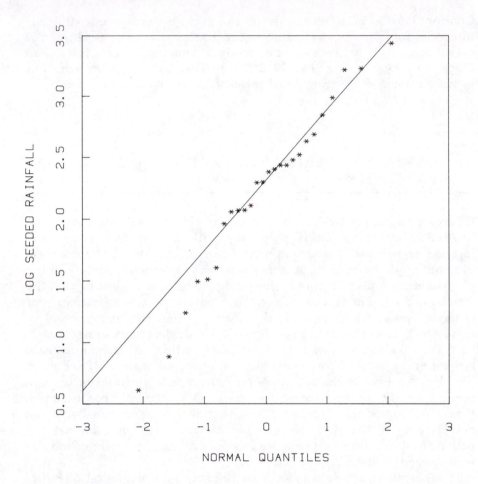

Figure 6.6 Judging departures from linearity in the normal quantile-quantile plot of the log seeded-rainfall data.

Commonly, although not inevitably, these observations will lie outside the typical range of the data. In trying to judge whether outliers have occurred, one must bear in mind that even well-behaved samples have observations in the tails. The question is whether the most extreme observations are even larger than could reasonably be expected for samples of this size from the distribution in question. The theoretical quantile-quantile plot provides an informal but effective answer. Figure 6.7 shows normal probability plots for two nearly identical sets of data. The first is a normal sample of size 75 (synthetically generated by computer), and the second is the same sample except that three of its points, randomly selected, have been multiplied by 10. The three points

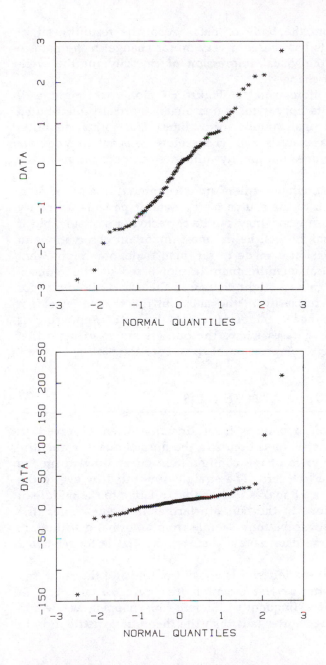

Figure 6.7 The top panel is a normal quantile-quantile plot of 75 values from a normal pseudo-random generator. The bottom panel shows the same data as in the top panel except that 3 values have been multiplied by 10.

have drifted away from the body of data. Also, the resulting slight reordering of the points has caused a very minor change in the pattern of the other 72, but the visual impression of linearity for the well-behaved points has not changed.

Looking at the bottom panel of Figure 6.7 alone, we might well conclude that these data appear to be reasonably normally distributed but contaminated by a small number of outliers. The normal quantile-quantile plot, as a data analysis tool, is therefore resistant to moderate outliers: their presence does not greatly influence our perceptions of the rest of the data.

We emphasize that, when outliers are encountered in a set of data, it is prudent to go back to the source of the data, if possible, to verify the values. If they are in error, they can be corrected or set aside, but if they are correct, they might well be the most important observations in the collection. If a decision is made to set them aside, one might want to redraw the theoretical quantile-quantile plot based on the reduced sample size. This will cause a slight change in the shape of the plot for the rest of the points, primarily in the tails, but the change is seldom large enough to alter one's judgment about the rest. Replotting is usually necessary only in cases where the outliers are so extreme that they have forced a severe compression of the rest of the plot.

LONG OR SHORT TAILS AT BOTH ENDS

A second common departure from linearity often observed in theoretical quantile-quantile plots occurs in the normal quantile-quantile plot in Figure 6.8; the ends of the configuration curve upward on the right and downward on the left. The straight line fitted by eye to the central portion in Figure 6.8 makes it clear that, relative to the middle of the data, the observations in the tails are farther from the center (the median) than they ought to be for a sample from a normal distribution. We would say that these data have a distribution that is longer-tailed than the normal.

It can happen that the left end is above the line and the right end is below, rather than the reverse situation in Figure 6.8, although in practice this is seen less frequently. Should this happen, we would judge the data as having shorter tails than the theoretical distribution in question.

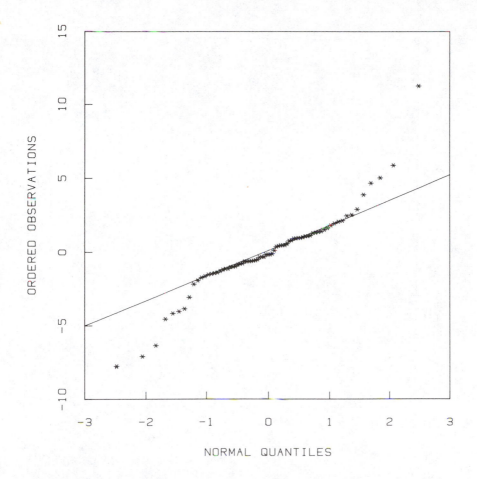

Figure 6.8 Normal probability plot of data generated by a distribution with longer tails than the normal distribution. A line has been drawn by eye through the points whose abscissas lie between −1 and 1.

ASYMMETRY

Another possibility is that the theoretical distribution is symmetric but the data are not. This happens in the normal probability plot of the seeded rainfall data in Figure 6.9. The configuration we see is a curve with slope increasing from left to right, reflecting the fact that the data have an asymmetric distribution that is skewed to the right. In other words, if we compare pairs of quantiles moving inward from the ends of the sorted data, we find that the quantiles above the median are farther from the median than their counterparts below. If the data were

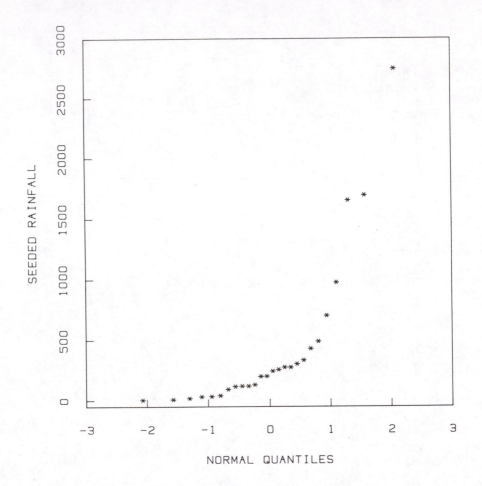

Figure 6.9 Normal probability plot of seeded rainfall data.

skewed to the left, then the lower-tail quantiles would be farther from the median than the upper-tail quantiles. Slight left skewness is observed in the log seeded rainfall data in Figure 6.6.

HORIZONTAL SEGMENTS, PLATEAUS, AND GAPS

A very common sight is a theoretical quantile-quantile plot like that in Figure 6.10, which contains a series of horizontal segments. A moment of reflection reveals that the data values all fall at multiples of 0.1. These data have been rounded to one decimal place, producing the horizontal segments. This granularity in the data is, of course, a

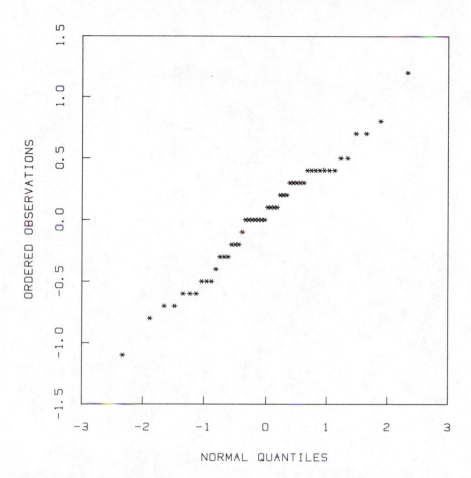

Figure 6.10 Plateau effect produced in a theoretical quantile-quantile plot when the data are rounded to a few significant digits or take only a limited number of values to begin with.

departure from normality, but one which the data analyst probably wants to ignore for most purposes. If granularity occurs at discrete values, but not simple ones, it may mean that the data were rounded at some earlier stage before being transformed to the present scale.

Figure 6.11 shows a related phenomenon. There are two rough plateaus, but the data have not been rounded to discrete values. This means that there are two distinct concentrations or clusters of points, centered approximately at 3.5 and at 5.5, which are not accounted for by the theoretical distribution. The opposite situation is shown in Figure 6.12. Here, instead of a cluster of points, there is a suspicious gap around zero in which no points have occurred.

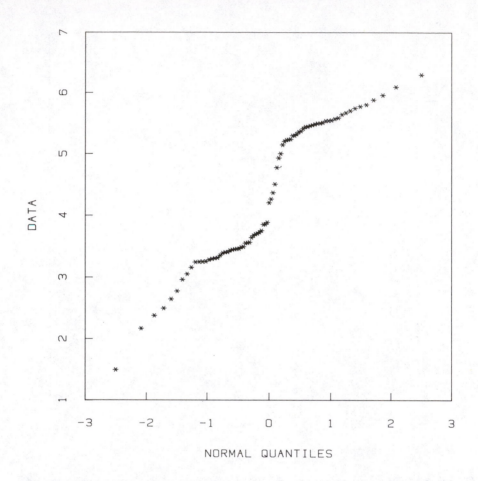

Figure 6.11 Normal quantile-quantile plot of data consisting largely of two separate tight clusters of values.

6.6 TWO CAUTIONS FOR INTERPRETING THEORETICAL QUANTILE-QUANTILE PLOTS

Theoretical quantile-quantile plots are a powerful tool for exploring distributional properties of data, but they must be used with care. Like any graphical or nongraphical summary, they present only a limited set of information. Trying to infer too much from them or ignoring their limitations can lead to bad conclusions about the data. Two important facts must be kept in mind:

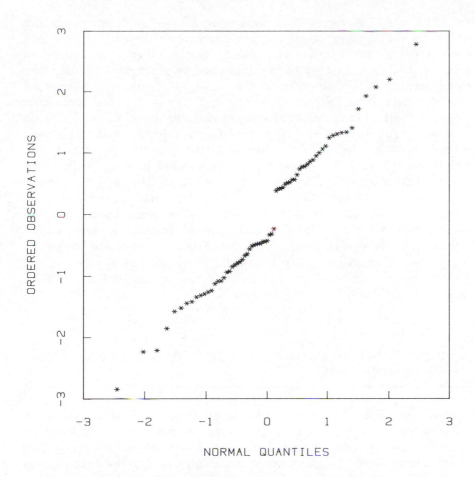

Figure 6.12 Theoretical quantile-quantile plot showing a gap, in this case caused by no values being near zero.

- the natural variability of the data, even if the distributional model is valid, generates departures from straightness, and

- each quantile-quantile plot only compares the empirical distribution of one variable with a theoretical distribution; all other information, in particular the relationship of this variable to others, is ignored.

The first point has been illustrated in Figure 6.3; the points on each panel do not exactly lie along a straight line, even though the data are pseudo-random normals. Section 6.9 contains some possibilities for calibrating the inherent variability.

The second point says that reasonably straight probability plots are no excuse for ignoring other possible structure in the data. Probability plots will sometimes detect such effects, but at other times important structure will not show up in the distributions of single variables. The cloud seeding data offer an instructive example. We saw in Figure 6.6 that the logarithms of rainfall for seeded clouds departed somewhat from normality, being mildly skewed to the left. In addition, we noted in Chapter 3 that there is a shift in the mean of the log data between seeded and unseeded clouds. However, if we combine the data for all 52 clouds, ignoring these two known departures from normality, and make a normal probability plot, the result in Figure 6.13 appears substantially straighter than Figure 6.6. The two departures from normality in these data mask each other. Had we started with this plot, noticed that it looks straight, and not looked further, we would have missed the important features of the data. The general lesson is important. Theoretical quantile-quantile plots are not a panacea and must be used in conjunction with other displays and analyses to get a full picture of the behavior of the data.

6.7   DISTRIBUTIONS WITH UNKNOWN SHAPE PARAMETERS

One advantage of the normal distribution is that the only parameters are location and spread (scale). Therefore, we can make the theoretical quantile-quantile plot without any estimation of parameters. This advantage is shared by many other families, including the uniform and exponential distributions. Some families, however, have other parameters for which values must be chosen before the plot can be drawn.

For example, the gamma distribution has a shape parameter as well as a spread parameter, and the shape parameter must be specified. The gamma probability density can be written

$$f(y;\alpha,\beta) = \beta^{-\alpha}y^{\alpha-1}\exp(-y/\beta)/\Gamma(\alpha),$$

where β is the spread parameter, α is the shape parameter, and Γ is the gamma function. In some applications, statistical estimation of the shape parameter is not needed. For instance the chi-square distribution, which is a member of the gamma family, is a model for a number of statistics arising in contingency table analysis and the analysis of variance. In these situations the number of degrees of freedom (which is the shape parameter for the chi-square) is usually known from the

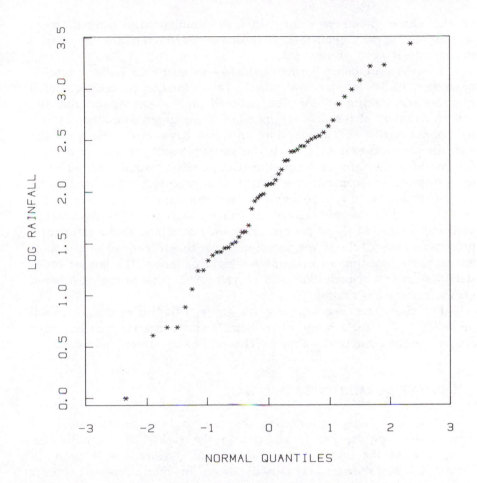

Figure 6.13 A misleadingly straight quantile-quantile plot. Merging all the log rainfall data obscures both nonnormality and differences in the seeded and control data.

extents of the contingency table or from the experimental design. However, if we know only that *some* gamma distribution might be a model, then estimation of the shape parameter is required.

To obtain a shape parameter estimate, we can use either formal (numerical) estimation or visual estimation by examining theoretical quantile-quantile plots for different parameter values. For the first approach, one needs statistical techniques for estimating parameters, preferably ones that produce a range of good values for the unknown parameters such as a confidence interval or a range based on maximum likelihood or Bayesian estimation (Cox and Hinkley, 1974). Estimation of the shape parameters may involve simultaneous estimation of location and spread, even though these two parameters are not needed to construct the probability plot.

However, in using formal estimates of shape to make quantile-quantile plots, we face a complication. The estimation procedure, which precedes the making of the plot, is based on the assumption that the true distribution of the data *is* a member of the given shape family, but we cannot verify the assumption until we have made the quantile-quantile plot and examined it. If the data are contaminated by a small fraction of outliers, for instance, they can have a dominant influence on the estimated shape parameter, which will cause the whole plot to be curved, and it will not be obvious that the curvature is due to the outliers. In other words, as a data analysis tool, the quantile-quantile plot with estimated shape parameters is only as robust as the estimation procedure used for the shape parameter. For this reason we might want to use resistant estimates that down-weight or ignore the largest order statistics. Wilk, Gnanadesikan and Huyett (1963) present such a method for the gamma distribution.

For the same reasons, a good strategy is to examine several probability plots for a range of reasonable shape estimates, rather than accept a single numerical estimate. This will be illustrated below.

POWER NORMAL DISTRIBUTIONS

Data that are amounts or counts, and therefore must be nonnegative, are frequently skewed to the right. We saw this in Chapter 2 for the ozone concentration data and we saw it again in Figure 6.9 for the seeded rainfall data. In many cases a power transformation of the data, defined by

$$
y^{(\theta)} = \begin{cases} y^\theta & \text{if } \theta > 0 \\ \log y & \text{if } \theta = 0 \\ -y^\theta & \text{if } \theta < 0, \end{cases}
$$

for some value of θ, might approximately symmetrize the data. In some fortunate cases, a symmetrizing power transformation might also make the data appear normal.

The reason that it makes sense to include log as a member of a "power transformation" family is that $\lim_{\theta \to 0}(y^\theta - 1)/\theta = \log_e y$. In terms of a set of data, the only difference between the expression $(y_i^\theta - 1)/\theta$ and our simpler formulation, $\pm y_i^\theta$, is a change of location and spread that depend on θ, but location and spread are not crucial to the quantile-

quantile plot construction. We find it more convenient to use log base 10 rather than base e, but the difference is only a change of scale since $\log_{10} x = c(\log_e x)$, where $c = \log_{10} e$.

If, for a random variable y, a power transformed variable $y^{(\theta)}$ has a normal distribution, we say that y has a *power normal distribution* with shape parameter θ. The *log normal distribution*, which has a particularly stretched upper tail, is of this kind with shape parameter equal to 0. The class of transformations also contains the *identity transformation* ($\theta = 1$), which leaves the data unchanged.

If there is a member of the power normal class that well approximates the distribution of the seeded rainfall data, it is certainly not $\theta = 1$, since we saw in Figure 6.9 that the untransformed data are very skewed and thus very nonnormal. The logarithms in Figure 6.6 appear to be somewhat skewed toward low values. In general, if θ_0 is a value that symmetrizes the data, then a power transformation with $\theta > \theta_0$ will usually result in right skewness, and a power transformation with $\theta < \theta_0$ will usually produce left skewness. For the seeded rainfall data, this suggests a value of θ between 0 and 1. In Figure 6.14 we try cube roots, or $y^{1/3}$. (This has a certain intuitive appeal, since the rainfall data are a measure of volume.) A small amount of right skewness remains in the plot. We might next try something less than 1/3 and greater than zero.

We could continue this process of guessing successively better values of θ and making additional theoretical quantile-quantile plots. But instead, we will switch at this point to a numerical estimation procedure, maximum likelihood, to estimate θ (Box and Cox, 1964). If $y^{(\theta)}$ has a normal distribution with mean μ and variance σ^2 then the log likelihood function of y_1 to y_n is

$$-\frac{n}{2} \log (2\pi\sigma^2) - \frac{1}{2\sigma^2} \sum_{j=1}^{n} \left[y_j^{(\theta)} - \mu \right]^2 + n \log |\theta| + (\theta-1) \sum_{j=1}^{n} \log |y_j|.$$

If we maximize over μ and σ^2 for any fixed value of θ the maximized log likelihood is

$$L_{\max}(\theta) = -\frac{n}{2} \log (2\pi\hat{\sigma}^2(\theta)) - \frac{n}{2} + n \log |\theta| + (\theta-1) \sum_{j=1}^{n} \log |y_j|$$

where $\hat{\sigma}^2(\theta)$ is the (biased) sample variance of $y_1^{(\theta)}$ to $y_n^{(\theta)}$. The maximum likelihood estimate of θ can now be obtained by finding the value of θ that maximizes $L_{\max}(\theta)$. One simple way to get an approximate maximum likelihood estimate is to evaluate $L_{\max}(\theta)$ at a sufficiently large number of θ values and pick the maximizing value by inspection. Once the maximum likelihood estimate $\hat{\theta}$ is found, the estimates of μ and σ^2 are just the mean and variance of $y_1^{(\theta)}$ to $y_n^{(\theta)}$.

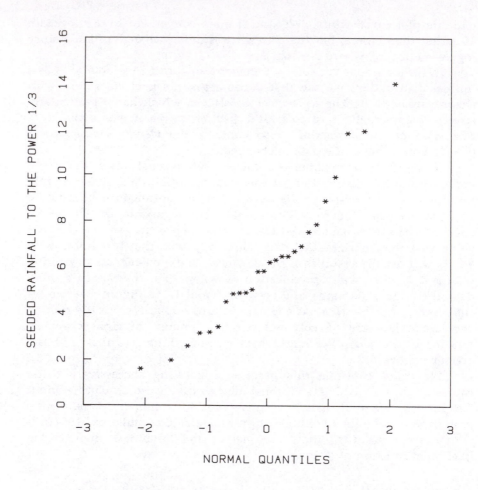

Figure 6.14 Normal probability plot of the cube roots of seeded rainfall data.

Using this procedure for the seeded rainfall data yields the estimate $\hat{\theta} = .12$. (Note that the value is between 0 and 1/3, as expected.) Figure 6.15 shows a normal probability plot of the data transformed with parameter .12. The power transformation has yielded a comfortably straight set of points.

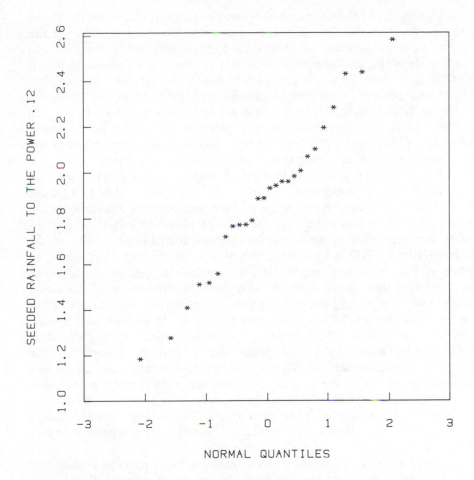

Figure 6.15 Normal probability plot of the seeded rainfall data to the .12 power.

GAMMA PROBABILITY PLOTS

In their published analysis of the rainfall data, Simpson, Olsen, and Eden (1975) assume the data are generated by gamma distributions. They hypothesize that the shape parameter, α, is the same for both seeded and unseeded clouds while the spread, or scale, parameter, β, varies. Thus there are three parameters: α, β_{seeded}, and $\beta_{control}$. Simpson *et al.* used Bayesian estimation to obtain a shape parameter estimate of $\hat{\alpha} = .6$, with most of the posterior distribution concentrated in the interval [.4, .8]. We will examine several probability plots to explore the adequacy of gamma distributions fitted to these data.

Figure 6.16 shows gamma quantile-quantile plots with shape parameter $\alpha = .6$ for the seeded data and for the control data. If the gamma model is suitable for these data, the two sets of observations will tend to lie along straight lines with slopes that are estimates of β_{seeded} and $\beta_{control}$. Both lines should pass through the origin. These plots illustrate a problem with simple gamma probability plots; the quantiles of the gamma distribution with $\alpha = .6$ are so unevenly spaced that much of the data is compressed into a small portion of the plot in the lower left. The eye tends to pick up the few large values on the right at the expense of virtually ignoring the detail in the rest of the data.

What can be done? One thing that helps is to use cube root scales for both x and y, producing Figure 6.17. We have selected the cube root scale (taken cube roots of both the ordinates and abscissas before plotting) since it is known that, for a large range of values of α, cube roots approximately symmetrize the gamma distribution. This is the Wilson-Hilferty (1931) transformation that is commonly thought of in terms of the chi-square distribution but applies to gamma distributions in general (since the gamma is simply a chi-square with fractional degrees of freedom). Unless α is small, the theoretical quantiles of the gamma distribution on the cube root scale are reasonably well spaced and do not cause the crowding problems seen in Figure 6.16. Furthermore, using cube root scales for x and y means that the reference configuration for the plot with transformed scales remains a straight line through the origin. This follows from the fact that if y_i is approximately βx_i then $y_i^{1/3}$ is approximately $\beta^{1/3} x_i^{1/3}$. (Had there been an undetermined location parameter, that is, had y_i been approximately $\beta x_i + \mu$, then cube root scales would transform a linear pattern into a curved pattern.)

There are departures from straightness on both plots in Figure 6.17 that lead us to question the appropriateness of the gamma distribution for these data. The control group has a distinct bend in the lower half of the data. The seeded data have a distinct bend in the upper tail. (The power normal probability plot of Figure 6.15 looks much better.)

Figure 6.18 shows gamma probability plots of the seeded rainfall data on the cube root scale with $\alpha = 0.4$ and $\alpha = 0.8$, which are the endpoints of the estimation interval obtained by Simpson *et al.* The shapes are not greatly changed from Figure 6.17, even though these values would be judged very unlikely in the formal estimation. Similar plots of the control data show similar results. The departures from straightness suggest that another distribution for the data might be sought, and indeed, the power normal with $\theta = .12$ in Figure 6.15 appeared to provide a better approximation to the seeded rainfall empirical distribution than any of the gamma distributions.

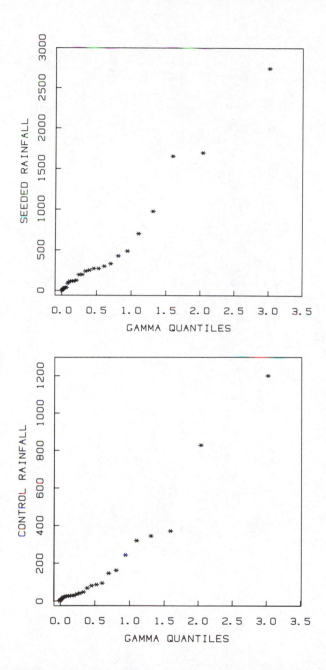

Figure 6.16 Gamma probability plot with $\alpha = .6$ of seeded rainfall data (top panel) and control rainfall data (bottom panel).

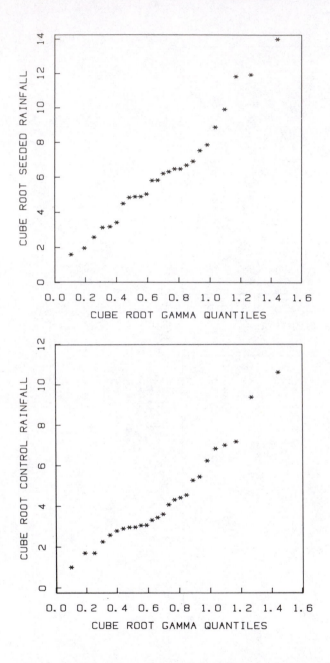

Figure 6.17 Gamma probability plots with $\alpha = .6$, on the cube root scale, of seeded rainfall data (top panel) and of control rainfall data (bottom panel).

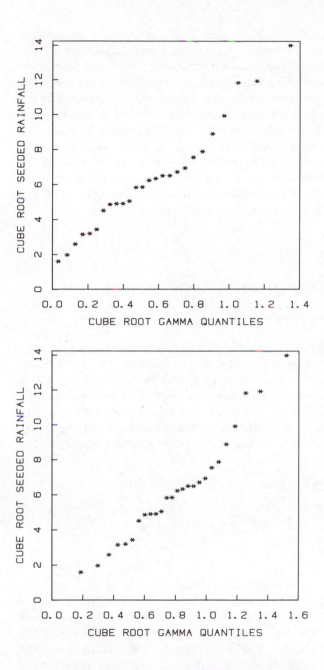

Figure 6.18 Gamma probability plots of seeded rainfall data on the cube root scale with $\alpha = .4$ (top panel) and $\alpha = .8$ (bottom panel).

The conclusions may sound prosaic, but the gamma probability plots in this example are performing a valuable role. Had we merely done the formal estimation, the results (particularly the sharp estimate of α) would have seemed misleadingly conclusive. The graphics have put the results in perspective: while the parameter estimates may be precise *if* we accept the gamma probability model, there is considerable evidence that the model as a whole is only barely adequate to make the estimates of the parameters individually useful. It is interesting to note, however, that the estimate obtained by Simpson *et al.* of the *ratio* of the scale parameters for seeded and unseeded clouds is 2.85, which is close to the value of 2.5 obtained in Chapter 3 through the simpler and less formal technique of empirical quantile-quantile plots.

6.8   CONSTRUCTING QUANTILE-QUANTILE PLOTS

Making a theoretical quantile-quantile plot involves three steps: sorting the data into ascending order; obtaining quantiles of the chosen theoretical distribution, that is, values of $Q_t(p_i)$ for $i = 1$ to n, where $p_i = (i-.5)/n$; and making a plot of the sorted data against the theoretical quantiles. The only step here that might pose difficulties in some cases is to obtain values of the theoretical quantile function, $Q_t(p)$. Depending on the distribution in question, the theoretical quantiles can be obtained by using

- exact closed-form formulas

- approximate formulas

- tables

- probability paper.

We will discuss these various approaches presently.

Tables 6.1 and 6.2 give some standard distributions that are frequently used in data analysis. Tables 6.3 and 6.4 give some information useful for the construction of theoretical quantile-quantile plots for these distributions. For each family the tables give the following: the general form of the distribution function; notes about symmetry and the interpretation of the parameters of the family; the range of possible data values; the quantities used as ordinates in the plot (sorted values of either the raw observations or power-transformed values); the quantities used as abscissas in the plot; and the parameters

Table 6.1. Distribution functions not in closed form. Φ is the standard normal distribution with mean 0 and variance 1. G_α is the standard gamma distribution with spread parameter 1 and shape parameter α; its density is $y^{\alpha-1}e^{-y}/\Gamma(\alpha)$. C_ν is the standard χ^2 distribution with ν degrees of freedom so that $C_\nu(y) = G_{\nu/2}(y/2)$. $y^{(\theta)}$ is equal to y^θ if $\theta > 0$, is equal to $\log y$ if $\theta = 0$, and is equal to $-y^\theta$ if $\theta < 0$.

			Parameters		
Family	*F(y|parameters)*	*Location*	*Spread*	*Power*	*Shape*
Normal	$\Phi(\frac{y-\mu}{\sigma})$	μ	σ		
Power Normal (Including Log Normal)	$\Phi\left\{\frac{y^{(\theta)}-\mu}{\sigma}\right\}$	(Note 1)		θ	μ
Gamma	$G_\alpha(\frac{y}{\lambda})$		λ		α
Chi-square	$C_\nu(\frac{y}{\lambda})$		λ		ν
Half-Normal	$2(\Phi(\frac{y}{\sigma})-.5)$		σ		

Family	*Symmetry*	*Data Restriction*
Normal	about μ	$-\infty < y < \infty$
Power Normal (Including Log Normal)	(Note 2)	$0 \leqslant y$ if $\theta > 0$ $0 < y$ if $\theta \leqslant 0$
Gamma	no	$0 \leqslant y$
Chi-square	no	$0 \leqslant y$
Half-Normal	no	$0 \leqslant y$

Note 1: μ and σ are location and spread parameters for $y^{(\theta)}$.

Note 2:   If $\theta = 1$ the distribution of y is normal and thus is symmetric. Otherwise y has an asymmetric distribution.

Table 6.2. Distribution functions in closed form.

Family	$F(y\|parameters)$	Location	Spread	Power	
		Parameters			
Uniform	$\dfrac{y-\mu}{\lambda}$	μ	λ		
One Parameter Exponential	$1 - \exp(-y/\lambda)$		λ		
Two Parameter Exponential	$1 - \exp\{-(y-\mu)/\lambda\}$	μ	λ		
Weibull	$1 - \exp\{-(\frac{y}{\lambda})^\theta\}$		λ	θ	(Note 1)

Family	Symmetry	Data Restriction
Uniform	about $\mu + \dfrac{\lambda}{2}$	$\mu \leqslant y \leqslant \mu+\lambda$
One Parameter Exponential	no	$0 \leqslant y$
Two Parameter Exponential	no	$\mu \leqslant y$
Weibull	no	$0 \leqslant y$

Note 1: $\theta > 0$.

Table 6.3. Information for quantile-quantile plot construction — distributions not in closed form. p_i is equal to $(i-.5)/n$.

Family	Plot Construction		What is Estimated by	
	Ordinate	*Abscissa*	*Intercept*	*Slope*
Normal	$y_{(i)}$	$\Phi^{-1}(p_i)$	μ	σ
Power Normal (Including Log Normal)	$y_{(i)}^{(\theta)}$	$\Phi^{-1}(p_i)$	μ	σ
Gamma	$y_{(i)}^{1/3}$	$[G_\alpha^{-1}(p_i)]^{1/3}$	0	$\lambda^{1/3}$
Chi-square	$y_{(i)}^{1/3}$	$[2\,G_{v/2}^{-1}(p_i)]^{1/3}$	0	$\lambda^{1/3}$
Half-Normal	$y_{(i)}$	$\Phi^{-1}(p_{(i)}/2+.5)$	0	σ

Table 6.4. Information for quantile-quantile plot construction — distributions in closed form. p_i is equal to $(i-.5)/n$.

Family	Plot Construction		What is Estimated by	
	Ordinate	*Abscissa*	*Intercept*	*Slope*
Uniform	$y_{(i)}$	p_i	μ	λ
One Parameter Exponential	$y_{(i)}^{1/3}$	$(-\log_e(1-p_i))^{1/3}$	0	λ
Two Parameter Exponential	$y_{(i)}$	$-\log_e(1-p_i)$	μ	λ
Weibull	$\log_e(y_{(i)})$	$\log_e\{-\log_e(1-p_i)\}$	$\log_e\lambda$	θ^{-1}

that would be estimated by the intercept and slope in the plot. All of the families appearing in Tables 6.2 and 6.4 have distribution functions with simple forms that are easily inverted, leading to closed-form expressions for the quantiles. For the families in Tables 6.1 and 6.3 including the normal, closed-form expressions cannot be written.

Note that all of the theoretical quantiles in Table 6.3, that is, all expressions in the Abscissa column, involve either $\Phi^{-1}(p)$, the normal quantile function, or $[G_\alpha^{-1}(p)]^{1/3}$, the cube-root gamma quantile function. Table 6.5 gives approximation formulas for these two functions. The normal approximation, which is due to Hastings (1955) and is discussed by Abramowitz and Stegun (1965), is an excellent rational function approximation. The cube-root gamma approximation, which is somewhat rougher but adequate for graphical purposes, is the well-known Wilson-Hilferty (1931) approximation in which the cube root gamma distribution is approximated by a normal distribution.

Plotting on power-transformed scales (either cube roots or logs) is recommended only in those cases where the distribution is very asymmetric and the reference configuration for the untransformed plot would be a straight line *through the origin*. (The suggested scale is indicated by *Ordinate* and *Abscissa* in Tables 6.3 and 6.4.) The second condition insures that the reference configuration for the transformed plot is still a straight line.

Working by hand, one can use tabulated values for several of the common distributions such as the normal and chi-square, although this may well require some interpolation by hand or by hand calculator. If the table available contains values of $F(y)$ tabulated against y, it can still be used in reverse, with interpolation, to get approximate values of $Q_t(p_i) = F^{-1}(p_i)$.

For the normal distribution, there is a special kind of commercially available graph paper, called probability paper, which is widely used in engineering and some other fields. Figure 6.19 shows the log seeded rainfall data plotted on graph paper of this kind. One of the axes is marked off by a series of unequally spaced grid lines which are labeled with 100 times p (lying between 0 and 100). However, their spacing is proportional to values of $Q_t(p)$ for the standard normal distribution function. Thus, to make a normal probability plot, which requires plotting the sorted data $y_{(i)}$ against $Q_t(p_i)$ with $p_i = (i-.5)/n$, one only needs to find each p_i among the grid labels (interpolating if necessary), and to plot a point above it at a height $y_{(i)}$. In effect, the probability paper does the "looking up" of the values of $Q_t(p_i)$, and it is very convenient to use when working by hand. (One minor complication is that slope calculations are more involved. This issue is explored in the exercises to this chapter.) Probability paper can also be constructed for distributions other than the normal. On the whole, however, the role of

Table 6.5. Approximation formulas for quantile functions

Normal with mean 0 and variance 1

$$\Phi^{-1}(p) \approx \{c - (2.30753 + .27061c)/(1 + .99229c + .04481c^2)\}\text{sign}(p - .5)$$

where

$$c = (-2 \log(\min(p, 1-p)))^{1/2}$$

$$\text{sign}(x) = +1 \quad \text{if } x > 0$$
$$= \quad 0 \quad \text{if } x = 0$$
$$= -1 \quad \text{if } x < 0.$$

Cube-root gamma with shape parameter α, *and* $\lambda = 1$

$$[G_\alpha^{-1}(p)]^{1/3} \approx \alpha^{1/3}\{1 - \frac{1}{9\alpha} + \frac{c}{3\sqrt{\alpha}}\}$$

where,

$$c = \Phi^{-1}(p).$$

---

probability paper (like slide rules) is diminishing due to the proliferation of computers with graphical capability.

If there are n observations, we have proposed plotting exactly n points in the theoretical quantile-quantile plot. When n is very large, this invariably produces a dense concentration of points over some stretch of the plot, usually at the center for symmetric data. In such cases, given the monotonicity of the plot, it is clearly unnecessary to plot every point — especially when working by hand. It will usually be sufficient to plot all of the largest few and smallest few points but only some selection of the points in the center, say every fifth or every tenth.

*6.9 ADDING VARIABILITY INFORMATION TO A QUANTILE-QUANTILE PLOT

Preceding sections included some discussion of the kinds of deviations from straightness typically seen in theoretical quantile-quantile plots,

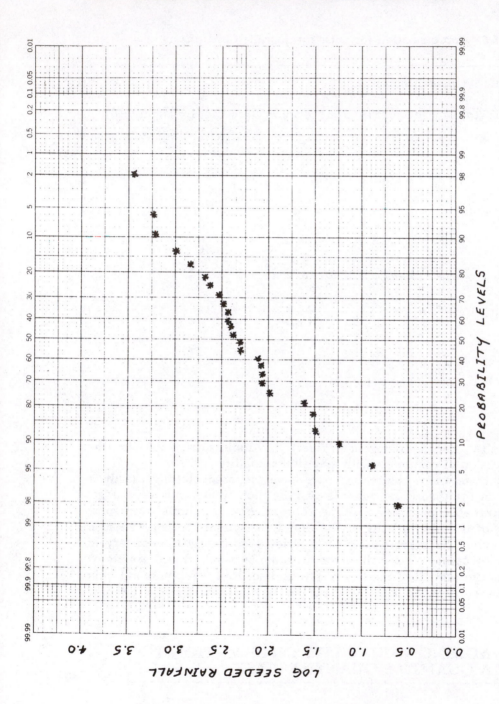

Figure 6.19 Theoretical quantile-quantile plot of log seeded rainfall data using normal probability paper.

but they did not give any clear-cut answer to the question "Are the data and the theoretical distribution compatible?" or "What is the variability of the plotted points when the theoretical distribution *is* a good approximation to the empirical distribution?" or, more succinctly, "How straight is straight?" The fact is that there are no simple or complete answers to these questions.

Nevertheless, it can be helpful in some circumstances to display variability information on a probability plot. One way to do this is to show, for each plotted point, plus and minus one standard deviation in the vertical direction from a line fitted to the plot; but to do so presents certain technical difficulties. To compute standard deviations it is appropriate to regard the plotted points as order statistics, but the standard deviations of order statistics depend on the underlying distribution, which must be estimated before we proceed.

We will let z_i be the values that are plotted on the vertical axis in a theoretical quantile-quantile plot, and as we did for other variables, we will let $z_{(i)}$ be the z_i ordered from smallest to largest. For each distribution in Tables 6.3 and 6.4 the $z_{(i)}$ are the values that appear in the *Ordinate* column for the distribution. Thus for a uniform distribution the $z_{(i)}$ are just the ordered data, $y_{(i)}$; for a gamma distribution they are $y_{(i)}^{1/3}$; and for a Weibull they are $\log_e y_{(i)}$. It is the values we plot, the $z_{(i)}$, whose standard deviations we want to portray.

We will proceed by giving a recipe for estimating the standard deviations of the $z_{(i)}$ and then indicate the source of the recipe at the end of this section. Suppose q_i is the value against which $z_{(i)}$ is plotted; for each distribution in Tables 6.3 and 6.4 the values of the q_i are given in the *Abscissa* column. Note that the q_i may involve some estimates of unknown parameters. Now let δ be the value that is estimated by the slope of the probability plot; the value of δ for each distribution in Tables 6.3 and 6.4 is given in the *Slope* column. Furthermore let $\hat{\delta}$ be an estimate of δ. Finally, in Table 6.6 we give, for each distribution in Tables 6.3 and 6.4, the form of a standardized density of the z_i. (By standardized density we mean the density of z_i with the value in the *Intercept* column equal to 0 and the value in the *Slope* column equal to 1.) Let $g(z)$ be this density with any unknown (shape) parameters set equal to estimates. Any such parameters would be the same unknown parameters that occur in the q_i and the same estimates used for the q_i would be used for g. Now an estimate of the standard error of $z_{(i)}$ is

$$\hat{sd}(z_{(i)}) = \frac{\hat{\delta}}{g(q_i)} \sqrt{\frac{p_i(1-p_i)}{n}}. \tag{6.3}$$

Table 6.6. Form of $g(z)$ for estimating standard deviations of order statistics

Family	$g(z)$
Uniform	1
One Parameter Exponential	$3z^2 e^{-z^3}$
Two-Parameter Exponential	e^{-z}
Weibull	$e^z e^{-e^z}$
Normal	$\dfrac{1}{\sqrt{2\pi}} e^{-\frac{1}{2}z^2}$
Power Normal	$\dfrac{1}{\sqrt{2\pi}} e^{-\frac{1}{2}z^2}$
Gamma	$3z^{3\alpha-1} e^{-z^3}/\Gamma(\alpha)$
Chi-square	$3(2)^{-\nu/2} z^{3\nu/2-1} e^{-z^3/2}/\Gamma(\alpha)$

Let us see how this formula works for the two-parameter exponential. From Tables 6.4 and 6.6 we have

$$q_i = -\log_e(1-p_i)$$

and

$$g(z) = e^{-z},$$

so that q_i and g have no unknown parameters for this family. Since $\delta = \lambda$ we have $\hat{\delta} = \hat{\lambda}$. Thus

$$s\hat{d}(z_{(i)}) = \frac{\hat{\lambda}}{\exp[-(-\log_e(1-p_i))]} \sqrt{\frac{p_i(1-p_i)}{n}}$$

$$= \hat{\lambda} \sqrt{\frac{p_i}{(1-p_i)n}}.$$

Figure 6.20 shows the exponential probability plots from Figure 6.5 with the standard deviation information added. As before, we suppose that μ has a fixed known value equal to 1 and we estimate $\hat{\lambda}$ by $\bar{y} - 1$. Let h_i be the height of the line $y = \hat{\lambda}x + 1$ at $x = q_i$. The dots in the figure are at heights $h_i \pm s\hat{d}(z_{(i)})$. It is clear that the random fluctuations of the points around the line have magnitudes similar to the standard deviations, so the configuration seems acceptably straight.

When looking at a theoretical quantile-quantile plot with standard deviation information superimposed, we must be careful not to try to turn such information into a formal test. The difficulty in using standard deviations to judge departures from the reference distribution is the familiar one of trying to make simultaneous inferences from many individual inferences, but compounded here by the high correlation that exists between neighboring order statistics. The probability that a particular $z_{(i)}$ deviates from h_i by more than, say, two standard deviations is small. But the probability that *at least one* of the $z_{(i)}$ deviates from h_i by two standard deviations is quite another matter and is likely to be much greater. What is worse, since there is a high correlation among neighboring order statistics, if one plotted point deviates by more than two standard deviations, there is a good chance that a whole stretch of them will.

The most important reason for portraying standard deviations is that they give us a sense of the relative variability of the points in different regions of the plot. In Figure 6.20 we see, for instance, that the standard deviations of the points near the high end are substantially larger than the standard deviations of the others.

The standard deviation estimation we have given requires estimating δ and any other unknown parameters involved in q_i and g. As we have stressed before it is important to have robust estimates of the parameters that are not distorted by a few outliers. In fact, the probability plot itself can be used to get an informal estimate of δ that is robust and that is quite sufficient for the task, since it is the relative values of the standard deviations that are most important; what we can do is use some robust measure of the slope of the points on the plot. For example, suppose $z_{(u)}$ and $z_{(\ell)}$ are the upper and lower quartiles of the $z_{(i)}$, and let q_u and q_ℓ be the corresponding abscissas on the plot. Then we can take as a slope measure

$$\hat{\delta} = \frac{z_{(u)} - z_{(\ell)}}{q_u - q_\ell}$$

which will clearly not be affected by a few outliers.

Now we will indicate the source of formula (6.3). Suppose $G(z;\phi)$ is the cumulative distribution function of the z_i, where ϕ represents all unknown parameters, and let $g(z;\phi)$ be the density function and

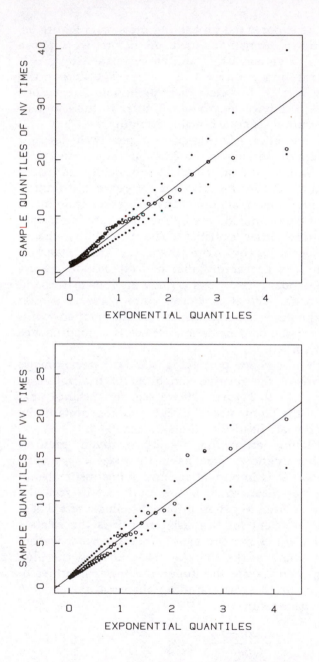

Figure 6.20 The exponential plots of Figure 6.5 with standard error information added.

$G^{-1}(p_i;\phi)$ the quantile function. For most continuous distributions, including those in Tables 6.1 and 6.2, a reasonable approximation for the standard deviation of $z_{(i)}$ (Kendall and Stuart, 1977, Section 10.10) is

$$sd(z_{(i)}) = \frac{1}{q(E(z_{(i)});\phi)} \sqrt{\frac{p_i(1-p_i)}{n}}$$

where $E(z_{(i)})$ is the expected value of $z_{(i)}$. Suppose $\hat{\phi}$ is a set of estimates of the unknown parameters, then a reasonable estimate of $E(z_{(i)})$ is $G^{-1}(p_i;\hat{\phi})$ which leads to the standard deviation estimate

$$\tilde{sd}(z_{(i)}) = \frac{1}{g(G^{-1}(p_i;\hat{\phi});\hat{\phi})} \sqrt{\frac{p_i(1-p_i)}{n}}.$$

Some simple algebra brings us from this formula to (6.3).

*6.10   CENSORED AND GROUPED DATA

In a number of application areas, data arise that are *censored*; that is, for some values of i we do not have exact observations, y_i, but only bounds on the true observations. Generally we have lower bounds on these data values, a situation that is called *right*-censoring. This happens frequently, for instance, when fitting lifetime distributions either in medicine or in the field of industrial quality control. In medicine, one might be measuring the amount by which some new drug prolongs the life of terminally ill patients. A certain number of the patients are still alive at the end of the experiment, so we do not know how much their lives have been prolonged overall, and certain others might have died of unrelated causes or have been removed from treatment prematurely. In quality control one might be measuring the distribution of times-to-failure for a sample of integrated circuit chips under conditions that accelerate aging. Again, many of the chips may not have failed by the end of the trial, while others may have failed at the very beginning due to manufacturing defects unrelated to the mechanisms which cause failures in the long term.

It is possible to adapt theoretical quantile-quantile plots to these situations. The basic approach is to take the view that the p_i (which we have consistently taken to be $(i - .5)/n$) are really values at the sorted data points of the empirical cumulative distribution function $\hat{F}$. With censored data we define an appropriately modified distribution function, one version of which is the Kaplan-Meier estimate, $\hat{F}_{KM}$ (Kaplan and

Meier, 1958). We then use values of $\hat{F}_{KM}(y_{(i)})$ at the complete observations (leaving out the censored ones) as the p_i, and proceed as before. This leads to values of p_i which can be written as follows: Suppose we have multiple right censoring and that $y_{(1)} \leqslant y_{(2)} \leqslant \cdots \leqslant y_{(n)}$ are the sorted observations, some of which are actually censored values. Let I be the indices of observations corresponding to complete (i.e., uncensored) observations. Then appropriate p_i are

$$p_i = 1 - \frac{n+.5}{n} \prod_{\substack{j \text{ in } I \\ j \leqslant i}} \frac{n-j+.5}{n-j+1.5}, \qquad \text{for } i \text{ in } I.$$

Only values of i in I are actually used for plotting. In other words, we only plot points for the complete observations, but their positions are affected by the presence of the censored observations. It is comforting to note that this formula for p_i reduces to $(i-.5)/n$ when no observations are censored. A more thorough discussion of theoretical quantile-quantile plots for censored data is given by Michael (1979).

The following is an example given by Michael. The data are from the lifetime testing of a batch of mechanical devices and are shown in the Appendix as Data Set 27 and reproduced along with two extra columns in Table 6.7. Each device has two components, A and B, either of which can fail. A device is taken off test as soon as either of its components fails, so an observed failure in one mode is a censored observation for the other failure mode. Also, three of the devices were still working at the end of the test. Since we are interested in the failure modes separately, the abscissas (i.e., values of p_i) for the two modes, with censoring taken into account, are also shown in Table 6.7. Figure 6.21 is a superimposed pair of normal quantile-quantile plots of the logs of failure times for the batches. Both are reasonably straight, supporting the log normal distributional model for the original data. We observe in the plot that component B has an expected log lifetime that is about 0.2 less than component A, but that its standard deviation (slope) is larger.

We note in passing that the Kaplan-Meier calculation of p_i values for censored data can be used as the basis for an empirical quantile-quantile plot (as in Chapter 3) for two censored samples.

The theoretical quantile-quantile plot can also be adapted to deal with grouped data, that is, data that have been reported in the form of frequency counts within cells defined by a set of cell boundaries. In a sense, this is another kind of censoring; it is also the kind of information that can be read from a histogram. One way to convert such data into a quantile-quantile plot is to plot one point for the right-hand boundary of each cell except the last. The location of the boundary is taken as the empirical quantile, and the p value associated with it is

Table 6.7. Life data for mechanical devices. The entries in the Abscissas columns are p_i values computed using the formula for censored data.

i	Time	Failure Mode A	Failure Mode B	Abscissas A	Abscissas B
1	1.151		x		.017
2	1.170		x		.042
3	1.248		x		.066
4	1.331		x		.091
5	1.381		x		.116
6	1.499	x		.020	
7	1.508		x		.141
8	1.534		x		.167
9	1.577		x		.192
10	1.584		x		.218
11	1.667	x		.052	
12	1.695	x		.084	
13	1.710	x		.116	
14	1.955		x		.246
15	1.965	x		.149	
16	2.012		x		.276
17	2.051		x		.305
18	2.076		x		.334
19	2.109	x		.187	
20	2.116		x		.365
21	2.119		x		.396
22	2.135	x		.228	
23	2.197	x		.269	
24	2.199		x		.430
25	2.227	x		.313	
26	2.250		x		.466
27	2.254	x		.360	
28	2.261		x		.505
29	2.349		x		.544
30	2.369	x		.415	
31	2.547	x		.470	
32	2.548	x		.524	
33	2.738		x		.597
34	2.794	x		.586	
35	2.883	Did not fail			
36	2.883	Did not fail			
37	2.910	x		.675	
38	3.015	x		.763	
39	3.017	x		.851	
40	3.793	Did not fail			

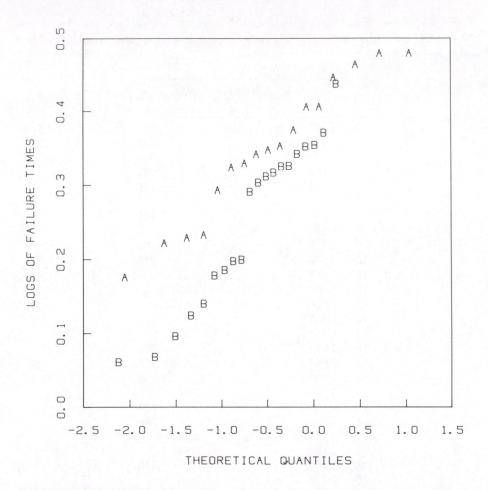

Figure 6.21 Normal probability plot of two groups of right-censored failure data.

$$\frac{\text{total of counts in cells to the left}}{\text{total count in all cells}}$$

We point out that the statistical fluctuations of the positions of the points in a quantile-quantile plot of this kind are different from those in an ordinary quantile-quantile plot with the same number of plotted points, because the effective n for assessing variability is not the number of cells but the total of all the counts.

6.11   SUMMARY AND DISCUSSION

In this chapter we have discussed the use of theoretical quantile-quantile plots as exploratory tools for learning about the distributional patterns of sets of data in relation to hypothesized theoretical distributions. Such plots provide an informal procedure for judging goodness-of-fit of distributional models to the data, but instead of yielding a formal test statistic, they give a wealth of diagnostic information about how and where the data deviate from the reference distribution. In looking at theoretical quantile-quantile plots, one must judge deviations from linear configurations, based on experience. Displaying standard deviation estimates as calibration can be helpful. As a data analytic technique, the plots are fairly robust since the presence of a few moderate outliers does not greatly affect one's judgment concerning the main body of data. Finally, they are quite versatile, since they can be constructed using virtually any theoretical distribution, and can be adapted to a number of nonstandard probability models and types of data, including censored data.

6.12   FURTHER READING

A good general exposition of both empirical and theoretical quantile-quantile plots was given by Wilk and Gnanadesikan (1968), who discuss the construction and interpretation of the plots and give some interesting examples.

The problem of calibrating the straightness of quantile-quantile plots has received some attention in the statistical literature. See, for example, Shapiro and Wilk (1965), LaBrecque (1977), Filliben (1975), Daniel (1959), Doksum and Sievers (1976), and Michael (1979). The last two of these references discuss ways to draw "acceptance" regions on quantile-quantile plots. Such regions look superficially like the curves traced by the plotted standard deviation points discussed in Section 6.9, but they have a different interpretation. In theory they provide an α-level test of the hypothesis that the data were generated by that distribution: if any point falls outside the region, then the hypothesis is rejected. This approach has some appealing theoretical properties, but it also has some practical drawbacks. In particular, it tends to lack power against many kinds of moderate but frequently encountered deviations from straightness, and it shifts the emphasis away from the diagnostic value of the plot and back to the rigid "accept versus reject" framework.

Michael (1983) describes a *stabilized quantile-quantile plot* that deals directly with the problem of unequal variability of the plotted points. In the spirit of the cube-root transformation for gamma quantile-quantile plots discussed in Section 6.7, the stabilized quantile-quantile plot is based on the arcsin transformation. One small complication is that the plot has neither the location nor scale invariance property, so that both location and scale must be estimated in advance.

Finally, although this chapter has described the use of quantile-quantile plots as the main graphical tool for comparing data to probability models, other entirely different strategies are possible. One classical approach is to rescale a histogram vertically to have total area equal to 1, and to superimpose a density function for the comparison theoretical distribution. Two variations of the idea are described by Tukey (1972) and by Velleman and Hoaglin (1981): First, the histogram and comparison density function can be plotted on a square-root (vertical) scale to make the random variability of the bar lengths more nearly equal (the *rootogram*). Second the bars can be "slid" vertically so that their top ends are attached to the curve, and the "residuals" are seen as discrepancies between the bottoms of the bars and the x-axis (the *hanging histogram*). The two ideas can be combined to produce the *hanging rootogram*. Although these techniques have some heuristic appeal, we feel that on the whole they are less sensitive and less effective for our needs than the theoretical quantile-quantile plot. The histogram or rootogram with a superimposed density curve requires the comparison of two curved patterns, which is hard to do visually. The hanging version improves matters, but it does not give discrepancies in the tails adequate visual impact.

EXERCISES

6.1. The quantile plot in Chapter 2 can also be regarded as a theoretical quantile-quantile plot. What is the implied theoretical distribution?

6.2. What would a normal quantile-quantile plot of data from a uniform distribution tend to look like? One way to study this question is to generate some pseudo-random data and make several such plots.

6.3. What would a normal probability plot of data from a t-distribution tend to look like?

6.4. What would a normal quantile-quantile plot of data from an exponential distribution tend to look like?

6.5. Make a normal quantile-quantile plot of the amount of headroom in 74 automobile models (Data Set 7). Comment on the plot.

6.6. Make a normal probability plot of the sepal width of all 150 irises (Data Set 14). Estimate location and spread of the underlying normal distribution from the plot and compare them with the sample mean and standard deviation.

6.7. Make a normal quantile-quantile of the first 48 average monthly temperatures in Newark (Data Set 9). Discuss the plot.

6.8. Make a normal quantile-quantile plot of the rear seat clearance of the automobile data (Data Set 7). What can you learn from the plot?

6.9. Make a normal probability plot of the rotor speed of the tar content data (Data Set 23). What can you see in the plot?

6.10. Make a normal probability plot of the percent population under 15 in 35 countries (Data Set 16). What does the plot reveal?

6.11. Make a normal quantile-quantile plot of the petal length of 150 irises (Data Set 14). Why does the plot look so strange?

6.12. For the disposable income in 35 countries (Data Set 16) find a power transformation that makes the distribution of the transformed data nearly normal.

6.13. Find a shape parameter α so that the resulting gamma distribution is a good approximation to the uncensored remission durations of leukemia patients (Data Set 28).

6.14. For the stereogram data with both verbal and visual information (Data Set 26) take logarithms and make normal probability plots. How well does the log normal distribution fit the data compared with the exponential distribution. To enhance the comparison make exponential probability plots on a log scale.

6.15. Find a power transformation of the graph areas (Data Set 13) that makes the empirical distribution nearly normal. Make a gamma probability plot. Which of the two theoretical distributions does a better job of describing the data.

6.16. Find a theoretical distribution in Table 6.1 or 6.2 that is a good approximation to the empirical distribution of the years since highest degree for all Bell Laboratories managers with a Ph.D. (Data Set 20).

6.17. Find a theoretical distribution in Table 6.1 or 6.2 that is a good approximation to the empirical distribution of the exponent data (Data Set 3).

6.18. Figure 6.11 showed a quantile-quantile plot for data from a mixture of normal distributions, with the same variance but different means.

    1. Why might a plot like this appear to be from a short-tailed distribution? What visual clues, other than the curvature, might distinguish the two cases?

    2. What would you expect a quantile-quantile plot to look like for a similar mixture with mean values equal but with standard deviations of 1 and 2? 1 and 5?

Note: you can approach these questions either by generating a number of examples or by studying the density function for a mixture distribution.

*6.19.   1. Why should the departure from normality seen in Figure 6.6 and a shift of the average value tend to cancel each other in the normal quantile-quantile plot of Figure 6.13?

    2. How would you supplement probability plots to detect (i) dependence of the distribution on the value of another qualitative variable? quantitative variable? (ii)

serial effects (i.e., x_{i+1} correlated with x_i)?

*6.20. Why is there greater variability in the tails than in the center of Figure 6.3?

6.21. Make a normal quantile-quantile plot of the exponent data (Data Set 3) by using normal probability paper.

6.22.   1. Make a normal probability plot of the catheter lengths for 12 children (Data Set 33) by using normal probability paper.

   *2. Fit a straight line by eye and estimate location and spread parameters from the plot.

   Note: For calculating a slope, it is inappropriate to use a difference of $100p$-values (the printed horizontal scale) as a denominator. Instead, one should use a difference of $\Phi^{-1}(p_i)$-values. A convenient device is to calculate the slope based on the two points for which $100p = 31$ and $100p = 69$. Then   the   correct   denominator   is $\Phi^{-1}(.69)-\Phi^{-1}(.31) = .991$ or, essentially, 1.

6.23. Select a page from the book and record the numbers of letters between successive occurrences of the letter "e". Continue until you have 35 values.

   1. Make an exponential probability plot.

   *2. Add standard error information.

*6.24. Make a normal probability plot of the square roots of the percent savings rate in 35 countries (Data Set 16) and add standard error information.

*6.25. Find a theoretical distribution which is a good approximation to the empirical distribution of the uncensored and censored observations on remission durations of 84 patients with leukemia (Data Set 28).

*6.26. Make a normal probability plot of the length of eggs of the common tern (Data Set 21).

*6.27.   Using the Kaplan-Meier p_i values from the Abscissa column of
Table 6.7, and suitable interpolation, devise a way to make an
empirical quantile-quantile plot of the A censored data against
the B censored (Data Set 27).

7

Developing and
Assessing Regression Models

7.1 INTRODUCTION

Regression models are used to describe how a response variable is
related to or can be "explained by" one or more explanatory variables.
In the words of Daniel and Wood (1971 or 1980), we are interested in
"fitting equations to data."

Graphical methodology provides powerful diagnostic tools for
conveying properties of the fitted regression, for assessing the adequacy
of the fit, and for suggesting improvements. There is seldom any prior
guarantee that a hypothesized regression model will provide a good
description of the mechanism that generated the data. Standard
regression models carry with them many specific assumptions about the
relationship between the response and explanatory variables and about
the variation in the response that is not accounted for by the
explanatory variables. In many applications of regression there is a
substantial amount of prior knowledge that makes the assumptions
plausible; in many other applications the assumptions are made as a
starting point simply to get the analysis off the ground. But whatever
the amount of prior knowledge, fitting regression equations is not
complete until the assumptions have been examined. The graphical
methods of this chapter help us to do this.

We make no attempt to teach regression but assume the reader has
a working knowledge of the basic concepts and techniques of
regression. (They can be found, for example, in Weisberg, 1980, or
Chatterjee and Price, 1977 or Draper and Smith, 1966.) Thorough
knowledge of detailed formulas and theory is not crucial. Most of the

basic plots in this chapter have been introduced in earlier chapters (for example, scatter plots); the emphasis here is on what variables are plotted and what information regarding the regression model is conveyed by the plots.

To begin the chapter we set out some concepts and notation and briefly consider simple regression. The rest of the chapter is organized into three parts, which present

- graphs for exploring the raw data *before* any serious regression analysis is done, to help understand peculiarities and potential difficulties with the particular set of data and to suggest models

- graphs for use *during* the analysis, after some intermediate stages of regression have been carried out, to examine components of the fit and suggest modifications to the model

- graphs to be employed *after* the model has been fit, to assess the quality of the fit and to diagnose deviations from the model assumptions.

In practice, these categories overlap, especially the last two. Diagnostic plots showing inadequacies after fitting will often suggest further model modifications and further fitting. Nearly all effective statistical model building is iterative in this way.

The main ideas of this chapter are discussed in the context of four examples. The first is a set of data taken from a survey of telephone cable splicing work. New telephone cables are placed in sections, and joining or splicing the sections together requires time-consuming manual work. In a survey of 842 splicing jobs the response variable was splicing time. The large number of potential explanatory variables included the number of pairs of wires in the cable to be joined and the type of cable.

The second example is taken from Davies (1957). Thirty rubber specimens were rubbed with an abrasive material and the amount of material rubbed off, the abrasion loss, was related to hardness and tensile strength. Thus the response is abrasion loss and the two explanatory variables are hardness and tensile strength. The data for this and for the examples in the two paragraphs below are given in the Appendix.

The third example, based on data from Badger (1946) and reproduced in Bennett and Franklin (1954), deals with a chemical process in which the tar content of an output gas was related to the temperature at which the chemical process was run and to the speed of a rotor. Since a curved dependence on speed was anticipated, speed-squared was considered as an additional explanatory variable along with temperature and speed. There are thirty-one observations.

The fourth example extends the example in Chapter 2 dealing with the psychological scales that people use to judge the relative areas of circles of varying sizes. A number of subjects were asked to judge the areas of a series of circles. The true and judged areas are taken as the explanatory and response variables, respectively (Cleveland, Harris, and McGill, 1982).

7.2 THE LINEAR MODEL

Linear regression is used to relate a response variable y_i to one or several explanatory or descriptive variables x_{ik} through a set of linear equations of the form

$$y_i = \beta_0 + \sum_{k=1}^{p} \beta_k x_{ik} + \epsilon_i , \quad \text{for } i = 1 \text{ to } n .\tag{7.1}$$

The y_i (for $i = 1$ to n) are the n observed values of the response variable, the x_{ik} (for $i = 1$ to n) are the n values of the kth explanatory variable (for $k = 1$ to p), and the parameters β_k are the unknown regression coefficients. The ϵ_i are the random "errors" or fluctuations. (The variables x_{ik} and y_i are sometimes called "independent" and "dependent" variables, but such terminology can be misleading since the x_{ik} variables are not statistically independent of the y_i, nor generally of each other.)

We will usually simplify (7.1) by defining an extra variable x_{i0} whose value is always 1 ($x_{i0} \equiv 1$), so the model with constant term can be written as

$$y_i = \sum_{k=0}^{p} \beta_k x_{ik} + \epsilon_i, \quad \text{for } i = 1 \text{ to } n .\tag{7.2}$$

In each application of such a model to data we are making three key assumptions:

- The x_{ik} are indeed the explanatory variables that influence y_i, or describe the behavior of y_i in some region.

- The relationship between the x_{ik} and y_i is well described by a linear equation as specified by (7.1).

- All other influences on y_i, together with all causes of fluctuations, are summed up by the error terms ϵ_i which have a joint probability distribution specified in some fashion, implicitly or explicitly.

Usually the ϵ_i are assumed to be statistically independent of each other with zero means and with a constant variance that does not depend on i or x_{ik}. Much of standard regression theory and methodology is based on the further assumption that the ϵ_i have normal distributions. In practice, some or all of these assumptions are often too optimistic. In applications, it is essential to check the validity of whatever important assumptions are made, in order to assess the accuracy and stability of the results. Most of the plots in this chapter are designed for this purpose.

In regression we usually want to compute estimates $\hat{\beta}_k$ of the regression coefficients from the data, either because we want to know and interpret the coefficients themselves, or because we will use them to predict future values of y_i. Ideally, the choice of estimation procedure for a particular situation should be based on the nature of the probabilistic assumptions appropriate for the ϵ_i. Simple least squares is widely used, but if the ϵ_i have a distribution with tails even slightly longer than the normal, which is a very common occurrence, least squares can perform very poorly and give highly variable estimates. In such situations, recently developed robust regression procedures may do better (e.g., Mosteller and Tukey, 1977). To a large extent, the graphical methods we present are suitable regardless of the type of estimation procedure used to calculate $\hat{\beta}_k$, even though several of the plots are motivated in terms of ordinary least squares and may require modification for weighted least squares or robust estimation. Some of the plots can help us decide when robust techniques are needed, and others can be more revealing if the estimation has been done robustly.

Replacing the β_k in the first term of (7.2) by their estimated values, $\hat{\beta}_k$, we obtain the fitted (or "predicted") values $\hat{y}_i$,

$$\hat{y}_i = \sum_{k=0}^{p} \hat{\beta}_k x_{ik} \ , \quad i = 1 \text{ to } n \ .$$

The residuals $\hat{\epsilon}_i$ are defined as the differences between the observed and fitted values,

$$\hat{\epsilon}_i = y_i - \hat{y}_i \ , \quad i = 1 \text{ to } n \ .$$

As we shall see, the residuals are used in many diagnostic displays because they contain most of the information regarding lack of fit of the model to the data. In terms of fitted values and residuals, we have

$$\text{data} = \text{fit} + \text{residual}$$

which in mathematical notation is expressed as

$$y_i = \sum_{k=0}^{p} \hat{\beta}_k x_{ik} + \hat{\epsilon}_i, \quad i = 1 \text{ to } n. \tag{7.3}$$

The top panel of Figure 7.1 shows a plot of a response against an explanatory variable in a simple regression situation (that is, with $p=1$) for a set of artificial data. When there is only one explanatory variable, linear regression consists of fitting a straight line to the data. The middle panel of Figure 7.1 shows the same set of points together with an oblique line which is the least squares line, and a number of short vertical lines to represent the residuals. The residuals are plotted against the explanatory variable in the bottom panel.

There is a close connection between this chapter and some of the graphical methods of Chapter 4 for studying the dependence of one variable on another. Regression analysis tries to find an average or typical value of the response variable for each possible value of the explanatory variables. The smoothing techniques of Section 4.6 can be thought of as a kind of regression analysis. However, this chapter deals with *linear* regression, so that the only "smooth" functions of the explanatory variables considered here are linear ones. Also, the primary interest here is in *multiple* linear regression with two or more explanatory variables, where simple scatter plots are inadequate. Finally, the smooth curves in Chapter 4 were used as an auxiliary guide for looking at the data, whereas this chapter focuses more on the fitted model itself.

The class of linear regression models discussed in this chapter is more general than it may seem. For instance, since the x_{ik} and y_i that appear in (7.1) may be transformed or reexpressed versions of other variables, many kinds of curved or nonlinear relationships can be studied. The essential thing is that (7.1) should be linear in the *parameters* β_k. Since these issues are not graphical and since they are discussed in most recent books on applied regression, they are not of major concern here. However, as some of the examples will illustrate, there are times when graphical displays will aid the choice of transformations, and there are times when the nature of the variables will govern the choice of displays.

7.3 SIMPLE REGRESSION

We first consider the case of simple linear regression in which there is only one explanatory variable:

Figure 7.1 A simple regression situation with artificial data. The top panel is a plot of y_i vs. x_i. The middle panel shows the least-squares regression line, and residuals as vertical lines. The bottom panel shows residuals plotted against x.

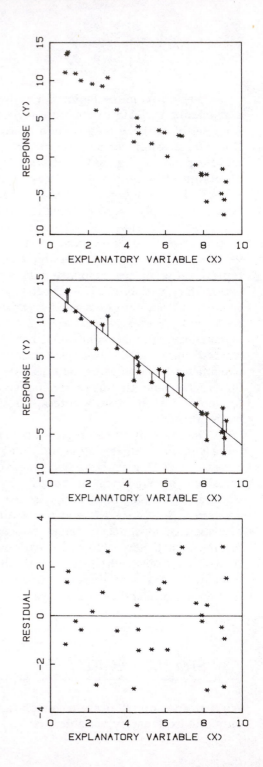

$$y_i = \beta_0 + \beta_1 x_i + \epsilon_i.$$

In a sense, the scatter plot of y_i against x_i tells the whole story since it displays all the data. But we now go farther and consider the implications that certain kinds of configurations have for regression fitting by looking at some simple cases with artificial data.

Figure 7.1 is an example of the most pleasant (but often quite unrealistic) circumstance: the values of x_i are well spread out, y_i and x_i have a high degree of linear association (correlation), the vertical deviations from the line show no outliers, and the residuals when plotted against x_i spread out in a band across the page with no other systematic structure.

Figure 7.2 shows nearly the same situation, but now the correlation between x_i and y_i is moderately weak. This is equivalent to saying that the amount of variation of the fitted values $\hat{y}_i$ is small compared to the residual variation. Unless there is a large amount of data, the regression coefficient $\hat{\beta}_1$ will probably be determined inaccurately, and we may not even be able to say with confidence whether the true β_1 is different from zero. Note that a value of zero for $\hat{\beta}_1$ would mean that x_i has no apparent linear bearing on y_i.

There is a curved relationship between y_i and x_i in Figure 7.3. If we fail to notice and take account of it, the residuals will exhibit the curvature even more strongly, showing a characteristic high-low-high (or low-high-low) pattern. If the curvature is strong enough, we will be led to fitting some curved function of x_i (perhaps a polynomial) in place of x_i.

In Figure 7.4, one data point is far removed from the others in the horizontal direction. Such a point is called a high-leverage point (Belsley, Kuh and Welsch, 1980), since changes in its y value will have a substantial effect on the estimation of β_1. In this example, the point seems consistent with the others because it falls in line with the linear configuration of the rest of the points; thus it need not be deemed an outlier.

Figure 7.5 shows a similar configuration, but now there is no high correlation in the remaining points. A "standard" least-squares regression and accompanying analysis might tell us that $\hat{\beta}_1$ is well-determined, but we should be cautious. Nearly all the information regarding slope is embodied in the single highly influential point, and the data themselves provide no confirmation that this point is reliable. When this happens we should return to the source of the data for confirmation.

A worse (but quite realistic) situation is shown in Figure 7.6. Here, the y value of the high-leverage point clearly contradicts the pattern of the rest. Nevertheless, the least-squares fit has tried to accommodate it,

Figure 7.2 Like Figure 7.1, but the residuals have larger dispersion.

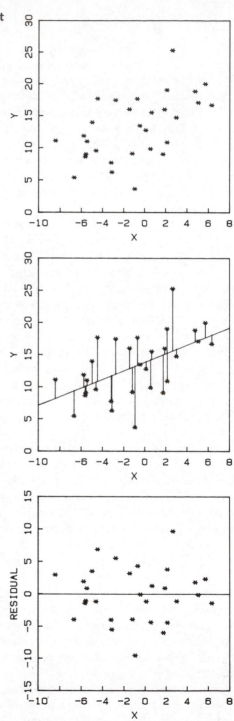

Figure 7.3 Like Figure 7.1, but the relationship of y_i to x_i is curved.

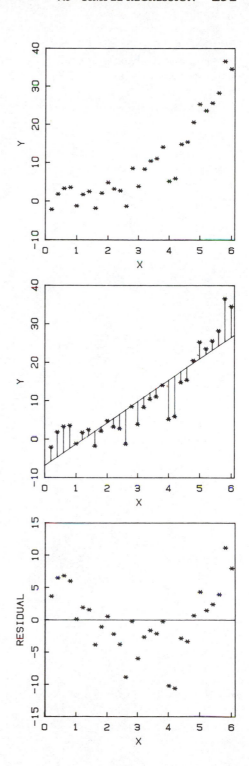

Figure 7.4 Like Figure 7.1, but there is one high-leverage point whose y_i value is in line with the rest.

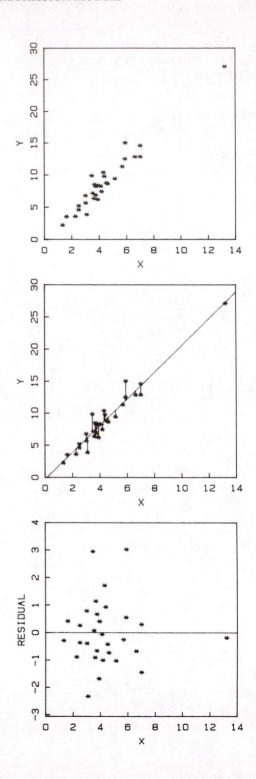

Figure 7.5 A simple regression situation with artificial data in which there is virtually no linear relationship between y_i and x_i, except for one highly influential point.

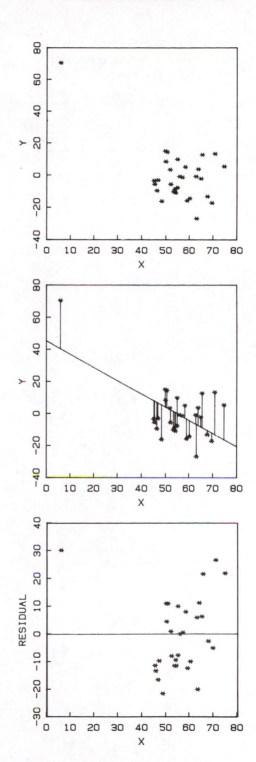

Figure 7.6 Like Figure 7.1, but there is one outlying point not in line with the rest.

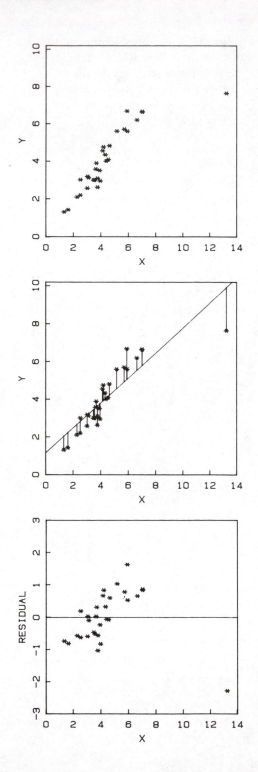

producing a characteristic strong linear pattern in most of the residuals, balanced by the one isolated residual. (This example shows the effect of a single outlier, but of course in a given set of data there could be two or several and they could act together in complicated ways to reinforce or to cancel each other's effects.)

In such a situation, we would have to think hard about such nongraphical questions as (1) whether the point is in error and could be corrected, (2) whether, if the point is correct, it should be set aside anyway with a suitable warning that the model does not seem to fit all the data, (3) whether additional data points could be obtained in the horizontal vicinity of the isolated one, or between it and the rest (or even beyond it), to see whether some curved function of the x_i would fit better, and (4) whether we ought to discard least-squares in favor of some robust regression fitting procedure that would automatically down-weight such a point, whether high-leverage, deviant, or both. Note that (4) is really a combination of (1) and (2).

The scatter plot in Figure 7.7 shows another common departure from the usual least-squares assumptions: the variability, or spread, or standard deviation of the points on the vertical axis does not remain constant from left to right. This is brought out more clearly by the residuals, but an even better way to study the change in spread is to plot the absolute values of the residuals and draw a smooth curve, as we discuss in Section 7.6. Nonconstant spread of residuals might lead us to transform the variables or to use weighted least-squares (or possibly robust regression) in place of ordinary least-squares.

Finally, in Figure 7.8 the density of points in the horizontal direction changes. This change in density does not violate any of the conventional assumptions of least-squares regression and is perfectly acceptable, however it may well have an undue influence on our visual assessment of the residuals. In checking for change of residual spread, it will be especially important here to plot absolute residuals accompanied by a smooth curve.

7.4 PRELIMINARY PLOTS

It is prudent to look closely at the raw data to get as much insight as possible before carrying out a multiple regression analysis. The objective is to discover any interesting relationships, unusual behavior, and exceptional points that, on the one hand, can help guide the choice of models and fitting procedures, and, on the other hand, can provide a key to understanding difficulties that may arise during the fitting and

Figure 7.7 A simple regression situation with artificial data in which there is a linear relationship between y_i and x_i, but an increasing spread of residuals.

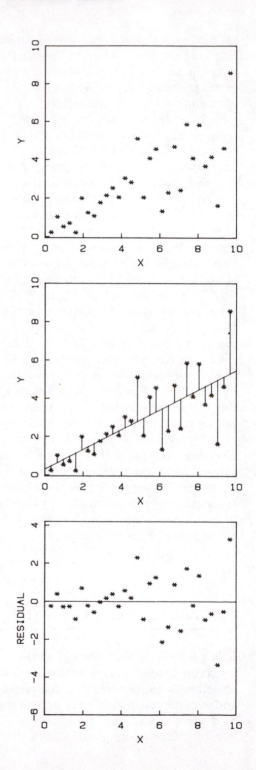

Figure 7.8 A simple regression situation in which there is a linear relationship between y_i and x_i and approximately constant spread of residuals, but decreasing density of x_i values.

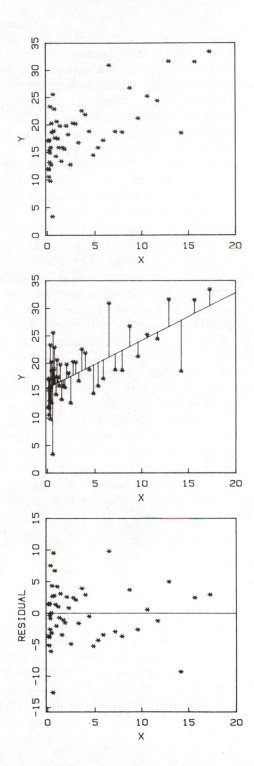

diagnostic stages. It is especially important for us to become familiar with the raw data because we are likely to fit the regression with a computer program that is blind to many obvious anomalies in the data.

There are many questions: Are there apparent outliers? Do variances appear constant? Do functional relationships look linear or curved? Would transformations (such as logarithms or square roots) help? Are there repeated values in some of the variables? Do the data cluster in interesting ways? How poorly balanced is the "design configuration"? (The design configuration is the collection of x_{ik} values, so called because the x_{ik} may have their values determined by an experimental design.) Answers to many of these questions must remain tentative, at least until we have made a preliminary fit, because of possible relationships involving several variables at once. For instance, an apparently outlying y_i value in a plot of y_i against x_{i1} may be perfectly well explained by that point having high values of x_{i3} and x_{i5}.

The bivariate graphical methods of Chapter 4 can be useful for exploring these questions, since we can look at any pair of variables separately. Also, we can use most of the multidimensional methods of Chapter 5, since we can think of the x_{ik} and y_i together as defining n points in $(p+1)$-dimensional space. (That is, we take $(y_1, x_{11}, x_{12}, \ldots, x_{1p})$ as a point, $(y_2, x_{21}, x_{22}, \ldots, x_{2p})$ as another, and so on.) Or we can think of the x_{ik} data alone as defining n points in a p-dimensional "design" space. We have at our disposal generalized draftsman's views, symbolic plots, casement displays, and the like.

When thinking about the separate terms in the regression model, it is tempting to look at the scatter plots of y_i against the separate x_{ik}, and to interpret them as in the simple-regression situation of Section 7.3. These plots can be useful, but they must be viewed with caution, for they can also be misleading. One of the dangers is highlighted by the following simple example with three variables and three points:

i	y_i	x_{i1}	x_{i2}
1	1	0	1
2	−1	1	−2
3	−1	2	−3

Figure 7.9 shows the three scatter plots of the variables. Since y_i equals x_{i1} plus x_{i2} exactly, the multiple regression coefficient of y_i on x_{i1} is 1, but if we look at the plot of y_i against x_{i1} alone, we see a negative slope. The reason is that x_{i1} and x_{i2} are highly negatively correlated. The regression coefficients of x_{i1} in the simple and multiple regressions have different meanings, and can have substantially different values!

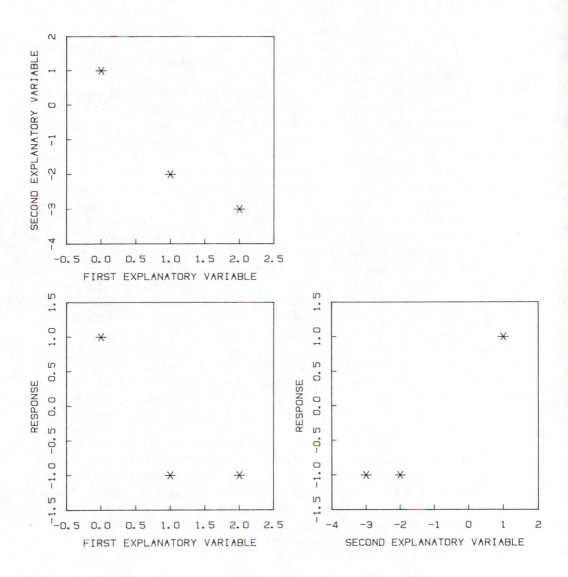

Figure 7.9 All pairwise scatter plots of points in 3-dimensional space illustrating a seeming negative relationship between the response and the first explanatory variable even though the true relationship is positive when the second explanatory variable is also considered.

Even when x_{ik} does not have a strong correlation with other explanatory variables, the true dependence of y_i on x_{ik} in the joint relationship of y_i and all the x_{ij} can be difficult to perceive in a plot of y_i against x_{ik} because a large amount of scatter can mask the functional or descriptive link between these variables. This is illustrated by the abrasion loss data. Figure 7.10 shows a draftsman's display of all pairs of variables in the abrasion loss example. We have labeled points by plotting with letters. The scatter plots of abrasion loss, y_i, against hardness, x_{i1}, and against tensile strength, x_{i2}, include smooth curves computed by robust locally weighted regression (Section 4.6). Such curves will be added to many of the plots in this chapter. The plot of abrasion loss, y_i, against tensile strength, x_{i2}, gives the impression that abrasion loss does not depend on tensile strength. However, as we will see in the next section, there is a strong relationship between abrasion loss and tensile strength when hardness is taken into account. The problem with the scatter plot of abrasion loss against tensile strength is that in going from one point to another the value of hardness is changing as well, so we cannot perceive the effect that tensile strength would have on abrasion loss if the linear effect of hardness were removed (or, crudely, "if hardness were held constant").

If there are enough data points available, one important improvement to the scatter plot of y_i against an individual x_{ik} is to plot subsets of the data for which other relevant variables are held constant or nearly constant, as we did in Chapter 5 when making casement and multiwindow displays. This will be illustrated in due course with the splicing data.

Although scatter plots of y_i against separate x_{ik} should be viewed with caution, scatter plots of the explanatory variables against each other are generally somewhat safer and capable of providing valuable insight into the design configuration. Of course, three or more of the explanatory variables may be involved in the kinds of relationships that we just described, but that is less serious here because we are not regarding one of the explanatory variables as a response variable to be "explained" in terms of the others. Our main interest is to see how the points spread out in the design space and to identify high-leverage points that lie at the periphery of the cloud of x_{ik} points, especially if they are separated by some distance from the rest. (Looking at two x_{ik} variables at a time may not be enough, but it is a good start.) In the abrasion loss example, the plot of hardness against tensile strength in Figure 7.10 characterizes the whole design configuration, since there are only two explanatory variables. It shows that the points are quite evenly deployed across a rectangular region and that there is no strong clustering or correlation. Note that we did not add a smooth curve to this plot, since we do not contemplate any link between the two explanatory variables.

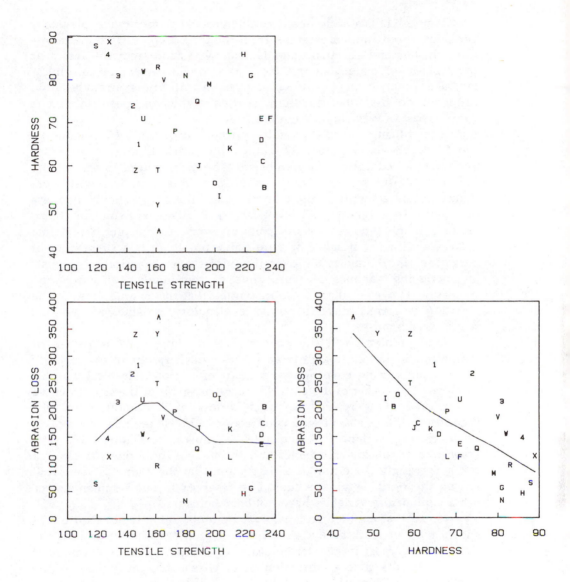

Figure 7.10 All pairwise scatter plots of the abrasion loss data, with point identifiers. The plots involving abrasion loss include robust smooth curves. The top panel shows the design configuration.

Figure 7.11 is a design-configuration scatter plot of two explanatory variables, speed and temperature, from the tar example. Here the points form clusters and one point stands somewhat apart from the rest near the right-hand margin of the plot. We should remember this high-leverage point in the ensuing analysis for it can exert substantial influence on the fitted equation, particularly when speed-squared is considered as a variable in the regression.

The splicing example provides further illustration of a number of the ideas above. Figure 7.12 shows the work time (the response variable) plotted against the number of wire pairs spliced in each of the 842 jobs of the survey. Before looking at this plot, it might seem plausible that a simple straight line through the origin should fit these data well, since, ignoring all other factors, it might take someone twice as long to splice twice as many pairs of wires. In the plot, work time increases with the number of wire pairs, but there is a suggestion of curvature. Furthermore, the overall wedge-shaped appearance suggests an increasing variance of work time as the number of wire pairs increases. However, there is no guarantee that this simple view of the situation is correct since the other explanatory variables are not yet being considered.

One problem with the scatter plot in Figure 7.12 is that both variables are skewed toward large values, which results in the majority of the points being concentrated into an uninterpretable black blob in the lower left corner of the plot. Even the behavior of the smooth curve is obscured. One remedy for such a loss of resolution is to take logarithms; this is also often a good way to address the related problem of increasing variance. A log plot is shown in Figure 7.13. The resolution is considerably better and the variability is more stable, but not surprisingly there now is a suggestion that the scatter is somewhat *less* on the right. Again we should be reserved in our judgments since other explanatory variables have not been considered.

Recall that another explanatory variable is cable type. Figure 7.14 shows plots of work time against number of wire pairs for each of the three cable types; in the terminology of Chapter 5, it is a casement display of work time against number of wire pairs, partitioned by the qualitative variable cable type. Figure 7.15 shows the same plot on the log scale. For the tagged and color types the smooth curves on Figure 7.15 suggest two straight lines with a break around 1.75 log number of pairs. Such a break might also be occurring for the random type, but there is no data in the left-hand region to judge this. What we are doing, in effect, is studying the dependence of work time on number of wire pairs with cable type held fixed. Clearly, the type of cable is a relevant variable. If we restrict ourselves to log number of wire pairs

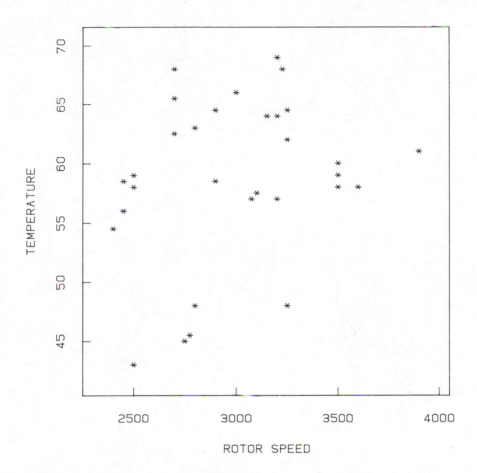

Figure 7.11 The design configuration scatter plot for the tar example.

greater than 1.75, we see a larger slope for the color cable than for the other two types, indicating that color cable is spliced less efficiently than the other two types.

Our initial graphical exploring of these data leads us strongly in the direction of modeling the data on the log scale, using cable type as an explanatory variable, and, for each cable type, relating log work hours to log number of wire pairs, possibly in a nonlinear way.

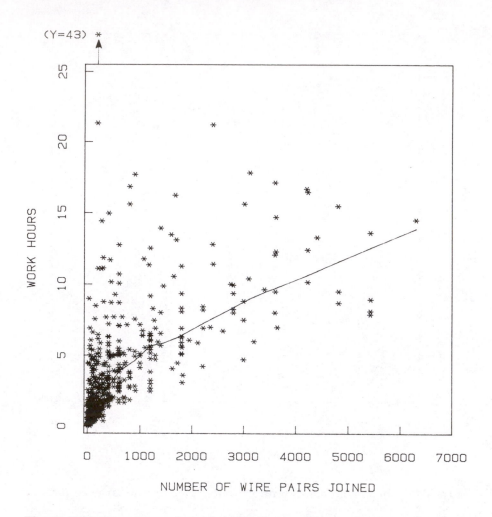

Figure 7.12 A scatter plot of work hours (the response) against the number of wire pairs joined. 842 points plotted. A robust smooth curve is plotted.

7.5 PLOTS DURING REGRESSION FITTING

This section focuses on diagnostic plots for use while the regression analysis is under way. The general strategy is to develop and fit the model in stages, making plots after each intermediate stage and letting the plots affect choices and decisions. We discuss graphics aimed at two specific objectives. The first is to study how well the individual coefficients β_k in a given regression model can be estimated with a

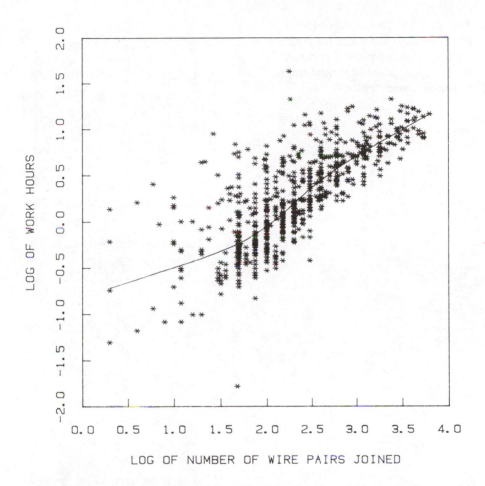

Figure 7.13 A scatter plot of the logarithms of work hours versus the logarithms of the number of wire pairs joined. A robust smooth curve is plotted.

given set of data. The second, for situations in which a number of potential explanatory variables are available, is to guide the choice of a reasonably small and effective subset of the variables for inclusion in the model.

To develop graphics for these objectives, it is helpful to consider an alternative interpretation of the meaning of regression. As we have seen in Section 7.2 the response can be written as

Figure 7.14 The scatter plot of splicing data from Figure 7.12 split into three plots according to the type of cable ("random", "tagged", and "color").

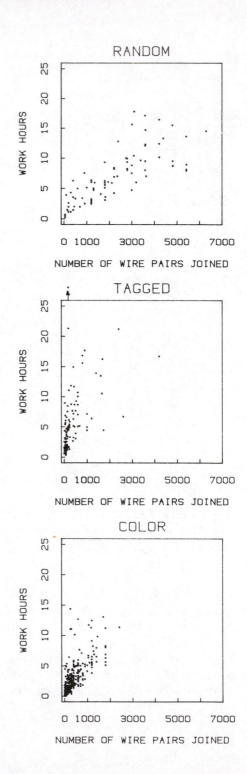

Figure 7.15 The log-log scatter plot of Figure 7.13 partitioned into a casement display according to cable type. This is also Figure 7.14 plotted on log scales. Robust smooth curves are plotted.

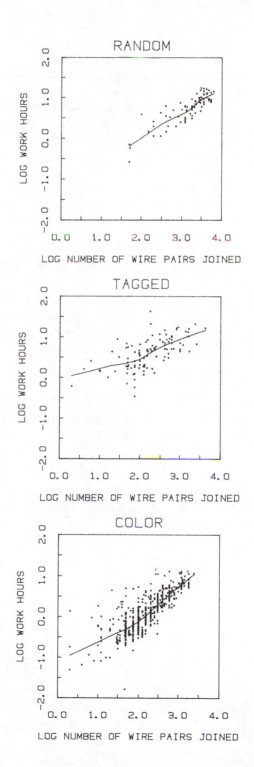

$$y_i = \hat{y}_i + \hat{\epsilon}_i, \quad i = 1 \text{ to } n$$

where $\hat{y}_i$ are the fitted values and $\hat{\epsilon}_i$ are the residuals. The model separates the observed y_i into the sum of two parts: the fitted values which are the part of y_i that is "related to", or "explained by", the x_{ik}, and the residuals which are the part of y_i that is not explained by the x_{ik}. The residuals can be regarded as quantities in the same units as y_i but with the influence or effect of the x_{ik} removed, and regression can be viewed as a way of "adjusting" the y_i values for the influence of the x_{ik} values to yield residuals $\hat{\epsilon}_i$. This interpretation is especially useful when we consider adjustment for (that is, regression on) several different subsets of explanatory variables.

ADJUSTED VARIABLE PLOTS

We have shown that a simple scatter plot of y_i against x_{ik} can be completely misleading when used to provide visual information about the estimation of β_k. A better alternative is based on the p pairs of *adjusted variables* defined as follows. For each k from 1 to p,

- adjust y_i for the effects of all explanatory variables except the kth, x_{ik}, producing a new *adjusted response variable*, y_{ik}^*

- adjust the kth explanatory variable, x_{ik}, for the effects of all the other explanatory variables (treating it as if it were a response variable), to produce an *adjusted explanatory variable*, x_{ik}^*.

In each case the adjustment is done by calculating a least-squares regression and taking the residuals as the adjusted variable. In symbols, we can write

$$y_i = \sum_{\substack{j=0 \\ j \neq k}}^{p} \hat{\alpha}_j x_{ij} + y_{ik}^*$$

and

$$x_{ik} = \sum_{\substack{j=0 \\ j \neq k}}^{p} \hat{\gamma}_j x_{ij} + x_{ik}^*$$

We then make a scatter plot of the adjusted variables y_{ik}^* against x_{ik}^*. (Adjusted variable plots were suggested by Gnanadesikan and are described by Larsen and McCleary (1969), who refer to them as G-partial residual plots.)

If there are p explanatory variables in the problem, there will be p adjusted variable plots to make and to study. The construction of each one formally requires two separate multiple regressions on $p - 1$ variables. Figures 7.16 and 7.17 are the two adjusted variable plots for the abrasion loss example. The first plot shows adjusted abrasion loss against adjusted tensile strength, where adjustment is for hardness, and the second shows abrasion loss against hardness adjusted for tensile strength. Both display more interesting structure than their counterparts in Figure 7.10. We will discuss these plots shortly.

The adjusted variable plot is, in effect, a plot of y_i against x_{ik}, but with the influences of the other explanatory variables accounted for or "removed" in a manner that permits us to interpret the plot in many of the ways that are appropriate in the simple-regression situation. The justification derives from the following remarkable fact. If the regressions to produce the adjusted variables are done with least squares, and if we then use least squares to fit a straight line to the points in the scatter plot of y_{ik}^* against x_{ik}^* leading to the fitted equation

$$y_{ik}^* = \hat{\alpha} x_{ik}^* + \hat{\epsilon}_i^* ,$$
(7.4)

then the simple regression coefficient $\hat{\alpha}$ of y_{ik}^* on x_{ik}^* is identical to the coefficient $\hat{\beta}_k$ of x_{ik} from the full multiple regression of y_i on all of the x_{ik}. Furthermore, the residuals $\hat{\epsilon}_i^*$ from the simple regression are identical to the residuals $\hat{\epsilon}_i$ from the full multiple regression. In symbols,

$$\left. \begin{array}{l} \hat{\alpha} = \hat{\beta}_k \\ \\ \hat{\epsilon}_i^* = \hat{\epsilon}_i, \quad \text{for } i = 1 \text{ to } n . \end{array} \right\}$$
(7.5)

A proof of this assertion, which requires a few lines of algebra, is included as an exercise. (Note that (7.4) is written without a constant term. If a constant term is included in both the full regression and the adjustment regressions, then a fitted constant term in (7.4) would be exactly zero.)

The consequences of (7.5) are several. First, if the points in the adjusted variable plot cluster around a line, we have a visual portrayal of a coefficient from the multiple regression, since the slope of the line is $\hat{\beta}_k$. (Recall that a plot of y_i against x_{ik} can have the wrong slope.)

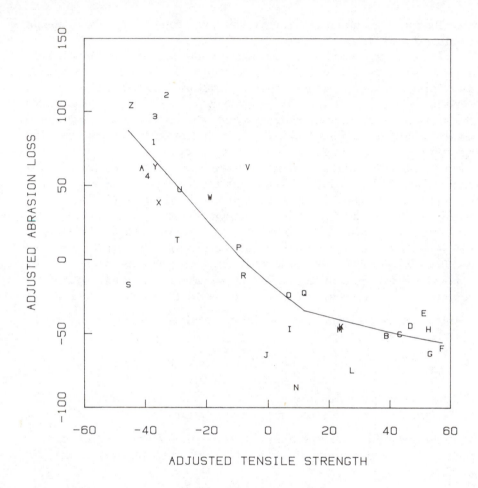

Figure 7.16 Adjusted variable plot of abrasion loss versus tensile strength, both variables adjusted for hardness, with a robust smooth curve.

Second, since the residuals from the simple regression (7.4) and the full regression (7.3) are identical, the adjusted variable plot gives a combined graphical presentation of two important components: the residuals and the fitted systematic effect of y_i on x_{ik}, isolated from the fitted effects of the other explanatory variables. This often allows us to judge whether the influence of x_{ik} on the response has practical significance relative to the residual (unexplained) random fluctuations in y_i over the range of the data, and might help us decide whether the term could reasonably be dropped from the regression model.

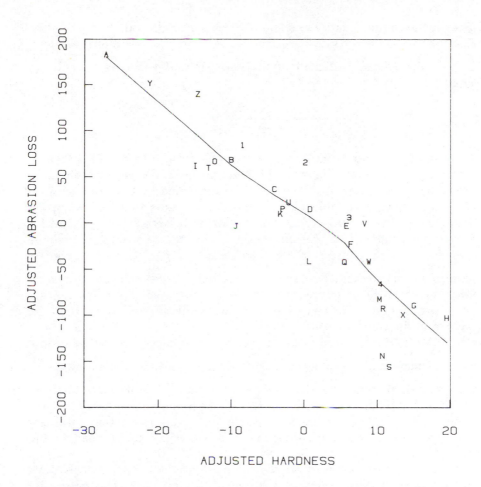

Figure 7.17 Adjusted variable plot of abrasion loss versus hardness, both variables adjusted for tensile strength, with a robust smooth curve.

A slightly different interpretation of this last idea is that the adjusted variable plot conveys information regarding the quality of the estimate $\hat{\beta}_k$. Standard least squares theory tells us that the t-value for $\hat{\beta}_k$ (that is, $\hat{\beta}_k$ divided by its standard error) is

$$t = \hat{\beta}_k \left(\frac{\sum_{i=1}^{n} \hat{\epsilon}_i^2}{(n-p-1) \sum_{i=1}^{n} x_{ik}^{*2}} \right)^{-\frac{1}{2}}$$

(See, for example, Draper and Smith, 1966.) A high value of $|t|$ means that the relative error in the estimate $\hat{\beta}_k$ is small. Now suppose we let r be the correlation coefficient of the two adjusted variables x_{ik}^* and y_{ik}^*. Then

$$t^2 = \frac{1}{n-p-1} \frac{r^2}{1-r^2}.$$

Thus as $|r|$ increases from 0 to 1, t increases from 0 to ∞. This tells us something important: the more highly correlated the two variables on the adjusted variable plot, the better β_k is estimated by the regression.

The adjusted variable plot also provides a good tool for seeing the distorting influence of outliers (i.e., points with large $|\hat{\epsilon}_i|$) on $\hat{\beta}_k$ and for detecting points in the design configuration that exert high leverage specifically with respect to the estimation of β_k. High leverage is potentially occurring when some x_{ik}^* are very large or small compared with the majority of points. On the adjusted variable plot we can see both the leverage and whether such an extreme point fits into the pattern of the other points.

Finally, the adjusted variable plot has relevance to model selection. The calculation of y_{ik}^* does not involve x_{ik} at all, so if the model is misspecified and the true dependence of y_i on x_{ik} is not linear, then y_{ik}^* will not have been distorted by fitting the wrong model. There is a good chance that the adjusted variable plot will reveal the nonlinear dependence and suggest a different function of x_{ik} to be used in the model.

With these ideas in mind, we can study the adjusted variable plots for the abrasion loss example in Figures 7.16 and 7.17. The latter plot shows that the regression coefficient for hardness is negative, and that it is well-estimated, since the points stay close to a line. The adjusted tensile strength plot, however, shows a number of unanticipated features. To begin with, in contrast to the lower left panel of Figure 7.10, there is now a clear relationship between abrasion loss and tensile strength. But the relationship is not linear; its shape could be approximated by two connected straight line segments (a "hockey stick" function). Also, the outlying point in the lower left of the plot (labeled S) will lead to a substantial distortion of the fit. We can gain some further insight into these difficulties by returning to the design configuration plot of the upper panel of Figure 7.10. Since point S has the smallest tensile strength value, we might think that it fails to conform to the general pattern simply by falling in a corner of the design configuration where the model breaks down, but we would have to reject that explanation because some fairly close neighbors do conform. We are not the experimenters and the experiment has long since ceased to be of any concern, save for pedagogical interest, so we cannot go back to verify this data point, and the outlier must forever remain a mystery.

The nonlinear effect is less mysterious. The seven points in Figure 7.16 with the largest values of adjusted tensile strength also have the largest unadjusted tensile strengths. In fact, the design configuration plot of the upper panel of Figure 7.10 shows a separation between these seven points and the others. The plots suggest that there is a limit to the influence of tensile strength; increasing tensile strength beyond the limit has little further effect on abrasion loss.

The foregoing plots and discussion lead us to two actions: to remove the deviant point, and to fit a new form of the model with three explanatory variables,

$$y_i = \beta_0 + \beta_1 x_{i1} + \beta_3 x_{i3} + \beta_4 x_{i4} + \epsilon_i, \quad i = 1 \text{ to } 30, (i \neq 19)$$

where

$$x_{i1} = \text{hardness (as before)}$$
$$x_{i3} = \min(0, x_{i2} - 196)$$
$$x_{i4} = \max(0, x_{i2} - 196)$$

piece wise linear

In this new model, the combined tensile strength term $\beta_3 x_{i3} + \beta_4 x_{i4}$ consists of two line segments with different slopes anchored together at $x_{i2} = 196$ on the tensile strength scale (196 was chosen by judgment). The new model fits the data far better than the original one; R^2 increases from .84 to .91 and the standard deviation of the residuals decreases from 36 to 28. This is a significant improvement for the price of including one more regression parameter in the model and deleting one point. The adjusted variable plots have led us directly to discover the nonlinearity and to improve the model. Of course, this one small set of data cannot conclusively establish the existence of a tensile strength limit; such data analysis should stimulate further experimentation.

Figure 7.18 is the adjusted variable plot for tar content against speed-squared in the regression of tar content on temperature, speed, and speed-squared. (We have not portrayed a smoothed value for the point on the extreme right since it does not have "neighbors" to locally estimate a smooth value in that region of the plot.) A mild dependence on speed-squared is suggested by the plot. The point identified in Figure 7.11 as having possibly high leverage in the design space is the one on the extreme right in Figure 7.18 and is plotted as "O". The fitting of the speed-squared regression depends heavily on this single point; the estimate of the regression coefficient for speed-squared with

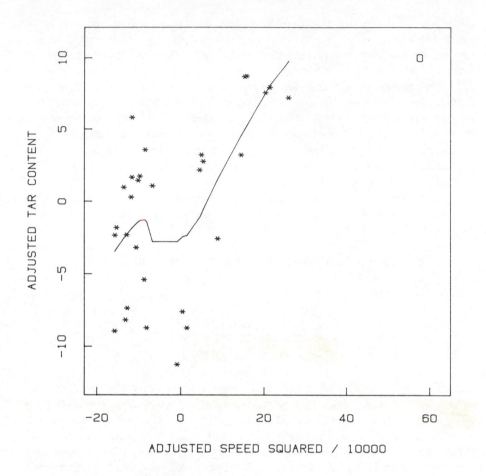

Figure 7.18 Adjusted variable plot of tar content versus speed-squared with (linear) adjustment for temperature and speed. A robust smooth curve is plotted. The point with the largest value of speed is plotted with an "O".

the leverage point included is 2.26×10^{-5} with standard error $.56 \times 10^{-5}$, while the estimate without this point is 2.83×10^{-5} with standard error $.82 \times 10^{-5}$. The reduction in standard error is a typical result of including a high leverage point. It may seem unwise to allow ourselves the luxury of a much lowered estimate of the standard error from a highly influential point in the design configuration at which the fit of the equation is in doubt.

A variation of the adjusted variable plot is obtained by taking a linear combination of some subset of the explanatory variables as a single explanatory variable to be adjusted for all explanatory variables not in the subset. For instance, we might combine all explanatory variables derived from one initial variable. (This is particularly useful when indicator or dummy variables have been used to represent the levels of some factor.) Consider, for example, the new representation for tensile strength in the modified abrasion loss model. If we want to ask whether we have indeed removed the nonlinearity detected earlier, we can treat

$$x_5 = \hat{\beta}_3 x_{i3} + \hat{\beta}_4 x_{i4}$$

as a single explanatory variable for tensile strength, with hardness as the other explanatory variable. The adjusted variable plot for this combined tensile strength variable is shown in Figure 7.19. (Point S is still set aside.) Tensile strength accounts for much of the variation in abrasion loss beyond that explained by hardness. We note again that this is the opposite of the impression given by Figure 7.10. There is a hint of nonlinearity remaining in Figure 7.19, but we will stop here since we have already extracted the main message in the data. The exact nature of the leveling off cannot be studied adequately with this small set of data.

It is important in using the adjusted variable plot to appreciate some of the things it will not do. If the model is misspecified in terms of two or more explanatory variables, each adjusted variable plot will make the wrong adjustment with regard to at least one variable, and the resulting systematic structure in y_{ik}^* may obscure the curved dependence that we might hope the plot will reveal, especially if the misspecified variables are correlated in the design space. If there is any misspecification involving two or more explanatory variables in a nonadditive way (for instance, if y_i really has a linear dependence on x_{i1}/x_{i2}), the plot can fail to diagnose it. Finally, any curvature in the plot of y_{ik}^* against x_{ik}^* shows a nonlinear dependence not on x_{ik} itself, but on x_{ik}^* which is x_{ik} adjusted by subtracting a linear combination of the other explanatory variables. This should be kept firmly in mind in altering the model to account for the nonlinearity.

*ADAPTATION TO ROBUST REGRESSION

Adjusted variable plots as presented above are based on least-squares estimation of the regressions. There is an easy way to extend the idea to one fairly large class of robust estimation procedures, the class of iteratively reweighted least-squares estimates (Andrews, 1974).

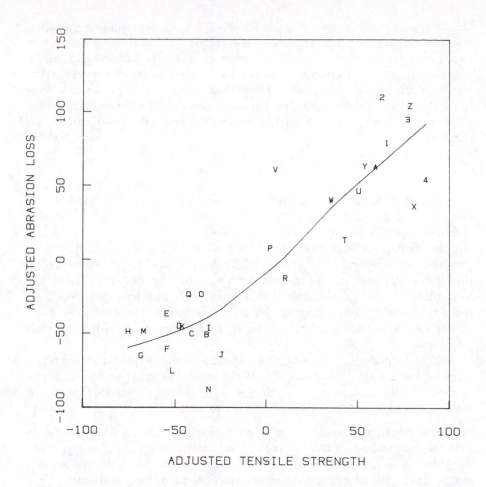

Figure 7.19 Adjusted variable plot of abrasion loss versus the revised tensile strength variable, that is, a piecewise linear function of raw tensile strength. Point *S* is not included. A robust smooth curve is plotted.

In an iterative reweighting scheme, the full regression is fitted several times using weighted least-squares. The weights at each iteration are taken as functions of the residuals from the previous stage (and possibly as functions of the x_{ik} values as well, if leverage is a concern), so that when points emerge as outliers they are down-weighted in subsequent stages. The final fit is formally expressed as a weighted least-squares regression, although the weights depend on the data.

If we have computed a robust regression in this manner using a regression program that is cooperative enough to return the final weights, we can compute adjusted variables as before, but using weighted least-squares in place of ordinary least-squares, taking the weights from the robust regression and treating them as if they were fixed. The connections between regression coefficients and residuals in the full and adjusted-variable regressions (7.5) remain the same. When viewing plots of these adjusted variables, we should bear the weights in mind; an outlier with a small weight has already had its influence reduced by the robust regression.

*THE C_p PLOT FOR MODEL SELECTION

In multiple regression applications we often have a large number of potential explanatory variables available, and are faced with the problem of choosing a reasonably small and effective subset of them to include in the regression equation. Mallows (1973) suggested a graphical method for judging the various possible regression equations in terms of total squared error at the n data points.

In considering a particular regression equation that contains p explanatory variables out of a possibly larger collection of K variables, we can write the expected total squared error of $\hat{y}_i$ at the n data points as the sum of two components, the total of the variances of $\hat{y}_i$ (the "variances of prediction") at the n points, plus the total of the squared biases at the n points due to leaving out x_{ik} variables that have systematic influence on y_i. As the regression equation is enlarged to include more explanatory variables (p increases), the total squared error of the fitted equation may improve (decrease) because more of the systematic variation in y_i is explained (the squared bias decreases), but the total variance of prediction increases by σ^2 for each new explanatory variable. Choosing a good regression equation (a subset of explanatory variables) usually means trading off a decrease in squared bias with an increase in the variance of prediction. It can also mean accepting some bias in order to obtain a simpler model, that is, one with fewer terms.

To help make these trade offs, Mallows defines a statistic, C_p, for each possible regression equation as

$$C_p = \frac{RSS_p}{s^2} - (n-2p)$$

where RSS_p is the residual sum of squares ($RSS_p = \sum_{i=1}^{n}(y_i - \hat{y}_i)^2$) for the regression equation and p is the number of explanatory variables in it. The quantity C_p is standardized by s^2, the usual estimate of σ^2 from the full regression containing all K variables, which is assumed to be unbiased. As a result, the average contribution to C_p from variance is 1 for each explanatory variable, and any regression equation that is unbiased will have an average C_p value of approximately p.

Mallows plots C_p against p for all possible regression equations (usually with identifiers, and usually leaving off-scale all points with $C_p > 2p$). For instance, Figure 7.20 shows the C_p plot for a small fictitious example with three explanatory variables a, b and c. For each point plotted, the vertical distance from the line up to the point estimates the total squared bias of the corresponding regression, and the distance from the line to the x axis estimates the total variance of prediction.

The best 2-variable equation is ab, the one containing x_{ia} and x_{ib}, which is essentially unbiased. (The full regression, abc in this case, always has $C_p = p$.) It is interesting to note that the regression bc has some bias, but in terms of total squared error of prediction it is better than the full regression.

We note that the C_p values of interest can be calculated more efficiently than simply by carrying out all 2^p possible regressions (see Furnival and Wilson, 1974). Also, Daniel and Wood (1971 or 1980) give a concise derivation of C_p and some illuminating examples.

7.6   PLOTS AFTER THE MODEL IS FITTED

Once a particular model has been fitted, it is essential to study the quality of the fit to determine how well the fitted model explains the observed variation in y_i. Traditionally, this is done with single-number summaries such as the multiple R^2 statistic or the standard deviation of the residuals. These two quantities measure, respectively, the fraction of variance of y accounted for by the model and the magnitude of unexplained variation. Neither is a satisfactory general purpose tool, since one or two numbers alone cannot characterize an entire distribution and be sensitive to all possible defects in the model's functional form. Well-chosen graphical displays, because of their ability to reveal the unexpected, are often far more powerful for diagnostic purposes.

The plots in this section all involve the residuals, $\hat{\epsilon}_i$. There are two main reasons for their fundamental diagnostic role. First, if the functional part of the model is misspecified and there is systematic lack of fit, this is embodied in the residuals. Second, if the dependence of y_i on the x_{ik} is correctly specified, the residuals $\hat{\epsilon}_i$ approximate the actual errors ϵ_i and can be used to check the probabilistic assumptions made about ϵ_i.

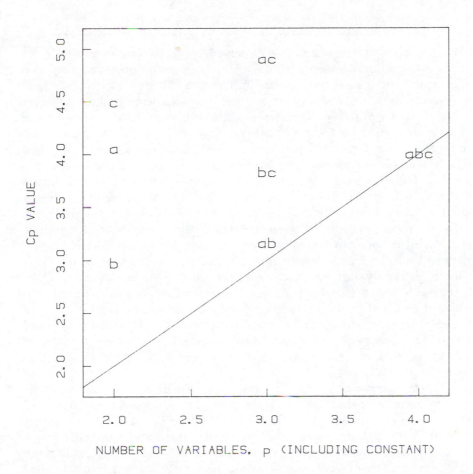

Figure 7.20 C_p plot for a regression example involving three explanatory variables, labeled a, b and c, and a constant term that enters all regressions (and is counted in p). Data are artificial.

Part of the strategy of regression modelling is to improve the model until the residuals look "structureless", or like a simple random sample. They should only contain structure that is already taken into account (such as nonconstant variance) or imposed by the fitting process itself. By plotting them against a variety of original and derived variables, we can look for systematic patterns that relate to the model's adequacy. Although we talk about graphics for use after the model is fit, if problems with the fit are discovered at this stage of the analysis, we should take corrective action and refit the equation or a modified form of it.

THE RESPONSE AGAINST THE FITTED RESPONSE

A graphical alternative — or supplement — to the multiple R^2 statistic is the scatter plot y_i against $\hat{y}_i$, which is the observed response against the fitted response. Figure 7.21 shows this plot for two versions of the tar model, one with and one without speed-squared included as an explanatory variable. For least-squares regression, the square of the simple correlation coefficient r^2 between y_i and $\hat{y}_i$ is exactly equal to the multiple R^2 for the full regression, so this plot gives a visual portrayal of the multiple R^2 statistic. An advantage of this type of plot is that the vertical deviations from the line $y = x$ shown in the plot are the actual residuals $\hat{\epsilon}_i$ from the full fit, so we can judge their magnitude relative to the systematic part of the fit (the line $y = x$). We can focus on outlying or high-leverage points, or we might see unequal variability suggesting that the fit is better or worse over certain ranges. A suspiciously curved pattern could lead us to try fitting some transformed version of y_i. (This plot is generally not good for detecting curved dependence of y_i on some x_{ik}; adjusted variable plots are better for that purpose.) In the two plots of Figure 7.21 the high-leverage point (having the largest value of speed) has been indicated by plotting with "O". This point is fitted better by the curved regression, but the overall improvement of the fit due to the curved term appears small, since the vertical scatter of points is not appreciably reduced.

It is important to note that the quadratic fit is only one possible way to describe the gentle curvature here. Equally good descriptions of the data over this range of values would be obtained by fitting, for instance, be^{cx} or bx^c instead. In particular, the fitted quadratic has a minimum value at some point outside the range of the data. As Bennett and Franklin (1954) point out, it would be a serious error to extrapolate the fitted function very far beyond the range of the data, or to give any credence to the minimum point on the quadratic curve.

RESIDUALS AND ABSOLUTE RESIDUALS AGAINST FITTED VALUES

Since the observed y_i is equal to the fitted y_i plus the residual $\hat{\epsilon}_i$, the plot of y_i against $\hat{y}_i$ that we have just seen is a plot of the residuals against fitted values with the line $y = x$ added in. The vertical axis of the plot can easily be dominated by the range of the systematic part, $\hat{y}_i$, so to look beyond $\hat{y}_i$ for discrepancies between the model and the data, it is often better to subtract out the line and display the residuals directly, plotting $\hat{\epsilon}_i$ against the fitted values $\hat{y}_i$. Figure 7.22 shows this plot for the tar model with speed-squared included. The plot looks

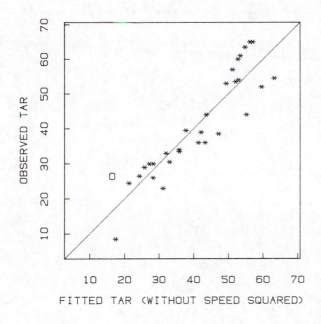

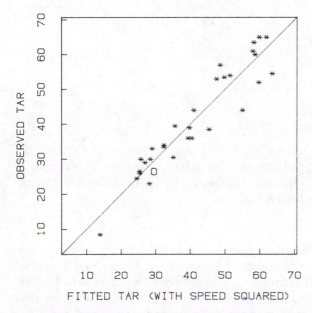

Figure 7.21 Scatter plots of observed tar versus fitted tar, from regression models without and with the speed-squared term. The point with the largest value of speed is plotted with an "O". The plotted line is $x = y$.

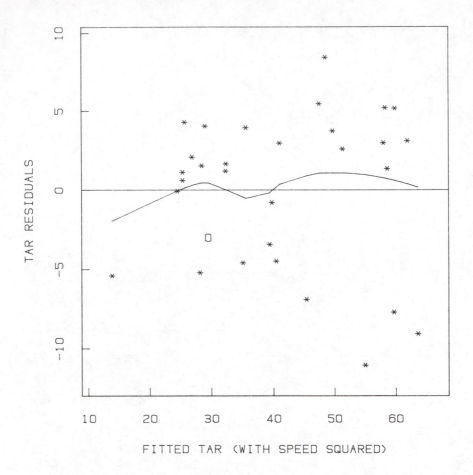

Figure 7.22 Tar content residuals plotted against fitted tar from the regression model with speed-squared included. The line $y = 0$ and a robust smooth curve are plotted. The point with the largest value of speed squared is plotted with an "O".

acceptable. A curved pattern in a plot like this might suggest replacing the observed y_i by some (nonlinear) function of y_i, say log y_i or y_i raised to some power, and refitting the model with the same set of x_{ik} as explanatory variables. With least squares, a single outlier will usually cause the plot of $\hat{\epsilon}_i$ against $\hat{y}_i$ to have a linear appearance balanced by one wild point, as in the bottom panel of Figure 7.6, since the correlation coefficient of the data in the plot must be exactly zero.

Figure 7.22 does suggest a mild increase in variance (that is, in the vertical scatter or spread of the points) from left to right. To

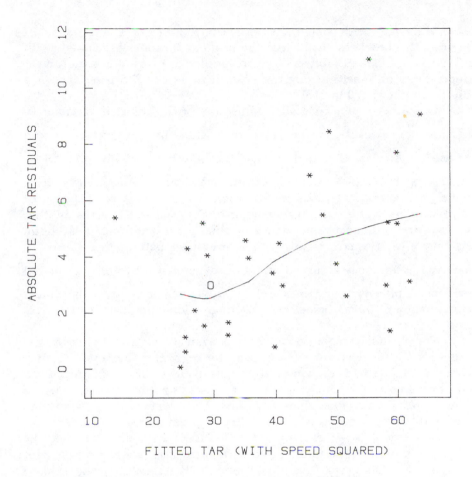

Figure 7.23 Absolute values of tar residuals plotted against fitted tar from the regression model with the speed-squared term. A robust smooth curve is plotted and the point with the largest value of speed squared is plotted with an "O".

concentrate on this feature of the data, it is better to plot the absolute residuals $|\hat{\epsilon}_i|$ and include a smooth curve, as in Figure 7.23. The increase in variance seems quite small.

RESIDUALS AGAINST VARIOUS VARIABLES

We can plot residuals against any of the explanatory variables ($\hat{\epsilon}_i$ against x_{ik}) and look for systematic patterns that may suggest replacing

x_{ik} in the model with some (nonlinear) function of x_{ik}. The top panel of Figure 7.24 shows residuals from the original abrasion-loss model (with all 30 data points) plotted against tensile strength. The nonlinear dependence on tensile strength discussed in Section 7.5 is evident as a dip in the range 170 to 210.

We can also plot residuals against any of the adjusted variables ($\hat{\epsilon}_i$ against x_{ik}^*). Because of the close connection between residuals and adjusted variables, this plot is like the adjusted variable plot of y_{ik}^* against x_{ik}^*, but with a fitted regression line subtracted out. The bottom panel of Figure 7.24 shows the abrasion loss residuals plotted against adjusted tensile strength. (Compare it to Figure 7.16.) It gives another view of the nonlinear dependence of abrasion loss on tensile strength. As with the adjusted variable plot, a nonlinear pattern in a plot of $\hat{\epsilon}_i$ against x_{ik}^* describes a curved response dependence not on one of the original explanatory variables but on x_{ik}^* which is a particular linear combination of them. Sometimes this distinction is important, often it is not.

The residuals can also be plotted against any variable from the same study that has not yet entered the regression model ($\hat{\epsilon}_i$ against some z_i). A trend or systematic pattern may be evidence of an additional term that should be included. An important special case is a plot of residuals against time ($\hat{\epsilon}_i$ against t_i). In many applications the data will have an ordering in time that is preserved in the index i (or can be restored by reordering). For instance, economic data may be taken from consecutive time periods. In such cases, we can simply plot $\hat{\epsilon}_i$ against i. Discovery of a time trend in the residuals may lead to including a new time-related explanatory variable in the model. Another common situation is to have experimental data that were gathered in a series of experimental runs made one after the other. If the plot of $\hat{\epsilon}_i$ against i reveals a time trend or an increase in the variance of the residuals when none was anticipated, the probable cause is a shift or a deterioration of experimental conditions, and corrective action might be required. For example, Figure 7.25 is a plot of $\hat{\epsilon}_i$ against i for the tar regression including the speed-squared term. If we assume that the original order of the data was preserved (although this was not mentioned by Bennett and Franklin), then this figure shows no time-dependency problems.

In all of the residual plots mentioned above, the ideal or "null" configuration — the pattern that indicates an adequate model and well-behaved data — is a horizontal band of points with constant vertical scatter as one looks from left to right. (Unequal *density* of points in different horizontal ranges may interfere with our visual perceptions,

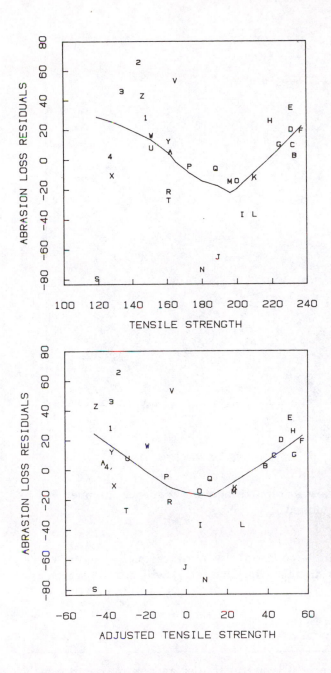

Figure 7.24 Abrasion loss regression residuals plotted first against raw tensile strength, then against tensile strength adjusted for hardness. Robust smooth curves are plotted.

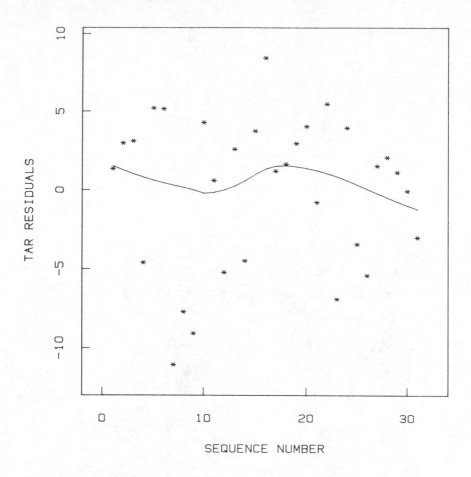

Figure 7.25 Tar residuals $\hat{\epsilon}_i$ plotted against sequence number i. A robust smooth curve is plotted.

but is otherwise of little concern.) In most cases, a smooth curve through the points (as discussed in Chapter 4) will aid the search for systematic patterns.

*ADJUSTED RESIDUALS

In some circumstances it is useful to display not the raw residuals themselves but some modified form of them. For instance, it frequently happens that the response variable used in the regression model is really some transformation of the variable of practical interest, and it may be more informative to explore the fit on the original scale. (If the response is $y_i = \sqrt{z_i}$, then the residuals on the original z scale are $y_i^2 - \hat{y}_i^2$.) We should not look for normality or compute sums-of-squares statistics for these restored residuals, but we may well want to see their pattern of behavior when plotted against other variables, predicted values, etc.

Another possibility is to standardize or weight the residuals to compensate for the fact that, although the true random fluctuations ϵ_i may indeed have constant variance, the least-squares residuals will not. Their variances depend on the values of the explanatory variables. If X is a matrix whose columns are the values of the explanatory variables (including a column of ones for the constant term), then the variance of $\hat{\epsilon}_i$ is σ^2 times $(1-h_i)$, where h_i is the ith diagonal element of the so-called hat matrix, H,

$$ H = X(X'X)^{-1}X' . $$

(A full discussion of H may be found in Belsley, Kuh, and Welsch, 1980.) We can compute weighted residuals $\hat{\epsilon}_i/(1-h_i)^{\frac{1}{2}}$ that have constant variance σ^2 (providing the ϵ_i have constant variance). This compensates for the differences in leverage, since a high-leverage point tends to produce a small residual, simply by virtue of its leverage. In many cases, weighting the residuals in this way produces only very small changes, especially if the design space is well-balanced and no points have excessive leverage. In the tar example weighting changes one residual by 16% and the rest by less than 9%, and the effect on the various residual plots is barely noticeable. The abrasion loss example is similar.

DISTRIBUTION OF THE RESIDUALS

Once we are satisfied that the systematic structure in the data has been extracted by fitting a suitable model, we can proceed to use the residuals (raw, or weighted) as sample-based surrogates for the errors, ϵ_i, and study their distributional pattern to test the assumptions made about the ϵ_i. We can use any of the techniques described in Chapters 2 and 6 to study the distribution of $\hat{\epsilon}_i$. For instance, if we had used a robust fitting procedure appropriate for symmetrically distributed errors, we could check the assumption with a symmetry plot of the residuals. Or, if we have assumed normality and plan to perform significance-level statistical calculations (t-based confidence intervals for the coefficients, F tests in an analysis of variance, etc.), then it may be useful to make a normal quantile-quantile plot of the residuals.

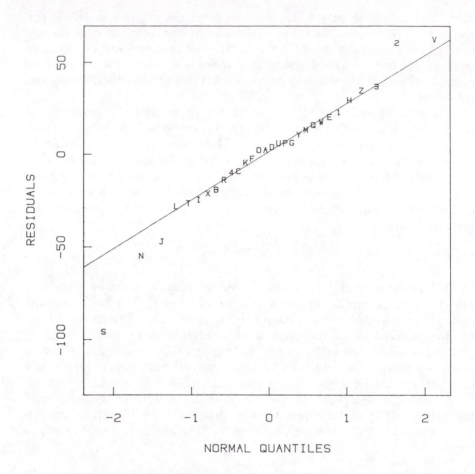

Figure 7.26 Normal quantile-quantile plot of abrasion loss residuals for the new model with all 30 data points. Least squares was used.

Figures 7.26 and 7.27 show two normal quantile-quantile plots of the residuals from the improved abrasion loss regression model. The first includes all 30 data points, and the second is from a fit with the most deviant point (S) removed from the fit. With the outlier present, a distinctly nonnormal pattern occurs in the residuals involving not only the deviant point but several others as well, which is typical of least-squares fits. With the outlier removed, the pattern is satisfactory. Figure 7.28 is a normal quantile-quantile plot of residuals from the same model with all data points included, this time fitted with a robust regression procedure. Unlike Figure 7.26, it conveys a strong suggestion of a single outlier.

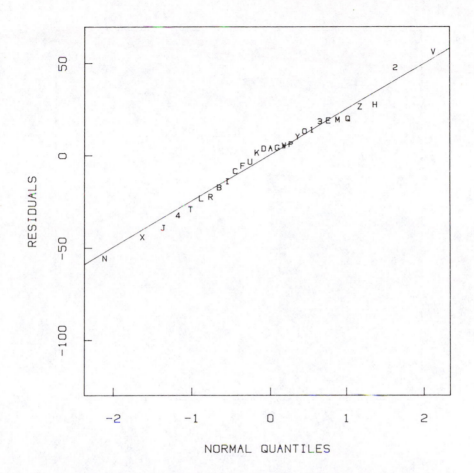

Figure 7.27 Normal quantile-quantile plot of abrasion loss residuals for the new model with point S not included in the fit. Least squares was used.

Anomalies in the pattern of residuals can lead to several courses of action. For one or two deviant points, we will probably go back to the original records or to the experimenter for verification or correction. If they seem correct, we will probably study their position in the design configuration. We may choose to set them aside and accompany our fitted model with a warning that a small fraction of the data do not comply. If the distribution of residuals looks even somewhat more long-tailed than normal, we may abandon least squares in favor of a more robust fit. In any case, whether we take corrective action or accept

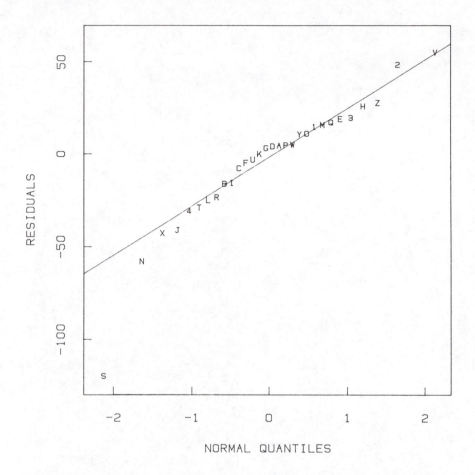

Figure 7.28 Normal quantile-quantile plot of abrasion loss residuals for the full data set. A robust regression was used.

the model despite anomalies, we should avoid making strong probability statements (involving significance levels, etc.) about the results.

7.7 A CASE STUDY

We illustrate the use of several kinds of residual plots with a more extended discussion of the perceptual psychological experiment introduced in Chapter 2 and mentioned in Section 7.1. Fourteen subjects were asked to judge the areas of 9 circles, whose diameters ranged from 2.74 mm to 15.39 mm, relative to a standard circle of diameter 9.3 mm which was said to have an area of 100 units. In a randomized presentation scheme, the subjects viewed a series of charts, each containing many circles including the standard circle and three to be judged. Each subject guessed the area of every test circle a total of 16 times. For each subject the simple linear regression model

$$y_i = \beta_0 + \beta_1 x_i + \epsilon_i \tag{7.6}$$

was fitted, where y_i is the natural logarithm of (*judged area* ÷ 100) and x_i is the natural logarithm of (*actual area* ÷ 100). A subject's values of $\hat{\beta}_0$ and $\hat{\beta}_1$ characterize the perceptual scale that he or she uses to judge circle sizes, while the residuals $\hat{\epsilon}_i$ from the fit characterize the individual's consistency or accuracy with respect to his or her personal perceptual scale. The fitted values $\hat{y}_i$ are fitted log areas; we shall define *fitted area* to be $\exp(\hat{y}_i)$, so that log(*fitted area*) = fitted (*log area*). We note that the systematic part of (7.6) corresponds to the model

$$judged\ area = \alpha(actual\ area)^\beta$$

that was mentioned in Section 2.1, where $\beta_1 = \beta$ and $\beta_0 = \log \alpha$. We have used logarithms to linearize the power-function relationship.

We can choose to study residuals either on the logarithmic scale on which we fitted the model (*log-scale residual* = log(*judged area*) − log(*fitted area*)) or on the original area scale (*residual* = *judged area* − *fitted area*). In this situation, the log scale seems preferable and produces the additional benefit of giving residuals a simple meaning in terms of percent deviations. Suppose that a judged area differs from a fitted area by 100δ% where δ is not too large (say $|\delta| < .4$) then

$$\frac{judged - fitted}{fitted} = \delta$$

and

$$log\text{-}scale\ residual = \log(judged) - \log(fitted)$$

$$= \log\left|\frac{judged}{fitted}\right| = \log(1 + \delta) \approx \delta.$$

(The maximum error of the approximation is about .09 for $|\delta| < .4$. Note that for this purpose *natural* logarithms must be used rather than base-10 logarithms.)

In Figure 7.29 residuals for one subject are plotted against x_i. (Since there is only one explanatory variable, plotting against x_i is equivalent to plotting against $\hat{y}_i = \hat{\beta}_0 + \hat{\beta}_1 x_i$; the only difference is a trivial linear change in the x scale of the plot.) This subject, like most, had a slope less than 1 ($\hat{\beta}_1 = .73$) and an intercept nearly equal to 0. Since there are many repeated values among the x_i and since there was a tendency for subjects to give repeated identical responses as well, a straightforward plot of $\hat{\epsilon}_i$ against x_i would result in considerable superposition of plotted points. To alleviate this problem the x_i were jittered horizontally by adding small random amounts. (See Chapter 4.) The data points are plotted as dots in Figure 7.29. The plot was enhanced by drawing the line $y = 0$ and plotting an asterisk at the midmean (that is, the mean of the values between the quartiles) of the ordinates for each of the nine distinct values of x_i. The asterisks serve as a simple set of smoothed values for this plot with its highly structured x_i.

What does Figure 7.29 reveal about this subject's deviations from his perceptual scale? First, there is no apparent systematic lack of fit since the midmeans show no consistent pattern. All but two of the residuals (relative deviations between judged and fitted) fall between $-.4$ and $+.4$. The two exceptions are both for the next-to-smallest test circle. The tendency for the subject to make identical guesses on repeated trials appears as repeated ordinates; this tendency is clearly more prevalent for the smaller circles than the larger ones.

A normal quantile-quantile plot of the residuals for all subjects combined is shown in Figure 7.30. (We cannot expect the pooled residuals to have a normal distribution, partly because subjects have different variances, but the plot is a useful summary of all the residuals.) The plot includes a horizontal scale at the top showing the cumulative fraction of the collection of observations, and residuals exceeding 1 in absolute value are shown in the margins. We can see, for example, that about 75% of the residuals fall between $-.2$ and $+.2$, which means that 75% of the judged areas were within 20% of the corresponding fitted areas.

Another summary of the residuals for all subjects is shown in Figure 7.31 which displays residuals for each of the nine values of the explanatory variable, circle size. Because of the large number of repeated x_i values, a box plot of the residuals for each circle size was drawn instead of the points themselves. (The five largest residuals have again been plotted schematically in the margins, but because of overplotting, they occur at only three distinct points in the margins.) We observe that the plots are consistent with the specification of the model, for the deviations of the medians from zero are small and show no consistent pattern. However, the spread of the residuals appears to

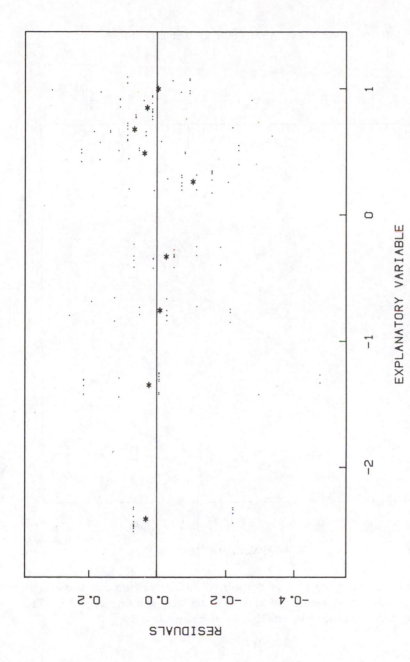

Figure 7.29 One subject's log-scale residuals from the perceptual experiment involving judged circle sizes, plotted (with horizontal jitter) against the explanatory variable, log(*actual area*). The model was fitted robustly to the logs of the raw data. An asterisk shows the midmean for each distinct circle size.

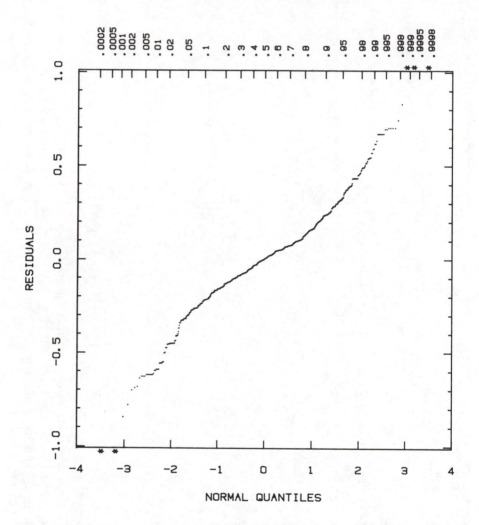

Figure 7.30 Normal Q-Q plot of combined residuals from all subjects in the perceptual experiment. Off-scale points are shown with *'s. The scale at the top is cumulative fraction of the sample.

change somewhat with circle size. The most extreme points seem to be more spread out for the small circles than for the large ones. We could conclude that the sizes of very small objects are not judged with the same relative precision as large objects. This may be due in part to the

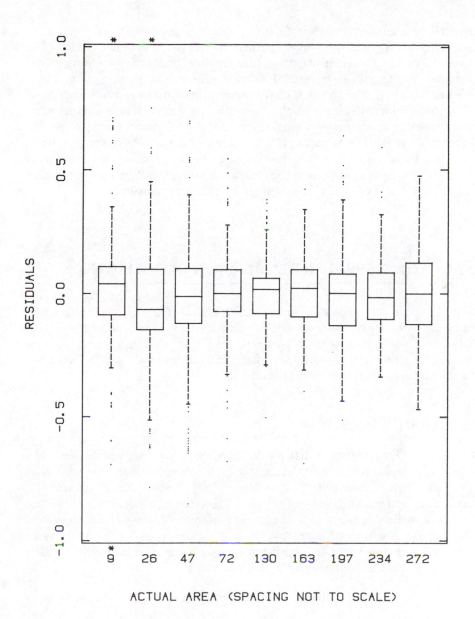

Figure 7.31 The log-scale residuals from all subjects in the perceptual experiment grouped according to the nine values of the actual areas. The horizontal axis shows the order, but not the relative magnitudes, of the actual areas.

natural tendency of subjects to give integer responses; rounding off to an integer represents a larger percent error for a smaller circle. The spread of the residuals as measured by the interquartile range (the vertical length of each box) does not show this pattern but rather reveals another. For the two circles with sizes closest to the standard of 100, there appears to be a slight reduction of the residuals compared to the others; this is not surprising since one would expect more consistent judgments when the sizes are close to the standard. These scale patterns and the large outliers would have caused some problems had we used least squares estimation, so the bisquare robust estimation procedure (Mosteller and Tukey, 1977) was used to fit the regressions.

*7.8   SOME SPECIAL REGRESSION SITUATIONS

This chapter has presented graphical methods for standard regression models with explanatory variables measured on continuous scales (for the most part) and with regression equations that are linear in the unknown parameters. However, many of the methods can be used for other kinds of regression situations.

NONLINEAR MODELS

If the regression equation is nonlinear in the parameters and cannot be made linear by rewriting it in terms of transformed variables and parameters, we can still fit the model, define fitted values and residuals, and make the residual plots described in Section 7.6. If the model equation consists of a nonlinear function of some variables added to a linear function of some others, we can even make limited use of adjusted variable plots by combining variables as mentioned in Section 7.5. For example, suppose the model equation is

$$y_i = \beta_0 + \beta_1 x_{i1} + \beta_4 \exp(\beta_2 x_{i2} + \beta_3 x_{i3}) + \epsilon_i .$$

Then, after an initial fit of the model to obtain values for $\hat{\beta}_2$ and $\hat{\beta}_3$, we can treat $\exp(\hat{\beta}_2 x_{i2} + \hat{\beta}_3 x_{i3})$ as a single explanatory variable and make adjusted variable plots as before. Alternatively, we can work with a "linearized" model. (This goes beyond the scope of this book. See Mosteller and Tukey, 1977.)

AUTOREGRESSIVE TIME SERIES MODELS

Autoregression is a basic tool in the field of time series analysis. With respect to graphics, it can often be treated just like ordinary regression. Suppose z_t, for $t = 1$ to T, is a time series or a set of observations of a random variable recorded at equally spaced points in time. The standard linear autoregressive model of order p is

$$z_t = \beta_0 + \sum_{k=1}^{p} \beta_k z_{t-k} + \delta_t,$$

where δ_t is a random error term. If we take $n = T - p$ and define

$$y_i = z_{i+p}, \qquad \text{for } i = 1 \text{ to } n,$$

$$\epsilon_i = \delta_{i+p}, \qquad \text{for } i = 1 \text{ to } n,$$

and

$$x_{ik} = z_{i+p-k}, \qquad \text{for } k = 1 \text{ to } p, \text{ and } i = 1 \text{ to } n,$$

then the autoregression can be written as an ordinary regression model where the kth "explanatory variable" is a copy of the response variable itself, but lagged by k time units. Thus we can use our collection of graphical tools described in earlier sections to probe the autoregressive model.

Autoregression was first formulated in the classic paper of Yule (1927) in which the yearly sunspot numbers from 1749 to 1924 were fitted by an autoregressive model with $p = 2$. Since then the sunspot data series has itself become classic, for it has been extensively used to illustrate time series methodology. To illustrate graphical methodology we shall continue this tradition, but contrary to tradition the graphics show that the standard linear autoregressive model does *not* fit these data well.

Figure 7.32 is an adjusted variable plot of sunspot number against the lag 2 explanatory variable, with adjustment for the lag 1 variable. It is quite clear that there is a substantial nonlinearity in the plot, so a linear model is inappropriate. Figure 7.33 is a plot of absolute residuals against fitted values. The plot shows that the variance increases with the level of the series so that the assumption of a constant variance for ϵ_i is also inappropriate. We have found that using the square roots of the sunspot numbers instead of the numbers themselves stabilizes the variance but unfortunately does not remove the nonlinearity.

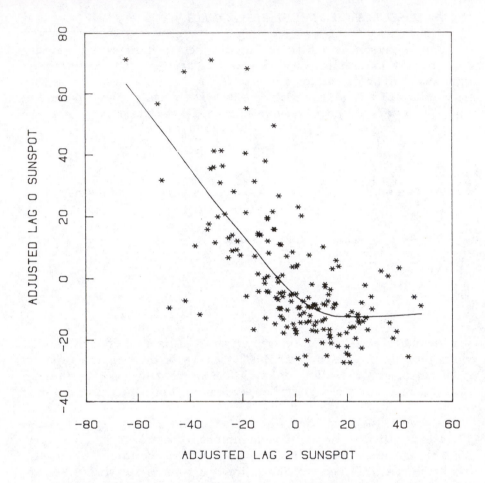

Figure 7.32 Adjusted variable plot of sunspot number versus lag 2 sunspot number, with adjustment for lag 1 sunspot number. A robust smooth curve is plotted.

A standard method for checking the adequacy of a fitted autoregressive model is to search for correlation in the residuals over time. Typically this is done by studying the autocorrelation of the residuals. (See, for example, Box and Jenkins, 1976.) In computing the autocorrelation at lag k we are looking for a linear dependence between $\hat{\epsilon}_i$ and $\hat{\epsilon}_{i-k}$; that is, a dependence between residuals separated by k time units. An important graphical adjunct to this search is to plot $\hat{\epsilon}_i$ against $\hat{\epsilon}_{i-k}$ just as we would plot any two variables whose relationship we wish to understand.

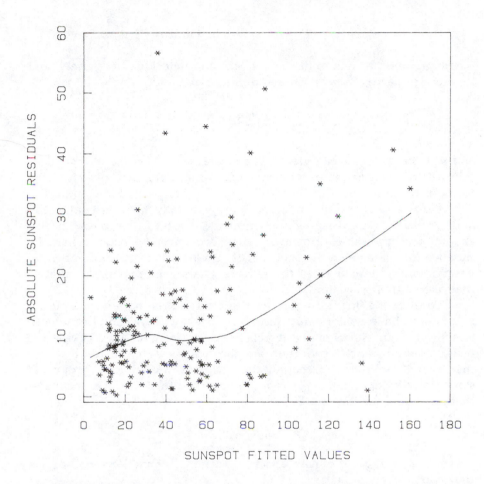

Figure 7.33 Absolute values of sunspot residuals from a second-order autoregressive model plotted against fitted values, with a robust smooth curve.

TWO-WAY AND MULTIWAY TABLES

We can use much of the graphical methodology for linear regression when fitting multiway tables or analyzing data from designed experiments in which the explanatory variables are factors that take only discrete or qualitative values. To be more concrete, consider an example given by Daniel (1976) consisting of a two-way table of total barley yields over a two-year period for 5 varieties of barley at each of 6 locations. The two factors are variety and location. The standard additive model for such a table is

$$y_{ij} = \mu + \alpha_i + \beta_j + \epsilon_{ij}, \quad i = 1 \text{ to } 5 \text{ and } j = 1 \text{ to } 6,$$

where α_i and β_j represent the effects on yield due to variety and location, respectively, with the requirement that

$$\sum_{i=1}^{5} \alpha_i = \sum_{j=1}^{6} \beta_j = 0,$$

and μ is the overall mean yield. The ϵ_{ij} are assumed to be independent (normal) random variables with mean 0 and and variance σ^2. The table layout is then as shown in Table 7.1.

For such a two-way table, and more generally for multiway tables and for data from designed experiments, most of the plots in this chapter are applicable. However, some care must be taken when the number of parameters is not small compared to the number of observations. In such cases the $\hat{\epsilon}_i$ have a large number of constraints that restrict their variation.

To illustrate this last point, we digress from the barley example for a moment and consider a full factorial design with two replications in which all main effects and interactions are estimated. In this case the residuals for the first replication are the negatives of the residuals for the second replication, although the residuals within each group are statistically independent. For example, suppose there are two factors so that the model for the data is

$$y_{ijk} = \mu + \alpha_i + \beta_j + \gamma_{ij} + \epsilon_{ijk}$$

where α_i and β_j are the main effects, γ_{ij} are the interactions, and ϵ_{ijk} are the errors. Then we have

$$\hat{\epsilon}_{ij1} = \frac{x_{ij1} - x_{ij2}}{2}$$

$$= \frac{\epsilon_{ij1} - \epsilon_{ij2}}{2}$$

$$= -\hat{\epsilon}_{ij2}.$$

Thus, the residuals $\hat{\epsilon}_{ij1}$ can give us information only about the distribution of the differences of the true errors, $\epsilon_{ij1} - \epsilon_{ij2}$. In particular, if we make the usual assumptions that the ϵ_{ijk} are independent and identically distributed, then the $\hat{\epsilon}_{ij1}$ must have a symmetric distribution even if the true ϵ_{ijk} do not. However, the $\hat{\epsilon}_{ij1}$ are normal if and only if

Table 7.1. Two-way table layout for the barley-yield data

			Yields			Variety effects
y_{11}	y_{12}	y_{13}	y_{14}	y_{15}	y_{16}	α_1
y_{21}	y_{22}	y_{23}	y_{24}	y_{25}	y_{26}	α_2
y_{31}	y_{32}	y_{33}	y_{34}	y_{35}	y_{36}	α_3
y_{41}	y_{42}	y_{43}	y_{44}	y_{45}	y_{46}	α_4
y_{51}	y_{52}	y_{53}	y_{54}	y_{55}	y_{56}	α_5
β_1	β_2	β_3	β_4	β_5	β_6	μ
		Location effects				Overall mean

ϵ_{ijk} are normal (assuming independence), so a normal quantile-quantile plot of $\hat{\epsilon}_{ij1}$ is a check of the normality of ϵ_{ijk}. Since the $\hat{\epsilon}_{ij1}$ have a symmetric distribution, the sign of $\hat{\epsilon}_{ij1}$ gives us no information, so in this case it would make sense to check normality by making a half-normal probability plot of the values $|\hat{\epsilon}_{ij1}|$.

Returning to the barley example, consider a factor that is orthogonal to all other factors, such as the variety factor. Let $\hat{\alpha}_i$ be the estimates of the main effects of this factor. If we combine the dummy variables and fitted coefficients for this factor into a single variable for an adjusted variable plot, as we did in Section 7.5, the result is simply a plot of the factor main effects plus the residuals against the factor main effects. Depending on our needs, we can also plot residuals or their absolute values against the main effects. For the variety factor in the barley example, this last plot, $|\hat{\epsilon}_{ij}|$ against $\hat{\alpha}_i$, is shown in Figure 7.34 as a scatter plot using dots. A smooth curve portrayed by asterisks (each asterisk is a midmean of the 6 absolute residuals) suggests that the scatter of the residuals increases linearly with increasing values of the variety main effect. Logarithms could be applied to the y_{ij} before analysis to stabilize variability, but we should bear in mind that an additive model on a log scale corresponds to a multiplicative model on the original scale.

Nonadditivity in a two-way table can sometimes be successfully modeled by including one nonlinear term in the model:

$$y_{ij} = \mu + \alpha_i + \beta_j + \gamma\alpha_i\beta_j + \epsilon_{ij}.$$

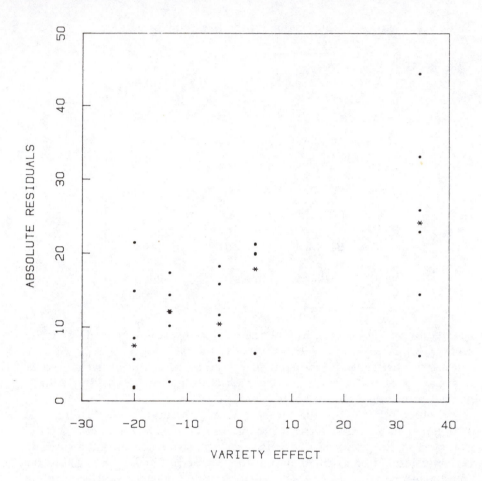

Figure 7.34 Absolute values of barley residuals plotted against fitted variety effects.

Estimates $\hat{\mu}$, $\hat{\alpha}_i$, and $\hat{\beta}_j$ can first be computed from the original additive model, and γ can be estimated as the regression coefficient from regressing the original residuals ($\hat{\epsilon}_{ij} = y_{ij} - \hat{\mu} - \hat{\alpha}_i - \hat{\beta}_j$) on the products $\hat{\alpha}_i\hat{\beta}_j$. Tukey (1949) showed that the usual analysis of variance may be used to test the presence of nonadditivity by testing whether $\hat{\gamma}$ is significantly different from zero. It is wise to accompany such a test with a scatter plot of $\hat{\epsilon}_{ij}$ against $\hat{\alpha}_i\hat{\beta}_j$. For example, the nonadditivity test applied to the barley data is statistically significant at the .025 level. But the scatter plot of $\hat{\epsilon}_{ij}$ against $\hat{\alpha}_i\hat{\beta}_j$ with a smooth curve in Figure 7.35

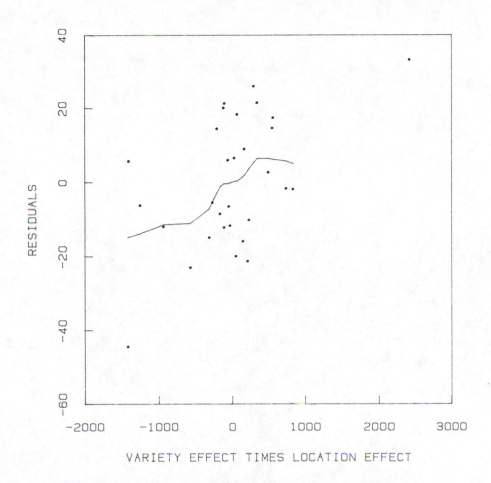

Figure 7.35 Barley residuals plotted against the product of the fitted effects for variety and location, for exploring nonadditivity.

reveals that the significance arises from two deviant data points and not from an overall nonadditive effect. Thus the nonlinear model appears to be inappropriate despite the "significance" of the test. Daniel reached the same conclusion, nongraphically, by comparing tables of residuals before and after the product term was fit.

All the components from fitting an additive two-way table can be portrayed in a diagram due to Tukey (1977) that we illustrate with the barley data. In Figure 7.36 the fitted values, $\hat{\mu} + \hat{\alpha}_i + \hat{\beta}_j = \hat{y}_{ij}$, are plotted against $\hat{\alpha}_i - \hat{\beta}_j = h_{ij}$, and points that share a common i or j are

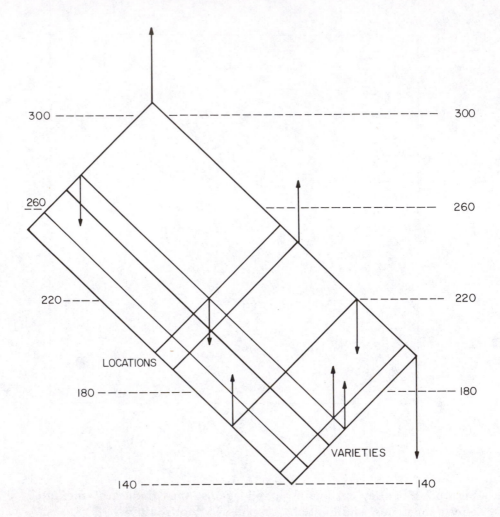

Figure 7.36 Two-way table plot of fitted effects and residuals for the barley example.

connected by line segments, forming a rectangular grid. In effect, this orders and spaces the rows according to the magnitudes of the row effects, does the same for column effects, and tilts the picture by 45°. Since the vertical coordinate in this plot represents fitted value, the horizontal dashed lines added to the picture are lines of constant fitted yield. (The horizontal coordinate, h_{ij}, has no important interpretation.)

One method for portraying the residuals is to code the values $\hat{\epsilon}_{ij}$ with symbols, using a symbol scale such as circle size, as was done in Chapter 5, and to place the symbol for $\hat{\epsilon}_{ij}$ at the position $(h_{ij}, \hat{y}_{ij})$. A second method, shown in Figure 7.36, is to use a vertical arrow emanating from the point $(h_{ij}, \hat{y}_{ij})$ with its head at (h_{ij}, y_{ij}). The sign and magnitude of $\hat{\epsilon}_{ij}$ are represented by the direction and the length of the arrow, respectively. In order to avoid cluttering the diagram, only the extreme residuals are shown in Figure 7.36. Notice that the two better-yielding varieties show numerically opposite trends, as a function of location, which suggests a location-variety interaction involving these two varieties.

7.9 SUMMARY AND DISCUSSION

We have discussed a number of graphical displays designed to aid a person using regression modeling methodology.

Various plots of the raw data can guide the choice of initially plausible models and appropriate procedures for fitting them, and will flag the anomalous behavior of unusual points.

Adjusted variable plots, which show certain components of the fit after intermediate stages of the fitting process, can help the analyst to assess the precision of the estimates of the separate regression coefficients, to judge the practical significance of individual terms, to see the impact of anomalous points on the fitted coefficients, and, often, to diagnose failures of the model in the form of nonlinear response dependencies not accounted for in the current regression equation.

Several kinds of plots made after regression fitting, most of which are based on the residuals, enable us further to diagnose failures of the regression equation. Even when the functional form seems adequate, they can throw light on the validity of the conventional distributional assumptions that are often made regarding the random error term in the model. Unanticipated structure discovered at this stage usually leads to remedial action, which often consists of modifying the model, refitting it, and doing further diagnostic checks.

Finally, we have shown some specialized graphical displays tailored to certain specific regression situations: nonlinear models, autoregression, and multiway tables.

Regression techniques are powerful tools, but ones that must be used with the utmost care and good sense, based on careful scrutiny of the data and results; they must be accompanied by a willingness to be flexible and to heed the structural messages hidden in the data. Automatic or blind use of regression models, especially in exploratory work, all too often leads to incorrect or meaningless results and to confusion rather than insight. At the very least, a user should be prepared to make and carefully study a number of plots of the data before, during, and after fitting the model.

7.10 FURTHER READING

Ezekiel (1924) suggested a graphical device for quantitative explanatory variables in a regression analysis in which $\hat{\epsilon}_i + \hat{\beta}_k x_{ik}$, the residual plus the component of the fit due to x_{ik}, is plotted against $\hat{\beta}_k x_{ik}$, for $i = 1$ to n. It has been argued by Larsen and McCleary (1972), who call these displays partial residual plots, and Wood (1973), who calls them component-plus-residual plots, that the method allows an assessment of nonlinear effects, patterns in the residuals, and the influence of the observations on the estimation of β_k. However, Feder (1975) has shown that considerable "leakage" can occur in these plots so that nonlinear effects due to one variable can make the plot for another variable look nonlinear, or, what seems even worse, nonlinear effects can cancel one another and give the false appearance that all is well. Overall, these plots appear less informative than the related adjusted variable plots described in Section 7.5.

One early article on residual plots and plots for multiway tables is Anscombe and Tukey (1963). Readers interested in a historical perspective and some additional plots should consult this paper.

Techniques for robust regression have been developed recently (e.g., Mosteller and Tukey, 1977) and are now an important part of regression methodology. Although we have mentioned the possibility of using adjusted variable plots in connection with robust regression, so far few graphical methods have been developed specifically to accompany robust regressions. Denby and Mallows (1977) have suggested a graphical method in connection with M-estimates using the Huber weight function, in which the behavior of the residuals is studied as a function of an adjustable parameter k that controls how many of the large residuals are downweighted.

The procedure of identifying deviant or high-leverage points and deleting them from the fit, as we did in the abrasion-loss example in Section 7.5, is a form of informal robust regression in which each point has either full weight or zero weight. Except for the normal probability plot, the graphical methods for regression described in this chapter can be used in this situation with the downweighted points included but shown by a different character. For the more general weighting schemes, such as iterated weighted least squares, the plots can also be made with, say, three plotting characters to indicate points with large, medium, and small weights.

Half-normal probability plotting was originally introduced by Daniel (1959) for the analysis of 2^n factorial experiments. Under a null hypothesis that assumes all true effects to be zero, the contrasts due to the 2^n-1 main effects and interactions are independently normally distributed. A half-normal probability plot is made of the absolute values, and those values that are large and deviate from the straight-line configuration of the majority of points are judged as corresponding to significant (nonzero) effects and interactions. The procedure has been extended to more general designs by Gnanadesikan and Wilk (1970).

EXERCISES

7.1. Regress length on turning diameter for the automobile data (Data Set 7). Make plots of y against x, residuals against fitted values, absolute residuals against fitted values, a normal quantile-quantile plot of the residuals.

7.2. Regress length on gear ratio for the automobile data (Data Set 7). How well does the line fit the data?

7.3. Regress the salaries of managers on the salaries of chauffeurs around the world (Data Set 11). Make a normal quantile-quantile plot of the residuals. Plot residuals against fitted values.

7.4. Regress the salaries of cashiers on the salaries of electrical engineers (Data Set 11). Plot residuals against fitted values. Plot absolute residuals against fitted values and smooth the data. What would you do next?

7.5. Regress weight on displacement of the automobile data (Data Set 7). Plot residuals against fitted values and superimpose a smooth curve. Make a normal quantile-quantile plot of the residuals.

7.6. Regress brain weight on body weight of 62 species of mammals (Data Set 19). Plot residuals against fitted values. Try some transformations of the variables. Which ones are best? Why?

7.7. Regress the salaries of cashiers on the salaries of teachers (Data Set 11). Plot residuals against fitted values. Redo the regression without the three largest fitted values. What happens to the regression coefficients and their variances? Why?

7.8. Regress age on years since highest degree for all Bell Laboratories managers with a BS (Data Set 20). Plot residuals against fitted values and make a normal probability plot. Redo the regression without the smallest fitted value. What happens to the regression coefficients and their variances? Why?

7.9. Based on Data Set 16, use regression and graphical displays to study the dependence of y = (per capita disposable income) on x_1 = (% population below age 15), x_2 = (% savings rate), and x_3 = (% contribution to manufacturing). Are there any peculiar points? Describe the relationships you see. Do a similar analysis on transformed data, using $\log(y)$ for y and $\text{logit}(x_i) = \log(x_i) - \log(100 - x_i)$ for the x's. Which analysis seems more satisfactory?

7.10. The data for the tar example in the text are given in Data Set 23.

   1. Make an adjusted variable plot of tar against temperature, adjusting for speed. Make another plot adjusting for both speed and speed squared. Can you draw any conclusions from these plots?

2. Plot tar against rotor speed using the raw data, and then using data adjusted for temperature. Comment on the evidence for a curved dependence on speed squared.

3. Compute residuals from a regression of tar on temperature, speed and speed squared. Also, compute residuals from a reduced model excluding the speed-squared term. Study and comment on the distributions of these two sets of residuals.

7.11. Identify some group of 15 to 30 people of mixed sex (e.g., a class or a department), and record their height, weight, age and sex (sex can be coded as 0 and 1). Use linear regression and graphical methods to study the dependence of weight on the other variables, both taking them singly, and adjusting for other subsets of the variables. Describe what you learn from each stage of the analysis.

7.12. Data Set 22 shows the famous stack loss data, which have been used as an example in many textbooks.

1. Regress stack loss on air flow, water temperature, and acid concentration using ordinary least squares. Make a normal quantile-quantile plot of the residuals.

2. Plot residuals against fitted values.

*3. Eliminate the outliers and make a C_p plot of all possible regressions.

4. Make an adjusted variable plot of the residuals from regressing stack loss on water temperature and acid concentration against the residuals from regressing air flow on the same variables (without the outliers).

5. Make a normal quantile-quantile plot of the residuals from the regression of stack loss on air flow and water temperature (without the outliers). Based on its appearance, comment on whether it seems appropriate to use least-squares fitting, and whether t-statistics would be justified for testing the significance of the regression coefficients.

7.13. Data Set 33 consists of data on catheter lengths (the response variable) and the heights and weights (the explanatory variables) of patients.

    1. Look at the design configuration. What can you say about the relationship between the explanatory variables? Are there any data points which might cause problems in the fitting stage?

    2. Make both adjusted variable plots. Does it look promising to add the other explanatory variable to the regression?

    *3. Make a C_p plot of all possible regressions.

    4. Plot the response variable against the fitted values from the best fitting regression equation determined in step 2 or 3.

    5. Plot the residuals from your best fit against the fitted values.

    6. Make a normal quantile-quantile plot of the residuals. Are there enough data points to make observations about the normality of the residuals?

7.14. We want to explain the ozone concentrations in Data Set 2 by means of the explanatory variables temperature, wind speed and solar radiation.

    1. If all days with missing data are eliminated, the ordinary least squares regression of ozone on temperature, wind speed and solar radiation yields negative fitted ozone values (a physical impossibility) on May 8, 9, 15, 18 and Sept. 25. Look at the relative positions of all values on these dates in the design configuration.

    *2. Make a C_p plot of all possible regressions. Which variables would you include?

    3. Study your best fit (based on step 1 or 2) by plotting the response variable against the fitted values, plotting residuals against fitted values, plotting absolute residuals

against fitted values, and making a normal quantile-quantile plot of the residuals.

4. Would transforming some of the variables improve the fit?

*7.15.   Fit an additive two-way table to the data on Fertility in Ireland shown in Data Set 31. Represent the table by a plot like the one in Figure 7.36. Would you use a more complicated model?

*7.16.   Fit an additive two-way table to the rubber data in Data Set 32. Make a plot like the one in Figure 7.36. Plot the residuals from the additive model against the product of fitted temperature and pressure effects. Plot absolute residuals against their corresponding pressure effect. What would your next model be?

*7.17.   Complete the following proof of Equation (7.5) in the text:

1. Two n-dimensional vectors u_i and v_i are said to be orthogonal if $\sum u_i v_i = 0$. Show that if vectors v_i and w_i are both orthogonal to a vector u_i, then their sum, $v_i + w_i$ is also orthogonal to u_i. Furthermore, show that if a set of vectors $v_{i1}, \ldots, v_{ip}$ are all orthogonal to u_i, then so is any linear combination, $\sum_{k=1}^{p} c_k v_{ik}$.

2. Show that when least squares is used to regress y_i on $x_{i0}, \ldots, x_{ip}$ producing the fitted equation

$$y_i = \sum_{k=0}^{p} \hat{\beta}_k x_{ik} + \hat{\epsilon}_i, \qquad (\text{e}1)$$

then the vector of residuals $\hat{\epsilon}_i$ is orthogonal to each of the x_{ik} vectors. That is,

$$\sum_{i=1}^{n} \hat{\epsilon}_i x_{ik} = 0 \qquad \text{for all } k=0 \text{ to } p. \qquad (\text{e}2)$$

(Hint: the objective of least squares is to find the values of $\hat{\beta}_0, \hat{\beta}_1, \ldots, \hat{\beta}_p$ that minimize $T = \sum_{i}^{n} \hat{\epsilon}_i^2$ $= \sum_{i=1}^{n} (y_i - \sum_{k=0}^{p} \hat{\beta}_k x_{ik})^2$. This can be done by setting the derivative of T with respect to each $\hat{\beta}_k$ to zero.)

3. The equations (e2) are called the normal equations. Written in terms of $\hat{\beta}_k$, they are

$$\sum_{i=1}^{n}(y_i - \sum_{k=0}^{p}\hat{\beta}_k x_{ik})x_{ik} = 0, \quad \text{for } k = 0 \text{ to } p. \tag{e3}$$

Show that these equations have exactly one solution for $\hat{\beta}_k$, $k=0$ to p.

4. In addition to the regression described by (e1), consider two other regressions, one of x_{ip} on the first $p-1$ x's,

$$x_{ip} = \sum_{k=0}^{p-1}\hat{\theta}_k x_{ik} + x_{ip}^* \tag{e4}$$

and the other of y_i on the same subset of the x's,

$$y_i = \sum_{k=0}^{p-1}\hat{\alpha}_k x_{ik} + y_{ip}^*. \tag{e5}$$

(Recall that in Section 7.5 we referred to the residuals from these regressions as the "adjusted variables" x_{ip}^* and y_{ip}^*, respectively.) Write down the normal equations for these two regressions.

5. Starting from

$$y_i - \hat{y}_i = \hat{\epsilon}_i$$

and adding $\hat{\beta}_p x_{ip}^*$ to both sides, show that

$$y_i - \sum_{k=0}^{p-1}\hat{\phi}_k x_{ik} = \hat{\beta}_p x_{ip}^* + \hat{\epsilon}_i \tag{e6}$$

where $\hat{\phi}_k = \hat{\beta}_p\hat{\theta}_k+\hat{\beta}_k$.

6. Using (e2) and the normal equations associated with (e4), show that the right hand side of (e6) is orthogonal to x_{ik} for each value of k from 0 to $p-1$.

7. Prove that $\hat{\phi}_k = \hat{\alpha}_k$ for $k=0$ to $p-1$ (hint: see step 3), and hence that the left hand side of (e6) is y_{ip}^*, so that

$$y_{ip}^* = \hat{\beta}_p x_{ip}^* + \hat{\epsilon}_i \qquad \text{(e7)}$$

8. Show that $\hat{\epsilon}_i$ is orthogonal to x_{ip}^* (hint: x_{ip}^* is a linear combination of $x_{i0}, \ldots, x_{ip-1}$) and thus that (e7) is the least squares regression equation of y_{ip}^* on x_{ip}^*.

9. Explain why a similar argument can be used to show that $y_{ik}^* = \hat{\beta}_k x_{ik}^* + \hat{\epsilon}_i$ for any other value of k besides $k=p$.

This completes the proof of (7.5) in the text.

8

General Principles
and Techniques

8.1 INTRODUCTION

Earlier chapters have discussed specific graphical methods to achieve a variety of data analytic and statistical goals. In this last chapter we consider the subject from a more general point of view and formulate general principles and techniques for graphical displays. Such principles and techniques allow us to employ graphics more incisively, to better tailor the choice of graphs for particular situations, to understand the messages as well as the pitfalls inherent in particular displays, and to think more critically about the results of graphical analyses. The principles and techniques also help guide a person who seeks to adapt existing graphical methods to new or special circumstances, or to develop wholly new styles of effective graphical displays.

Cox (1978) has issued his challenge for developing a theory of graphical methods that "will bring together in a coherent way things that previously appeared unrelated and which also will provide a basis for dealing systematically with new situations." Although we do not propose to offer a comprehensive theory here, we will discuss a number of general issues and illustrate how they may or may not be fulfilled by many of the plots in earlier chapters. We refrain from calling the principles and techniques of this chapter a theory, partly because they often contradict each other in specific applications (trade-offs among them are necessary), and partly because we need much more experience, information, and thought before the truly important principles can be unequivocally identified. Indeed as the reader will shortly see, we present the principles as a very loosely connected sequence of discussions about a variety of topics.

We will proceed from general issues to more focused ones. Section 8.2 is a discussion of general strategies for using and designing graphs. In Section 8.3 some conjectures about human visual perception of graphs are used to suggest certain design criteria; but the investigation of the human factors of graphs is in its infancy (Cleveland, Harris, and McGill, 1983) and the reader should not expect too much. In Section 8.4 some suggestions are made about what to plot on a graph, and in the final section, 8.5, we discuss how to make scales for graphs.

8.2   OVERALL STRATEGY AND THOUGHT

ITERATION

In any serious application we should look at the data in several ways, construct a number of plots, and do several analyses letting the results of each step suggest the next. There are many times when we choose to make a certain kind of plot to highlight or confirm some feature that was suggested by an earlier plot or analysis. For example, in Figure 4.7 we plotted weight against price for the automobile data, and the two branches suggested that another variable was partitioning the data. So we made the scatter plot in Figure 5.7 with U.S. cars coded "O" and cars of other countries coded by "×" and found this two-valued variable did do a good job of explaining the branches.

Effective data analysis is iterative, as in the automobile example. We cannot expect the first plot we make, nor any single plot, to be the "right" plot for the data; we must carefully examine and reflect upon each plot that we make, letting it influence our course of action and the plot that we make next.

MATCHING GOALS AND PLOTS

The information on a plot should be relevant to the goals of the analysis. This means that in choosing graphical methods we should match the capabilities of the methods to our needs in the context of each application. For instance, if linear relationships among the variables in a set of multidimensional data are relevant, we are unlikely to find them using stars, trees, or other types of symbolic representation discussed in Chapter 5; those methods are better suited for informal clustering and spotting peculiar points. Scatter plots, with the views carefully selected as in draftsman's displays, casement displays, and multiwindow plots, are likely to be more informative.

We must be careful, however, not to confuse what is relevant with what we expect or want to find. Often wholly unexpected phenomena constitute our most important findings.

TRUE MESSAGES AND ARTIFACTS

In using graphs for data analysis we need to recognize what kinds of perceived structure are attributable to the data, and what kinds are artifacts of the display technique itself. As a nearly trivial example, the empirical quantile-quantile plots in Figures 3.1 to 3.5 are forced to be monotonic regardless of the data. Another simple example is the histogram; we do not often believe that the true underlying data distribution is a coarse step function, so we quickly learn to ignore the square corners. The smooth density summaries in Figures 2.20 to 2.22 tend to better match our beliefs about the data density. In extreme cases, when looking at derived data that is very far removed from the original, we may sometimes wonder whether we are seeing only things that have been inadvertently introduced at various stages of analysis. While it seems sensible to prefer graphical techniques that introduce a minimum of artifact, we should remember that it is often by imposing some regularity that the message in the data is made evident.

A danger of graphical data analysis is what we might call the Rorschach effect: seeing things that are not there, or that are there but only by accident in our present set of data. This is a problem of all data analysis (all empirical science, really), but it can be acute when we are looking at plots. We must always exercise a healthy skepticism about conclusions, especially when based on weak indications. Part of the solution is to calibrate our thinking by gaining enough familiarity with the graphical techniques to know what kinds of apparent structure typically turn up when the data are really structureless. This was discussed in relation to probability plots in Chapter 6.

Another possibility is to do some confirmatory analysis (calculate test statistics, etc.) on the results; but we must be warned that reusing the same data in the tests modifies the significance levels, often substantially. The real answer is that we should not feel certain about results until we can show some or all of the following: (1) that they are very convincing, (2) that they are reproducible in other independent data sets taken under similar conditions, or (3) that they can be explained by theory or well-understood phenomena in the application context, even if we did not understand the connections before we looked at the data.

FLEXIBILITY

The most valuable graphical methods are flexible enough to be useful on a wide variety of data. Graphs have the ability to reveal the unexpected, and many we have presented do not collapse to an uninformative state if, for example, a small subset of the data is grossly in error. They remain useful if a large amount of data is encountered, and they are reasonably unaffected by such minor changes in the data as changing the units of measurement of some variable. Often the simpler displays are the more flexible, for example, quantile plots and scatter plots. They tend to be less tied to particular analyses or notions about the data, and more likely to be useful in the initial stages of looking at a data set.

Many of the plots in the book have been designed with flexibility in mind. For instance, in place of the box plot described in Chapter 2 we might have plotted a point with error bars showing the sample mean plus and minus one sample standard deviation. But the box plot is more flexible because it reveals possible asymmetry and long tails in the distribution. For example, in Figure 3.6 the box plots of the SO_2 data show asymmetry and outliers. In some situations, even a box plot may not be flexible enough; for instance it cannot show clustering in the data.

Another flexible procedure is to draw a lowess curve through the middle of a scatter of points, as shown in Figure 4.13 for the hibernation data and in Figure 4.20 for the graph area data. The curve helps guide our perception of the middle of the local distribution of y and helps us decide whether this middle goes up or down as a function of x or is constant. We could also take a more classical approach and smooth a scatter plot by fitting straight lines, quadratic curves, or higher order polynomials. However, to do this would work against one of the essential strengths of graphs as an exploratory device; they are not committed in advance to any particular shape of curve. Once we draw a curve, that curve is likely to dominate our subsequent impressions. The lowess smoothing provides a more flexible curve through the data. But even this is a compromise, since there is a price for smoothness. A curve computed in this way cannot track abrupt changes in level, even if they are genuine.

INTERPRETABILITY

When some interesting structure is seen in a plot, it is an advantage to be able to relate that structure back to the original data in a clear, direct, and meaningful way. Although this seems obvious, interpretability is at once one of the most important, difficult, and controversial issues.

An extreme position is that a graph must be simple and that the variables plotted should have clear-cut physical interpretations. This is desirable when feasible, but it is easy to go too far in this direction. We certainly want the simplest kind of plot that will show us clearly the phenomenon that is to be shown. But if the phenomenon is itself subtle, it may only be revealed in a plot of derived values with less directly interpretable axes. Restricting ourselves to the most directly interpretable plots would prevent us from using graphs for their most important analytical and exploratory uses. For these uses, a graph should be regarded first and foremost as a picture, and only secondarily as something with axes.

The abrasion loss data of Chapter 7 are a good example. When we plotted the three variables abrasion loss, hardness, and tensile strength in Figure 7.10 we learned little about how abrasion loss depended on the other two variables. But when we made the tensile strength adjusted variable plot in Figure 7.16, which involves highly derived values that are much less easily interpreted than the original data, we found a substantial nonlinearity that was important for the analysis.

The probability plot in Chapter 6 is quite easily interpretable — after some initial training and experience. This is partly because every point displayed is an original data point and the vertical scale is the original measurement scale. Thus, while showing the shape of the distribution, the plot also lets us see the data in a very direct sense. By contrast, since the empirical quantile-quantile plot of Chapter 3 compares two samples that are generally of different sizes, the individual points have a less clear-cut interpretation. Each plotted point corresponds to an observation in the smaller data set, but the other plotting coordinate is obtained by interpolating between ordered observations of the larger set.

As with quantile-quantile plots, the interpretability of nearly every graphical method in this book hinges to some extent on the user's familiarity with the technique. Perhaps the correct question to ask is not how inherently interpretable a display is, but how much background and training — of a general or specific nature — is required to make interpretation easy. It may well be that showing clearly by example how to interpret a number of diverse instances of a plot is more effective than describing, in detailed words and formulas, the plot's construction. Displays that are tied closely to the details of complicated analyses, such as the adjusted variable plots in Chapter 7, obviously demand more background and training. On the other hand, the multiwindow display of Chapter 5, as a scatter plot within a scatter plot, can be readily interpreted with only a brief introduction, despite its dealing with four-dimensional data.

Although clear interpretability is an advantage, Tukey and Wilk (1966) point out that "one great virtue of good graphical representation is that it can serve to display clearly and effectively a message carried by quantities whose calculation or observation is far from simple."

8.3   VISUAL PERCEPTION

We can gain further insight into what makes good plots by thinking about the process of visual perception. The eye can assimilate large amounts of visual information, perceive unanticipated structure, and recognize complex patterns; however, certain kinds of patterns are more readily perceived than others. If we thoroughly understood the interaction between the brain, eye, and picture, we could organize displays to take advantage of the things that the eye and brain do best, so that the potentially most important patterns are associated with the most easily perceived visual aspects in the display.

Knowledge about the psychology of visual perception of statistical displays can help us appreciate the strengths and weaknesses of graphs. For instance, when we are asked to judge the linear association in a scatter of points, do we actually see the Pearson product-moment correlation coefficient or do we perceive some other measure of association? Experiments run by Cleveland, Diaconis, and McGill (1982) show that most people do not see r, but rather some perceptual scale that is much better described by r^2 if r is positive and $-r^2$ if r is negative. Furthermore, the experiments show that construction factors, such as the size of the point cloud relative to the size of the frame around it, can affect our perception. But, unfortunately, there are very few such experiments on graphical perception and so our knowledge about the psychology of visual perception of graphs is limited.

Given this state of knowledge, we must base our graphical principles on a set of plausible assertions. In particular, we conjecture that the eye is able to perceive

- location along an axis more easily than other graphical aspects, such as size

- straight lines more clearly than curves

- simple patterns more quickly than complex ones

- large or dark objects, or clusters of objects, with greater impact than small, light, or isolated ones

- symmetry, especially bilateral and circular symmetry.

To this list we add two more points that have more to do with the associated mental processes:

- We can sometimes perceive several different aspects in one plot, simply by switching attention from one aspect to another.

- Accumulated visual evidence is roughly additive.

In this section we will explore these ideas and see what principles and techniques of graph construction they suggest.

LOCATION, SHAPE, AND MOTION

In designing displays, we have to choose not only where to plot things, but what to plot there, implying choices of shape, size, texture, color, darkness, orientation, and so on. Nevertheless, among all of these graphical aspects, it is location along an axis that has the most immediate visual impact. In any one plot we are free to associate just two numerical aspects of our data with the horizontal and vertical plotting positions. Any other numerical aspects either must be left out, (as in a simple scatter plot of 2 out of p raw variables), must be confounded with the first two (as in the multiwindow plots of Figure 5.29), or must be relegated to other graphical aspects, as in the coding of the automobile data by Kleiner-Hartigan trees in Figure 5.26.

Although location dominates our perceptions, we can rank other graphical aspects in terms of their relative impact, and take advantage of the ranking. For instance, shape, especially of large objects, is closely connected with location and is easily perceived. This is one reason why the quantile plot of Stamford ozone in Figure 2.4 is more effective than the jittered one-dimensional scatter plot of Figure 2.8 for communicating the empirical density; the quantile plot has us look at the shape of a curve, but the jittered scatter plot asks us to judge the changing density (darkness) of a series of points, which is harder to do. But the density trace in Figure 2.20 is easiest of all to perceive since we are judging location along an axis.

There is one other visual aspect that is at least as compelling as location — motion. We have deliberately avoided any discussion of moving displays in this book because of the difficultly of putting examples into a book. But active data displays are certainly an important area for data analysis (Fisherkeller, Friedman, and Tukey, 1974).

LINEAR REFERENCE PATTERNS

Straight line configurations play a central role in many graphical methods, partly because of the conceptual simplicity of linear relationships, but also because of our ability to perceive lines more readily than other kinds of patterns. When we perceive curvature — especially if it is gentle or moderate — we probably see it more as a departure from linearity than as any particular kind of curve. Imagine, for instance, the difficulty of judging visually whether a particular curve $y = f(x)$ over the range $x = 1$ to $x = 2$ is more like $y = x^2$ or $y = (3x^3+4)/7$. (Both functions are 1 at $x = 1$ and 4 at $x = 2$.) It would be easier to perform the logically equivalent task of judging which of the curves $y = f(x) - x^2$ or $y = f(x) - (3x^3+4)/7$ is more nearly linear.

It may also be true that curved departures from horizontal lines are easier to see than curved departures from slanted ones. Of course, if there is an oblique linear pattern in a plot drawn on a piece of paper, we can always turn the paper to view it horizontally. (Furthermore, when we want to see subtle deviations from a line, it is helpful to sight along the configuration from the edge of the plot at a shallow angle from the paper.)

Most statistical analyses have one or several reference situations (models, in one sense of the word) against which deviations are to be judged. A basic way of designing a graphical display is to arrange for reference situations to correspond to straight lines in a plot. This principle is embodied in many of the displays in the book. Two general ways to link reference situations to straight lines are (i) to plot some set of observed quantities against a set of fitted or standard values, that is, values that they can be anticipated to have on average under the reference assumptions and (ii) to plot residuals from some fitted model against fitted values, or against a variety of other things. The first approach produces a plot in which the reference situation corresponds to the line $y = x$, and the second approach has the reference line $y = 0$.

The theoretical quantile-quantile plot in Chapter 6 is an example of the first approach. On a normal probability plot the points have a straight line pattern if the empirical distribution of the data is well-approximated by a normal distribution. Another way to judge normality would be to judge the similarity of the patterns of a quantile plot of the data and a quantile plot of a normal distribution, as in Figure 6.2 for the log seeded rainfall data. By making a probability plot we replace this difficult visual task with a much easier one: looking for a straight line reference pattern.

Plotting residuals against fitted values, as we described in Chapter 7, is an example of the second approach. If there is no dependence of the response on the explanatory variables we expect to see the points follow a horizontal reference line pattern.

There are examples of other specialized ways of focusing on particular relationships by straightening them out or making them horizontal. For instance, the empirical quantile-quantile plot of Figure 3.5 suggested that the distributions of Stamford and Yonkers ozone data differed by a multiplicative constant. Had the idea been true, the subsequent plot of the ratios in Figure 3.13 would have displayed a horizontal linear configuration.

VISUAL IMPACT

Generally speaking, a good display is one in which the visual impact of its components is matched to their importance in the context of the analysis. Consider the issue of overplotting. Most plotting devices will cause two or more identical points in a data set to appear as a single plotted point (perhaps slightly darkened), and therefore to have less visual impact than they deserve. Jittering — both for the one-dimensional scatter plot of ozone in Figure 2.8 and for the scatter plot of the iris data in Figure 4.22 — is an effort to restore the proper visual impact, since the duplicates will then appear as a small cluster. The practice of using digits to indicate multiplicity has the disadvantage that digits are not properly graded for visual impact. Another approach might be to plot a suitably larger character, but before doing this, one would have to face two questions: (1) If the data are on continuous scales, how close should two points have to be (i.e., how much should their plotting characters overlap) before we consider them identical? (2) How much larger should we make a plotted character to double its impact (or triple, etc.)?

The latter question invariably arises when we try to control visual impact in a quantitative way. For example it complicates the design of graded character scales that code the values of additional variables, as for those in Chapter 5. One view holds that area is proportional to impact; but experimental evidence (for instance, the example in Chapter 7 on the assessment of circle sizes) suggests that when people try to judge area, they actually perceive some power of area that is less than 1.

This is one of the unsettled psychological issues. Nevertheless, to design good graphics we must deal with the issue of visual impact as best we can.

In choosing good character scales, we sometimes face the additional complication of representing both positive and negative values; an example is the residuals in the two-way table plot of the barley data in Figure 7.36. Large positive and small negative residuals are equally important and deserve equal visual impact, but they must be visually distinct. We would conjecture that using up arrows for positive residuals and down arrows for negative residuals achieves this equality in Figure 7.36. Another example is Figure 5.35 which uses solid and dashed circles for positive and negative values.

The principle of matching visual impact to importance underlies the design of the box plot in Chapter 2. The central 50% of the data, stretching from the first to the third quartile, is considered the most important part for seeing generally where the data lie and what their spread is; it is represented by the box with median line, which has a large visual impact. The tails are regarded as less important, and are shown in a way that has less visual impact. Distant stragglers are shown as isolated points, having the least impact of all, unless they are deliberately plotted with large symbols. The effectiveness of this scheme is especially apparent when we scan across several schematic plots placed alongside each other as in Figure 3.6. We can pick up the changing distributional patterns at a glance.

When we enhance scatter plots with smooth curves, as in Figures 4.13 and 4.20, we should keep in mind the principle of proper visual impact. If the points are the real message and the curve is only a gentle guide, the curve should probably be drawn lightly so that it does not dominate. If the curve is the message, it should be heavy and the points light. The decision depends on our objectives at the moment. Not all of the examples of enhanced scatter plots in the book achieve high marks on this criterion, partly because of the limitations of the plotting devices used.

The principle of visual impact also explains why it can be unwise to put legends, grid lines, and other "chartjunk" (Tufte, 1978) inside the plotting region of the display. Such things tend to become part of the pattern that we see, despite our efforts to ignore them.

EQUAL VARIABILITY

The concept of matching importance and visual impact has one other more subtle but important consequence. A deviation of a certain magnitude of a plotted point from a reference curve or reference pattern in one part of the plot should have the same importance as a similar deviation in another part of the plot. This means that ideally the variability of the points should remain constant across the plot; otherwise there is a danger that regions with higher variability will have greater visual impact.

Equal variability is not always achieved in plots. For instance, if the theoretical distribution for a probability plot has a density that drops off gradually to zero in the tails (as the normal density does), then the variability of the data in the tails of the probability plot is greater than in the center. Another example is provided by the histogram. Since the height of any one bar has a binomial distribution, the standard deviation of the height is approximately proportional to the square root of the expected height; hence, the variability of the longer bars is greater.

A transformation can often be devised that (at least approximately) stabilizes the variability, but usually only at the expense of some other criterion, such as interpretability. For example, in Chapter 6 we suggested plotting cube roots for gamma probability plots which reduces but does not eliminate the unequal variability.

As another illustration, Tukey (1972) suggests improving the histogram by making the plot on a square-root vertical scale (the square-root is an approximate variance-stabilizing transformation for the binomial distribution), producing a *rootogram*. To do this means giving up the direct interpretation of bar lengths as frequencies. Whether the price is tolerable depends on our objectives in making the plot.

ACCUMULATED VISUAL EVIDENCE

Generally, two points on a plot will receive roughly twice as much attention as a single point. In this sense, the various bits of visual evidence that we gather from a plot tend to add up in our minds. For the combined message to be accurate, the pieces of evidence should be independent of each other; to the extent they are not, we will be giving added weight to essentially redundant information. This means that a good graphical display is one in which the plotted points, curves, etc., are as statistically independent of each other as conveniently possible.

This is a difficult technical issue. It is usually hard to assess the dependencies, and even harder to take corrective action. For instance, what is the correlation between the values of the locally weighted robust smooth curve at $x = 10$ and $x = 15$ for the hamster data in Figure 4.13? Or how much correlation is there between two points on a smooth density summary? Although we cannot answer these questions in a quantitative way, it is clear that we must usually pay for smoothness by introducing more dependence. At the other extreme, the histogram is quite unsmooth, but its bar lengths are often nearly statistically independent.

One of the criticisms of probability plots is that the plotted points are correlated with each other, and adjacent points are the most highly correlated. In a sense, this is a consequence of the very fact that the plot is forced to be monotonically increasing.

As with remedies for unequal variability, devices to improve statistical independence usually force us to compromise other principles, often interpretability. In the case of the probability plot, Andrews and Tukey (1973) suggest computing the gaps between consecutive ordered observations and plotting them in various ways, since they are nearly statistically independent. If we do that, we can no longer interpret one of the axes as a data axis, nor will the individual plotted points correspond to original observations. Andrews and Tukey, however, argue that the loss is small.

8.4 GENERAL TECHNIQUES OF PLOT CONSTRUCTION

REMOVING GROSS STRUCTURE

Frequently we can increase the informativeness of a graph by removing structure from the data once we have identified it, so that subsequent plots are free of its dominating influence and can help us see finer structure or subtler effects. This usually means (1) partitioning the data, or (2) plotting differences or ratios, or (3) fitting a model and taking the residuals as a new set of data for further study.

We will first illustrate (1). If the data contain one or a small number of deviant points, we usually want to make another plot that concentrates on the remaining data by setting aside the outliers, since they are likely to dominate the plot and obscure other effects by decreasing substantially the resolution of the other points. Generalizing this idea, if preliminary plots or analyses reveal two or several distinct clusters of points, we may well want to analyze and plot the points in each cluster separately.

To illustrate (2) consider Figure 3.5, the empirical quantile-quantile plot of Stamford and Yonkers ozone data. The overall dominant effect of the points is a straight line through the origin. When we plotted the ratios of the quantiles in Figure 3.13 we removed the line and were able to see the subtler departures from linearity.

We can apply (3), for instance, when one variable, y, has a linear dependence on another variable, x. Plots of y against x may show the linearity nicely, but plotting the residuals from a fitted line against x can be more informative when we are looking beyond the initial linear fit for curved effects. This is illustrated in Figure 7.3.

REDUCING CLUTTER

The amount of uninformative detail and clutter in a plot should be minimized, since they interfere with our perception of the important information. Clutter can be caused by grid lines (which are usually unnecessary except perhaps on archival plots), overly ornate axes or plotting characters, arrows and legends within the plotting area, and other adornments. But clutter can also be caused by overburdening the plot with too many data points, or coding too many aspects into the plotted characters, or using too many superimposed curves. Just getting all the data into a plot does not necessarily make it informative.

Selectivity is important, but in addition, some of the methods in the book are specifically designed to reduce clutter from large data sets. For example, the sunflowers of Chapter 4 can help to reduce clutter in scatter plots. In the examples we gave, each petal represented one point, as did the dot; but for a scatter plot with a large number of observations we could have a dot represent 1 to 5 points, a dot and a single petal represent 6 to 10 points, a dot and two petals represent 11 to 15 points and so forth. For an ordinary scatter plot with a large number of points, simply reducing the size of the plotting character can reduce the clutter, but some care is necessary because very small dots can be overlooked or confused with dirt specks, or not be reproduced when the plot is copied.

Sometimes a set of data to be plotted along the scale of a plot has a very skewed empirical distribution, which can cause great clutter because the majority of the points are forced into a small region of the plot. We encountered this with the gamma probability plot of the rainfall data in Figure 6.16 and the scatter plot of work hours and number of wire pairs in Figure 7.12. In both cases transforming the data by a power transformation made the data less skewed and reduced the clutter; in Figure 6.17 we plotted cube roots for the rainfall data and in Figure 7.13 we plotted logs for the wire pair data.

LABELING

Making effective graphs frequently demands the effective use of labels. If we are to interpret a plot at all, we must know what we are looking at. Axes that are to be interpreted should be clearly labeled with names or descriptions of the variables. If nothing else, this helps us to remember the variables when we look at it again a week, a month, or a decade later. Sometimes, as in the abrasion loss plots (Figures 7.10, 7.16, 7,17, 7.19, 7.24, and 7.26 to 7.28), we want to label individual points in a display so that we can easily link them up with points in other plots or with other information about them. If there are so many points that labeling them all would create too much clutter, we may choose to label only the isolated or outlying ones. Of course, in some applications we can relax these requirements when the context of the plot makes it very clear what is plotted.

8.5   SCALES

All graphical methods involve the representation of numerical values by encoding them into some visual aspect of a display. The techniques for doing this encoding or scaling share some basic features, regardless of the graphical method. Scaling is often taken for granted, but a clear understanding of some underlying issues can help us make more effective displays.

LINEAR RESCALING

A common task in constructing plots is to rescale, or map, a set of values linearly into a different numerical range. We do this, for instance, when we plot points in Cartesian coordinates; we map our data values into physical positions on the plot, measured perhaps in centimeters. We also do this when we code a variable, such as weight in Figure 5.8, by the area of a circle.

The task can be accomplished easily by identifying the largest and smallest data values to be mapped, say $xmin = \min_i(x_i)$ and $xmax = \max_i(x_i)$, deciding what the extremes should be on the new scale, say $umin$ and $umax$, and then calculating the rescaled values with the formula

$$u_i = \frac{x_i - xmin}{xmax - xmin} (umax - umin) + umin.$$

CHOOSING COORDINATE AXIS SCALES

When preparing to plot in Cartesian coordinates we face several scaling complications. In addition to finding values of $xmin$ and $xmax$ that accommodate our data, we usually want a moderate number of reference values running through the range of the data that we can print as numerical labels along the axis, and we usually want the reference values to be pretty, or round, numbers so that the labels are easy to read. A common practice is to choose values that are consecutive integer multiples of an increment δ that is a simple number, either 1, 2, or 5 times some appropriate power of 10. A reasonable number of reference values might be between four and twelve. We cannot always have exactly the number we might ask for, unless we are prepared to extend the ends of the axis by some multiples of δ and waste some plotting space. A Fortran algorithm for doing these computations has been published by Lewart (1973). Note that when plotting in two coordinates all of the scaling decisions and computations must be made twice, once for the horizontal axis and once for the vertical axis.

If we plan to draw an axis at the edge or a box around the plot, we should not allow a plotted point to fall exactly on the edge of the plot. To avoid this we can, after choosing δ, replace $xmin$ and $xmax$ in the scaling function by values $xmin^*$ and $xmax^*$ that are the next smaller and next larger multiples of δ, respectively. All of the data points will then lie strictly inside the extended range, and the ends of the axis will be among the reference values. A second approach, called α-extended axes, is to push out $xmin$ and $xmax$ by a small fraction α of the range, say

$$xmin^* = xmin - .02(xmax - xmin)$$

$$xmax^* = xmax + .02(xmax - xmin).$$

Although the ends of the axis will no longer be among the reference numbers, this approach has the advantage of always using nearly all the available plotting area.

Certain situations occur frequently that require modifications to the basic scaling algorithm. Among them are the following:

- Two or more sets of points are to be plotted in the same display, perhaps with different characters. In this case, *all* the data sets must be scanned for overall values of *xmin*, *xmax*, *ymin*, and *ymax* before the first set is plotted.

- A series of plots are to be made, and their scales should be the same to facilitate visual comparisons. Again, all the data sets must be scanned in advance, and the same scaling values used in all the plots.

- *x* and *y* are measured in the same units and we want the plot to be scaled in such a way that the number of units per centimeter is the same on the two axes. This can be accomplished by taking

$$r = \max(ymax - ymin, xmax - xmin)$$

$$xmin^* = (xmin + xmax)/2 - r/2$$

$$xmax^* = (xmin + xmax)/2 + r/2$$

$$ymin^* = (ymin + ymax)/2 - r/2$$

$$ymax^* = (ymin + ymax)/2 + r/2$$

and making the plot square.

- The situation is so inherently symmetric that the origin should be in the center of the plotted axis. We can take $xmin^* = -xmax^* = \min(xmin, -xmax)$.

When plotting by hand, we usually make all such scaling decisions and computations without much conscious thought; when we use a high level plotting program in a computer they are usually made for us automatically (often not flexibly enough). The issues that we have discussed become especially important when we are writing new plotting programs, and when we are judging whether existing programs meet our needs or require modification.

CHOOSING SYMBOL SCALES

In this book, the main alternative to graphical representation of data as coordinate positions has been the use of graphical symbols. Data values are encoded into some visible feature of the plotted object that can be varied. We have argued in the section on visual perception that no way of coding information into a character allows us to see data values as quantitatively and precisely as we can see location in a plot. Usually, the most we can hope to convey is an impression of the relative sizes of the coded quantities.

Many different types of character scales have been proposed. Some are discussed in Chapter 5, and others are mentioned in Tukey and Tukey (1981). In order to use symbols effectively, we must make careful choices after considering both the demands of the particular application and the capabilities of each symbolic scale, bearing in mind the graphical principles that we have outlined. A long and detailed discussion is possible; we shall only indicate a few of the kinds of considerations that can be relevant.

Although symbols are generally not good for conveying quantitative information, some do better than others. For instance, we can perceive lengths and directions of short line segments somewhat more quantitatively than darkness on a grey scale.

Some symbolic scales are inherently one-ended (such as circles of varying sizes, ranging down to a point), and are not suitable for data (such as residuals) in which very negative values and very positive values are equally important.

Certain symbolic scales provide only a small number of distinct symbols (such as a grey-level scale produced by overstriking characters), while others (such as circle size) allow variation on a more nearly continuous scale. Given the limitations of our perceptual abilities, representing continuous data on a discrete symbolic scale instead of a more continuous symbolic scale often does not sacrifice much information.

Some symbols convey order information very well (such as size scales), while others are only able to make groups of points visibly distinct without suggesting any order (such as the set {+, Δ, ×}). A scale that provides order information only through the lexical meaning of the symbols (such as digits, or letters) is not effective in graphical terms.

The scale produced by the direction of a whisker emanating from a circle or a dot is ideal for data that is on a circular scale (such as wind direction).

Color is potentially one of the most effective coding methods, but also one of the most difficult to use well. Most current computer technology does not let us control color with precision, nor can we inexpensively reproduce colored plots. Moreover, our insufficient knowledge of color perception does not yet allow us to use it in an effective and quantitative way. For now, we most often regard color as an excellent way to display qualitative differences (for example, when we want to plot four partially overlapping clouds of points in a single scatter plot).

Scales on plots, while seemingly mundane, carry much weight in determining our ability to interpret graphs.

References

Abramowitz, M. and Stegun, I. A. (1965). *Handbook of Mathematical Functions.* Dover Publications, New York. [Chapter 6]

Allison, T. and Chiccheti, D. V. (1976). Sleep in mammals: Ecological and constitutional correlates. *Science* **194**, 732-734. [Chapters 4, 7]

Anderson, E. (1935). The irises of the Gaspe Peninsula. *Bulletin of the American Iris Society* **59**, 2-5. [Chapter 5]

Anderson, E. (1957). A semigraphical method for the analysis of complex problems. *Proceedings of the National Academy of Sciences* **13**, 923-927. Reprinted in *Technometrics* (1960) **2**, 387-391. [Chapter 5]

Andrews, D. F. (1972). Plots of high-dimensional data. *Biometrics* **28**, 125-136. [Chapter 5]

Andrews, D. F. (1974). A robust method for multiple linear regression. *Technometrics* **16**, 523-531. [Chapters 4, 7]

Andrews, D. F. (1982). Exploiting 3-dimensional graphics with micro-computers. *Talk presented at the Joint Statistical Meetings of the American Statistical Association and Biometric Society.* Cincinnati, Ohio. [Chapter 5]

Andrews, D. F. and Tukey, J. W. (1973). Teletypewriter plots for data analysis can be fast: 6-line plots, including probability plots. *Journal of the Royal Statistical Society, Series C* **22**, 192-202. [Chapter 8]

Andrews, H. P., Snee, R. D., and Sarner, M. H. (1980). Graphical display of means. *The American Statistician* **34**, 195-199. [Chapter 3]

Anscombe, F. J. (1973). Graphs in statistical analysis. *The American Statistician* **27**, 17-21. [Chapter 4]

Anscombe, F. J. and Tukey, J. W. (1963). The examination and analysis of residuals. *Technometrics* **5**, 141-160. [Chapter 7]

Ashton, E. H., Healey, M. J. R., and Lipton. S. (1957). The descriptive use of discriminant functions in physical anthropology. *Proceedings of the Royal Society, Series B* **146**, 552-572. [Chapter 5]

Bachi, R. (1968). *Graphical Rational Patterns: A New Approach to Graphical Presentation of Statistics.* Israel University Press, Jerusalem. [Chapter 5]

Badger, E. H. M. (1946). Part II. The value and the limitations of high-speed turbo-exhausters for the removal of tar-fog from carburetted water-gas. *Journal of the Society of Chemical Industry* **65**, 166-168. [Chapter 7]

Barnett, V. (ed.) (1981). *Interpreting Multivariate Data.* Wiley, Chichester, U. K. [Chapter 5]

Belsley, D. A., Kuh, E., and Welsch, R. E. (1980). *Regression Diagnostics.* Wiley, New York. [Chapter 7]

Bennett, C. A. and Franklin, N. L. (1954). *Statistical Analysis in Chemistry and the Chemical Industry.* Wiley, New York. [Chapter 7]

Benzecri, J.-P. (1973). L'analyse des correspondances (Vol. 2 of *L'analyse des Donnees*). Dunod, Paris. [Chapter 5]

Bertin, J. (1973). *Semiologie Graphique. Second edition.* Mouton, Paris & The Hague. (In French). [Chapter 5]

Bertin, J. (1977). *La Graphique et le Traitement Graphique de l'Information.* Flammarion, Paris. (In French). [Chapter 5]

Bertin, J. (1980). *Graphics and the Graphical Analysis of Data.* (Translated by W. Berg). DeGruyter, Berlin. [Chapter 5]

Box, G. E. P. and Cox, D. R. (1964). An analysis of transformations. *Journal of the Royal Statistical Society B* **26**, 211-252. [Chapter 6]

Box, G. E. P. and Jenkins, G. M. (1976). *Time Series Analysis Forecasting and Control*. Holden Day, New York. [Chapter 7]

Bradu, D. and Gabriel, K. R. (1978). The biplot as a diagnostic tool for models in two-way tables. *Technometrics* **20**, 47-68. [Chapters 5, 7]

Carmichael, J. W. and Sneath, P. N. A. (1969). Taxonometric maps. *Systematic Zoology* **18**, 402-415. [Chapter 5]

Carroll, J. D. and Arabie, P. (1980). Multidimensional scaling. *Annual Review of Psychology* **31**, 607-49. [Chapter 5]

Carroll, J. D. and Kruskal, J. B. (1978). Multidimensional scaling of two-way and three-way arrays. *The Encyclopedia of Statistics*, (W. H. Kruskal and J. M. Tanur, eds.). Free Press, New York. [Chapter 5]

Chambers, J. M. (1977). *Computational Methods for Data Analysis*. Wiley, New York. [Chapter 5]

Chambers, John M. and Kleiner, B. (1982). Graphical techniques for multivariate data and for clustering. *Handbook of Statistics. Volume II*. (P. R. Krishnaiah, ed.) North-Holland, New York. [Chapter 5]

Chatterjee, S. and Price, B. (1977). *Regression Analysis by Example*. Wiley, New York. [Chapter 7]

Chernoff, H. (1973). The use of faces to represent points in k-dimensional space graphically. *Journal of the American Statistical Association* **68**, 361-368. [Chapter 5]

Chernoff, H. (1978). Graphical representation as a discipline. *Graphical Representation of Multivariate Data*. (P. C. C. Wang, ed.) 1-11. Academic Press, New York. [Chapter 5]

Cleveland, W. S., Diaconis, P., and McGill, R. (1982). Variables on scatterplots look more highly correlated when the scales are increased. *Science* **216**, 4550, 1138-1141. [Chapter 8]

Cleveland, W. S., Harris, C. S., and McGill, R. (1983). Experiments on quantitative judgements of graphs and maps. *Bell System Technical Journal*, to appear. [Chapter 8]

Cleveland, W. S., Harris, Charles S., and McGill, R. (1982). Judgments of circle sizes on statistical maps. *Journal of the American Statistical Association* **77**, 541-547. [Chapters 2, 5, 7]

Cleveland, W. S. (1979). Robust locally weighted regression and smoothing scatterplots. *Journal of the American Statistical Association* **74**, 829-836. [Chapter 4]

Cleveland, W. S. (1981). LOWESS: A program for smoothing scatterplots by robust locally weighted regression. *The American Statistician* **35**, 54. [Chapter 4]

Cleveland, W. S. (1982). Graphs in scientific publications. (Submitted for publication.) [Chapter 4]

Cleveland, W. S. and Guarino, R. (1978). The use of numerical and graphical statistical methods in the analysis of data on learning to see complex random-dot stereograms. *Perception* **7**, 113-118. [Chapter 6]

Cleveland, W. S. and McGill, R. (1982). The many faces of a scatterplot. (Submitted for publication.) [Chapter 4]

Cox, D. R. (1978). Some remarks on the role in statistics of graphical methods. *Journal of the Royal Statistical Society, Series C* **27**, 4-9. [Chapter 8]

Cox, D. R. and Hinkley, D. V. (1974). *Theoretical Statistics*. Chapman and Hall, London. [Chapter 6]

Dallal, G. and Finseth, K. (1977). Double dual histograms. *The American Statistician* **31**, 39-41. [Chapter 3]

Daniel, C. (1959). Use of half-normal plots in interpreting factorial two-level experiments. *Technometrics* **1**, 311-341. [Chapters 6, 7]

Daniel, C. (1976). *Applications of Statistics to Industrial Experimentation*. Wiley, New York. [Chapter 7]

Daniel, C. and Wood, F. S. (1971). *Fitting Equations to Data*. Wiley, New York. [Chapters 6, 7]

Daniel, C. and Wood, F. S. (1980). *Fitting Equations to Data. Second edition*. Wiley, New York. [Chapter 7]

Davies, O. L. (ed.), Box, G. E. P., Cousins, W. R., Hinsworth, F. R., Henney, H., Milbourn, M., Spendley, W., and Stevens, W. L. (1957). *Statistical Methods in Research and Production. Third edition*. Oliver and Boyd, London. [Chapter 7]

Denby, L. and Mallows, C. L. (1977). Two diagnostic displays for robust regression. *Technometrics* **19**, 1-13. [Chapter 7]

Diaconis, P. and Freedman, D. (1981). On the maximum deviation between the histogram and the underlying density. *Zeitscrift fur Wahrscheinlichkeitstheorie* **57**, 453-476. [Chapter 2]

Doksum, K. A. and Sievers, G. L. (1976). Plotting with confidence: graphical comparisons of two populations. *Biometrika* **63**, 421-434. [Chapter 6]

Donoho, D. L., Huber, P. J., Ramos, E., and Thoma, H. M. (1982). Kinematic display of multivariate data. *Proceedings of the Third Annual Conference and Exposition of the National Computer Graphics Association* **1**, 393-400. [Chapter 5]

Draper, N. R. and Smith, H. (1966). *Applied Regression Analysis*. Wiley, New York. [Chapter 7]

Dunn, D. M. and Landwehr, J. M. (1980). Analyzing clustering effects across time. *Journal of the American Statistical Association* **75**, 8-15. [Chapter 5]

Erickson, B. H. and Nosanchuk, T. A. (1977). *Understanding Data*. McGraw-Hill Ryerson Limited, Canada. [Chapter 7]

Everitt, B. (1978). *Graphical Techniques for Multivariate Data*. North-Holland, New York. [Chapter 5]

Ezekiel, M. (1924). A method of handling curvilinear correlation for any number of variables. *Journal of the American Statistical Association* **19**, 431-453. [Chapter 7]

Feder, P. I. (1975). Computer plots for more informative regression analysis. (Unpublished notes). [Chapter 7]

Fienberg, S. E. (1979). Graphical methods in statistics. *The American Statistician* **33**, 165-178. [Chapter 5]

Filliben, J. J. (1975). The probability plot correlation coefficient test for normality. *Technometrics* **17**, 111-117. [Chapter 6]

Fisher, R. A. (1936). The use of multiple measurements in taxonomic problems. *Annals of Eugenics* **7**, 179-188. [Chapters 4, 5, 8]

Fisherkeller, M. A., Friedman, J. H., and Tukey, J. W. (1974). PRIM-9: An interactive multidimensional data display and analysis system. **Pub 1408**, Stanford Linear Accelerator Center, Stanford, California. [Chapters 5, 8]

Fowlkes, E. B., Gabbe, J. D., and McRae, J. E. (1976). A graphical technique for making a two dimensional display of multidimensional clusters. *American Statistical Association 1976 Proceedings of the Business and Economic Statistics Section.* 308-312. [Chapter 5]

Friedman, H. P., Farrell, E. S., Goldwyn, R. M., Miller, M., and Sigel, J. H. (1972). A graphic way of describing changing multivariate patterns. *Proceedings of the Sixth Interface Symposium on Computer Science and Statistics* 56-59. University of California, Berkeley. [Chapter 5]

Friedman, J. H., McDonald, J. A., and Stuetzle, W. (1982). An introduction to real-time graphical techniques for analyzing multivariate data. *Proceedings of the Third Annual Conference and Exposition of the National Computer Graphics Association* **1**, 421-427. [Chapter 5]

Friedman, J. H. and Rafsky, L. C. (1981). Graphics for the multivariate two-sample problem. *Journal of the American Statistical Association* **76**, 277-295. [Chapter 5]

Friedman, J. H. and Stuetzle, W. (1982). Smoothing of scatterplots. (Submitted for publication.) [Chapter 4]

Friedman, J. H. and Stuetzle, W. (1982). Projection pursuit methods for data analysis. *Modern Data Analysis* (R. L. Launer and A. F. Siegel, eds.). Academic Press, New York. [Chapter 5]

Friedman, J. H. and Tukey, J. W. (1974). A projection pursuit algorithm for exploratory data analysis. *IEEE Transactions on Computers* **C-23**, 881-890. [Chapter 5]

Frisby, J. P. and Clatworthy, J. L. (1975). Learning to see complex random-dot stereograms. *Perception* **4**, 173-178. [Chapter 6]

Furnival, G. M. and Wilson, R. W. (1974). Regression by leaps and bounds. *Technometrics* **16**, 499-511. [Chapter 7]

Gabriel, K. R. (1971). The biplot graphic display of matrices with applications to principal components analysis. *Biometrika* **58**, 453-467. [Chapter 5]

Gabriel, K. R. (1981). Biplot display of multivariate matrices for inspection of data and diagnosis. *Interpreting Multivariate Data.* (V. Barnett, ed.) 167-173. Wiley, Chichester, U. K. [Chapter 5]

Gabriel, K. R. (1983). Multivariate graphics. *Encyclopedia of Statistical Science.* Wiley, New York. [Chapter 5]

Gnanadesikan, R., Kettenring, J. R., and Landwehr, J. M. (1977). Interpreting and assessing the results of cluster analyses. *Bulletin of the International Statistical Institute* **47**, 451-463. [Chapter 5]

Gnanadesikan, R. (1977). *Methods for Statistical Data Analysis of Multivariate Observations.* Wiley, New York. [Chapters 2, 5]

Gnanadesikan, R. and Wilk, M. B. (1970). A probability plotting procedure for general analysis of variance. *Journal of the Royal Statistical Society, Series B* **32**, 88-101. [Chapter 7]

Greenacre, M. J. (1981). Practical correspondence analysis. *Interpreting Multivariate Data.* (V. Barnett, ed.) 119-146. Wiley, Chichester, U. K. [Chapter 5]

Hartigan, J. A. (1975a). Printer graphics for clustering. *Journal of Statistical Computation and Simulation* **4**, 187-213. [Chapter 5]

Hartigan, J. A. (1975b). *Clustering Algorithms.* Wiley, New York. [Chapter 5]

Hastings, C., Jr. (1955). *Approximations for Digital Computers.* Princeton University Press, Princeton, New Jersey. [Chapter 6]

Huber, P. J. (1973). Robust regression: asymptotics, conjectures, and Monte Carlo. *Annals of Statistics* **1**, 799-821. [Chapter 4]

Immer F. R., Hayes, H. K., and Powers, LeRoy (1934). Statistical determination of barley varietal adaptation. *Journal of the American Society of Agronomy* **May**, 403-419. [Chapter 7]

Joiner, B. L. (1975). Living histograms. *International Statistical Review* **43**, 339-340. [Chapter 3]

Julesz, B. (1965). Texture in visual perception. *Scientific American* **212**, 38-48. [Chapter 6]

Julesz, B. (1971). *Foundations of Cyclopean Perception.* University of Chicago Press, Chicago. [Chapter 6]

Kaplan, E. L. and Meier, P. (1958). Nonparametric estimation from incomplete observations. *Journal of the American Statistical Association* **53**, 457-481. [Chapter 6]

Kendall, M. G. and Stuart A. (1977). *The Advanced Theory of Statistics, Volume 1. Fourth edition.* Hafner, New York. [Chapter 6]

Kennedy, R. E., Jr. (1973). Minority status and fertility. *American Sociological Review* **38**, 85-96. [Chapter 7]

Kleiner, B. and Hartigan, J. A. (1981). Representing points in many dimensions by trees and castles (with discussion). *Journal of the American Statistical Association* **76**, 260-276. [Chapter 5]

Knuth, D. E. (1969). *The Art of Computer Programming, Volume 1. Second edition.* Addison-Wesley, Reading, Massachusetts. [Chapter 5]

Kruskal, J. B. (1969). Toward a practical method which helps uncover the structure of a set of multivariate observations by finding the linear transformation which optimises a new 'index of condensation'. *Statistical Computation,* (R. C. Milton and J. A. Nelder, eds.). Academic Press, New York. [Chapter 5]

Kruskal, J. B. and Wish, M. (1978). *Multidimensional Scaling.* Sage Publications, Beverly Hills, California. [Chapter 5]

LaBrecque, J. (1977). Goodness-of-fit tests based on nonlinearity in probability plots. *Technometrics* **19**, 293-306. [Chapter 6]

Larsen, W. A. and McCleary, S. J. (1969). The use of partial residuals in regression analysis. Bell Laboratories Memorandum, Murray Hill, N. J. Unedited version of Larsen and McCleary (1972). [Chapter 7]

Larsen, W. A. and McCleary, S. J. (1972). The use of partial residual plots in regression analysis. *Technometrics* **14**, 781-790. [Chapter 7]

Lewart, C. R. (1973). Algorithm 463: Algorithms SCALE1, SCALE2 and SCALE3 for determination of scales on computer generated plots. *Communications of the Association for Computing Machinery* **16**, 639-640. [Chapter 8]

Lyman, C. P., O'Brien, R. C., Greene, G. C., and Papafrangos, E. D. (1981). Hibernation and longevity in the Turkish hamster *Mesocricetus brandti*. *Science* **212**, 668-670. [Chapter 4]

Mallows, C. L. (1973). Some comments on C_p. *Technometrics* **15**, 661-675. [Chapter 7]

Matthew, D. E. and Farewell, V. T. (1982). On testing for a constant hazard against a change-point alternative. *Biometrics* **38**, 463-468. [Chapter 6]

McGill, R. Tukey, J. W., and Larsen, W. A. (1978). Variations of box plots. *The American Statistician* **32**, 12-16. [Chapters 2, 3]

Michael, J. R. (1979). Fundamentals of probability plotting with applications to censored data. Bell Laboratories Memorandum [Chapter 6]

Michael, J. R. (1983). The stabilized probability plot. *Biometrika*, to appear. [Chapter 6]

Mosteller, F. and Tukey, J. W. (1977). *Data Analysis and Regression*. Addison-Wesley, Reading, Massachusetts. [Chapters 5, 6, 7]

Newton, C. M. (1978). Graphics: from alpha to omega in data analysis. *Graphical Representation of Multivariate Data*. (P. C. C. Wang, ed.) 59-92. Academic Press, New York. [Chapter 5]

Phillips, D. P. (1978). Airplane accident fatalities increase just after newspaper stories about murder and suicide. *Science* **201**, 748-750. [Chapter 4]

Playfair, W. (1786). *The Commercial and Political Atlas*. London. [Chapter 2]

Scott, D. W. (1979). On optimal and data-based histograms. *Biometrika* **66**, 605-610. [Chapter 2]

Shapiro, S. S. and Wilk, M. B. (1965). An analysis of variance test for normality (complete samples). *Biometrika* **52**, 591-611. [Chapter 6]

Simpson, J., Olsen, A., and Eden, J. C. (1975). A Bayesian analysis of a multiplicative treatment effect in weather modification. *Technometrics* **17**, 161-166. [Chapters 3, 6]

Stone, C. J. (1977). Consistent nonparametric regression. *Annals of Statistics* **5**, 595-620. [Chapter 4]

Tarter, M. E. and Kronmal, R. A. (1976). An introduction to the implementation and theory of nonparametric density estimation. *The American Statistician* **30**, 105-112. [Chapter 2]

Tippett, L. H. C. (1952). *The Methods of Statistics. Fourth Edition*. Wiley, New York. [Chapters 4, 6]

Tufte, E. (1978). Data graphics. *First General Conference on Social Graphics*. Leesburg, Virginia. [Chapter 8]

Tukey, J. W., Friedman, J. H., and Fisherkeller, M. A. (1976). PRIM-9, an interactive multidimensional data display and analysis system. *Proceedings of the 4th International Congress for Stereology* Gaithersburg, Maryland. [Chapter 5]

Tukey, J. W. (1949). One degree of freedom for nonadditivity. *Biometrics* **5**, 232-242. [Chapter 7]

Tukey, J. W. (1972). Some graphic and semigraphic displays. *Statistical Papers in Honor of George W. Snedecor*. (T. A. Bancroft, ed.) 292-316. Iowa State University Press, Ames, Iowa. [Chapters 6, 8]

Tukey, J. W. (1977). *Exploratory Data Analysis*. Addison-Wesley, Reading, Massachusetts. [Chapters 2, 3, 4, 7]

Tukey, J. W. and Tukey, P. A. (1983). Some graphics for studying four-dimensional data. *Computer Science and Statistics: Proceedings of the 14th Symposium on the Interface*. 60-66. Springer-Verlag, New York. [Chapter 5]

Tukey, J. W. and Wilk, M. B. (1966). Data analysis and statistics: an expository overview. *AFIPS Conference Proceedings* **29**, 695-709. [Chapter 8]

Tukey, P. A. (1980). Unpublished notes. [Chapter 4]

Tukey, P. A. and Tukey, J. W. (1981). Graphical display of data sets in 3 or more dimensions. Chapters 10, 11, and 12 in *Interpreting Multivariate Data*. (V. Barnett, ed.) Wiley, Chichester, U. K. [Chapters 4, 5, 8]

Velleman, P. F. and Hoaglin, D. C. (1981). *Applications, Basics, and Computing of Exploratory Data Analysis*. Duxbury Press, North Situate, Massachusetts. [Chapters 2, 3, 6]

Wachter, K. W. (1975). Harvard University Research Report **W-75-1**, Cambridge, Massachusetts. [Chapter 5]

Wainer, H. and Thissen, D. (1981). Graphical data analysis. *Annual Review of Psychology* **32**, 191-241. [Chapter 5]

Wakimoto, K. and Taguri, M. (1978). Constellation graphical method for representing multi-dimensional data. *Annals of the Institute of Statistical Mathematics* **30**, 97-104. [Chapter 5]

Wang, P. C. C. (ed.) (1978). *Graphical Representation of Multivariate Data.* Academic Press, New York. [Chapter 5]

Wegman, E. J. (1972). Nonparametric probability density estimation: I. A summary of available methods. *Technometrics* **14**, 533-546. [Chapter 2]

Weisberg, S. (1980). *Applied Linear Regression.* Wiley, New York. [Chapter 7]

Wilk, M. B., Gnanadesikan, R., and Huyett, M. J. (1963). Separate maximum likelihood estimation of scale or shape parameters of the gamma distribution using order statistics. *Biometrika* **50**, 217-221. [Chapter 6]

Wilk, M. B. and Gnanadesikan, R. (1968). Probability plotting methods for the analysis of data. *Biometrika* **55**, 1-17. [Chapters 2, 3, 6]

Wilson, E. B. and Hilferty, M. M. (1931). The distribution of chi-square. *Proceedings of the National Academy of Sciences* **17**, 684-688. [Chapter 6]

Wood, F. S. (1973). The use of individual effects and residuals in fitting equations to data. *Technometrics* **15**, 677-695. [Chapter 7]

Yule, G. U. (1927). On the method of investigating periodicity in disturbed series, with special reference to Wolfer's sunspot numbers. *Philosophical Transactions of the Royal Statistical Society, Series A* **226**, 267-298. [Chapter 7]

Appendix - Data Sets

CONTENTS

1. Maximum Daily Ozone Concentrations 346
2. Air Quality Measurements for the New York Metropolitan Area 347
3. Exponent Data 349
4. Singers' Heights 350
5. Rainfall from Cloud-Seeding 351
6. Ages of Signers of the Declaration of Independence 351
7. Statistics of Automobile Models 352
8. Baseball Batting Averages 356
9. Average Monthly Temperatures 357
10. Graph Areas 1 359
11. Salaries Around the World 360
12. Hibernation Data 362
13. Graph Areas 2 363
14. Anderson's Iris Data 365
15. Wheat Data 367
16. Socioeconomic Data for 35 Countries 368
17. Murder-Suicides by Deliberately Crashing Private Airplanes 369
18. Number of Telephones in the United States 370
19. Average Brain and Body Weights for 62 Species of Mammals 371
20. Bell Laboratories Managers' Data 373
21. Egg Sizes of the Common Tern 374
22. Stack Loss Data 376
23. Tar Content Data 377
24. Tooth Measurements of Humans, Apes and Fossils 378
25. Rubber Specimen Data 379
26. Stereogram Data 380
27. Life Times of Mechanical Devices 381
28. Remission Durations of 84 Leukemia Patients 382
29. Wölfer's Sunspot Numbers, 1749-1924 383
30. Barley Yield 384
31. Fertility in Ireland 385
32. Rubber Compressibility 385
33. Heart Catheterization 386

1. Maximum Daily Ozone Concentrations

Daily maximum ozone concentrations at Stamford, Connecticut (Stmf) and Yonkers, New York (Ykrs), during the period May 1, 1974 to September 30, 1974, recorded in parts per billion (*ppb*). Missing observations are shown as "—". Source: Stamford, Connecticut Department of Environmental Protection. Yonkers, Boyce Thompson Institute. [Chapters 2, 3, 4]

May		June		July		August		September	
Stmf	Ykrs	Stmf	Ykrs	Stmf	Ykrs	Stmf	Ykrs	Stmf	Ykrs
66	47	61	36	152	76	80	66	113	66
52	37	47	24	201	108	68	82	38	18
—	27	—	52	134	85	24	47	38	25
—	37	196	88	206	96	24	28	28	14
—	38	131	111	92	48	82	44	52	27
—	—	173	117	101	60	100	55	14	9
49	45	37	31	119	54	55	34	38	16
64	52	47	37	124	71	91	60	94	67
68	51	215	93	133	—	87	70	89	74
26	22	230	106	83	50	64	41	99	74
86	27	—	49	—	27	—	67	150	75
52	25	69	64	60	37	—	127	146	74
43	—	98	83	124	47	170	96	113	42
75	55	125	97	142	71	—	56	38	—
87	72	94	79	124	46	86	54	66	38
188	132	72	36	64	41	202	100	38	23
118	—	72	51	75	49	71	44	80	50
103	106	125	75	103	59	85	44	80	34
82	42	143	104	—	53	122	75	99	58
71	45	192	107	46	25	155	86	71	35
103	80	—	56	68	45	80	70	42	24
240	107	122	68	—	78	71	53	52	27
31	21	32	19	87	40	28	36	33	17
40	50	114	67	27	13	212	117	38	21
47	31	32	20	—	25	80	43	24	14
51	37	23	35	73	46	24	27	61	32
31	19	71	30	59	62	80	77	108	51
47	33	38	31	119	80	169	75	38	15
14	22	136	81	64	39	174	87	28	21
—	67	169	119	—	70	141	47	—	18
71	45			111	74	202	114		

2. Air Quality Measurements for the New York Metropolitan Area

Daily readings of the following air quality values from May 1, 1973 (a Tuesday) to September 30, 1973: mean ozone in parts per billion from 1300 to 1500 hours at Roosevelt Island, solar radiation (Sol R) in Langleys in the frequency band 4000-7700 Å from 0800 to 1200 hours at Central Park, average wind speed (Wind) in miles per hour at 0700 and 1000 hours at LaGuardia Airport, maximum daily temperature (Temp) in degrees Fahrenheit at La Guardia Airport. Source: ozone data — New York State Department of Conservation; meteorological data — National Weather Service. [Chapters 2, 3, 4, 5, 7]

May 1973				June 1973			
Ozone ppb	Sol R lang	Wind mph	Temp °F	Ozone ppb	Sol R lang	Wind mph	Temp °F
41	190	7.4	67	—	286	8.6	78
36	118	8.0	72	—	287	9.7	74
12	149	12.6	74	—	242	16.1	67
18	313	11.5	62	—	186	9.2	84
—	—	14.3	56	—	220	8.6	85
28	—	14.9	66	—	264	14.3	79
23	299	8.6	65	29	127	9.7	82
19	99	13.8	59	—	273	6.9	87
8	19	20.1	61	71	291	13.8	90
—	194	8.6	69	39	323	11.5	87
7	—	6.9	74	—	259	10.9	93
16	256	9.7	69	—	250	9.2	92
11	290	9.2	66	23	148	8.0	82
14	274	10.9	68	—	332	13.8	80
18	65	13.2	58	—	322	11.5	79
14	334	11.5	64	21	191	14.9	77
34	307	12.0	66	37	284	20.7	72
6	78	18.4	57	20	37	9.2	65
30	322	11.5	68	12	120	11.5	73
11	44	9.7	62	13	137	10.3	76
1	8	9.7	59	—	150	6.3	77
11	320	16.6	73	—	59	1.7	76
4	25	9.7	61	—	91	4.6	76
32	92	12.0	61	—	250	6.3	76
—	66	16.6	57	—	135	8.0	75
—	266	14.9	58	—	127	8.0	78
—	—	8.0	57	—	47	10.3	73
23	13	12.0	67	—	98	11.5	80
45	252	14.9	81	—	31	14.9	77
115	223	5.7	79	—	138	8.0	83
37	279	7.4	76				

2. Air Quality Measurements for New York, (cont'd)

July 1973				August 1973			
Ozone ppb	Sol R lang	Wind mph	Temp °F	Ozone ppb	Sol R lang	Wind mph	Temp °F
135	269	4.0	84	39	83	6.9	81
49	248	9.2	85	9	24	13.8	81
32	236	9.2	81	16	77	7.4	82
—	101	10.9	84	78	—	6.9	86
64	175	4.6	83	35	—	7.4	85
40	314	10.9	83	66	—	4.6	87
77	276	5.1	88	122	255	4.0	89
97	267	6.3	92	89	229	10.3	90
97	272	5.7	92	110	207	8.0	90
85	175	7.4	89	—	222	8.6	92
—	139	8.6	82	—	137	11.5	86
10	264	14.3	73	44	192	11.5	86
27	175	14.9	81	28	273	11.5	82
—	291	14.9	91	65	157	9.7	80
7	48	14.3	80	—	64	11.5	79
48	260	6.9	81	22	71	10.3	77
35	274	10.3	82	59	51	6.3	79
61	285	6.3	84	23	115	7.4	76
79	187	5.1	87	31	244	10.9	78
63	220	11.5	85	44	190	10.3	78
16	7	6.9	74	21	259	15.5	77
—	258	9.7	81	9	36	14.3	72
—	295	11.5	82	—	255	12.6	75
80	294	8.6	86	45	212	9.7	79
108	223	8.0	85	168	238	3.4	81
20	81	8.6	82	73	215	8.0	86
52	82	12.0	86	—	153	5.7	88
82	213	7.4	88	76	203	9.7	97
50	275	7.4	86	118	225	2.3	94
64	253	7.4	83	84	237	6.3	96
59	254	9.2	81	85	188	6.3	94

2. Air Quality Measurements for New York, (cont'd)

September 1-15, 1973				September 16-30, 1973			
Ozone ppb	Sol R lang	Wind mph	Temp °F	Ozone ppb	Sol R lang	Wind mph	Temp °F
96	167	6.9	91	46	237	6.9	78
78	197	5.1	92	18	224	13.8	67
73	183	2.8	93	13	27	10.3	76
91	189	4.6	93	24	238	10.3	68
47	95	7.4	87	16	201	8.0	82
32	92	15.5	84	13	238	12.6	64
20	252	10.9	80	23	14	9.2	71
23	220	10.3	78	36	139	10.3	81
21	230	10.9	75	7	49	10.3	69
24	259	9.7	73	14	20	16.6	63
44	236	14.9	81	30	193	6.9	70
21	259	15.5	76	—	145	13.2	77
28	238	6.3	77	14	191	14.3	75
9	24	10.9	71	18	131	8.0	76
13	112	11.5	71	20	223	11.5	68

3. Exponent Data

Measured exponents for 24 people from a perceptual psychological experiment. The values have been multiplied by 100, rounded to the nearest integer, and ordered from smallest to largest. Source: Cleveland, Harris and McGill (1982). [Chapters 2, 6, 7]

58	63	69	72	74	79
88	88	90	91	93	94
97	97	99	99	99	100
103	104	105	107	118	127

4. Singers' Heights

Heights in inches of the singers in the New York Choral Society in 1979. The data are grouped according to eight voice parts; the vocal range of each voice parts decreases in pitch in the order in which the voice parts are given in the table. Soprano 1 is highest, soprano 2 is next highest, and so forth. The four highest parts are female voices and the four lowest parts are male voices. [Chapters 2, 3]

Soprano 1

64 62 66 65 60 61 65 66 65 63 67 65 62 65 68 65 63 65
62 65 66 62 65 63 65 66 65 62 65 66 65 61 65 66 65 62

Soprano 2

63 67 60 67 66 62 65 62 61 62 66 60 65 65 61 64 68 64
63 62 64 62 64 65 60 65 70 63 67 66

Alto 1

65 62 68 67 67 63 67 66 63 72 62 61 66 64 60 61 66 66
66 62 70 65 64 63 65 69 61 66 65 61 63 64 67 66 68

Alto 2

70 65 65 65 64 66 64 70 63 70 64 63 67 65 63 66 66 64
64 70 70 66 66 66 69 67 65

Tenor 1

69 72 71 66 76 74 71 66 68 67 70 65 72 70 68 64 73 66
68 67 64

Tenor 2

68 73 69 71 69 76 71 69 71 66 69 71 71 71 69 70 69 68
70 68 69

Bass 1

72 70 72 69 73 71 72 68 68 71 66 68 71 73 73 70 68 70
75 68 71 70 74 70 75 75 69 72 71 70 71 68 70 75 72 66
72 70 69

Bass 2

72 75 67 75 74 72 72 74 72 72 74 70 66 68 75 68 70 72
67 70 70 69 72 71 74 75

---

5. Rainfall from Cloud-Seeding

Rainfall in acre-feet from 52 clouds, of which 26 were chosen randomly and seeded with silver oxide. Source: Simpson, Olsen and Eden (1975). [Chapters 2, 3, 6]

Rainfall from Control Clouds		Rainfall from Seeded Clouds	
1202.6	41.1	2745.6	200.7
830.1	36.6	1697.8	198.6
372.4	29.0	1656.0	129.6
345.5	28.6	978.0	119.0
321.2	26.3	703.4	118.3
244.3	26.1	489.1	115.3
163.0	24.4	430.0	92.4
147.8	21.7	334.1	40.6
95.0	17.3	302.8	32.7
87.0	11.5	274.7	31.4
81.2	4.9	274.7	17.5
68.5	4.9	255.0	7.7
47.3	1.0	242.5	4.1

Reproduced by permission of the American Statistical Association.

6. Ages of Signers of the Declaration of Independence

Fifty-six men signed the Declaration of Independence. The birthdates of 47 were known accurately, day, month, year; but for 8 only the year was known and for one no birthdate was available. Their ages as of July 4, 1776 are shown. Signers for whom only the year was known have two possible ages shown. The signer of unknown age is omitted. [Chapter 2]

26	34	39	44	46	53	32 or 33
26	35	39	45	47	53	34 or 35
29	35	40	45	48	55	43 or 44
30	35	41	45	49	60	49 or 50
31	37	41	45	50	63	51 or 52
33	37	42	46	50	69	59 or 60
33	38	42	46	50	70	61 or 62
34	38	42	46	52		62 or 63

7. Statistics of Automobile Models

The data give the following statistics for 74 automobiles in the 1979 model year as sold in the United States: price in dollars, mileage in miles per gallon, repair records for 1978 and 1977 (rated on a 5-point scale; 5 best, 1 worst), headroom in inches, rear seat clearance (distance from front seat back to rear seat back) in inches, trunk space in cubic feet, weight in pounds, length in inches, turning diameter (clearance required to make a U-turn) in feet, displacement in cubic inches, and gear ratio for high gear. Data is from various sources, primarily *Consumers Reports*, April 1979, and the United States Government EPA statistics on fuel consumption. [Chapters 2, 4, 5, 6, 7]

Make & Model	Price $	Mileage mpg	Repair Record 1978	Repair Record 1977	Head-room in	Rear Seat in	Trunk Space cu ft	Weight lbs	Length in	Turn Circle ft	Displace-ment cu in	Gear Ratio
AMC Concord	4099	22	3	2	2.5	27.5	11	2930	186	40	121	3.58
AMC Pacer	4749	17	3	1	3.0	25.5	11	3350	173	40	258	2.53
AMC Spirit	3799	22	—	—	3.0	18.5	12	2640	168	35	121	3.08
Audi 5000	9690	17	5	2	3.0	27.0	15	2830	189	37	131	3.20
Audi Fox	6295	23	3	3	2.5	28.0	11	2070	174	36	97	3.70
BMW 320i	9735	25	4	4	2.5	26.0	12	2650	177	34	121	3.64
Buick Century	4816	20	3	3	4.5	29.0	16	3250	196	40	196	2.93
Buick Electra	7827	15	4	4	4.0	31.5	20	4080	222	43	350	2.41
Buick Le Sabre	5788	18	3	4	4.0	30.5	21	3670	218	43	231	2.73
Buick Opel	4453	26	—	—	3.0	24.0	10	2230	170	34	304	2.87
Buick Regal	5189	20	3	3	2.0	28.5	16	3280	200	42	196	2.93
Buick Riviera	10372	16	3	4	3.5	30.0	17	3880	207	43	231	2.93
Buick Skylark	4082	19	3	3	3.5	27.0	13	3400	200	42	231	3.08
Cad. Deville	11385	14	3	3	4.0	31.5	20	4330	221	44	425	2.28
Cad. Eldorado	14500	14	2	2	3.5	30.0	16	3900	204	43	350	2.19
Cad. Seville	15906	21	3	3	3.0	30.0	13	4290	204	45	350	2.24

7. Statistics of Automobile Models, (cont'd)

Make & Model	Price $	Mileage mpg	Repair Record 1978	Repair Record 1977	Head-room in	Rear Seat in	Trunk Space cu ft	Weight lbs	Length in	Turn Circle ft	Displace-ment cu in	Gear Ratio
Chev. Chevette	3299	29	3	3	2.5	26.0	9	2110	163	34	231	2.93
Chev. Impala	5705	16	4	4	4.0	29.5	20	3690	212	43	250	2.56
Chev. Malibu	4504	22	3	3	3.5	28.5	17	3180	193	41	200	2.73
Chev. Monte Carlo	5104	22	2	3	2.0	28.5	16	3220	200	41	200	2.73
Chev. Monza	3667	24	2	2	2.0	25.0	7	2750	179	40	151	2.73
Chev. Nova	3955	19	3	3	3.5	27.0	13	3430	197	43	250	2.56
Datsun 200-SX	6229	23	4	3	1.5	21.0	6	2370	170	35	119	3.89
Datsun 210	4589	35	5	5	2.0	23.5	8	2020	165	32	85	3.70
Datsun 510	5079	24	4	4	2.5	22.0	8	2280	170	34	119	3.54
Datsun 810	8129	21	4	4	2.5	27.0	8	2750	184	38	146	3.55
Dodge Colt	3984	30	5	4	2.0	24.0	8	2120	163	35	98	3.54
Dodge Diplomat	5010	18	2	2	4.0	29.0	17	3600	206	46	318	2.47
Dodge Magnum XE	5886	16	2	2	3.5	26.0	16	3870	216	48	318	2.71
Dodge St. Regis	6342	17	2	2	4.5	28.0	21	3740	220	46	225	2.94
Fiat Strada	4296	21	3	1	2.5	26.5	16	2130	161	36	105	3.37
Ford Fiesta	4389	28	4	—	1.5	26.0	9	1800	147	33	98	3.15
Ford Mustang	4187	21	3	3	2.0	23.0	10	2650	179	42	140	3.08
Honda Accord	5799	25	5	5	3.0	25.5	10	2240	172	36	107	3.05
Honda Civic	4499	28	4	4	2.5	23.5	5	1760	149	34	91	3.30
Linc. Continental	11497	12	3	4	3.5	30.5	22	4840	233	51	400	2.47
Linc. Cont Mark V	13594	12	3	4	2.5	28.5	18	4720	230	48	400	2.47
Linc. Versailles	13466	14	3	3	3.5	27.0	15	3830	201	41	302	2.47

7. Statistics of Automobile Models, (cont'd)

Make & Model	Price $	Mileage mpg	Repair Record 1978	Repair Record 1977	Head-room in	Rear Seat in	Trunk Space cu ft	Weight lbs	Length in	Turn Circle ft	Displacement cu in	Gear Ratio
Mazda GLC	3995	30	4	4	3.5	25.5	11	1980	154	33	86	3.73
Merc. Bobcat	3829	22	4	3	3.0	25.5	9	2580	169	39	140	2.73
Merc. Cougar	5379	14	4	3	3.5	29.5	16	4060	221	48	302	2.75
Merc. Cougar XR-7	6303	14	4	4	3.0	25.0	16	4130	217	45	302	2.75
Merc. Marquis	6165	15	3	2	3.5	30.5	23	3720	212	44	302	2.26
Merc. Monarch	4516	18	3	—	3.0	27.0	15	3370	198	41	250	2.43
Merc. Zephyr	3291	20	3	3	3.5	29.0	17	2830	195	43	140	3.08
Olds. 98	8814	21	4	4	4.0	31.5	20	4060	220	43	350	2.41
Olds. Cutlass	4733	19	3	3	4.5	28.0	16	3300	198	42	231	2.93
Olds. Cutl Supr	5172	19	3	4	2.0	28.0	16	3310	198	42	231	2.93
Olds. Delta 88	5890	18	4	4	4.0	29.0	20	3690	218	42	231	2.73
Olds. Omega	4181	19	3	3	4.5	27.0	14	3370	200	43	231	3.08
Olds. Starfire	4195	24	1	1	2.0	25.5	10	2720	180	40	151	2.73
Olds. Toronado	10371	16	3	3	3.5	30.0	17	4030	206	43	350	2.41
Peugeot 604 SL	12990	14	—	—	3.5	30.5	14	3420	192	38	163	3.58
Plym. Arrow	4647	28	3	3	2.0	21.5	11	2360	170	37	156	3.05
Plym. Champ	4425	34	5	4	2.5	23.0	11	1800	157	37	86	2.97
Plym. Horizon	4482	25	3	—	4.0	25.0	17	2200	165	36	105	3.37
Plym. Sapporo	6486	26	—	—	1.5	22.0	8	2520	182	38	119	3.54
Plym. Volare	4060	18	2	2	5.0	31.0	16	3330	201	44	225	3.23

7. Statistics of Automobile Models, (cont'd)

Make & Model	Price $	Mileage mpg	Repair Record 1978	Repair Record 1977	Head-room in	Rear Seat in	Trunk Space cu ft	Weight lbs	Length in	Turn Circle ft	Displacement cu in	Gear Ratio
Pont. Catalina	5798	18	4	4	4.0	29.0	20	3700	214	42	231	2.73
Pont. Firebird	4934	18	1	2	1.5	23.5	7	3470	198	42	231	3.08
Pont. Grand Prix	5222	19	3	3	2.0	28.5	16	3210	201	45	231	2.93
Pont. Le Mans	4723	19	3	3	3.5	28.0	17	3200	199	40	231	2.93
Pont. Phoenix	4424	19	—	—	3.5	27.0	13	3420	203	43	231	3.08
Pont. Sunbird	4172	24	2	2	2.0	25.0	7	2690	179	41	151	2.73
Renault Le Car	3895	26	3	3	3.0	23.0	10	1830	142	34	79	3.72
Subaru	3798	35	5	4	2.5	25.5	11	2050	164	36	97	3.81
Toyota Celica	5899	18	5	5	2.5	22.0	14	2410	174	36	134	3.06
Toyota Corolla	3748	31	5	5	3.0	24.5	9	2200	165	35	97	3.21
Toyota Corona	5719	18	5	5	2.0	23.0	11	2670	175	36	134	3.05
VW Rabbit	4697	25	4	3	3.0	25.5	15	1930	155	35	89	3.78
VW Rabbit Diesel	5397	41	5	4	3.0	25.5	15	2040	155	35	90	3.78
VW Scirocco	6850	25	4	3	2.0	23.5	16	1990	156	36	97	3.78
VW Dasher	7140	23	4	3	2.5	37.5	12	2160	172	36	97	3.74
Volvo 260	11995	17	5	3	2.5	29.5	14	3170	193	37	163	2.98

8. Baseball Batting Averages

1979 batting averages (times 1000) of all baseball players in the American League and the National League who were at bat 100 times or more. A player's batting average is his total number of hits divided by his total number of official times at bat. [Chapters 2, 3]

1979 National League Batting Averages Times 1000

150	162	164	167	192	197	202	207	207	210	217	216
211	217	216	211	225	224	227	227	221	227	231	239
233	239	238	234	232	238	238	249	249	248	248	249
248	248	245	243	243	241	241	247	248	243	249	241
259	259	258	254	254	250	250	256	253	252	259	253
259	257	254	253	251	265	262	268	265	262	268	268
262	260	264	268	263	260	276	273	272	276	273	272
270	274	274	271	276	276	275	270	275	271	276	273
279	276	273	289	288	285	284	283	283	281	289	287
282	281	283	286	281	280	288	288	282	281	284	283
287	287	286	290	290	297	298	298	293	295	291	294
304	302	307	306	303	304	301	300	308	314	310	318
318	316	315	310	314	327	321	335	333	331	344	

1979 American League Batting Averages Times 1000

167	171	179	188	186	198	203	200	206	203	200	200
211	212	215	215	218	211	224	229	220	223	222	229
224	223	229	222	239	230	230	236	233	237	230	233
231	239	239	237	249	248	247	248	242	240	246	245
240	246	243	246	244	249	248	246	248	243	248	247
243	247	257	254	254	254	257	254	253	254	252	259
255	254	254	253	256	255	253	256	261	266	265	261
269	264	263	264	264	262	267	266	267	266	263	267
267	262	261	265	260	278	274	272	270	276	276	274
275	275	277	279	275	270	270	276	271	271	271	270
279	278	278	271	271	273	270	277	275	273	273	274
277	274	288	285	287	280	286	285	280	280	288	287
283	282	284	282	289	285	281	287	283	288	288	280
285	288	288	287	295	295	297	296	294	293	290	296
295	295	291	293	297	297	299	293	292	300	309	308
300	305	301	311	318	318	313	318	315	313	316	319
325	326	329	325	322	321	323	337	333	358		

9. Average Monthly Temperatures

Average monthly temperatures in degrees Fahrenheit, from January 1964 to December 1973 in Eureka, California (Eurk), Lincoln, Nebraska (Linc) and Newark, New Jersey (Newk). Source: Local Climatological Data, U. S. Department of Commerce, National Oceanic and Atmospheric Administration, Environmental Data Service. [Chapters 2, 3, 6]

Year	Eurk	Linc	Newk	Year	Eurk	Linc	Newk
1964	46.6	31.6	34.3	1967	47.4	25.2	36.9
	47.0	31.3	31.9		47.6	29.3	29.4
	45.7	35.3	42.6		46.7	43.6	37.6
	47.1	53.2	49.1		46.2	54.1	50.9
	50.4	67.9	65.4		51.9	59.0	54.3
	54.8	71.7	71.2		54.6	70.1	72.0
	56.6	82.0	76.0		56.5	74.9	74.2
	57.0	72.0	73.9		56.8	72.8	73.5
	55.2	65.7	68.9		59.1	63.5	66.6
	54.9	54.8	55.9		56.9	53.7	56.4
	50.0	42.2	49.4		53.3	39.4	42.2
	48.5	26.5	35.9		45.1	29.9	38.3
1965	47.3	24.4	28.3	1968	46.6	24.9	27.8
	45.7	22.6	32.4		53.2	28.2	29.9
	48.5	26.7	39.0		50.6	46.0	43.1
	50.1	52.5	50.0		48.1	52.9	54.0
	49.9	66.7	67.3		52.4	58.8	59.6
	51.9	70.8	71.6		55.5	74.6	69.7
	54.8	75.8	75.7		56.3	77.8	78.2
	58.9	74.8	74.5		59.3	76.0	76.9
	53.9	60.1	68.4		57.5	66.2	70.7
	55.7	57.8	54.0		53.3	57.2	59.7
	54.6	42.9	44.4		51.8	38.1	45.7
	47.0	36.2	38.8		46.5	24.1	32.5
1966	47.7	18.4	30.4	1969	44.0	19.6	31.3
	46.5	28.3	33.2		46.2	27.1	31.3
	48.0	43.2	41.7		48.3	31.6	38.8
	50.4	46.7	48.2		49.8	54.1	54.6
	50.4	61.4	59.3		53.4	64.3	64.1
	55.5	72.5	73.8		56.6	68.5	72.8
	56.6	81.4	79.6		55.6	79.1	74.2
	55.9	72.6	76.5		55.8	76.8	77.3
	58.0	63.9	66.6		56.5	68.7	67.5
	53.2	55.6	55.5		55.2	50.4	56.2
	52.6	40.5	48.9		51.3	42.7	45.5
	49.5	28.2	36.5		51.3	27.0	33.1

9. Average Monthly Temperatures, (cont'd)

Year	Eurk	Linc	Newk	Year	Eurk	Linc	Newk
1970	52.1	18.6	24.2	1972	44.6	20.8	35.4
	51.4	33.2	33.0		49.0	26.1	31.3
	49.9	36.0	39.0		51.2	41.5	40.5
	47.4	53.4	51.9		49.1	49.7	50.0
	52.3	68.3	64.6		51.2	60.7	63.0
	54.3	74.9	70.9		54.6	71.2	68.8
	54.8	79.1	77.2		57.8	74.1	77.9
	55.3	78.0	77.3		58.2	72.2	75.9
	55.7	66.0	70.6		55.8	65.1	69.8
	52.6	52.0	59.5		54.2	49.0	53.3
	53.5	39.0	49.1		51.8	36.2	44.8
	47.4	31.2	35.3		45.7	21.6	39.7
1971	45.7	19.9	27.3	1973	47.3	23.4	35.5
	46.3	26.3	35.2		50.7	28.4	33.3
	47.1	37.5	41.2		47.4	42.6	48.6
	48.1	54.3	51.4		50.1	49.6	54.2
	50.6	60.4	60.6		52.0	59.0	60.4
	54.3	78.0	74.8		55.1	73.4	74.6
	55.2	74.6	77.8		55.6	75.0	78.7
	60.0	76.2	76.0		54.8	77.2	79.6
	56.7	68.1	71.8		57.1	63.2	71.0
	50.6	58.8	63.2		52.1	56.1	60.3
	49.4	41.8	46.2		51.4	39.0	48.8
	45.0	31.2	41.4		51.2	21.8	39.4

10. Graph Areas 1

Average areas of graphs in square centimeters for 50 articles, in each of 21 scientific journals printed in one column format and 29 scientific journals printed in multi-column format. Source: Cleveland (1982). [Chapter 3]

One-Column Format Journals

Journal	Area cm^2	Journal	Area cm^2
Geogr Rev	247	Am J Sociol	117
Comput Gra Im Proc	174	Biometika	116
Geogr J	148	Profess Geogr	115
Br J Psychol	140	Proc R Soc (Ser B)	111
J Exp Biol	129	Econometrica	109
Am Math Mo	125	Bell Syst Tech J	108
Life Sciences	124	Bell J Econ	107
J R Stat Soc (Ser C)	123	J Appl Polym Sci	103
J Chem (Faraday Trans)	122	J Exp Med	101
J Physics (C)	118	J Polit Econ	99
Am Educ Res	117		

Multi-Column Format Journals

Journal	Area cm^2	Journal	Area cm^2
Scientific Am	199	Rev Econ Stat	87
Educ Res	140	Percept Psychophys	87
J Geophys Res	139	J Clin Investigation	85
Ann As Am Geogr	125	Cell	84
Am Sociol Rev	123	J Appl Physics	81
Computer J	111	Science (Articles)	79
J Am Stat As (Theory)	108	J Phys Chem	79
Nature (London)	107	Science (Reports)	78
Computer	104	New Eng J Med	78
J Am Stat As (Applic)	101	Phys Rev (A)	75
IEEE Trans Commun	100	Phys Rev (Lett)	73
J Exp Psychol	96	J Am Chem Soc	68
IEEE Comm Radar Sig	96	Lancet	68
IBM J Res Develop	91	Am Econ Rev	57
Commun ACM	89		

11. Salaries Around the World

Salaries as of 1979, quoted in Swiss francs, of seven different professions in 44 cities around the world. Source: *Prices and Salaries Around the World*, 1979/80 edition. Union Bank of Switzerland, Zurich. [Chapters 3,4,5,7]

City	Teacher	Chauffeur	Mechanic	Cook	Manager	Elect. Engineer	Cashier
Abu Dhabi	16800	15336	8996	31562	26520	31635	11960
Amsterdam	34125	29820	26642	37067	59280	47730	32200
Athens	11025	10650	12456	19451	31980	18870	16100
Bahrain	10500	5112	6574	14680	56940	44955	18400
Bangkok	3150	3408	3460	12478	14820	7770	3680
Bogota	4725	3408	3806	12478	14040	14430	3220
Brussels	28350	26412	25258	24589	59280	33855	38640
Buenos Aires	5775	6390	6574	36333	21060	36075	13800
Caracas	11550	14058	20068	35232	45240	42180	17940
Chicago	33600	36636	39790	30094	60060	48285	24380
Copenhagen	32550	31950	34946	46976	67080	53280	33120
Dublin	18375	13206	13840	20919	23400	25530	17020
Dusseldorf	33600	33228	23528	31562	63180	44400	30360
Geneva	56700	44304	37022	31929	71760	53835	45080
Helsinki	19950	19596	17646	16515	48360	33855	17940
Hongkong	11550	7668	5882	14680	20280	17205	11500
Istanbul	4725	5964	6228	9909	13260	12210	5980
Jakarta	2625	2130	2422	5505	8580	6105	3220
Jeddah	21000	20360	20760	26057	60060	32745	22540
Johannesburg	14700	13206	16608	19818	31200	36630	13800
London	20475	18318	17646	14680	31200	21090	17020

11. Salaries Around the World, (cont'd)

City	Teacher	Chauffeur	Mechanic	Cook	Manager	Elect. Engineer.	Cashier
Los Angeles	32550	29394	36330	32296	59280	46065	17940
Luxemburg	42000	35784	20068	24956	63960	63270	38640
Madrid	14700	14058	12110	18717	32760	31635	24380
Manila	2100	2982	1730	4771	20280	4440	4140
Mexico City	6825	6816	8304	27892	28860	22200	11040
Milan	12600	14910	13494	16148	17160	31080	23920
Montreal	29400	25560	23528	20185	51480	34410	15180
New York	27300	26838	32870	48444	67080	53280	20240
Oslo	25200	25560	25258	31195	42900	42735	28060
Panama	4725	4260	7266	12478	22620	24420	10120
Paris	24150	24282	15916	30828	40560	43845	21160
Rio de Janeiro	7350	7242	8650	15047	53040	42735	9660
San Francisco	32025	30246	34946	50279	65520	46065	16560
Sao Paulo	9450	8520	11072	12845	64740	29970	11040
Singapore	8925	4260	5190	10276	24960	8325	9200
Stockholm	28875	24708	25950	33397	54600	33855	26680
Sydney	28350	19596	20068	21286	34320	31080	19780
Teheran	12600	11076	13840	24956	26520	37185	18400
Tel-Aviv	7875	11928	9688	9542	14040	14430	6440
Tokyo	30450	26412	16954	25690	63180	34410	40940
Toronto	29925	25986	25950	20919	44460	39960	14260
Vienna	19425	23430	19722	18717	42900	38850	26220
Zurich	52500	42600	34600	36700	78000	55500	46000

12. Hibernation Data

Percent of lifetime spent in hibernation (Hib) and age at death in days, for 144 hamsters, from an experiment to investigate whether increased hibernation results in increased life span. Data were digitized from a graph in the article. Source: Lyman et al. (1981). [Chapter 4]

Hib %	Age days	Hib %	Age days	Hib %	Age days	Hib %	Age days
0	116	9	711	15	1107	21	942
0	612	9	678	15	843	21	860
0	711	9	446	15	760	21	843
0	744	10	579	15	711	22	645
0	760	10	694	15	512	22	727
0	579	10	810	16	1388	22	1107
0	562	11	1107	16	826	23	1421
0	545	11	826	16	810	23	1306
0	496	11	760	16	777	23	1273
0	364	11	744	16	331	23	1256
0	314	11	727	17	760	23	1174
1	826	12	1207	17	893	23	1074
1	975	12	1124	17	909	23	1025
1	893	12	876	17	1289	23	760
1	826	12	843	18	1289	24	1587
1	727	12	826	18	1207	24	1504
1	678	12	793	18	1124	24	1289
1	579	12	545	18	1058	24	1041
1	430	12	364	18	1041	25	909
2	826	12	264	18	1008	25	1190
2	860	13	1289	18	909	25	1207
2	1074	13	1140	18	860	25	1256
3	760	13	678	18	562	25	1587
3	975	13	446	19	545	26	760
4	959	14	1289	19	1008	26	1091
4	810	14	1273	19	1174	27	1372
4	678	14	1157	19	1438	28	264
6	397	14	1132	20	1256	28	1107
6	496	14	1124	20	1174	28	1124
6	727	14	1107	20	1140	29	760
6	1008	14	893	20	1074	29	1107
7	1058	14	884	20	810	29	1273
8	876	14	876	20	711	29	1620
8	975	14	860	21	1223	30	760
9	975	14	760	21	1140	32	1355
9	810	15	1223	21	992	33	1074

13. Graph Areas 2

The sum of graph areas for 50 articles divided by the sum of the total article areas, for each of 57 scientific journals (1980-1981), and the standard errors of these fractional areas. Data are rounded to three decimal places. Source: Cleveland (1982). [Chapters 4, 6]

Journal	Graph Area (fr. of total)	Standard Error
J Geophys Res	0.310	0.019
J Appl Polym Sci	0.264	0.017
J Exp Biol	0.207	0.019
J Chem (Faraday Trans)	0.200	0.021
J Appl Physics	0.199	0.013
IEEE Comm Radar Sig	0.164	0.020
Bell Syst Tech J	0.158	0.021
Life Sciences	0.157	0.015
J Phys Chem	0.149	0.017
IEEE Trans Commun	0.139	0.014
J Clin Investigation	0.127	0.012
J Physics (C)	0.122	0.016
Proc R Soc (Ser B)	0.114	0.015
Scientific Am	0.108	0.019
Phys Rev (Lett)	0.108	0.010
J Exp Med	0.106	0.012
J R Stat Soc (Ser C)	0.105	0.020
J Am Chem Soc	0.098	0.014
Phys Rev (A)	0.097	0.014
Nature (London)	0.091	0.016
Percept Psychophys	0.089	0.014
Profess Geogr	0.089	0.018
Lancet	0.084	0.014
J Exp Psychol	0.082	0.020
Science (Reports)	0.078	0.013
IBM J Res Develop	0.070	0.012
New Eng J Med	0.068	0.009
J Am Stat As (Applic)	0.067	0.013
Ann As Am Geogr	0.066	0.016
Geogr J	0.063	0.012
Comput Gra Im Proc	0.059	0.018
J Am Stat As (Theory)	0.057	0.020
Geogr Rev	0.055	0.015
Science (Articles)	0.053	0.010
Br J Psychol	0.045	0.012
Computer J	0.045	0.021

13. Graph Areas 2, (cont'd)

Journal	Graph Area (fr. of total)	Standard Error
Am Educ Res	0.041	0.011
Am Econ Rev	0.038	0.007
Bell J Econ	0.038	0.008
Am Math Mo	0.034	0.010
J Polit Econ	0.034	0.008
Cell	0.034	0.007
Educ Res	0.032	0.012
Econometrica	0.025	0.008
Commun ACM	0.023	0.008
Biometrika	0.019	0.009
Rev Econ Stat	0.014	0.004
Am J Sociol	0.014	0.005
Am Sociol Rev	0.014	0.004
Computer	0.014	0.005
Social Forces	0.009	0.005
Ann Statist	0.006	0.003
Rev Educ Res	0.004	0.002
Br J Sociol	0.004	0.002
T Am Math Soc	0.002	0.002
Oxford Rev Educ	0.001	0.001
J Soc Psychol	0.000	0.000

14. Anderson's Iris Data

Sepal and petal lengths (l) and widths (w) in centimeters for three species of iris. The data were collected, but not published, by Edgar Anderson, and his methods of collecting information about irises are described in Anderson (1935). Source: Fisher (1936). [Chapters 4, 5, 6]

Iris setosa				*Iris versicolor*				*Iris virginica*			
Sepal		Petal		Sepal		Petal		Sepal		Petal	
l	*w*	*l*	*w*	*l*	*w*	*l*	*w*	*l*	*w*	*l*	*w*
5.1	3.5	1.4	0.2	7.0	3.2	4.7	1.4	6.3	3.3	6.0	2.5
4.9	3.0	1.4	0.2	6.4	3.2	4.5	1.5	5.8	2.7	5.1	1.9
4.7	3.2	1.3	0.2	6.9	3.1	4.9	1.5	7.1	3.0	5.9	2.1
4.6	3.1	1.5	0.2	5.5	2.3	4.0	1.3	6.3	2.9	5.6	1.8
5.0	3.6	1.4	0.2	6.5	2.8	4.6	1.5	6.5	3.0	5.8	2.2
5.4	3.9	1.7	0.4	5.7	2.8	4.5	1.3	7.6	3.0	6.6	2.1
4.6	3.4	1.4	0.3	6.3	3.3	4.7	1.6	4.9	2.5	4.5	1.7
5.0	3.4	1.5	0.2	4.9	2.4	3.3	1.0	7.3	2.9	6.3	1.8
4.4	2.9	1.4	0.2	6.6	2.9	4.6	1.3	6.7	2.5	5.8	1.8
4.9	3.1	1.5	0.1	5.2	2.7	3.9	1.4	7.2	3.6	6.1	2.5
5.4	3.7	1.5	0.2	5.0	2.0	3.5	1.0	6.5	3.2	5.1	2.0
4.8	3.4	1.6	0.2	5.9	3.0	4.2	1.5	6.4	2.7	5.3	1.9
4.8	3.0	1.4	0.1	6.0	2.2	4.0	1.0	6.8	3.0	5.5	2.1
4.3	3.0	1.1	0.1	6.1	2.9	4.7	1.4	5.7	2.5	5.0	2.0
5.8	4.0	1.2	0.2	5.6	2.9	3.6	1.3	5.8	2.8	5.1	2.4
5.7	4.4	1.5	0.4	6.7	3.1	4.4	1.4	6.4	3.2	5.3	2.3
5.4	3.9	1.3	0.4	5.6	3.0	4.5	1.5	6.5	3.0	5.5	1.8
5.1	3.5	1.4	0.3	5.8	2.7	4.1	1.0	7.7	3.8	6.7	2.2
5.7	3.8	1.7	0.3	6.2	2.2	4.5	1.5	7.7	2.6	6.9	2.3
5.1	3.8	1.5	0.3	5.6	2.5	3.9	1.1	6.0	2.2	5.0	1.5
5.4	3.4	1.7	0.2	5.9	3.2	4.8	1.8	6.9	3.2	5.7	2.3
5.1	3.7	1.5	0.4	6.1	2.8	4.0	1.3	5.6	2.8	4.9	2.0
4.6	3.6	1.0	0.2	6.3	2.5	4.9	1.5	7.7	2.8	6.7	2.0
5.1	3.3	1.7	0.5	6.1	2.8	4.7	1.2	6.3	2.7	4.9	1.8
4.8	3.4	1.9	0.2	6.4	2.9	4.3	1.3	6.7	3.3	5.7	2.1
5.0	3.0	1.6	0.2	6.6	3.0	4.4	1.4	7.2	3.2	6.0	1.8
5.0	3.4	1.6	0.4	6.8	2.8	4.8	1.4	6.2	2.8	4.8	1.8
5.2	3.5	1.5	0.2	6.7	3.0	5.0	1.7	6.1	3.0	4.9	1.8
5.2	3.4	1.4	0.2	6.0	2.9	4.5	1.5	6.4	2.8	5.6	2.1
4.7	3.2	1.6	0.2	5.7	2.6	3.5	1.0	7.2	3.0	5.8	1.6
4.8	3.1	1.6	0.2	5.5	2.4	3.8	1.1	7.4	2.8	6.1	1.9
5.4	3.4	1.5	0.4	5.5	2.4	3.7	1.0	7.9	3.8	6.4	2.0
5.2	4.1	1.5	0.1	5.8	2.7	3.9	1.2	6.4	2.8	5.6	2.2
5.5	4.2	1.4	0.2	6.0	2.7	5.1	1.6	6.3	2.8	5.1	1.5

14. Anderson's Iris Data, (cont'd)

Iris setosa				Iris versicolor				Iris virginica			
Sepal		Petal		Sepal		Petal		Sepal		Petal	
l	*w*	*l*	*w*	*l*	*w*	*l*	*w*	*l*	*w*	*l*	*w*
4.9	3.1	1.5	0.2	5.4	3.0	4.5	1.5	6.1	2.6	5.6	1.4
5.0	3.2	1.2	0.2	6.0	3.4	4.5	1.6	7.7	3.0	6.1	2.3
5.5	3.5	1.3	0.2	6.7	3.1	4.7	1.5	6.3	3.4	5.6	2.4
4.9	3.6	1.4	0.1	6.3	2.3	4.4	1.3	6.4	3.1	5.5	1.8
4.4	3.0	1.3	0.2	5.6	3.0	4.1	1.3	6.0	3.0	4.8	1.8
5.1	3.4	1.5	0.2	5.5	2.5	4.0	1.3	6.9	3.1	5.4	2.1
5.0	3.5	1.3	0.3	5.5	2.6	4.4	1.2	6.7	3.1	5.6	2.4
4.5	2.3	1.3	0.3	6.1	3.0	4.6	1.4	6.9	3.1	5.1	2.3
4.4	3.2	1.3	0.2	5.8	2.6	4.0	1.2	5.8	2.7	5.1	1.9
5.0	3.5	1.6	0.6	5.0	2.3	3.3	1.0	6.8	3.2	5.9	2.3
5.1	3.8	1.9	0.4	5.6	2.7	4.2	1.3	6.7	3.3	5.7	2.5
4.8	3.0	1.4	0.3	5.7	3.0	4.2	1.2	6.7	3.0	5.2	2.3
5.1	3.8	1.6	0.2	5.7	2.9	4.2	1.3	6.3	2.5	5.0	1.9
4.6	3.2	1.4	0.2	6.2	2.9	4.3	1.3	6.5	3.0	5.2	2.0
5.3	3.7	1.5	0.2	5.1	2.5	3.0	1.1	6.2	3.4	5.4	2.3
5.0	3.3	1.4	0.2	5.7	2.8	4.1	1.3	5.9	3.0	5.1	1.8

Reprinted by permission of the *Annals of Human Genetics* published by Cambridge University Press.

15. Wheat Data

The protein content of 100 commercial Ohio wheats and truncated volume in cubic centimeters of standard loaves of bread baked from them. Source: Tippett (1952). [Chapter 4]

Loaf Volume	Protein Content								
	9%	10%	11%	12%	13%	14%	15%	16%	17%
1600	2	—	1	—	1	—	—	—	—
1700	—	2	1	—	2	—	—	—	—
1800	6	5	5	2	1	—	—	—	—
1900	5	4	6	7	—	—	—	—	—
2000	2	3	9	10	2	1	—	—	—
2100	1	—	3	3	5	2	1	—	—
2200	—	—	1	2	—	2	1	—	—
2300	—	—	—	—	—	—	—	1	1

16. Socioeconomic Data for 35 Countries

Percent of population below age 15 and above age 75, per capita disposable income in U. S. dollars, percent savings rate, and percent contribution to the gross domestic product (GDP) of agriculture (Agr), manufacturing and construction (Mfg), and service including government (Ser) for 35 countries. Data are believed to be for 1970. Source: Various unspecified U. S. Government publications. [Chapters 4, 5, 6, 7]

Country	Below Age 15	Above Age 75	Disp Inc $	Save Rate	Contribution to GDP Agr	Mfg	Ser
Australia	29	3	2330	11	6	36	58
Bolivia	42	2	189	6	16	34	50
Brazil	42	1	728	13	12	26	62
Canada	32	3	2983	9	4	31	65
Chile	40	1	663	1	7	43	50
Costa Rica	48	1	471	11	23	24	53
Denmark	24	4	2497	17	7	38	55
Ecuador	46	1	288	4	27	22	51
Finland	28	2	1681	11	12	38	50
Germany	23	3	2457	13	3	54	43
Greece	26	3	871	11	16	27	57
Honduras	47	1	232	8	31	21	48
India	41	1	89	9	43	20	37
Italy	25	3	1391	14	9	42	49
Japan	27	2	1257	21	6	45	49
Korea	42	1	208	4	28	31	41
Libya	44	2	124	9	2	70	28
Luxembourg	22	4	2449	10	4	52	44
Malaysia	47	1	243	5	30	28	42
Netherlands	25	3	1741	15	6	39	55
Nicaragua	45	1	326	7	25	26	49
Panama	44	1	569	4	19	24	57
Paraguay	41	1	221	2	32	21	47
Peru	44	1	400	13	17	35	48
Portugal	29	3	580	12	16	41	43
South Africa	32	2	651	11	8	41	51
Spain	28	3	769	12	11	37	52
Sweden	21	5	3299	7	4	39	57
Turkey	43	1	390	5	27	29	44
Tunisia	46	1	250	3	17	21	62
United Kingdom	23	4	1814	8	2	42	56
United States	30	3	4002	8	3	35	62
Uruguay	28	3	767	9	11	25	64
Venezuela	46	1	813	9	7	40	53
Zambia	45	1	138	19	11	55	34

17. Murder-Suicides by Deliberately Crashing Private Airplanes

These data were used to investigate the hypothesis that newspaper and television publicity of murder-suicides through the deliberate crashing of private airplanes triggers further similar murder-suicides. They consist of an index of newspaper coverage (Index) of 17 crashes known to be murder-suicides and the number of multi-fatality plane crashes (Crash) during the week following each of the 17 crashes. Source: Phillips (1978). [Chapter 4]

Index	Crash	Index	Crash	Index	Crash	Index	Crash
376	8	98	4	63	2	5	2
347	5	96	8	44	7	0	4
322	8	85	6	40	4	0	3
104	4	82	4	5	3	0	2
103	6						

18. Number of Telephones in the United States

Number of telephones in thousands (Bell and Independent Companies) in the United States, for the years 1900 through 1970. Source: *Historical Statistics of the United States: Colonial Times to 1970*, Bicentennial Edition Part 1, U. S. Bureau of the Census (1975). [Chapter 4]

Year	Number	Year	Number	Year	Number	Year	Number
1900	1356	1918	12078	1936	18433	1954	52806
1901	1801	1919	12669	1937	19453	1955	56243
1902	2371	1920	13273	1938	19953	1956	60190
1903	2809	1921	13817	1939	20831	1957	63624
1904	3353	1922	14294	1940	21928	1958	66645
1905	4127	1923	15316	1941	23521	1959	70820
1906	4933	1924	16015	1942	24919	1960	74342
1907	6199	1925	16875	1943	26381	1961	77422
1908	6484	1926	17680	1944	26859	1962	80969
1909	6996	1927	18446	1945	27867	1963	84453
1910	7635	1928	19256	1946	31611	1964	88793
1911	8349	1929	19970	1947	34867	1965	93656
1912	8730	1930	20103	1948	38205	1966	98787
1913	9543	1931	19602	1949	40709	1967	103752
1914	10046	1932	17341	1950	43004	1968	109256
1915	10524	1933	16628	1951	45636	1969	115222
1916	11241	1934	16869	1952	48056	1970	120218
1917	11717	1935	17424	1953	50373		

19. Average Brain and Body Weights for 62 Species of Mammals

Data were taken from a larger study, Allison and Ciccheti (1976). Brain weight was measured in grams and body weight in kilograms. Source: Weisberg (1980), Chapter 6. [Chapters 4, 7]

Species (Common Name)	Body Weight kg	Brain Weight g
African Elephant	6654.000	5712.00
Asian Elephant	2547.000	4603.00
Giraffe	529.000	680.00
Horse	521.000	655.00
Cow	465.000	423.00
Okapi	250.000	490.00
Gorilla	207.000	406.00
Pig	192.000	180.00
Donkey	187.100	419.00
Brazilian Tapir	160.000	169.00
Jaguar	100.000	157.00
Gray Seal	85.000	325.00
Man	62.000	1320.00
Giant Armadillo	60.000	81.00
Sheep	55.500	175.00
Chimpanzee	52.160	440.00
Gray Wolf	36.330	119.50
Kangaroo	35.000	56.00
Goat	27.660	115.00
Roe Deer	14.830	98.20
Baboon	10.550	179.50
Patas Monkey	10.000	115.00
Rhesus Monkey	6.800	179.00
Raccoon	4.288	39.20
Red Fox	4.235	50.40
Vervet	4.190	58.00
Yellow-Bellied Marmot	4.050	17.00
Rock Hyrax (*Procavia habessinica*)	3.600	21.00
Nine-Banded Armadillo	3.500	10.80
Water Opossum	3.500	3.90
Arctic Fox	3.385	44.50
Cat	3.300	25.60
Echidna	3.000	25.00
Rabbit	2.500	12.10

19. Average Brain and Body Weights for 62 Species of Mammals, (cont'd)

Species (Common Name)	Body Weight kg	Brain Weight g
Tree Hyrax	2.000	12.30
N. American Opossum	1.700	6.30
Phalanger	1.620	11.40
Genet	1.410	17.50
Slow Loris	1.400	12.50
Mountain Beaver	1.350	8.10
Guinea Pig	1.040	5.50
African Giant Pouched Rat	1.000	6.60
Arctic Ground Squirrel	0.920	5.70
Tenrec	0.900	2.60
European Hedgehog	0.785	3.50
Rock Hyrax (*Heterohyrax brucci*)	0.750	12.30
Desert Hedgehog	0.550	2.40
Owl Monkey	0.480	15.50
Chinchilla	0.425	64.00
Rat	0.280	1.90
Galago	0.200	5.00
Mole Rat	0.122	3.00
Golden Hamster	0.120	1.00
Tree Shrew	0.104	2.50
Ground Squirrel	0.101	4.00
Eastern American Mole	0.075	1.20
Star Nosed Mole	0.060	1.00
Musk Shrew	0.048	0.33
Big Brown Bat	0.023	0.30
Mouse	0.023	0.40
Little Brown Bat	0.010	0.25
Lesser Short-Tailed Shrew	0.005	0.14

20. Bell Laboratories Managers' Data

Age in 1982, years since highest degree (Yrs) and highest degree (Deg) for 136 managers at Bell Laboratories. [Chapters 4, 5, 6, 7]

Age	Yrs	Deg	Age	Yrs	Deg	Age	Yrs	Deg	Age	Yrs	Deg
35	12	MS	44	18	PhD	50	28	BS	57	32	PhD
36	10	PhD	44	19	MS	51	22	PhD	57	37	BS
36	12	MS	44	19	MS	51	27	PhD	58	23	MS
36	14	BS	44	20	MS	52	19	MS	58	27	PhD
37	10	PhD	45	13	PhD	52	25	PhD	58	28	MS
37	12	PhD	45	15	MS	52	25	PhD	58	31	BS
38	10	PhD	45	20	MS	52	26	PhD	58	32	PhD
38	14	MS	45	20	MS	53	22	PhD	58	33	BS
39	10	PhD	45	21	MS	53	23	PhD	58	33	MS
39	14	PhD	45	21	MS	53	24	MS	58	33	PhD
39	15	MS	46	18	MS	53	27	PhD	58	34	BS
40	12	PhD	46	18	PhD	53	30	MS	58	34	MS
40	14	PhD	46	19	PhD	53	31	BS	59	25	PhD
41	10	PhD	46	20	PhD	53	32	BS	59	28	PhD
41	17	MS	46	21	PhD	54	21	PhD	59	29	PhD
42	8	PhD	47	18	MS	54	27	PhD	59	30	PhD
42	12	PhD	47	21	MS	54	28	BS	59	30	PhD
42	16	PhD	47	21	MS	54	28	MS	59	31	PhD
42	19	MS	47	21	MS	54	29	PhD	59	32	PhD
43	15	PhD	47	21	MS	54	29	PhD	59	33	PhD
43	17	PhD	47	21	MS	54	30	MS	59	34	BS
43	17	PhD	47	23	MS	55	25	MS	59	35	MS
43	17	PhD	47	25	BS	55	27	PhD	60	27	PhD
43	17	PhD	47	26	BS	55	29	BS	60	28	PhD
43	20	MS	48	18	PhD	55	29	PhD	60	33	PhD
43	21	MS	48	21	MS	55	30	PhD	61	34	MS
44	9	PhD	48	23	MS	55	31	MS	61	40	BS
44	12	PhD	48	26	MS	55	31	PhD	62	34	MS
44	14	PhD	49	20	MS	55	33	BS	62	35	MS
44	16	PhD	49	22	PhD	55	33	MS	63	30	PhD
44	16	PhD	50	17	MS	56	27	PhD	63	41	MS
44	17	PhD	50	21	MS	56	28	PhD	64	40	MS
44	17	PhD	50	23	PhD	56	28	PhD	64	41	MS
44	18	MS	50	24	PhD	56	30	BS	66	43	MS

21. Egg Sizes of the Common Tern

Length in centimeters, longitudinal girth in centimeters, and the number of occurrences of each size for 955 eggs of the common tern. Source: Tippett (1952). [Chapters 4, 6]

Occur	Length	Girth	Occur	Length	Girth	Occur	Length	Girth
1	3.55	9.8	7	3.95	11.2	1	4.20	11.0
1	3.70	10.3	1	3.95	11.6	3	4.20	11.1
1	3.70	11.0	1	4.00	10.7	11	4.20	11.2
1	3.75	10.4	8	4.00	10.8	23	4.20	11.3
2	3.75	10.5	11	4.00	10.9	29	4.20	11.4
1	3.75	10.6	20	4.00	11.0	20	4.20	11.5
1	3.75	10.8	20	4.00	11.1	8	4.20	11.6
1	3.75	10.9	6	4.00	11.2	2	4.20	11.7
2	3.80	10.5	2	4.00	11.4	1	4.20	11.9
6	3.80	10.6	1	4.00	11.9	1	4.25	11.1
2	3.80	10.7	1	4.05	10.5	5	4.25	11.2
3	3.80	10.8	2	4.05	10.8	13	4.25	11.3
1	3.80	10.9	5	4.05	10.9	21	4.25	11.4
1	3.85	10.4	23	4.05	11.0	27	4.25	11.5
1	3.85	10.5	20	4.05	11.1	15	4.25	11.6
2	3.85	10.6	21	4.05	11.2	9	4.25	11.7
4	3.85	10.7	7	4.05	11.3	2	4.30	11.1
3	3.85	10.8	3	4.05	11.4	5	4.30	11.3
1	3.85	10.9	1	4.05	11.5	9	4.30	11.4
1	3.85	11.0	2	4.05	11.7	22	4.30	11.5
1	3.85	11.1	1	4.10	10.8	30	4.30	11.6
1	3.85	11.2	1	4.10	10.9	25	4.30	11.7
1	3.85	11.8	10	4.10	11.0	9	4.30	11.8
1	3.90	10.3	25	4.10	11.1	4	4.30	11.9
4	3.90	10.6	37	4.10	11.2	1	4.35	11.1
8	3.90	10.8	38	4.10	11.3	1	4.35	11.3
11	3.90	10.9	10	4.10	11.4	2	4.35	11.4
2	3.90	11.0	5	4.10	11.5	9	4.35	11.5
3	3.90	11.1	1	4.10	11.6	12	4.35	11.6
1	3.90	11.2	1	4.15	11.0	16	4.35	11.7
2	3.95	10.6	8	4.15	11.1	10	4.35	11.8
3	3.95	10.7	29	4.15	11.2	2	4.35	11.9
9	3.95	10.8	25	4.15	11.3	1	4.35	12.0
7	3.95	10.9	25	4.15	11.4	1	4.40	11.2
20	3.95	11.0	11	4.15	11.5	1	4.40	11.3
6	3.95	11.1	2	4.15	11.6	1	4.40	11.5

21. Egg Sizes of the Common Tern, (Cont'd)

Occur	Length	Girth	Occur	Length	Girth	Occur	Length	Girth
5	4.40	11.6	4	4.45	11.9	3	4.55	12.0
10	4.40	11.7	4	4.45	12.0	1	4.55	12.1
15	4.40	11.8	1	4.50	11.6	1	4.55	12.2
5	4.40	11.9	1	4.50	11.8	1	4.60	12.0
2	4.40	12.0	6	4.50	11.9	1	4.60	12.1
1	4.45	11.3	5	4.50	12.0	3	4.65	12.1
2	4.45	11.5	1	4.50	12.1	1	4.65	12.2
1	4.45	11.6	1	4.50	12.2	1	4.65	12.3
2	4.45	11.7	1	4.55	11.8			
11	4.45	11.8	6	4.55	11.9			

22. Stack Loss Data

Data from operation of a plant for the oxidation of ammonia to nitric acid on 21 consecutive days: flow of air to the plant (x_1); temperature of the cooling water (x_2); concentration of nitric acid in the absorbing liquid as a percentage (coded by subtracting 50 and then multiplying by 10) (x_3). The response (y) is 10 times the percentage of ingoing ammonia lost as unabsorbed nitric oxides (an indirect measure of nitric acid yield). Units of air flow and temperature are not reported. Source: Brownlee (1965). Also in Draper and Smith (1966), Chapter 6, and Daniel and Wood (1971, 1980), Chapter 5. [Chapters 5, 7]

Air Flow x_1	Water Temp x_2	Acid Conc. x_3	Stack Loss y	Air Flow x_1	Water Temp x_2	Acid Conc. x_3	Stack Loss y
80	27	89	42	58	17	88	13
80	27	88	37	58	18	82	11
75	25	90	37	58	19	93	12
62	24	87	28	50	18	89	8
62	22	87	18	50	18	86	7
62	23	87	18	50	19	72	8
62	24	93	19	50	19	79	8
62	24	93	20	50	20	80	9
58	23	87	15	56	20	82	15
58	18	80	14	70	20	91	15
58	18	89	14				

23. Tar Content Data

Results of 31 observations of a chemical process in which tar content of an output gas was related to the temperature at which the process was run and to the speed of a rotor. Rotor speed squared divided by 1000 and rounded is also shown. Source: Badger (1946). Part II. [Chapters 5, 6, 7]

Obs. Number	Tar Content gr/100 cu ft	Temp °F	Rotor Speed rpm	Speed^2/1000 rpm^2/1000
1	60.0	54.5	2400	5760
2	61.0	56.0	2450	6003
3	65.0	58.5	2450	6003
4	30.5	43.0	2500	6250
5	63.5	58.0	2500	6250
6	65.0	59.0	2500	6250
7	44.0	62.5	2700	7290
8	52.0	65.5	2700	7290
9	54.5	68.0	2700	7290
10	30.0	45.0	2750	7563
11	26.0	45.5	2775	7701
12	23.0	48.0	2800	7840
13	54.0	63.0	2800	7840
14	36.0	58.5	2900	8410
15	53.5	64.5	2900	8410
16	57.0	66.0	3000	9000
17	33.5	57.0	3075	9456
18	34.0	57.5	3100	9610
19	44.0	64.0	3150	9923
20	33.0	57.0	3200	10240
21	39.0	64.0	3200	10240
22	53.0	69.0	3200	10240
23	38.5	68.0	3225	10401
24	39.5	62.0	3250	10563
25	36.0	64.5	3250	10563
26	8.5	48.0	3250	10563
27	30.0	60.0	3500	12250
28	29.0	59.0	3500	12250
29	26.5	58.0	3500	12250
30	24.5	58.0	3600	12960
31	26.5	61.0	3900	15210

24. Tooth Measurements of Humans, Apes and Fossils

The data give group means of eight canonical variates of measurements on the permanent first lower premolar over eight groups: three types of human beings, two pairs (male, female) of apes, and one fossil. Source: Ashton, Healey and Lipton (1957). Also in Andrews (1972). [Chapter 5]

Group	Means of Groups							
1	+3.05	−4.21	+0.17	+0.28	+0.04	+0.02	−0.06	−0.06
2	+1.86	−4.28	−2.14	−1.73	+2.06	+1.80	+2.61	+2.48
3	−8.09	+0.49	+0.18	+0.75	−0.06	−0.04	+0.04	+0.03
4	+6.28	+2.89	+0.43	−0.03	+0.10	−0.14	+0.07	+0.08
5	−9.37	−0.68	−0.44	−0.37	+0.37	+0.02	−0.01	+0.05
6	+3.46	−3.37	+0.33	−0.32	−0.19	−0.04	+0.09	+0.09
7	+4.82	+1.52	+0.71	−0.06	+0.25	+0.15	−0.07	−0.10
8	−8.87	+1.44	+0.36	−0.34	−0.29	−0.02	−0.01	−0.05

25. Rubber Specimen Data

Thirty rubber specimens were rubbed with an abrasive material. The data are hardness in degrees Shore, tensile strength in kilograms per square centimeter, and abrasion loss (the amount of material rubbed off) in grams per horsepower-hour, for each specimen. Source: Davies, ed. (1957). [Chapters 5, 7]

Spec.	Hardness deg Shore	Tensile Strength kg/cm^2	Abrasion Loss g/hp hour	Spec.	Hardness deg Shore	Tensile Strength kg/cm^2	Abrasion Loss g/hp hour
A	45	162	372	P	68	173	196
B	55	233	206	Q	75	188	128
C	61	232	175	R	83	161	97
D	66	231	154	S	88	119	64
E	71	231	136	T	59	161	249
F	71	237	112	U	71	151	219
G	81	224	55	V	80	165	186
H	86	219	45	W	82	151	155
I	53	203	221	X	89	128	114
J	60	189	166	Y	51	161	341
K	64	210	164	Z	59	146	340
L	68	210	113	1	65	148	283
M	79	196	82	2	74	144	267
N	81	180	32	3	81	134	215
O	56	200	228	4	86	127	148

26. Stereogram Data

Lengths of time in seconds taken by subjects to see a three dimensional object, (a spiral ramp coming out of the page), in a random dot stereogram. The subjects were given varying prior information about the object; 42 receiving either no information or verbal information only (*NV*), and 35 receiving both verbal and visual information (*VV*). Standard errors are also shown (*NVSE* and *VVSE*). Data were digitized from the article and rounded. Source: Frisby and Clatworthy (1975). [Chapter 6]

NV	NVSE	NV	NVSE	VV	VVSE	VV	VVSE
22.0	9.335	6.3	1.001	19.7	6.391	3.5	0.727
20.4	5.324	6.1	0.954	16.2	3.636	3.3	0.686
19.7	4.073	5.6	0.909	15.9	2.774	3.3	0.647
17.4	3.398	4.7	0.866	15.4	2.308	2.9	0.610
14.7	2.958	4.7	0.824	9.7	2.003	2.8	0.573
13.4	2.640	4.3	0.784	8.9	1.782	2.7	0.538
13.0	2.395	4.2	0.744	8.6	1.611	2.4	0.504
12.3	2.198	3.9	0.705	8.6	1.473	2.3	0.470
12.2	2.034	3.4	0.667	7.4	1.358	2.0	0.436
10.3	1.895	3.1	0.629	6.3	1.260	1.8	0.402
9.7	1.775	3.1	0.592	6.1	1.175	1.7	0.367
9.7	1.669	2.7	0.554	6.0	1.100	1.7	0.332
9.5	1.574	2.4	0.516	6.0	1.032	1.6	0.296
9.1	1.489	2.3	0.478	5.9	0.971	1.4	0.256
8.9	1.411	2.3	0.438	4.9	0.915	1.2	0.213
8.9	1.340	2.1	0.398	4.6	0.863	1.1	0.163
8.4	1.274	2.1	0.355	3.8	0.815	1.0	0.093
8.1	1.212	2.0	0.309	3.6	0.769		
7.9	1.155	1.9	0.258				
7.8	1.101	1.7	0.197				
6.9	1.049	1.7	0.112				

27. Life Times of Mechanical Devices

Time to failure, measured in millions of operations, of 40 mechanical devices. Failure was caused by either switch A or B. In three cases, indicated by "—" under Failure Mode, the device did not fail. Source: Michael (1979). [Chapter 6]

	Failure Mode			Failure Mode			Failure Mode	
Time	A	B	Time	A	B	Time	A	B
1.151		x	1.965	x		2.349		x
1.170		x	2.012		x	2.369	x	
1.248		x	2.051		x	2.547	x	
1.331		x	2.076		x	2.548	x	
1.381		x	2.109	x		2.738		x
1.499	x		2.116		x	2.794	x	
1.508		x	2.119		x	2.883	—	—
1.534		x	2.135	x		2.883	—	—
1.577		x	2.197	x		2.910	x	
1.584		x	2.199		x	3.015	x	
1.667	x		2.227	x		3.017	x	
1.695	x		2.250		x	3.793	—	—
1.710	x		2.254	x				
1.955		x	2.261		x			

28. Remission Durations of 84 Leukemia Patients

Time in days from remission induction to relapse for 84 patients with acute nonlymphoblastic leukemia who were treated on a common protocol at university and private institutions in the Pacific Northwest. Source: Matthews and Farewell (1982). [Chapter 6]

		Uncensored Observations					
24	46	57	57	64	65	82	89
90	90	111	117	128	143	148	152
166	171	186	191	197	209	223	230
247	249	254	258	264	269	270	273
284	294	304	304	332	341	393	395
487	510	516	518	518	534	608	642
697	955	1160					

		Censored Observations					
68	119	182	182	182	182	182	182
182	182	182	182	182	182	182	182
182	182	182	182	182	182	182	182
182	182	583	1310	1538	1634	1908	1996
2057							

Reproduced from D. E. Matthews and V. T. Farewell, "On Testing for a Constant Hazard Against a Change-Point Alternative." *Biometrics* 38: 463-468. 1982. With permission from the Biometric Society.

29. Wölfer's Sunspot Numbers, 1749-1924

Daily relative sunspot numbers are based on counts of spots and group entities of spots on the sun's surface. Wölfer's numbers reduce these observations to a common basis: $k(f + 10g)$, where g is the number of groups, for a given day, f is the total number of component spots in these groups and k is a factor dependent on the estimated efficiency of the observer and his telescope. Data are the mean of daily values for each year. Source: Yule (1927). [Chapter 7]

Year	Sunspot Number	Year	Sunspot Number	Year	Sunspot Number	Year	Sunspot Number
1749	80.9	1780	84.8	1811	1.4	1842	24.2
1750	83.4	1781	68.1	1812	5.0	1843	10.7
1751	47.7	1782	38.5	1813	12.2	1844	15.0
1752	47.8	1783	22.8	1814	13.9	1845	40.1
1753	30.7	1784	10.2	1815	35.4	1846	61.5
1754	12.2	1785	24.1	1816	45.8	1847	98.5
1755	9.6	1786	82.9	1817	41.1	1848	124.3
1756	10.2	1787	132.0	1818	30.4	1849	95.9
1757	32.4	1788	130.9	1819	23.9	1850	66.5
1758	47.6	1789	118.1	1820	15.7	1851	64.5
1759	54.0	1790	89.9	1821	6.6	1852	54.2
1760	62.9	1791	66.6	1822	4.0	1853	39.0
1761	85.9	1792	60.0	1823	1.8	1854	20.6
1762	61.2	1793	46.9	1824	8.5	1855	6.7
1763	45.1	1794	41.0	1825	16.6	1856	4.3
1764	36.4	1795	21.3	1826	36.3	1857	22.8
1765	20.9	1796	16.0	1827	49.7	1858	54.8
1766	11.4	1797	6.4	1828	62.5	1859	93.8
1767	37.8	1798	4.1	1829	67.0	1860	95.7
1768	69.8	1799	6.8	1830	71.0	1861	77.2
1769	106.1	1800	14.5	1831	47.8	1862	59.1
1770	100.8	1801	34.0	1832	27.5	1863	44.0
1771	81.6	1802	45.0	1833	8.5	1864	47.0
1772	66.5	1803	43.1	1834	13.2	1865	30.5
1773	34.8	1804	47.5	1835	56.9	1866	16.3
1774	30.6	1805	42.2	1836	121.5	1867	7.3
1775	7.0	1806	28.1	1837	138.3	1868	37.3
1776	19.8	1807	10.1	1838	103.2	1869	73.9
1777	92.5	1808	8.1	1839	85.8	1870	139.1
1778	154.4	1809	2.5	1840	63.2	1871	111.2
1779	125.9	1810	0.0	1841	36.8	1872	101.7

29. Wölfers Sunspot Numbers, 1749-1924, (cont'd)

Year	Sunspot Number	Year	Sunspot Number	Year	Sunspot Number	Year	Sunspot Number
1873	66.3	1886	25.4	1899	12.1	1912	3.6
1874	44.7	1887	13.1	1900	9.5	1913	1.4
1875	17.1	1888	6.8	1901	2.7	1914	9.6
1876	11.3	1889	6.3	1902	5.0	1915	47.4
1877	12.3	1890	7.1	1903	24.4	1916	57.1
1878	3.4	1891	35.6	1904	42.0	1917	103.9
1879	6.0	1892	73.0	1905	63.5	1918	80.6
1880	32.3	1893	84.9	1906	53.8	1919	63.6
1881	54.3	1894	78.0	1907	62.0	1920	37.6
1882	59.7	1895	64.0	1908	48.5	1921	26.1
1883	63.7	1896	41.8	1909	43.9	1922	14.2
1884	63.5	1897	26.2	1910	18.6	1923	5.8
1885	52.2	1898	26.7	1911	5.7	1924	16.7

Reprinted by permission of the Royal Society, London.

30. Barley Yield

Total yields in bushels per acre of 5 varieties of barley grown in 1/40 acre plots at six experimental stations in Minnesota in the two year period 1930-1931. Source: Immer, Hayes and Powers (1934). Reproduced in part in Daniel (1976). [Chapter 7]

	Station					
Variety	1	2	3	4	5	6
Manchuria	162	247	185	219	165	155
Svansota	187	258	182	183	139	144
Velvet	200	263	195	220	166	146
Trebi	197	340	271	267	151	194
Peatland	182	254	220	201	184	190

Adapted from the *Journal of the American Society of Agronomy*, May 1934, pages 403-419, by permission of the American Society of Agronomy.

31. Fertility in Ireland

Average number of children born alive per woman aged 25-29 at marriage and married 20-24 years. Row category is husband's occupational status and column category is a combination of religion and part of Ireland. Source: Kennedy (1973). Also in Erickson and Nosanchuk (1977). [Chapter 7]

Occupational Status of Husband	Catholic		Non-Catholic		Row Means
	Northern Ireland	Repulic of Ireland	Northern Ireland	Repulic of Ireland	
Upper	4.02	3.80	2.13	2.19	3.04
Middle	4.14	3.91	2.2	2.44	3.17
Lower	4.82	4.33	2.65	2.81	3.65
Agriculture	5.25	4.57	3.37	3.08	4.07
Column Means	4.56	4.15	2.59	2.63	3.48

Reprinted by permission of the American Sociological Society.

32. Rubber Compressibility

Specific volumes in cubic centimeters per gram of natural rubber was measured at four temperatures in degrees Centigrade and five pressures in kilograms per square centimeter to determine its compressibility. Source: Brandu and Gabriel (1978). [Chapter 7]

Temp °C	Pressure (kg/cm^2)					
	500	400	300	200	100	0
0	137	178	219	263	307	357
10	197	239	282	328	376	427
20	256	301	346	394	444	498
25	286	330	377	426	477	532

Reprinted by permission of the American Statistical Association.

33. Heart Catheterization

In heart catheterization a catheter is passed into a major vein or artery at the femoral region and moved into the heart and maneuvered to specific regions to provide information concerning physiology and function. For 12 children, the proper length (y) in centimeters, was determined by checking with a fluoroscope (X-ray) that the catheter tip has reached the aortic valve. The patients' height (x_1) in inches and weight (x_2) in pounds were recorded as a possible help in predicting catheter length. Source: Weisberg (1980), Chapter 9. [Chapters 6, 7]

Catheter y	Height x_1	Weight x_2	Catheter y	Height x_1	Weight x_2
37	42.8	40.0	37	43.0	38.5
50	63.5	93.5	20	22.5	8.5
34	37.5	35.5	34	37.0	33.0
36	39.5	30.0	30	23.5	9.5
43	45.5	52.0	38	33.0	21.0
28	38.5	17.0	47	58.0	79.0

Index

abrasion loss data 244, 260, 269-273, 282-285, 286-290, 311, 319, 328, 379

absolute residuals, against fitted 283-284

adjusted residuals 286

    variable plot 268-277, 297-298

        plot, and nonlinearity 273

            limitations 275

    variables, against residuals 283-284

        compared to partial residuals 306

        derivation of 311-313

ages data 46, 351

air quality data 187-188, 347

area data 245, 290-296

artifacts of plotting methods 317

asymmetry in probability plot 203, 207

automobile data 81, 86, 116-120, 130-144, 149-168, 172-180, 307-308, 352-355

autoregressive time series models 297

barley data 299-305, 384

baseball data 356

biplot 185

bivariate graphical methods, for regression 258

box plot 21-24, 41, 43-45, 57

and hypothesis testing 62
quantile-quantile plot 58
computer programs 69
in strips on scatter plot 89
notched 60-63
significance of different locations 60
visual impact of 324
box-and-whisker plot 69
boxcar weight function 35
brain data 371
cable splicing data 244, 262-267
casement displays (see partitioning)
censored data, probability plot for 233
chi-square distribution, probability plot 212
circles, for symbolic scatter plot 139
cloud-seeding data (see rainfall data)
cluster analysis 186
clutter, reducing graphical 327
co-ordinate axis scales 329-330
coding for symbolic plots 178
color, as a coding method 331
component-plus-residual plot 306
compressibility data 385
confirmatory analysis 317
constellation plot 185
correlation coefficient, product-moment 77
correspondence analysis 185
cosine weight function 36
C_p plot 277
cumulative distribution function 193
distribution, compared to probability plot 195
curvature in probability plot 203, 206
data sets, for scatter plot 77
guide to 7
data, abrasion loss 244, 260, 269-273, 282-285, 286-290, 311, 319, 379
ages 46, 351
air quality 187-188, 347
area 245, 290-296
automobile 81, 86, 116-120, 130-144, 149-168, 172-180, 307-308, 352-355
barley 299-305, 384
baseball 356
brain 371
cable splicing 244, 262-267
compressibility 385
egg 127, 241, 374

exponent 11, 22, 349
fertility 311, 385
graph area 80, 86, 101-104, 359, 363
hamster 80, 86-93, 362
heart 310, 386
iris 82, 87, 107-109, 130, 170-172
leukemia 382
lifetime 234-236, 381
managers 127, 187, 308, 373
murder 369
ozone 11, 14, 21, 23, 26, 48, 64, 80, 83, 86, 110-117, 310-311, 326, 346
perceptual psychology (see exponent data)
rainfall 43, 47, 50-51, 193, 212-222, 351
salary 125-127, 360-361
singers' height 42-44, 350
socioeconomic 127, 187-189, 239, 307-308, 368
stack loss 188, 309, 377
stereogram 193, 199-203, 380
sulfur dioxide 58
sunspot 383
tar 239, 244, 273-275, 280-286, 377
telephone 370
temperature 53, 58, 125, 357
tooth 378
wheat 367
data matrix 130
dendrogram 186
density traces, for comparing distributions 63
density, local 32
in scatter plot 111
trace 33
design configuration plot 260, 272
diagnostic tools 1
differences, used in quantile-quantile plot 64-67
discriminant analysis 184
distribution, cumulative 194
empirical bivariate 83
of the residuals 287
two-parameter exponential 201
distributional assumptions, reasons for 191
testing 192
distributions, comparing 47
many sets of data 57
plots for portraying 9
draftsman's display 136

generalized 145
with symbols 171
dynamic displays for multivariate data 182
ecdf 41
egg data 127, 241, 374
empirical bivariate distribution 83
cumulative distribution function 41
quantile-quantile plot (see quantile-quantile plot)
quantiles and theoretical quantiles 194
estimation, for probability plot 212
exercises 42-46, 69-73, 125-127, 187-190, 238-242, 307-313
exponent data 11, 21, 349
exponential probability plot 201
with standard deviation 231
factor-response data 80
fertility data 311, 385
flexibility of graphical methods 318
gamma distribution, probability plot 212
gaps 326
generalized draftsman's display 145
glyphs 184
graph area data 80, 86, 101-104, 359, 363
graphical methods, and equal variability 325
flexibility 318
interpretability 319
visual perception of 320
grouped data, probability plot for 234
half-normal plot 307
hamster data 80, 86-93, 362
heart data 310, 386
high-leverage points 249, 274, 307
histogram 24-26, 39, 58, 69
choice of interval 41
equal variability violated 325
vs. probability plot 238
horizontal segments in probability plot 203, 208
iris data 82, 87, 107-109, 130, 145-148, 170-172
iteration, in graphical analysis 316
jittering for automobile data 133
overlap 20
in scatter plot 106
Kaplan-Meier estimate 233
labeling plots 328
leukemia data 382
lifetime data 234-236, 381
linear reference patterns 322-323

local density 15, 32
            from quantile plot 15
logarithms in regression 262
lowess mathematical details 121
        method for smoothing 125-127
                        scatter plot 94
managers data 127, 187, 308, 373
matrix of data 130
maximum likelihood estimation 215
median 14
motion in displays 322
multidimensional scaling 186
multiple-code symbols 157
multivariate data, dynamic displays for 182, 186
                plotting 129
                symbolic matrix 184
            planing 185
multiwindow plot 167
murder data 369
negative values in symbols 179
nonadditivity test 302
nonlinear models 296
normal distribution 19
                    probability paper 226
        probability plot 194-199, 238-241
notches and hypothesis testing, and box plot 62
one variable methods for multivariate data 131
one-dimensional scatter plot 19-21, 38, 43
order statistics 193
outliers in iris data 148
            probability plot 203
overlap 87
        in automobile data 131
        one-dimensional scatter 20
overplotting, visual impact of solutions 323
ozone data 11, 14, 21, 23, 26, 48, 64, 80, 83, 86, 110-117, 310-311, 326, 346
pairwise scatter plots 136
partial residual plot 306
partitioning and draftsman's display 174
            data 326
            for scatter plot 141
            in four-dimensions 167
perception, and plotting methods 320-326
plot, theoretical Q-Q (see probability plot)
plots, their value in statistics 1

power normal distributions 214
  transformations 30
preliminary plots for regression 255-264
prerequisites for reading the book vi
principal components 184
probability paper 226, 241
  plot 193
    by hand 226
    censored and grouped data 233
    construction 222-227
    departures from straightness 203-210
    effect of natural variability 211
      other factors 212
    estimation from 199
    exponential 201
    for factorial experiments 307
     mixtures 240
     regression 288, 293-294
    interpretability 319
    location and spread 199
    stabilized 238
    summary 237
    transformations to normality 214
    using gaps 326
    variability information for 227-233
    with estimation 212-222
profile plot for multivariate data 156-159
properties of probability plot 197
Q-Q plot (see probability plot)
quality of plots 8
quantile plot 11, 14, 37
  plot, for local density 16
    to examine symmetry 17
quantile, definition of 12-14
quantile-quantile plot, and box plot 58
    compared to scatter plot 53
    empirical 48-57
    of positive measurements 49
    ratios and differences to improve 65-67
    seeing details 56
    straight-line pattern 52
    theoretical (see probability plot)
    unequal numbers of observations 55
quantiles, empirical and theoretical 194
quartiles, lower and upper 14
rainfall data 43, 47, 50-51, 193, 212-222, 218, 351

data, normal probability plot 194
ratios, in quantile-quantile plot 65-67
regression, adjusted residuals 286
              variable plot 268-277
    C_p plot 277
    danger of scatter plot 258
    distribution of residuals 287
    high-leverage points 249
    logarithms of explanatory variables 262
    model for 245
        selection 277
    need for graphics 243
    nonlinear models 296
    plots after fitting 278
       during fitting 264-278
       for robust estimation 275
    plotting explanatory variables 260
    preliminary plots 255-264
    quality of the estimated coefficients 270
    relation to Chapter 4 247
    residuals against adjusted variables 283-284
                fitted 280
    response against fitted 280
    simple 247-255
    varying spread 255
    weighted residuals 287
residuals, adjusted 286
    against adjusted variables 283-284
             fitted in regression 280
             various variables 283-284
    distribution of 287
    from many-parameter models 300
    or absolute residuals 283
right censoring, and probability plot 234
robust regression 306
robustness, for smoothing scatter plot 98
rootogram 325
salary data 125-127, 360-361
scales for plots 328-331
    several data sets 330
    symbols 330
scales, cube root for gamma plot 218
    for positive and negative data 324
scatter plot 75-127
    compared to quantile-quantile plot 53
    defined 75

distinguishing clusters in 136
for multivariate data 131
further reading 124
importance of smoothing 101
local density on 111
of explanatory variables in regression 260
one-dimensional 19-21, 43
overlap in 87, 106
partitioning for 141
sharpening for 114
smoothing 90-110
by local regression 94
studying spread of dependence 105
summary of techniques 123
symbolic 136-141
schematic plot 69
shape parameters, for probability plot 212
sharpened scatter plot 114
signed data in symbols 179
simple regression 247-255
simultaneous inferences, in probability plot 231
singers' height data 42-44, 350
smoothing scatter plot 91-110
socioeconomic date 127, 187-189, 239, 307-308, 368
spread of dependence, in scatter plot 105
stabilized probability plot 238
stack loss data 188, 309, 377
standard deviations, for probability plot 227-233
star plot for multivariate data 155-159
stem-and-leaf diagram 26-29, 40-41, 44, 58
for multivariate data 131-132
stereogram data 193, 199-203, 380
stragglers in probability plot 203
structure, removing it from plots 326
subsets, plotting for regression 260
sulfur dioxide data 58
summary of contents 4
sunflowers, in scatter plot 106
sunspot data 383
symbolic generalized draftsman's display 171
matrix 184
plot, coding for 178
profile plot 157-159
scatter plot 136-141
plot, for several variables 157
star plot 157-159

tree plot for multivariate data 164
symbols, scales for 330
symmetry, and transformations 29-32
      from box plot 22
      importance of 17-18
      plots to examine 16-19
tables, compared to plots 10
    plots for fitting 299
tar data 239, 244, 273-275, 280-286, 377
telephone data 370
temperature data 53, 58, 125, 357
theoretical Q-Q plot (see probability plot)
      quantile-quantile plot (see probability plot)
three variable data, plotting 135-145
tooth data 378
transformations, for several-variables 175
        power 30, 214
        to produce symmetry 30
two-parameter exponential 199, 230
two-way table, plotting components 301
units, the same on both axes 330
variability, shown on probability plot 227-233
vertical strips, on scatter plot 87
visual impact 323
weather map symbols 157
weighting, for local density 35
wheat data 367